Nº 5
MAP OF THE
UNITED STATES
Engraved to Illustrate
MITCHELL'S
School and Family Geography.
EXPLANATION.
The Capitals of Countries are represented thus ✱
of States ⊛ Rail Roads ——— Canals ———
The figures attached to the Cities and Towns indicate
the number of thousands of the population
thus New York 516 signifies 516,000 inhabitants.
The figures attached to the Rivers indicate the number
of hundreds of miles of their length of course thus
the Mississippi River 41 signifies 4100 miles long.
These characters ⚓ ⇸ ⚓ signify steam boat ship and
sloop navigation the distance of which from the sea
in miles is pointed out by the annexed figures.
The words underscored are the names of Indian Tribes.
Longitude West from Greenwich
Longitude 12 West from 10 Washington
Longitude 2 East
ATLANTIC OCEAN
GULF OF MEXICO
1000 miles long and 800 wide
LAKE SUPERIOR
LAKE MICHIGAN
LAKE HURON
L. ONTARIO
LAKE ERIE
CANADA
PENNSYLVANIA
OHIO
VIRGINIA
KENTUCKY
TENNESSEE
NORTH CAROLINA
SOUTH CAROLINA
GEORGIA
ARKANSAS
IOWA
To Portugal 3400 m.
To the Azores Is. 2500 m.
To Portugal 3700 miles
To the Straits of Gibraltar 3900 m.
To Madeira 3600 miles
To Bermuda 900 miles
To Morocco 4200 miles.
To the Canary Is. 3800 miles
Engraved by W. Williams

A Short Illustrated
HISTORY of the UNITED STATES

A Short Illustrated

Men of the Union Pacific and Central Pacific meet in northwestern Utah, May 10, 1869.

HISTORY *of the* UNITED STATES

By James Munves

GROSSET & DUNLAP • NEW YORK

ACKNOWLEDGMENTS

The author would like to express his gratitude to all those historians who have found meaning in diaries, letters and journals, the raw materials of our nation's past, in particular to those whose works are listed in the bibliography and, preeminently, to Arthur M. Schlesinger, Sr., and Dixon Ryan Fox, whose "History of American Life" served as a base stratum of social and economic information.

For specific help, encouragement, loading heavy bound periodicals on library carts, advice, photography and criticism, he thanks the following, with the usual reminder that judgments expressed, and errors, in *"A Short Illustrated History of the United States"* remain the author's responsibility: Professors John A. Garraty and David Brody, Columbia University; Charles K. O'Neill; William Knapp; Frederick H. Jackson; Sidney Ravitz; Dr. Joseph Turner; Mrs. Richard Harris; Stanley Crane and the staff of the Pequot Library, Southport, Conn.; Dr. James J. Heslin, Geraldine Beard, A. Rachel Minick, Betty J. Ezequelle, Arthur B. Carlson and Paul Bride of the New-York Historical Society; Karl Kup of the New York Public Library; Henry E. Edmunds, Ford Motor Co.; and Sandak, Inc., N. Y. C.

To Eli Moschcowitz, M.D., 1880-1964; and Margaret Munves, 1954-; the living past and the living future.

Library of Congress Catalog Card Number: 65-14748

Published simultaneously in Canada Printed in the United States of America.

CONTENTS

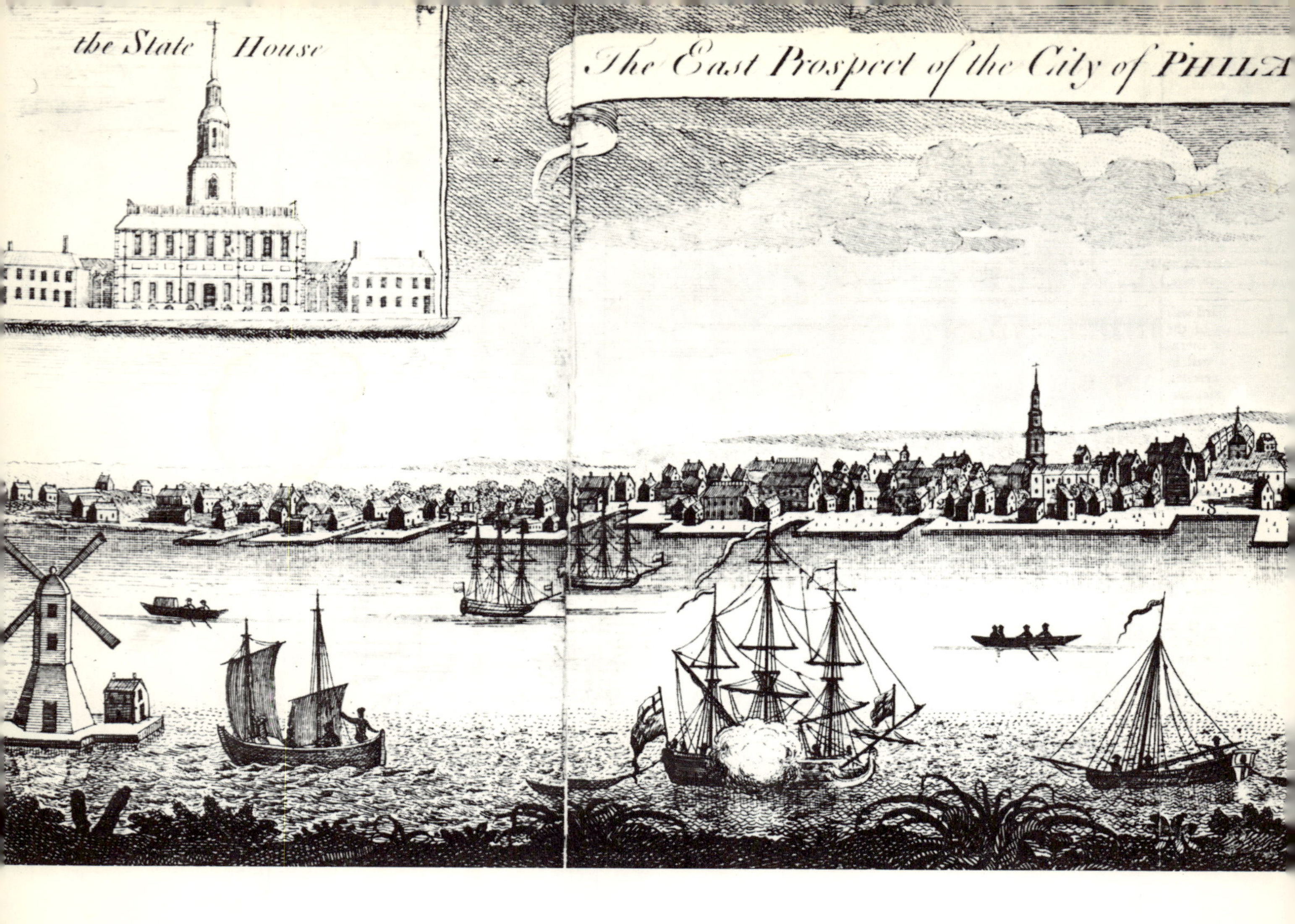

REVOLUTION

In recent years, many new nations have emerged. In each case, a people has exchanged colonial servitude for the perilous privilege of deciding its own destiny.

This book tells the story of one nation that emerged two hundred years ago when some people living between the Atlantic Ocean and the Appalachian Mountains found they could no longer defer to eight million Englishmen three thousand miles away.

Let us go back to 1776. Only one person out of twenty does not live on a farm, and no one is far from the sweet scent of the hay loft, and whinnying of horses, the trembling of the wooden handle as the plow opens the damp soil. It is a world of wood and leather; of wooden wheels slowly turned by animals and men, water or wind; of the clop clop of horseshoes on cobblestones between two-story dwellings bordering city streets; of muddy roads sticky and impassable in April. Against the cold are open fireplaces (iron stoves are a luxury). Against the night are guttering candles (whale oil is for the few who can afford it). Death stands at the elbow, as familiar as cut fingers that turn black,

Seaboard towns became small cities. In 1763, the population of the colonies was 1,500,000, six times that of 1690. Trade (fish, rum, and slaves) had grown even faster.

as crimson blood coughed, as fevers that chase men from swamps and cities. Most children die before they grow up. Gentlemen wear powdered wigs, often shaving the natural hair from their heads to rid themselves of fleas. Bathing is rare, the heating of water is cumbersome, and even cold water must be fetched from a pump.

1776, a year of violence and doubt. The heart of revolution is Philadelphia. A rarity among cities, her streets glow at night from oil lamps on poles. Some sixty men meet here: around tables at their lodgings, assembling in Mechanics Hall. Letters are read and pens scratch paper under flickering candle shadows.

These men, delegates chosen by revolutionary committees in thirteen colonies, are the Second Continental Congress. The Congress recognizes no authority but its own. There is no executive. Business is carried on, slowly and bumblingly by committees. Everything is done by committees: buying supplies, choosing officers, negotiating with foreign powers, deciding the design of a flag. Committees of Congress argue about the price of bacon, the supply of salt, the weave of cloth.

Everything comes before the Congress: a request that three prisoners of war be allowed to exercise in a prison yard; a report from the Committee of Claims that there is due "To *Melchior Meng,* for twenty-one days' hire of his Wagon and Horses, carrying Money to Virginia, the sum of 42 Dollars." The Secret Committee delivers seventy-five pounds of gunpowder here, fifty pounds there, or "three tons of Saltpetre, to be . . . manufactured into Gunpowder for the use of the United Colonies. . . ."

Congress will do everything by committee and recognize no other authority because the rebellion has its roots in opposition to the authority of the British ministry and parliament. British power has been manifest in British customs officers searching colonial homes for contraband, in suspending colonial legislatures, in shutting the port of Boston, in removing prisoners for trial in England. The rebels have come to know power as an engine of oppression. Yet they need power themselves to face the British power.

Can power exist and *not* be oppressive? The Congress rations power, giving it out in small portions hedged with restrictions. George Washington is commissioned to command the army, but when he requests blankets he must explain why they are needed. The members of committees watch each other and Congress watches the committees. On desperate occasions, the restrictions must be lowered. Washington is given power to extend enlistments. This opens up the danger that he will build a personal army that can be used against Congress. But if he is not given the power, there will be no army at all. Either course is hazardous. Too little power is as dangerous as too much. Will the United States lose the war with committees or win it with a leader who will prove as odious as the British authority that had brought them to rebellion?

Power and liberty. Congress will strive to reconcile them all through the sombre years of revolution. Power and liberty are the warp and woof of American history. They are the two poles that make the dynamo spin. In 1861, seventy-eight years after the end of the revolution, an American President would ask: "Must a government, of necessity, be too strong for the liberties of its own people or too weak to maintain its own existence?" Each generation of Americans has had to find its own answer to this momentous question. We will watch this precious liberty make its American debut, but first, let's pause to look at two "stars" in the drama, Benjamin Franklin and George Washington.

BENJAMIN FRANKLIN

Essentially, what made America different from Europe was the ocean and the wilderness. Three thousand miles of water loosened the weight of tradition; in the forest, a man had only his inner resources. If such conditions defeated men of certain abilities, men with different talents might find them favorable. One such was Benjamin Franklin.

Born in Boston in 1706, Franklin arrived in Philadelphia in October, 1723, with a few cents in his pocket. Twenty-two years later, he was the publisher of the best and most widely circulated newspaper in America, the celebrated author of the most popular almanac, and clerk of the Pennsylvania Assembly. He introduced street lighting in Philadelphia and founded the first library, fire company, college, and hospital in the city. He was

The scientist Franklin observes the motion of two pith balls bearing the same charge. As the two suspended from the upside-down cup indicate, they repel each other. In such experiments, Franklin demonstrated that there are two different kinds of electricity, which he named positive and negative.

easily the most respected man in Philadelphia and one of the wealthiest.

Franklin had educated himself. Following one year of schooling, he had "often . . . sat up in [his] room reading the greatest part of the night, when the book was borrowed in the evening and to be returned early in the morning."

In his autobiography he told how he had taught himself to be a writer. He had found some copies of The Spectator, an English magazine. "I thought the writing excellent," Franklin noted, "and wished if possible to imitate it. With this view I took some of the papers and, making short hints of the sentiment in each sentence, laid them by a few days, and then, without looking at the [*Spectator*] try'd to complete the papers again . . ."

Franklin invented a stove which, unlike any then in use, warmed the air instead of merely radiating heat a short distance around. It heated whole rooms instead of mere corners, and it used less wood in the bargain. With the same originality, he discovered the ways of gaining influence in America.

In older societies, public and state matters were decided by aristocrats at dinner parties. Franklin perceived that in America, public matters could be decided by members of a club. His Leatherapron Club, or *Junto,* was able to organize public support for his library, fire department, and other schemes. ("Is not one-half the property in the city of Philadelphia owned by men who wear leather aprons?" a Philadelphia newspaper once asked. "Does not the other half belong to men whose fathers wore leather aprons?") And the Freemasons, of which he became grandmaster, helped him to extend his influence throughout the colony.

But Franklin's originality was not confined to merely practical affairs. At the age of forty-two, he was able to retire from active business with a comfortable income. Turning to scientific investigation, he discovered that there are two kinds of electricity, positive and negative — a major scientific achievement. After proving that lightning is a form of electricity, he invented the lightning rod. As the man responsible for lifting an ancient scourge, Franklin gained a world reputation as a kind of magician. He became the first American member of the British Royal Academy and was later elected to the French Academy of Science.

Politically, Franklin had been an ardent supporter of the King. When the Stamp Act was passed, he was in London petitioning to have Pennsylvania taken from the Penns and made a royal colony. When American resistance to the act caused Parliament to consider its repeal, Franklin was questioned by the House of Commons. His explanation of American grievances helped bring about repeal of the act and made him the outstanding American of the time. Three other colonies made Franklin their agent. During the revolution he became Congress's principal agent in Europe.

GEORGE WASHINGTON

In December, 1753, a party of eight white men and three Indians approached a crude log fort on a creek some ten miles south of Lake Erie. Over the fort fluttered the white *fleur-de-lis* of France.

Inside Fort Le Boeuf, the leader of the small party talked with the French commander, St. Pierre, and handed him a letter from Governor Dinwiddie of Virginia. The letter warned the French to return to Canada.

The man who handed St. Pierre the letter was a tall, raw-boned youth. He had big hands and big feet and a handsome pock-marked face. His name was George Washington.

George Washington had been born twenty-one years before in a farmhouse on the Potomac River. The land on which the farm stood had been purchased by George's father, Augustine, from the owners of the fertile northern neck.

George was the oldest son of his father's second wife, Mary Ball. By his first wife, Augustine Washington had had two other sons. Since, in Virginian and English law, the bulk of property was left to the oldest child, George could not expect much of an inheritance. Ambitious for wealth, George Washington early equipped himself to obtain it. By the time he was fifteen, he was a full-fledged surveyor, a measurer and definer of the principal source of Virginian wealth — land. He spent the summer of his sixteenth year helping to survey the western boundaries of the huge Fairfax Grant. This trip took him to the headwaters of the Rappahannock River, high in the Appalachians.

As Washington wrote his friend John Posey, ". . . the greatest estates were made . . . by taking up and purchasing at very low rates the rich back lands." It was in the West, as Washington saw it, that his great opportunity lay. The lands east of the mountains had all been taken up. In 1749, King George II had given away 20,000 acres of land on the Ohio River, and promised 300,000 more, to a company of Virginians, among them George's half-brother Lawrence.

The sensible and hard-working young Washington won the confidence of his elders. His familiarity with the West and his willingness to endure the hardships of the frontier recommended him to Governor Dinwiddie for the important mission to the French commander, St. Pierre.

Fort Le Boeuf was situated a good 400 miles northwest of Williamsburg, Virginia; but Virginia claimed the valley of the Ohio and all the great wilderness reaching an unknown distance to the Pacific.

The French felt that the voyages of La Salle and Father Marquette and the use of the valley by a host of their woodsmen gave them a clear claim to the region. Washington returned to Williamsburg with the knowledge that the French intended to make good their claim. They would proceed southward from Fort Le Boeuf and erect a string of fortifications along French Creek and the Allegheny River to the mighty Ohio.

The Ohio is formed by the junction of the Allegheny with the Monongahela, which flows up from the South. Washington noted that a fort built at this junction could prevent the French from moving into the Ohio Valley.

Governor Dinwiddie set a party of Virginia recruits to constructing the fort. In April, 1754, George Washington left Alexandria with 150 men. His instructions were to help complete the fort and "to act on the defensive, but in case any attempts are made to obstruct the works . . . you are to restrain all such offenders, and in case of resistance to make prisoners of or kill and destroy them. . . ."

A few weeks later, he received news that the French had come down the Allegheny and seized the uncompleted fort. Washington pushed westward through the mountains to the valley of the Monongahela. Hearing that French tracks had been seen a few miles away, he set out to find the intruders. With Washington were forty Virginians and the frontiersman Christopher Gist.

Sunrise the following day found Washington leading his column of men through the leaf-shaded woods. They walked in single file, heel-first to avoid crackling the twigs underfoot — 40 Virginians in leather hunting clothes and a dozen friendly Indians. The French were surprised in a boulder-littered hollow. Washington shouted "Fire!" and discharged his musket. Indians dropped to the ground, Virginians crouched behind trees. The French returned the volley and the woods shook with sharp, uneven thunder. In a quarter of an hour, eleven of the French were dead and fifteen had managed to crawl unseen into the underbrush. The remaining twenty-two were taken prisoners. The date was May 28, 1754.

The French and British had been fighting for world supremacy for 65 years. This little skirmish reopened the struggle. During the next seven years, France would lose India, Canada, Louisiana, and much of the West Indies. The French and Indian War changed the balance of world

Charles Willson Peale, a young saddler who showed promise as an artist, was sent by several wealthy Annapolis families to study in London. Two years after he returned to America, he painted the master of Mount Vernon. The year was 1772. Washington, then 40 years old, is wearing the uniform of a colonel of the Virginia militia.

power and set the stage, as we shall see, for American independence. And George Washington fired the first shot.

Young Washington served four years, as an aide to British officers and as commander of the Virginia militia. The frontier Indian raids ended in 1758, after the Moravian missionary, Frederick Post, convinced the Indians that the English would win the war; and Washington returned to civilian life. "Thear was no end to my troble while george was in the army butt he has now given it up," his mother noted.

His brother Lawrence had left George Mt. Vernon, and by purchase, by hard work, and through marriage to the wealthy widow Martha Custis, Washington had greatly extended his holdings. He had achieved his ambition of acquiring cheap Western lands. A few years after the end of the French and Indian War, he held 32,385 acres of bounty land along the Ohio River.

With wealth came responsibility. "For what with my own business, my present Wards', my mother's . . . Colonel Colville's, Mrs. Savage's, Colonel Fairfax's, Colonel Mercer's . . . and the little assistance I have undertaken to give in the management of my brother Augustine's affairs. . . ." he wrote in January, 1775. Washington was the kind of man people wanted as a guardian of children, as trustee of an estate. He spent many weary hours protecting Mrs. Savage's money from her grasping second husband. He sent the son of an impoverished friend through college. In addition to assuming these private burdens, Washington was a Justice of the County Court, a warden of his parish, and a member of the House of Burgesses.

Washington also had to manage his plantation. He was not content to lose money growing tobacco on tired land, as other planters did. He grew wheat, built a mill, and sold hundreds of barrels of flour. He also sold herring and whitefish, netted in the Potomac.

From the beginning, George Washington was anxious to improve himself morally as well as materially. ". . .'tis with pleasure I receive reproof when reproof is due," he had told Governor Dinwiddie in 1757, "because no man can be readier to accuse me than I am to acknowledge an error when I am guilty of one . . ."

This native sternness of character was softened by years of care and concern. He had disappointments as well as successes. As judge, warden, trustee, and friend he grew used to the failings and weaknesses of others. He found good in bad men and meanness in good men. Above all he learned patience and, that in working for others, a man must forget himself.

Perhaps some of his qualities showed as he dined or played cards with fellow delegates at the Continental Congress. He talked little, but what he said always made sound sense.

"I have been with him for a great part of the last forty-eight hours in Congress," a Connecticut delegate said of Washington, "and the more I am acquainted with, the more I esteem him." Washington had been wearing his old French and Indian War uniform to sessions, as if saying "It's too late for *words.*" John Adams, a delegate from Massachusetts, recommended him as Commander in Chief. The fighting, in the spring of 1775, was all near Boston and Adams felt that the selection of a Southern leader would warm the enthusiasm of the Southern colonies. Also in Washington's favor was the circumstance that,

This emblem first appeared in newspapers in December, 1774, following the Continental Congress' non-trade agreement. It was probably originated by Benjamin Franklin.

as a delegate, he would know how to work with Congress.

The French and Indian War had taught Washington that the glory for which he once thirsted was but the tinsel wrapping around a very ugly and burdensome package — wagons stuck in the mud, the digging of latrines, "the dead, the dying, the groans . . . and cries along the road . . ." that he had heard the night after Braddock's defeat beside the Monongahela in 1755.

To lead farmers and millhands against a trained professional army would be, as Washington well knew, a difficult task, even for a man who had spent his life in military service. How much more difficult it would be, then, for a man who had been nothing more than an aide to a general and who had merely led some small raiding parties some twenty years before. Command of the American Army, as Washington saw it, could only ruin what little reputation he had been able to build up for himself. The future would prove this forecast incorrect.

THE DECLARATION

Tuesday, July 9, 1776. 6 P.M. New York City. A hot yellow sun glares from the western sky. On a soft meadow broken by outcroppings of granite stand several hundred soldiers. One guesses they are soldiers because they have muskets. Their uniforms vary. Some wear blue coats with red facings, others blue coats with buff facings, others have coats of green or brown. Some stand in fringed leather hunting gear, or in dun-colored or checkered shirts of coarse cloth. Their formation is uneven, their long shadows irregular, and they continue to move and talk after drummers have rolled the call to attention. A major, dressed like the others, his rank marked only by a pink cockade in his hat, unfolds a piece of paper between his hands and begins reading:

"When in the Course of human events it becomes necessary for one people to dissolve the political bonds which have connected them with another . . ."

Some of the words are obscured by the sea breeze, by untimely chatter, by the moo of a cow grazing in the distance. "We hold these truths to be self-evident, that all men are created equal, that they are endowed by their Creator with certain unalienable Rights, that among these are Life, Liberty and the pursuit of Happiness. That to secure these rights, Governments are instituted among Men, deriving their just powers from the consent of the governed . . ." If these truths had indeed, in 1776, been self-evident, they need not have been so forcefully asserted. In 1776, men were ruled by divine right and it was "self-evident" that kings were superior to lords and nobles to commoners in accordance with heavenly design. Civilized governments had derived their just powers from the consent of the governed in just a few isolated cities for a few brief periods in the past (in Athens, for instance, twenty-two hundred years before).

Seven minutes later, the major is still reading (in accordance with the orders of his commander, General George Washington): ". . . We, therefore, the Representatives of the united States of America, in General Congress, Assembled, appealing to the Supreme Judge of the world for the rectitude of our intentions, do in the Name and by Authority of the good People of these Colonies solemnly publish and declare, That these United Colonies are, and of Right ought to be Free and Independent States; that they are Absolved from all allegiance to the British Crown, and that all political connection between them and the State of Great Britain, is and ought to be totally dissolved; and that as Free and Independent States, they have full Power to levy war, conclude Peace, contract Alliances, establish Commerce, and do all other Acts and Things which Independent States may of right do . . ."

The power from which "the good People of these United Colonies" sought freedom was represented a few miles to the south, in New York harbor, by a fleet of 130 vessels, ". . . something resembling a wood of pine trees trimmed," in the words of one awed observer.

The words "When in the Course of human events" and all the rest are largely the work of a tall, red-haired Virginian named Thomas Jefferson. For two and a half weeks, he had worked at a small folding desk in the second floor parlor of a brick house on Market Street, Philadelphia. Jefferson was a member of a committee appointed by Congress to prepare a declaration of independence. The declaration gives the reasons for independence. It states the principles for which the rebels fought, and lists colonial grievances against King George III. Its purpose was to inspire Americans and to win the sympathy of other countries.

There has never been a definition of nationhood to which all men could agree. Whether or not a people is a nation has, generally, depended on their ability to prove it by force of arms. The delegates hoped an announcement of nationhood would make it easier for other countries to come to their aid. Agents had been in touch with ministers of England's arch enemy, France. France, and other continental powers, would prefer allying with an independent nation to assisting rebellious colonies in a British civil war. (There was *secret* aid: about $400,000 and 30,000 army coats from Spain; more money from France; and experienced volunteers: among them, the

German officers, Von Steuben and De Kalb; the Pole, Kosciusko; the Frenchmen, Lafayette and Duportail.)

On July 2, Congress had voted for independence. On the third of July, Jefferson's document was submitted for approval. Discussion of the declaration continued on the fourth, following a resolution that the Pennsylvania Committee of Safety be asked to supply flints to troops in New York. That same day Jefferson, curious about a great many things, had paid nineteen dollars for a thermometer. Temperatures in Philadelphia that day, recorded by Jefferson, were: 6 A.M., 68; 9 A.M., 72¼; 1 P.M., 76; 9 P.M., 73½.

The delegates considered every word in every sentence. They deleted a condemnation of the King's upholding of the slave trade (it condemned, by inference, American slave traders and even slavery itself). They also tempered Jefferson's criticism of the English people for supporting the Parliament that oppressed the colonies. Altogether they eliminated about a quarter of Jefferson's 1800 words. Approving the revised declaration, they (except for New York, which approved later) ordered that it be authenticated and printed and "Resolved, That copies of the Declaration be sent to the several Assemblies, Conventions, and Committees or Councils of Safety, and to the several Commanding Officers of the Continental Troops; that it be proclaimed in each of the *United States,* and at the head of the Army."

Printed, the declaration was read to a crowd of Philadelphians from a circular platform in the yard of the State House, on Monday, July 8. It is reported that cheers rose to the sky, bells rang for hours, volleys of musketry were fired, and the King's coat of arms burned.

On the following day, as we have seen, the declaration was broadcast to the several brigades of General Washington's troops in New York. And, down in New York's Battery Park, in sight of the British fleet, a statue of King George himself was destroyed.

Nassau Hall was illuminated on the evening of the 10th, while the document was read to a crowd in Princeton, New Jersey. On Tuesday, the 16th, it was read to Indians in Watertown, New York, and sent by the Maryland Council of Safety to local Committees of Observation. On the 20th: its publication was ordered in Virginia; it was heard by a great parade of militia and citizens in Portsmouth, New Hampshire; and by a noisy gathering in Newport, Rhode Island. On Monday, July 22, the North Carolina Council of Safety resolved that the Committees of the respective towns and counties proclaim the Declaration of Independence. Colonel St. Clair read it to the men under his command at Ticonderoga, New York, on July 28. It was read from the Baltimore Courthouse on the 30th, reached Richmond, Virginia, on August 10th, and was published in the churches of Boston on the 15th.

At about the same time it was being posted in Boston, Philadelphia newspapers in which the declaration was printed were reaching the backwoods of North Carolina: in particular, a big, raw, white house in the Waxhaw country. About two dozen horses were hitched along the rail fence outside. Within, a nine year-old boy stood on a table looking over the heads of bearded farmers, men in coonskin caps smoking pipes and chewing tobacco. The boy was reading out loud from the newspaper because few of these men could read themselves:

"When in the Course of human events,

it becomes necessary for one people to dissolve the political bonds which have connected them with another, and to assume among the Powers of the earth, the separate and equal station to which the Laws of Nature and of Nature's God entitle them, a decent respect for the opinions of mankind requires that they should declare the causes which impel them to the separation.

"We hold these truths to be self-evident, that all men are created equal, that they are endowed by their Creator with certain unalienable rights, that among these are Life, Liberty and the pursuit of Happiness. That to secure these rights, Governments are instituted among Men, deriving their just powers from the consent of the governed . . ."

The boy's name is Andrew Jackson. The big white house belongs to Captain Robert Crawford. Captain Crawford is a relative of Andrew's uncle, James Crawford. Andrew's own father is dead. The boy, his mother, older brother, and sister live at the home of Uncle James Crawford.

The redcoats are far away, but Loyalist Carolinians are on guard against rebels like Captain Crawford. Eventually the redcoats will come to these hills and men will be hunted and killed. A British officer will demand that Andrew polish his boots, the boy will refuse, and the officer will slash his cheek with a sword.

On August 2, as the declaration made its way to remote backwoods, Georgia farmhouses, and shacks of Maine fishermen, an engrossed (decoratively handwritten) parchment copy was presented to the Congress for formal signing. Some of the men who had voted for the Declaration on the 4th never returned to Philadelphia to put their names beside John Hancock's. Others signed it months later, some as late as 1777. Not all voted or signed free of regret or doubt. Every one of the 56 men who did sign the Declaration was a criminal in the eyes of the British. The delegates made grim jokes about hanging. Justices of His Most Gracious Majesty George III, King of Great Britain and Ireland, swore out warrants for their arrest, and parties of redcoats were dispatched to their homes.

In agitating for liberty and, finally, declaring their independence from King and Parliament, members of Congress doomed themselves to years of uncertainty and danger.

The British regulars who had gone to Lexington and Concord on April 19, 1775, had been seeking Samuel Adams as well as stores of munitions. Elbridge Gerry, another member of the Massachusetts delegation to the first, the 1774 Congress, escaped from the redcoats by fleeing in his nightclothes from an Arlington inn. The Long Island home of delegate Francis Lewis was burned by the British and his wife was taken captive. Richard Stockton of New Jersey was betrayed by neighbors and his health ruined by months of brutal imprisonment. John Hart, another New Jersey signer, was hunted by German mercenaries through the winter of 1776-77. He had to sneak into a friend's house to visit his sick wife. The home of Pennsylvania signer, George Clymer, was looted and burned by British troops, as was the Newport residence of William Ellery. Other delegates lost property and had to move their families to safety.

OF HUMAN EVENTS

The men in the city of Philadelphia claim to represent rebels against British

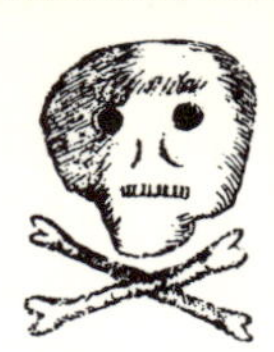

A LIST of the Names of the
PROVINCIALS who were Killed and
Wounded in the late Engagement with
His Majeſty's Troops at *Concord*, &c.

KILLED.

Of *Lexington*.

* Mr. Robert Munroe,
* Mr. Jonas Parker,
* Mr. Samuel Hadley,
* Mr. Jona[n.] Harrington,
* Mr. Caleb Harrington,
* Mr. Iſaac Muzzy,
* Mr. John Brown,

Mr. John Raymond,
Mr. Nathaniel Wyman,
Mr. Jedediah Munroe.

Of *Menotomy*.

Mr. Jaſon Ruſſel,
Mr. Jabez Wyman,
Mr. Jaſon Winſhip,

Of *Sudbury*.

Deacon Haynes,
Mr. —— Reed.

Of *Concord*.

Capt. James Miles.

Of *Bedford*.

Capt. Jonathan Willſon.

Of *Acton*.

Capt. Davis,
Mr. —— Hoſmer,
Mr. James Howard.

Of *Woburn*.

* Mr. Azael Porter.

Mr. Daniel Thompſon.

Of *Charleſtown*.

Mr. James Miller,
Capt. William Barber's Son.

Of *Brookline*

Iſaac Gardner, Eſq;

Of *Cambridge*.

Mr. John Hicks,
Mr. Moſes Richardſon,
Mr. William Maſſey.

Of *Medford*.

Mr. Henry Putnam.

Of *Lynn*.

Mr. Abednego Ramſdell,
Mr. Daniel Townſend,
Mr. William Flint,
Mr. Thomas Hadley.

Of *Danvers*.

Mr. Henry Jacobs,
Mr. Samuel Cook,
Mr. Ebenezer Goldthwait,
Mr. George Southwick,
Mr. Benjamin Daland, jun.
Mr. Jotham Webb,
Mr. Perley Putnam.

Of *Salem*.

Mr. Benjamin Peirce.

WOUNDED.

Of *Lexington*.

Mr. John Robbins,
Mr. John Tidd,
Mr. Solomon Peirce,
Mr. Thomas Winſhip,
Mr. Nathaniel Farmer,
Mr. Joſeph Comee,
Mr. Ebenezer Munroe,
Mr. Francis Brown,
Prince Eaſterbrooks,
(A Negro Man.

Of *Framingham*.

Mr. —— Hemenway.

Of *Bedford*.

Mr. John Lane.

Of *Woburn*.

Mr. George Reed,
Mr. Jacob Bacon.

Of *Medford*.

Mr. William Polly

Of *Lynn*.

Joſhua Feit,
Mr. Timothy Munroe.

Of *Danvers*.

Mr. Nathan Putnam,
Mr. Dennis Wallis.

Of *Beverly*.

Mr. Nathaniel Cleaves.

MISSING.

Of *Menotomy*.

Mr. Samuel Froſt,
Mr. Seth Ruſſell.

Thoſe diſtinguiſhed with this Mark [*] were killed by the firſt Fire of the Regulars

Sold in Queen Street.

authority in thirteen colonies south of Canada. They call themselves a Continental Congress, "Representatives of the united States of America in General Congress Assembled." This is a resounding title, but a good many colonists are indifferent to these pretensions. At least as many Americans are opposed to Congress and what it stands for, as favor it; and even those who favor independence differ on other issues.

Aristocrats had fought Parliament out of jealousy of the rights of their own colonial assemblies. Mechanics and tradesmen joined the attacks on Parliament as prelude to reforming the assemblies (which were often as arbitrary toward most Americans as Parliament was toward the colonies).

Each colony is in a condition of civil war. There are Committees of Safety, Councils of Safety, meeting secretly where the Loyalists are strong. Where the Crown officers have been driven off, the revolutionary committees organize new state governments.

There are fathers on one side and sons on the other. The president of Congress, Peyton Randolph, has a brother loyal to the King. Benjamin Franklin's son is the Loyalist (Tory) governor of New Jersey.

The failure of civil authority gives scope to old antagonisms. Western Americans had often found themselves at odds with the older communities to the east. In Pennsylvania, for instance, Lancaster County was allowed only half as many General Assembly votes as the older counties. Tidewater residents sneered at frontiersmen as uncivilized "buckskins." The people of the back country replied that "clustering into Towns [was] a great and mighty evil . . ." Where men of the Tidewater favored revolution, Westerners were likely to be

Tories. Where Easterners were loyal, Westerners would be rebels. Barns were burned. Fences were broken so that cattle would destroy fields of corn. Americans fought Americans in bitter little backwoods battles.

This is revolution — the seams of society torn, no one sure who can be trusted, words changing their meanings, everything changing its shape.

The revolution, like all revolutions, has followed a break in the connection between what rulers think the situation is and what is really happening. King George and his ministers have persisted in seeing the thirteen communities across the Atlantic as requiring the protection of British arms and the privilege of belonging to the great world-wide emporium that was the British Empire; and as possessed of insufficient talent, education, and restraint to govern themselves.

In reality, the colonies have not required the protection of British arms since 1763 when, at the conclusion of the Seven Years (French and Indian) War, the French were driven from North America. They are self-sufficient, possessing a large and thriving merchant fleet and producing more iron than Great Britain. Thirteen colonial legislatures, local town and country governments, a system of courts, and the traditions of English common law have trained thousands of Americans in the arts of regulating their own affairs.

The difficulty of King George and his ministers in comprehending America, however, was not purely that they had not kept up with their colonies' growth. Things had happened to Americans that made them react differently from the way Englishmen expected. Americans were not simply Englishmen three thousand miles to the west. (Indeed, one out of five

Mobs of rowdies tarred and feathered Tories and hung them by the heels; in other places, they treated Revolutionaries the same. In a land torn by civil strife, one cannot comfortably act according to beliefs, or even express opinions. Yet neither mob rule nor civil law, where it was established, prevented Loyalists from giving the English forces the support without which they would not long have remained in the field. (It is possible that more Americans wore redcoats than served the Continental Congress and the states.) After the war, many Loyalists moved to Canada.

was German, Dutch, French, or from some other part of the world.)

New conditions forced settlers to think anew and act anew. The Puritans acted out their dream of a holy church state in Massachusetts. Preachers became judges and the Bible a source of civil law. Refugees from Puritan oppression and Old World tyranny found in tolerance their only safety. Catholics in Maryland permitted Protestant worship to insure that Protestants would not restrict *them.* Rhode Island, founded by the Puritan dissenter Roger Williams, permitted all men to worship as they pleased. And going beyond mere liberty of conscience, the little colony also did not permit the establishment of an official state religion.

This complete separation of church and state was a startling experiment. Everywhere else in the world it was believed that without religious sanction a government could not command the loyalty of its citizens. The Aztec King of Mexico, conquered by Cortez, had been descended from gods; England's King was head of the Anglican Church. Rhode Island demonstrated that without an official religion, order could be maintained. Conditions were changing men. And the shape of the land itself was changing men, as they changed it.

The effect of land on people was most evident in differences between Americans in different parts of their continent. South of Pennsylvania, mild climate, a broad coastal plain, and easy water transportation had all contrived to make large-scale planting of tobacco and rice staples profitable for export. In New England, a narrow coastal plain and other harsh conditions had forced men to the sea. Months of loneliness on the ocean and the smell of salt air in the rigging changed men. Life on isolated farms, the

management of estates, and the ownership of slaves changed men; the amassing of fortunes by buying land wholesale and selling it retail also changed them. The merchants, sailors, and fishermen of Salem, Boston, and Gloucester had grown as different from the masters of Potomac plantations as the inhabitants of any two European nations (and neither were much like the people of the remote green isles their ancestors had left). The yeoman farmers numerous in all the colonies were another distinctive breed, and strangest of all to European eyes appeared the lanky men in Indian style leather breeches moving beyond the river falls (that impeded shipping and halted flour, salt and civilization) into the forest.

Taming the forest was not a task for Europeans. Some thousand years of civilization had to be shed, some new things learned. What was lost was the impulse to finish something just a little better — to carve a scroll in a chest, to paint a door. Refinements fell before the brutal

To the European who could only rent land from some noble, America seemed a kind of paradise. From left to right we can trace one man's progress: clearing the forest; building a log cabin (a Scandinavian invention); becoming a comfortable manor owner. It wasn't easy for an American to build up a fine estate, but in Europe it was vastly more difficult. Ownership of land breeds independence.

necessities of the frontier. "The country now consists of Natives, few of which have read much . . ." wrote Governor Nicholson of Virginia. In 1690, the Connecticut legislature noted that many men were "unable to read the English tongue." In Natick, Massachusetts, only one child in seventy could read; eight of thirteen Proprietors of Manchester, New Hampshire, could not write.

What was gained was Indian lore. Boys living at the edge of the wilderness hunted and fished in the forest, sometimes with Indian friends. They set Indian traps, learned the shapes of certain healing leaves and the tastes of certain sustaining roots, how to snare rabbits, squirrels or pigeons; how to stalk deer. They grew into men different from their fathers.

The attack on the forest had begun as a team effort. Towns were laid out within fortified palisade fences (like the camps the Romans had built in France, Germany, and England eighteen centuries before). From farms outside, the townspeople would retire within the fence when Indians threatened.

Now, having mastered the arts of blazing trails and turning trees and deer into canoes and clothes, small groups, even single men, were moving into the forest. The pioneer cleared his field like an Indian, killing standing trees by removing bark and soft wood, planting an Indian crop of beans, corn, and squash.

The pioneer woman, in a buckskin dress, worked beside her husband. She raised her children, swept her cabin with an Indian broom made from a birch log, made fat and ashes into soap, and bear grease into candles.

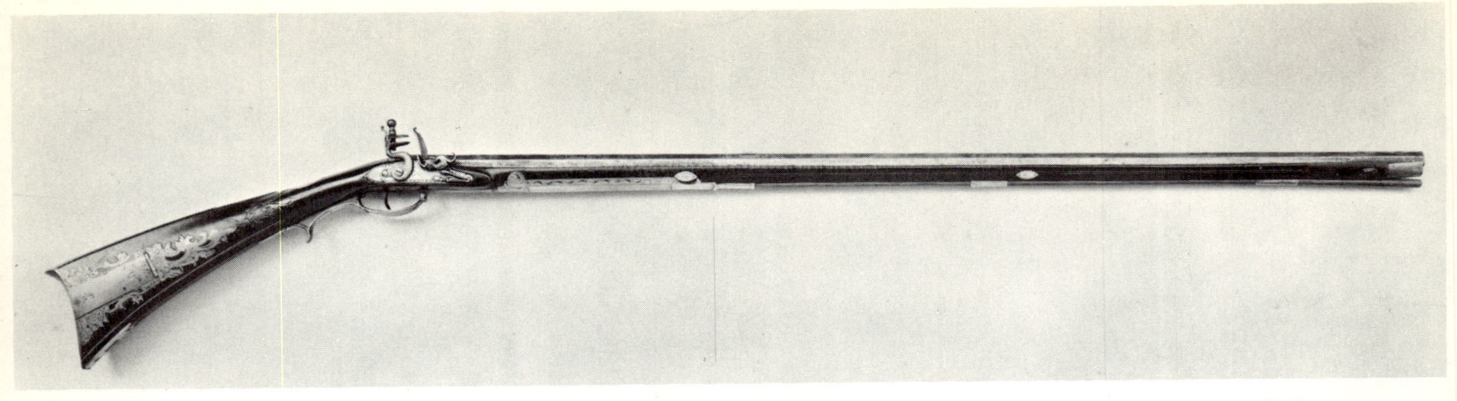

The clumsy rifle German gunsmiths brought here fired heavy bullets. They turned it into a light weapon that fired bullets so small that a hundred could be carried easily. The Pennsylvania (or Kentucky) rifle enabled a man to exist in the forest for months.

The loneliness of this forest life was harder on women than on men. And between the woman and the man there was often the long struggle between the forest and the farm: the man finding hunting easier than breaking the land, the woman wanting to build a home; the man neglecting the fields and then having to go off into the forest to feed his family. If her husband became a hunter, the woman was doomed to endless hardship. The settlement that the woman craved meant an end to the forest. The hunter would move his family farther into the wilderness as soon as there were neighbors. And all there would be was what William Byrd was to come upon one afternoon in western Virginia: ". . . a dirty poor house with hardly anything in it but children, that wallowed around like so many pigs."

As men change their language changes. In 1775, Americans use many words strange to Englishmen. What Englishmen call "autumn," they usually call "fall." A stream running across a road is a "branch." The colonists have borrowed words from the Indians: "skunk, hickory, squash, raccoon, canoe, moccasin, tomahawk." They have borrowed words from the French: "bureau, gopher, bogus, prairie, chowder"; and from the Dutch: "cruller, stoop, waffle, boss, cooky." They have invented new words, too: "bullfrog, eggplant, cold-snap, schooner, kinky, chunky."

The colonies displayed the same differences between rich and poor that prevailed in the Old World. One out of every three Americans was not even free: a slave, a defaulted debtor, a convict, an indentured servant (who sold up to five years of labor in return for his passage across the Atlantic) or a vagrant sold by court order. Among the two out of three who were self-supporting, however, differences broke down more readily than in Europe. High pay for skills and cheap land enabled tailors to buy fine houses and former indentured servants to build plantations. In Europe, landowning was a privilege for the few. In America, even the landless came to expect the privileges that went with landowning.

The key to much that Britain's rulers did not understand is contained in this statement, penned some years after the revolution, by a resident of Orange County, New York: "The instant I enter on my own land, the bright idea of property, of exclusive right, of independence exalts my mind."

"THE TIMES THAT TRY MEN'S SOULS"

As has already been pointed out, the expulsion of the French in 1763 greatly lessened the colonists' need for British protection. The conclusion of this same war also changed Great Britain.

For one thing, the world-wide struggle had won all Canada and India for Great Britain, and left her without a serious rival. For another, the great cost of the war had resulted in a British national debt of 130 million pounds. The acquisition of an immense empire forced the English to change methods of administration. As part of a bigger empire, the thirteen American colonies were bound to be treated differently from the way they had been treated when they comprised the principal portion of England's overseas possessions. The acquisition of an immense debt caused the Government to seek ways of increasing revenues.

Taxes and trade regulations to increase revenues looked different on each side of the Atlantic. The Stamp Tax, the import duties on glass, paints, paper, and tea, and the later decision to sell tea directly to American wholesalers, seemed sensible and moderate in England, and arbitrary and oppressive in America. Colonial defiance of British measures (boycotts, buyers' strikes, smuggling) brought British retaliation. Retaliation brought more defiance. The colonists misunderstood the purposes of their King and Parliament, and King and Parliament misjudged the temper of the colonists. "Your majesties will observe there are some resolves which show a little ill humour in the House of Burgesses," Governor Dunmore of Virginia wrote in 1773, "but I thought them so insignificant that I took no notice of them."

In these misunderstandings not the smallest part was played by the 3,000 miles of ocean between Dover and the Virginia capes. The six months required for a message to be dispatched and answered, had long given the colonial legislatures freedom from effective home control. It now meant that at least half a year must pass between colonial news of an unpopular measure and the earliest report of English reaction to their displeasure. The Atlantic Ocean acted as a great magnifier of disputes.

By 1775, the difference between what Britains thought America and Americans were, and what they really were, was so great that Americans and Englishmen could hardly talk in any terms that both could comprehend. Bullets took the place of words.

The first shots were fired in the early hours of Wednesday, April 19, 1775, at the common green in the middle of Lexington, Massachusetts, about ten miles northwest of Bóston. The fighting that day, between Lt. Colonel Francis Smith's seven hundred redcoats and, eventually, about two thousand armed farmers of Lexington, Concord, and the surrounding region was followed by the Battle of Bunker Hill, which showed that American militia would not break before an

On the frontier there was little time for frills. But as this powder horn shows, the artistic impulse remained.

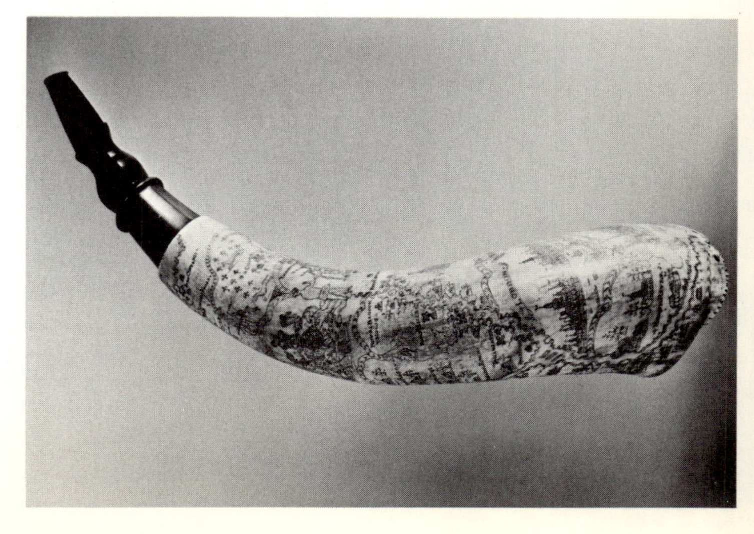

attack by British regulars, and then by the siege of Boston.

George Washington assumed command of the American Army at Cambridge, Massachusetts, on July 3, ten weeks after the affair at Lexington. He found a rabble in arms. There was no organization at all, no system of supplying or paying the troops. The men ate what they could buy, shoot, or steal. It took Washington eight days to get reports on the number of men present and the arms in the various units, a procedure which, he would sadly write, "in a regular army would have been done in an hour." The Army dissolved and almost disappeared as enlistments ran out; but sufficient remained to drive the redcoats away. In March, 1776, the 5,000-man British garrison sailed from Boston.

In July of 1776, the Continental Congress addressed some 30,000 soldiers, mostly farmers who would go home when it was time for the fall harvest. Against these amateur soldiers stood an empire of vast resources (a private British company had conquered the sub-continent of India). And there were 280 British ships in New York Harbor.

On the 12th and 13th of August, this awesome 280-ship forest of pine masts was reinforced by about a hundred more warships and transports. Two weeks later, 32,000 British regulars and marines and German mercenaries in their hire were put ashore on Long Island. After one day of battle, 20,000 Americans were lucky to escape back to Manhattan. There were more disasters and it seemed that the rebellion had all but collapsed. In September, the remnants of Washington's small army retreated northward into Westchester and up the Hudson, southward down New Jersey. December 21: General Washington with only 5,000 men was encamped on the chill fields south of the Delaware River; the Congress had fled from Philadelphia to Baltimore; an ex-English corset-maker named Thomas Paine was writing: "These are the times that try men's souls: The summer soldier and the sunshine patriot will, in this crisis, shrink from the service of his country; but he that stands it NOW, deserves the love and thanks of man and woman. Tyranny, like hell, is not easily conquered . . ."

Every great enterprise has its dark night of the soul and the December of the year 1776 was the dark night of the

In PROVINCIAL CONGRESS,

NEW-YORK, May 31, 1775.

RESOLVED, That it be recommended to the inhabitants of this Colony in general, immediately to furniſh themſelves with neceſſary arms and ammunition, to uſe all diligence to perfect themſelves in the military art; and if neceſſary, to form themſelves into companies for that purpoſe, until the further order of this Congreſs.

A true copy from the minutes,

ROBERT BENSON, Secretary.

Printed by JOHN HOLT, in WATER-STREET, near the Coffee Houſe.

American Revolution. For the months since the defeats in New York, General Washington had been acting muddled and indecisive. But beneath the indecision, there was iron. In late December, with almost all the men scheduled to be discharged at the end of the year, there remained the opportunity for one desperate move. A Christmas raid on Trenton, across the Delaware, resulted in the capture of 918 Germans and forced the British to pull back from western New Jersey. More important, it encouraged Washington's men to renew their enlistments until the spring.

The turning point of the war came the following summer. The capture of Burgoyne's 6,000 redcoats and Indians near Saratoga, New York, by rebel troops and guerrilla fighters convinced the French that the rebellion deserved serious consideration. France recognized American independence and French fleets and armies were sent across the Atlantic. In Europe, the French and Spanish, later joined by the Dutch, proceeded to raid the seas around the British Isles, to threaten Minorca, the West Indies and India, and to lay siege to Gibraltar. (American privateers also helped disrupt British commerce. One court in Massachusetts condemned 818 prize ships.)

The winters were always hard; the men were cold in their huts, ill-clothed, ill-fed. The small rebel armies fell apart as short enlistments ran out. There were mutinies and smallpox. General Washington spent most of his time just trying to keep his army together.

The war ended in America in September, 1781, with the capture of Cornwallis' English and German veterans on Yorktown Peninsula, Virginia, after a one-month siege by Washington's army and a French army and naval fleet.

Following the surrender of Cornwallis, there were rumors of peace. But until there was peace, the army had to be kept together and the authority of Congress upheld. Some officers sought to make their commander King of America, a suggestion that George Washington viewed "with abhorrence. . . ." At Newburgh, New York, in February, 1783, Washington barely prevented his officers from rebelliously marching on Philadelphia to demand half-pay pensions from Congress.

A treaty of peace was signed in Paris on September 3. On November 25, the British left New York after seven years of occupation, to be followed by a parade of American troops.

Washington rode south to Virginia, to his plantation and to his mills. He was fifty-one years old, an upright figure in the prime of life. More than any other man, he had contributed to his country's independence. He had been patient when patience was required. He had been daring when boldness was demanded. And above all, he had possessed the wisdom to know when each quality was needed. If he enjoyed the adulation of his fellow citizens, he always felt indebted to the Providence that had provided the fog and the north winds on the night of the defeat on Long Island and the obscuring snow on the morning before Trenton.

He had lived too long to believe that anyone "lived happily ever after."

"It remains only for the States to be wise," he said, "and to establish their independence on the basis of inviolable, efficacious union and firm confederation, which may prevent their being made the sport of European policy."

If one trial was over with, another was just beginning.

NEW SOUTH WALES
JAMES BAY
KRIS or CHRISTINAUX
Nation of the Bear
CANADA
MONSONIS
Eastern Sioux
Chipewas
SUPERIOR
Algom quins
Nipisin Lake
Lake Abitibis
Temiscaming Lake
HURONS LAKE
MICHIGAN LAKE
ONTARIO L.
ERIE
Outagamis
Mascoutins
CHIKTACHIKS
TWIGTWEES
ILINOIS
MIYAMIS
LOUISIANA
Kaskakias
Ohio River
Missisipi River
VIRGINIA
NEW YORK
PENSILVANIA
Long Island
NORTH CAROLINA
SOUTH CAROLINA
CHARLESTOWN
CHEROKEES
UPPER CREEKS
CHACTAWS
MIDDLE CREEKS
GEORGIA
LOWER CREEKS
WEST FLORIDA
EAST FLORIDA
Mobile Bay
Balise Fr. I.
Mouths of the Missisipi
GULF OF MEXICO
THE ATL
SCALES.
Sea Leagues 20 to a Degree
English Miles 69½ to a Degree
100
95
90
85
80
75
70
50
45
40
35
30

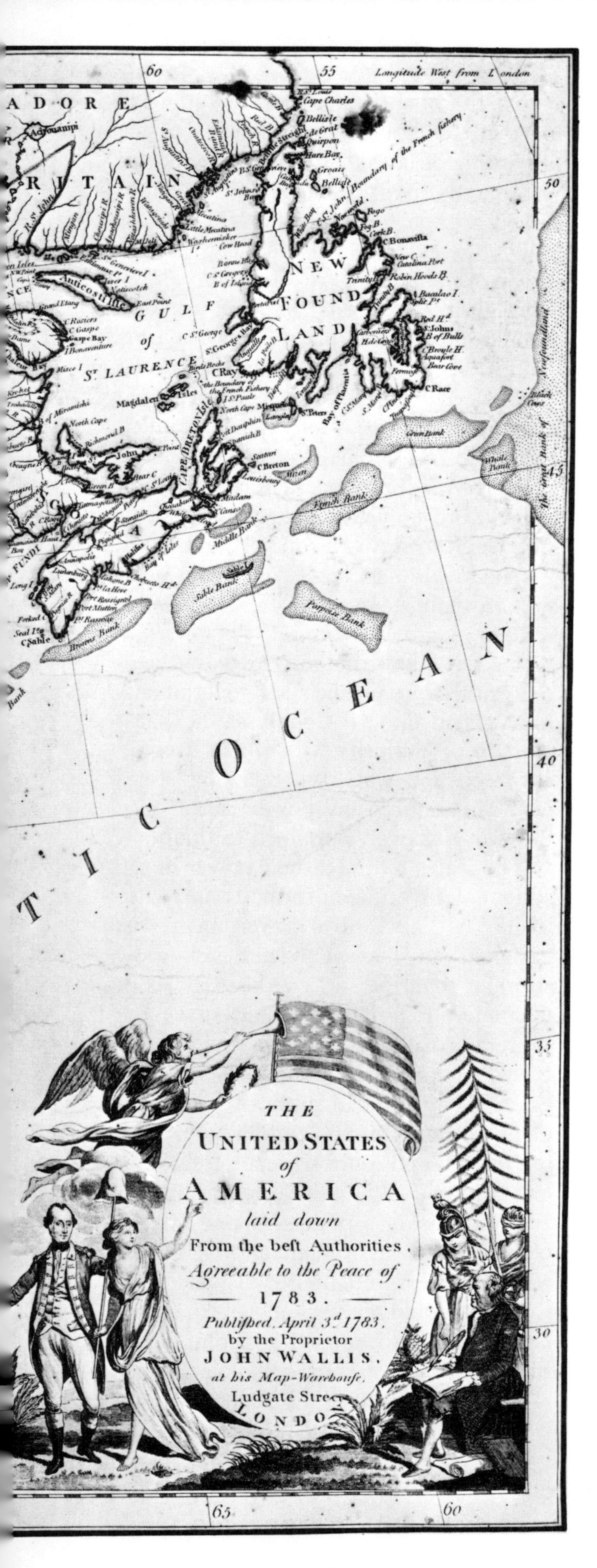

Notice that the further west, the less accurate is this map of 1783. Missing are the Kentucky and Tennessee Rivers, among others.

INDEPENDENCE

THE United States of America consisted of all the lands south of Canada and north of Florida, between the Atlantic Ocean and the Mississippi River. This was an immense empire, larger than all of western Europe. And since western Europe had for more than a thousand years been divided up into dozens of warring states, it can readily be seen why there was little expectation anywhere that America would survive as a single nation.

Of the million square miles, about one-third consisted of the thirteen colonies along the Atlantic Seaboard. The remainder, stretching from the Appalachian Mountains to the Mississippi, was wild, unsettled forest country. Here and there, in green valleys and on the other side of the mountains, in western Virginia and west of North Carolina, small settlements were rising and crops were being planted. But the trees that were cut down were erected into palisade forts to defend against the Indians. There were clearings in the woods called Lexington, Boonesboro, Harrodsburg, Louisville, and Nashboro. There were rivers called Kentucky, Tennessee, Ohio, Wabash, Miami, Illinois, Kanawha, Muskingum, Kankakee, Maumee — Indian names for Indian rivers. The hills had Indian names and also the places for crossing the rivers, the salt licks, the springs, the creeks, and the dim trails through the dark forest.

West of the Mississippi was the vast, vague area known as Louisiana. At the mouth of the Mississippi River was the Spanish settlement of New Orleans. Just south of where the great Missouri River met the Mississippi stood the small trading post of St. Louis. On the eastern shore of the Mississippi were two small American forts and trading posts — Kaskaskia and Cahokia. Detroit, and other posts northwest of the Ohio River were still occupied by British soldiers in violation of the Treaty of Peace.

THE ARTICLES OF CONFEDERATION

In freeing themselves from British rule, Americans did not win liberty. Liberty is not a prize, it is a condition of life — the condition of being able to choose how one will live and of being responsible for the consequences.

Even as they fought Great Britain, patriots wondered if victory would bring any measure of freedom. On the one hand, the war had brought into being a Continental Army and a Continental Government. There were fears that, "at the close of a struggle for liberty, a triumphant army, elated with victory, and headed by a popular general may become more formidable than the tyrant that has been expelled." There were fears that an American central government would impose taxes on the thirteen states as unjust as any invented by Parliament.

On the other hand, the revolutionary overturn of courts and judges, the disregarding of laws, had raised the spectre of anarchy. To the citizen of an established regime, government is a fact of daily life as visible as the flag or the shape of money. The revolutionary, however, has broken this tissue of custom. Would men who had taken up arms against the soldiers of their King have reverence for any officer sent to enforce unpleasant laws? "A long time and much prudence," as one patriot put it, "will be necessary to reproduce a spirit of union and that reverence for government without which society is a rope of sand."

The loyalties of rebel Americans went first to their states. Revolutionary committees, fugitives from British law, had erected new governments. New and jealous of their power, the state governments had given up to Congress the least amount of authority with which it could carry on the war. Whether the states would relinquish any power at all, once the war was over, remained in doubt.

The states retained their power in the system of government formally agreed to in 1781. The central government was designed so that it would not grow stronger than the states. The Articles of Confederation named Congress as the supreme governing body. Instead of executives, there were committees of Congress. Congress had authority over the Continental Army; its care in apportioning money and authority had created at least as many difficulties for Washington as the redcoats; Congress spoke for the United States in foreign affairs. Otherwise its powers were limited at every turn. Congress could not pass acts of trade and navigation — to impose duties or make rules about whose ships could carry what — nor could it force the states to do its bidding. If a state did not choose to pay taxes levied by Congress, Congress could do nothing about it.

Some Americans were happy with this arrangement and some were not. Those who favored the Federal system of Confederation were becoming known as "Federalists." Believers in a stronger central government called themselves "Nationalists." (Later, as we shall see, the strong-government men would come to call themselves "Federalists.")

The Federalists had been particularly concerned that the Confederacy did not have an income of its own. They knew that it could act independently of the states only if it had money of its own. But the Nationalists saw that if the Confederacy owed people money, these creditors would want the government to have an income so that they would be paid. The separate states had emerged from the war owing their citizens a total of at least $100,000,000. The Nationalists tried to have the Confederation assume these debts. They were unsuccessful in this, but the national debt of $34,000,000, which the Confederation owed various citizens, served somewhat the same purpose.

The composition of Congress changed with successive annual elections. Nationalists sought to strengthen the government — even going so far as to delegate great power to one man, Robert Morris. He was put in charge of all the financial affairs of the Confederacy. When Federalists regained control, they were more restrained.

But the practical problems of running a government tended to change the views of the more extreme proponents of weakness. Government by committee was gradually replaced by government by executive heads of departments. Despite its lack of coercive force, the Confederation took in between $400,000 and $3,000,000 a year and managed to pay off $27,000,000 of its $34,000,000 domestic debt in eight years, and to resolve much of the financial tangle of the Revolutionary War.

As promise of future resources and stability, the Confederation had the Western lands the states had ceded to it. The Northwest Ordinances, passed in 1784 and 1787, prescribed a growing union in which territories would be converted into new states. The sale of the Western lands assured the Confederation a revenue that would permit it to retire its debts and meet its needs without oppressing the states.

But there were men who wanted a government that would do more for them, and others who found themselves excluded from power.

EQUALITY

Forces had been set in motion. There was no telling what might happen. The rebels had proclaimed that "all men are created equal." To show they meant it, they had abolished all hereditary titles. (This, Tories on both sides of the Atlantic predicted, must surely create lawlessness, mob rule, anarchy. No man would be safe.)

The business of daily life — buying and selling and passing property on to heirs and the methods of settling lawsuits — was carried over from the English rules as developed in the colonies. The Constitution of the State of New York announced that, "such parts of the common law of England, and of the statute law of England and Great Britain, and of the acts of the Legislature of the colony of New York, as together did form the law of said Colony" were to "be and continue the law of this State."

Yet the laws of Europe, Thomas Jefferson recognized, led to the privileges of European society. The system of entail and primogeniture was the basis of the landed aristocracy. Land in entail was as inseparable from the owner in life as his own head, and equally inseparable from his heir. Primogeniture is the exclusive handing on of the estate to the most direct heir in line of descent. Like entail, it prevented the breaking up of large estates and, as Jefferson said, "raised up a distinct set of families . . . privileged by law in the perpetuation of their wealth. . ." Thus far the practices had not been followed in Virginia. Laws aimed at keeping estates together could only have hampered the transfer of property. They would have interfered with land speculation. To insure that Virginia's mobile society of buyers and sellers of property would not some day freeze into the European, ancestral pattern, Jefferson had laws passed against entail and primogeniture.

The establishment of religion, the support of a single sect by the state, also smacked of special privileges. The tendency was to disestablish churches. Only in Massachusetts, Connecticut, and New Hampshire did religion (always Protestant, usually Congregational) remain tax-supported. Restrictions against Jews and Catholics were gradually lifted. Catholics could hold office anywhere but in New Jersey and some of the New England States. Full religious equality was not yet a fact, but the trend was unmistakably in the direction of complete separation of church and state, after the example of Rhode Island.

The revolutionary, leveling tendency went on. Quitrents, fixed rents paid as a kind of tax to the original landowner even after the purchaser had paid for his land, were abolished in one state after another. In Virginia, the gradual ending of slavery was considered. In 1783, a Massachusetts court outlawed slavery as inconsistent with the Massachusetts Bill of Rights.

The vote, long considered the exclusive privilege of the man of property, was extended to men who paid more than a certain amount of taxes, whether they owned real estate or not. This opened elections to many tradesmen and manufacturers.

But certainly everyone did not approve these changes. The New Yorker John Jay is supposed to have told his son that "those who own the country ought to govern it." And there were Virginians who believed that the first clause of the State Bill of Rights which read, "that all men are by nature equally free and independent, and have certain inherent rights . . ." embodied subversive doctrine, "the forerunner or pretext of civil convulsion."

But surely and steadily, more men were winning the right to vote. If an ordinary workman had not yet won the right, his life improved as the labor shortage forced wages up. This resulted in more, rather than less, equality. The time would come when even debtors, the habitual victims of the old society, would not be kept in prison, there was so much work to be done and so few to do it.

The speculator William Grayden, thinking of his great tracts of unoccupied lands, compained that "the want of inhabitants [is] perhaps our only calamity." To help attract more settlers, Pennsylvania offered foreigners voting citizenship after two years of residence.

"It is our business to render our country an Asylum worthy to receive all who may wish to fly to it," John Adams wrote.

THE VALUE OF MONEY

The absolute sovereignty of states with regard to the issuance of money and to taxation meant that the policies of a state could affect the value of its money and its property. A holder of a state's money, or its debts, or of a debt of one of its citizens, always had some uncertainty about the value of his holdings. There were a number of disputes over property during the years of the Confederation. The most notorious occurred in western Massachusetts in the fall of 1786.

On September 11, more than 200 farmers entered the courtroom at Concord and forced the justices of the Sovereign State of Massachusetts to close the court. Within a few weeks, the state government had been driven from all the towns of western Massachusetts. The rebellion came to a head under the leadership of a former captain in the Continental Army named Daniel Shays. More than 12,000 men appeared ready to take up arms, and there was talk of marching on an armory in Springfield where the Continental Congress stored arms and ammunition. In 1775, the aroused militia of Massachusetts had started a war against the mighty British Empire. In 1786, it seemed likely that this same militia would destroy the government of Massachusetts.

What had brought the farmers to violence was a high tax rate and a shortage of money. The taxes were payable only in money, and the shortage put the farmers in debt and led to the seizure of their property and their farms.

To gain relief the farmers had advocated that the state print paper money. As this money went into circulation, the farmers would be able to pay their taxes. Such an increase in the supply of money often brings about an inflation.

Too little money forces people to barter, makes business difficult, and slows down the pulse of trade. But too much money can be just as harmful. If the supply of money increases faster than the things it buys, then more money is needed to buy each thing. Prices rise. If the price of a pound of potatoes goes from one cent to two cents, it means that the purchasing power (value) of the penny has gone down from one pound of potatoes to half a pound. A rise in price is a cheapening of money.

The value of money always stands between the debtor, the one who owes the money, and the creditor, the man who lends the money. If money rises in value, the creditor stands to gain. If money falls in value, it is the debtor who gains.

In all the states, creditors and debtors struggled to control the price of money. In Massachusetts, the creditors were in control of the state legislature. Among their credits were the notes issued by Massachusetts during the war, and representing the bulk of the war debt of the state. They had bought these notes at a low price, when there was little confidence they would be paid, and had then proceeded to legislate themselves a profit by having the state repay them at a much higher price.

Payment in paper money, the creditors feared, would give them less value than payment in specie (gold or other money that was legal tender throughout the world). In Massachusetts, as in a number of other states, proposals to increase the supply of money were defeated. The situation was further complicated by the fact that elements over which neither group had any control could affect the value of money. An unfavorable balance of trade (imports exceeding exports) could drain a state of its specie. A war or a tightening of trade regulations, by contracting trade, could make money scarce and drive it upward in value.

In Massachusetts in 1786, the specie shortage had resulted from a siege of bad weather that had cut off trade with the West Indies. The Massachusetts farmers had stopped the courts as a last resort, after other relief — paper money or changes in the laws — had been denied them. The power of Massachusetts proved sufficient to quell the disturbance, the rebels were easily put down. But an uneasy feeling remained. Economic disputes could lead to violence. If order was restored in Massachusetts, it might be overturned in some other state, with a cancellation of debts or destruction of money. And where violence did not occur, paper money was one solution to internal differences that could seriously affect people outside the state. By 1786, seven states, a majority, had resorted to this solution, with varying results.

THE NEED FOR COOPERATION

George Washington, viewing these disturbances from Virginia, sent a questioning letter to his former aide, David Humphreys. "What is the cause of all these commotions?" he asked. "If (real grievances) why were they delayed until the popular mind had become so much agitated? If (licentiousness) why are not the powers of government tried at once?"

The General had also written to John Jay, "That it is necessary to revise and amend the Articles of Confederation, I entertain *no* doubt . . ."

As the above letters indicate, George Washington had not lost interest in the world beyond Mount Vernon. With other farsighted men of his region, Washington had become involved in a company to improve transportation up the Potomac River, to the mouth of Stony Creek, forty-five miles inland from Fort Cumberland. As early as 1784, Washington saw that unless the headwaters of the Potomac and the Ohio were somehow linked, New York State, by opening an easy route westward from the Hudson River, would become the market and supplier for the pioneers of the West.

In May, 1785, the Potomac Company was formed to build the necessary canals, roads, and locks. George Washington was president of the company, and $200,000 of stock were sold.

But such a vast scheme required support beyond a single state. Massachusetts and Connecticut claimed portions of the western territory watered by the Ohio and its tributaries. The Potomac River, which the company sought to improve, was as much the concern of the state of Maryland as it was Virginia's.

In November, 1784, at the General's request, both the Maryland and Virginia legislatures passed acts for the improvement of their common river. Four months later, at Mount Vernon, representatives of the two states signed a pact allowing equal rights to Chesapeake Bay and the Potomac to the two sovereign states. The statesmen of Maryland and Virginia, now perceiving that their destinies were firmly attached, agreed to meet annually to discuss their commercial relations.

Other men of vision were confronted

with similar situations. A single state was too small a sphere for their schemes.

Maryland decided to invite neighboring Delaware and Pennsylvania to the next conference with Virginia. Virginia, in turn, decided to invite *all* the states.

The conference in Mt. Vernon in March, 1785, led directly to a convention in Philadelphia in May, 1787, to "take into consideration the situation of the United States, to devise such further provisions as shall appear to them necessary to render the constitution of the federal government adequate to the exigencies of the Union; and to report such an Act for that purpose to the United States in Congress assembled . . ."

As the proposed meeting had broadened from two states to all thirteen, and as the rebellion in Massachusetts demonstrated the manner in which the prospects of trade were mixed with every aspect of life, the scope of the convention had become enlarged.

THE DELEGATES

Not all Americans were, of course, represented at the convention in Philadelphia. At least one-quarter of the people of the states were either slaves, or bonded servants or jailed debtors — not free citizens in any sense. Among the remaining three quarters were many small farmers, tradesmen, and Western settlers who looked upon any government as an instrument of oppression. They did not approve of the convention at all.

The delegates in Philadelphia, elected by state legislatures, had a common interest in protecting their property against men like the followers of Captain Shays and in devising better means of carrying on and increasing commerce among the states, but they were divided by their local interests. A tariff on shoes, for instance, would improve the business of the shoe manufacturers of Lynn, Massachusetts; but it would raise the price of shoes in South Carolina.

Thirteen sovereign states, then, were assembling in Philadelphia. Their object — to improve conditions without giving up any existing benefits. No wonder each of the states wished to send the best available men.

James Madison contributed more to the ideas and wording of the Constitution than any other delegate. Later, during the great debate over its adoption, he, Hamilton, and John Jay, in their Federalist Papers, *ably explained and defended the new plan of government.*

Of the thirty-seven delegates from nine states who began deliberations in Independence Hall in the State House on May 29, twenty-nine were lawyers or judges; twenty-one were college graduates; and twenty-six served as officers in the War against Great Britain, four on Washington's staff. Ultimately, all the states except Rhode Island were represented in the convention. Of the fifty-five delegates, almost all had helped to write the constitutions of their states; half had served in the Continental Congress; eight had signed the Declaration of Independence; and at least six had at one time or another headed the governments of their states. George Washington was unanimously elected president of the convention.

Never had so many able men — with such broad experience of human nature and of laws and their effects on life — met together to try to draw up a frame of government.

War is a great dissolver of human pretension. Just as those who had been exposed to the rigors of war had seen the extremes of human nature, so other delegates, like lawyers and judges in circuit courts, had seen all the vagaries of their fellow citizens in all the far counties of their states. "The law," as Thomas Jefferson once noted, "gives a man a view of the dark side of humanity."

"PASSIONS... SUBSERVIENT TO THE PUBLIC GOOD"

The powers of government had been reserved to the States by men determined never again to suffer the oppression of the British Parliament. But lack of government, it now appeared, also has its dangers. As one pamphleteer noted, "The ambition of the poor, and the avarice of the rich demagogue can never be restrained upon the narrow scale of a state government."

Was there not some middle course? Could not a government be formed that would be able to preserve the peace without being oppressive? Could not men invent a system that would give the benefits of strong government without the evils of power?

The members of the parliament who had voted for the Townshend Acts and other oppressive measures had been, after all, men much like the members of the colonial legislatures. The same man who, as a member of the Virginia House of Burgesses, bitterly opposed the Stamp Act might, as a British member of parliament, have voted *for* the Stamp Act. It was not that the member of parliament was any worse a man than the Virginia Burgess — *it was where he lived that caused him to act as he did.*

Any legislator would rather tax people whose votes and support he did not directly need, as he would certainly rather have others pay taxes than himself. It was the acceptance of this selfishness of human nature that was behind the colonial insistence that taxation without representation was wrong.

The delegates in Philadelphia, as practical men of affairs, started with the knowledge that the actions of government proceed from human nature, and that human beings are not perfect.

As Madison said, ". . . what is government itself but the greatest of all reflections on human nature? If men were angels, no government would be necessary."

People are weak and selfish. By and large, they look after their own interests before those of their neighbors. They will work together only insofar as they see that by working together they stand to gain more than they lose. This is the way of human nature and an unalterable condition. The only thing that can be changed is the form of government in which human nature will operate.

A government is a kind of machine that harnesses or organizes this elemental human nature. Would it be possible to set up a government in which the selfish impulses of the people *in* the government would benefit, rather than injure, the people it governed?

"Take mankind as they are," Hamilton told the convention. "And what are they governed by? Their passions . . . One great error is that we suppose mankind more honest than they are. Our prevailing passions are ambition and interest; and it will ever be the duty of wise government to avail itself of those passions, in order to make them subservient to the public good . . ."

The way in which this could be done was to divide the government into separate parts that would constantly struggle with each other. If the powers of government were carefully divided, no single part of the government would be able to act without the cooperation of the other parts. And each would be careful not to let the other parts grow so powerful that its own powers were endangered. Such a divided system of government is complicated and slow-moving; but its divisions prevent that concentrated exertion of power that causes oppression and subsequent rebellion.

The frame of government devised in Philadelphia placed the administration of the new government in the hands of an elected President who, like the king or the royal governors, was dependent on the legislature for his money. The legislature could make laws and raise money, but had no powers of enforcement. The independence of the courts was insured by making the salaries and terms of office of federal judges impregnable to executive or legislative interference.

The smaller states feared that any powers transferred to the new government would be used to their disadvantage. On the other hand, if all the states were treated alike, the more populous states would suffer at the expense of the less populous states. A system that gave Rhode Island, with 80,000 people, an equal vote in all things with Massachusetts' 300,000 would, in effect, give each Rhode Islander almost four votes to the citizen of Massachusetts' one.

These jealousies and reservations of the states were resolved by compromise. Again, the method used was the division of power. The legislature was divided into two houses. In the Senate, each of the states would have an equal vote. In the House of Representatives, representation would be in proportion to population, and the larger states would have the bigger voice.

The powers of the legislature were then divided. Money bills, which affect all people equally, originated in the lower House. Reserved for the upper House was the responsibility of approving treaties and major appointments. This provision, and the required concurrence of the Senate in all legislation assured each of the states an important voice in the affairs of the nation.

As the small states were mollified by their Senate powers, the framers of the Constitution were able to use the undemocratic Senate to strengthen the government against perhaps the most dangerous of all oppressors — the majority.

If the Representatives elected for two-year terms would be sensitive to the

wishes of their constituents, the Senators chosen for six-year terms would hold the government back from yielding too readily to such popular pressures. The Senate would act, in the words of George Washington, as a "saucer" into which legislation could be "poured" for cooling.

Yet no mere design of government, no matter how clever, could insure liberty. As Jefferson had written, "Mankind soon learn to make interested uses of every right and power which they possess . . ."

If the Constitution admitted selfishness and greed, it did not pretend that scoundrels could govern. Ultimately, no system could be better than the men who composed it. It was foolish to suppose, Madison wrote, "that any form of government will secure liberty or happiness without any virtue in the people. . . ."

The delegates met to change the Articles of Confederation. They had, instead, framed a new form of government. For it to be adopted, it had to be approved by special conventions of nine of the thirteen states.

"JURISDICTIONS TO BE . . . IN EVERY STATE . . ."

"We contended with Great Britain . . . because they claimed a right to tax and bind us in all cases whatever. And does

Revolutions offer unusual opportunities to able young men. Alexander Hamilton, trusted aide to Washington before he was 20, was an early advocate of strong central government.

not this Constitution do the same?" Amos Singletary asked in the Massachusetts Constitutional Convention.

Opposition to the Constitution was powerful and widespread. The criticism by the Governor of Virginia, Patrick Henry, began with the document's very first words. Why, he demanded, did it say, "We, the people?" Why was it not, "We, the States?" A New York Manifesto would declare that the Constitution was "monarchical, aristocratical, oligarchical, tyranical, diabolical . . ."

Most of those who were dissatisfied with the Constitution worried that it did not sufficiently safeguard individual liberty.

"The rights of conscience, trial by jury, liberty of the press . . . all pretensions to human rights and privileges, are rendered insecure . . ." said Patrick Henry.

Most of the old leaders in Virginia agreed with him. Benjamin Harrison distrusted "jurisdictions to be established in every state altogether independent of their laws."

Jefferson, writing his friend Madison from France, took a middle course. He favored "very energetic government," but felt that Shays' rebellion had "given more alarm than it should have." On the other hand, "the will of the majority should prevail. If they approve the proposed Constitution in all its parts, I shall concur in it cheerfully, in hopes they will amend it, whenever they shall find it works wrong."

In favor of the Constitution in Massachusetts, as Washington's old friend Henry Knox reported, was "all the commercial part of the community."

The Constitution was adopted by the State of Delaware on December 7, 1787. Pennsylvania and New Jersey gave their approval shortly afterwards. Then followed Georgia, Connecticut, Massachusetts, Maryland and South Carolina. New Hampshire, on June 21, 1788, had the honor of being the ninth and decisive State.

In many of the states, ratification came only after a close and bitter struggle. The vote in Massachusetts was 187 to 168; in Virginia, 89 to 79; in New York, 30 to 27. What seemed to have gained most support for the new government was that both Washington and Franklin favored it. As the *Pennsylvania Herald* stated: "If the plan is not a good one, it is impossible that either . . . would have recommended it."

THE UNITED STATES OF AMERICA

When the first Congress of the United States, sitting in a hall on Wall Street in New York City, counted the votes sent in by the electors of the eleven states that had ratified the Constitution, they found that George Washington had been unanimously elected President. This had been expected from the beginning. For, as one of the general's former aides had written to him, a "universal opinion of your being elected President of the United States" had persuaded many to favor the new system.

In accordance with the terms of the Constitution, each of the Presidential electors voted for two men, without indicating who was to be President and who was to be Vice President. George Washington received sixty-nine votes, one from each elector. John Adams received the next highest number of votes, thirty-four, and so became Vice President. Governor George Clinton of New York would have been elected Vice President, except for the opposition of Washington.

Washington did not want Clinton as Vice President because Clinton had opposed ratification of the Constitution in his state. Men like Clinton in New York and Patrick Henry in Virginia, who had opposed ratification, were becoming known as Anti-Federalists; Washington, Adams, Hamilton, and James Madison, who during Confederation days had been called Nationalists, now adopted the name of their former antagonists. "Federalist" once had meant a friend to the Confederation. Now it was coming to mean a friend of the Constitution, a proponent of strong national power.

The division between those who favored more centralized power and those who feared it; between those who put order before liberty and those who put liberty before order, had now become the difference between Federalists and Anti-Federalists.

Following his election on April 6, 1789, Washington made a magnificent triumphal tour north from Mount Vernon to New York. Along roadsides, at fords, bridges and ferries he was greeted by joyous crowds. He was escorted over flower-strewn roads by mounted veterans of the War of Independence, presented with bouquets by little girls in ribbons, toasted and feasted by the leading citizens of each city and village between the Potomac and the Hudson. Bells pealed, bands serenaded, guns fired salutes.

If Washington was universally admired, there were still men who favored the new government and those who viewed it with suspicion. As Fisher Ames, a young Federalist Congressman from Massachusetts noted, "Tranquility has smoothed the surface [but] faction glows within like a coalpit."

AN EMERGING NATION

During the struggles over ratification the Federalists had gained support by promising to change the Constitution.

Specifically, what many Americans demanded were certain guarantees against oppression similar to those they had written into their state constitutions.

The effect of these guarantees, which the states called "Bills of Rights," was to erect the people into a separate branch of government. Individuals were protected from interference in the same way the courts, the legislatures and the executives were protected.

The first eight amendments expressly forbid the passage of laws limiting expression, religion or the right to bear arms; the courts could not imprison men without giving reason nor deny a special trial, usually by jury, nor, by accepting testimony by an individual against himself, benefit from torture. The people were secured against search and seizure and the quartering of soldiers in their houses. In the ninth and tenth amendments, the people made clear their supremacy by retaining other rights, and by reserving to themselves, and their states, all powers not given to the United States by the Constitution.

The ten amendments made people feel better about the Constitution, but they could not really guarantee their liberties. As the revolutionary generation well knew, freedom was not that easy. In the states Bills of Rights had proved of little value when they were most needed.

"Repeated violations of these parchment barriers have been committed by . . . majorities in every State," Madison warned. "In Virginia I have seen the Bill of Rights violated in every instance where it has been opposed to a popular current . . . Wherever the real power of government lies, there is the danger of oppression. In our Governments . . . the invasion of private rights is *chiefly* to be apprehended . . . from acts in which the Government is the mere instrument of the major number of the Constituents..."

THE PRESIDENT

President Washington acted very much like a king. He entertained at formal weekly levees, kept twelve to sixteen horses in his stable in New York and often rode about on a white steed embellished with leopard skin and gold. He and his family were waited on by fourteen white servants and seven slaves, and wine and champagne flowed freely. Washington was naturally an austere, commanding and kingly person, but these royal manners were partly policy. Since the nation was new and weak, respect for the Presidency could only come from the way Washington acted.

As he created the manner in which the President was to appear to the public, Washington also had to invent the means by which the office would operate. He created rules and precedents that would be followed by all his successors.

To carry out the different executive responsibilities outlined in the Constitution, Washington set up separate departments.

The new government inherited a considerable staff of experienced administrators from the Confederation. Many, including General Henry Knox, who had been in charge of army affairs, were continued in office. Besides Knox, as Secretary of War, Washington named Thomas Jefferson Secretary of State (foreign affairs). He put Alexander Hamilton at the head of the Treasury Department, made Edmund Randolph Attorney General, and Samuel Osgood Postmaster General.

The three Secretaries of State, Treasury and War, and the Attorney General became Washington's principal advisers and the President met with them regularly, much as he had met with his military staff during the war. They became known as the Cabinet, after an English term used to describe similar meetings of the King of England with his principal ministers.

YOUNG AND DEFENSELESS

At the same time that he was working out the nature of the Presidency, Washington was faced with a whole series of difficult problems, any one of which could have brought the infant Republic to ruin. He was like a man trying to build a house during a blizzard. He had only some rough plans to go by, and if he did not build the house fast enough the blizzard would have him.

Not the least of the Federal Government's difficulties was the vast size of its domain in terms of slow and unreliable communications. From New York to Charleston was a week's sail. Overland, a mounted messenger spent three weeks reaching Savannah from Philadelphia. East-west, the situation was even worse. The few roads dissolved into mere forest trails at the foothills of the Alleghenies. The Cumberland Road went through to Pittsburgh, but the Mississippi outposts were a month further on, by boat traveling with the current. Washington and the Congress in New York were as removed from the Americans of the interior as had been the English King and Parliament from the seaboard colonies. Westerners, carving new settlements out of the wilderness, had the same opportunities for disobedience and independence that had been enjoyed by the eastern colonies. And with the mouth of their outlet to the sea — the Mississippi — in Spanish hands, some were tempted to switch allegiance.

Washington's, and America's, freedom of action was also hampered by the circumstance that the newly formed Republic would not survive the strains of a full-scale war. The new institutions needed a period of peace in which to develop. But keeping the United States out of war would not be easy. The United States was a weak nation surrounded by the possessions of England, Spain and France. In the event that these powers became involved in a war, the United States would be unable to prevent them from making use of her territory. An alliance with France formed during the Revolution was almost certain to bring America into any conflict. Nor was there any way that American ships could be protected on the high seas.

Pioneers from Pennsylvania, Virginia and the Carolinas passed beyond the Appalachians into the rich valley of the Ohio and cleared farms and plantations in Tennessee and Kentucky. They placed their produce on the westward-flowing rivers on the far side of the Appalachians and found themselves and their hams and whisky on rafts floating southward through Spanish Louisiana to the busy city of New Orleans. Even as Washington and Secretary of State Jefferson negotiated for American rights to the Mississippi River, it was heard that five Spanish regiments of 600 men each had landed in New Orleans, to be followed by another 3,000 soldiers from Havana. Spain claimed considerable territory between the Mississippi and the Appalachians. Spanish agents were active in the Creek country, west of Georgia and Tennessee, trying to "check, as far as they can, the rapid increase, extension and consequence of this country."

While Spain was stirring up the Indians to the south, England was keeping the northern frontier in a state of unrest. The six nations of the Iroquois remained peaceful, but Miami and Wabash tribes attacked boats on the Ohio and Wabash Rivers. All along the north bank of the Ohio, settlers' cabins were burned, men and women killed, their children stolen. It was getting so bad that the westward movement had come to a halt. On November 4, 1791, General Josiah Harmar lost 900 of his 1,500 men in a Miami surprise attack. If the new Constitution had given the Federal Government exclusive power of dealing with Indians, it was

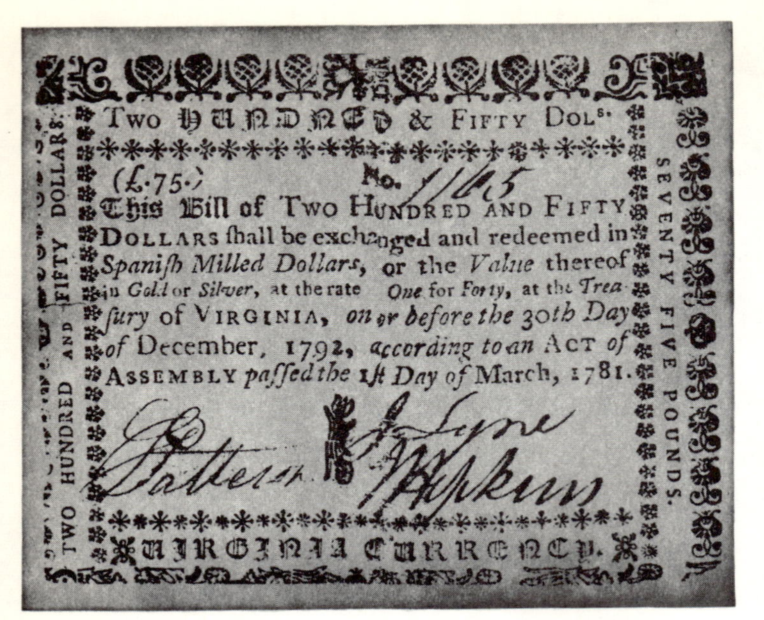

Paper money of such states as Virginia, Massachusetts, and Rhode Island was to be redeemed in silver or gold some years after issue.

having difficulty in exercising its authority. Nor did it seem capable of protecting the Indians' lands against the depredations of American citizens. The Yazoo Company, for instance, in which Patrick Henry was interested, threatened to raise its own army and drive the Indians from the lands along the Yazoo River, unless the Federal Government did it for them.

THE WAR DEBT

At the head of the newly-formed government that was weak in the affections of the people, that was surrounded by powerful enemies and possessed but feeble means of exercising authority, Washington was soon faced by deep divisions within the government.

These first showed themselves in Congressional opposition to a proposal by Alexander Hamilton that the United States assume responsibility for repaying all money that had been borrowed for the War for Independence.

This was a renewal of the old nationalist proposal, defeated during the Confederation. The Nationalists, now Federalists, expected to strengthen the national government by making Americans look to it for payment of the debts assumed by states during the war. (Three quarters of the national debt — money borrowed by Congress — had already been paid — as we have seen.)

Since the people, through taxes, must pay all the expenses of their government, they must eventually repay any money that their government borrows. A state that borrows money is people agreeing to pay taxes in the future. It is people borrowing money from themselves or their children.

The logical question about all this is: why don't people just give what is needed for a war? If farmer A gives one hundred bushels of wheat to the state and farmer B does not, it is unfair to farmer A. But if farmer A sells one hundred bushels to the state and farmer B does not, there is no injustice even if the money farmer A receives is, in effect, borrowed from the future. For when the debt is paid, in the form of taxation, farmer B will have to pay taxes, too.

Hamilton's proposal was complicated by the fact that the several states had already repaid various amounts of their debts to their citizens and to the national government. The states that had, like Virginia, paid a good part of their debts, naturally resented having to assume a share of the debts of states that had not made as great an effort at payment. There was also the fact that assumption would benefit some people out of all proportion to their help to the Revolution. During the long years of war the paper representing the debts had fallen in value. Soldiers and their families had often been relieved to find that a cobbler, for instance, would take even $100 or $200 in such paper for a pair of shoes.

Against the circumstance that in redeeming the debts of the states, the Federal Government might greatly benefit certain individuals who had happened to accumulate great amounts of these inflated securities, Hamilton had to weigh the fact that people of other nations, particularly America's ally France, were among the creditors.

The issue was finally settled. At the same time that this matter of debt assumption was being debated, the Congress was also considering the location of the new national capital. The southern states were able to get the northern states to agree to have the national capital moved south, in return for their agreement to Federal assumption of debts. Each group of states lost something and each gained. Fortunes were made by sharp traders who raced through the back country to stuff their saddlebags with old securities.

On a tour of the southern states in 1791, Washington had found, "The country appears to be in a very improving state, and industry and frugality are becoming much more fashionable. . . . Tranquility reigns among the people, with that disposition towards the general government which is likely to preserve it. They begin to feel the good effects of equal laws and equal protection. The farmer finds a ready market for his produce, and the merchant calculates with more certainty on his payments."

Oddly enough, commerce with Britain was as heavy as if no separation had occurred. In 1789, seven out of every eight foreign ships in American ports were British, and Americans were buying five times as many goods from the British, on easy credit terms, as the British were buying from them. Hamilton wanted to change this trend by increasing American manufactures and placing duties on British goods.

VIGOR VS. LIBERTY

Shortly after the Federal Government agreed to pay the remaining costs of the Revolution, Alexander Hamilton proposed to have the Federal Government support the formation of a private national bank.

As Federal taxes were collected they would be deposited in a Bank of the United States. But the bank would not just hold the funds idle, while waiting to pay salaries and the Government's bills. The money would be put to work. It would be lent out at interest, contributing to the commerce and prosperity of the nation. A merchant, for instance, who knew he could sell wine from the Canary Islands at a profit in New Orleans, could borrow money from the bank to purchase the wine in the Canary Islands.

Of course, the Government could have deposited the money in private banks with similar results. But Hamilton saw that a powerful part of the business community could be firmly attached to the new Government if it needed the favors of the Bank.

Hamilton and his followers saw the Federal Government as a great instrument for the promotion of wealth. It should, they thought, build roads and canals, deepen harbors and open one section of the nation to another so that trade could proceed where none had gone before. As the creation of a national bank would put the otherwise idle money of the nation into the hands of merchants who would bring more wealth and trade into the country, industry might be encouraged by tariffs that raised the price of foreign products. The power of the Federal Government was to be applied to make money flow as did water from the rock at the touch of Aaron's rod!

On the other hand, there were many Americans who viewed any extensions of the Federal Government's activities with suspicion and as against the principles of the Constitution. They viewed the entrance of the Federal Government into the mercantile life of the nation as an enlargement of Federal influence at the expense of the states and the individual citizen. Give the Federal Government the power to lend money to private individuals, they argued, and you give it another means of controlling and influencing their decisions.

The mercantile and banking interests in the different states influenced enough Congressmen to gain passage of the Bank Bill. The Bank was chartered in February, 1791 for a twenty-year period, to be managed by twenty-five directors, only five of whom were Government-chosen. Private stockholders selected the remainder.

If many Anti-Federalists had been mollified by the adoption of the first ten amendments, they now saw in the actions of Hamilton and his followers a plot to impose an unnecessarily strong central government on the country. "The creatures that surround [George Washington]," said Senator William Maclay of Pennsylvania, "would place a crown on his head, that they may have the handling of its jewels."

As the end of Washington's first four years in office drew near, the administration and country seemed more and more to be drifting into two opposing camps. As Alexander Hamilton was the leader of those who wished to strengthen the power of the Federal Government, James Madison and Thomas Jefferson of Virginia had become the leaders of the opposition. They had been against the assumption of state debts and had engineered the compromise that brought the new capital to the Potomac. Jefferson, in the cabinet, and Madison as a leader of Congress, had opposed the plan of a national bank.

Between the views of his Secretary of State and his Secretary of the Treasury, Washington saw nothing irreconcilable. The nation needed both the vigorous central government that Hamilton advocated and the conservative protection of individual liberties that Jefferson sought. There was no reason, as Washington saw it, why the vigor of the government should jeopardize the rights of individuals. The Federal Government had been founded on this balance between power and liberty, and there was no reason why it could not operate on these principles.

Washington was sixty years old in 1792. His hearing was failing, and he could not read without spectacles. More than anything else, he longed to retire to his Virginia plantations. ". . . the life of a husbandman of all others is the most delectable," he had written. Yet he was desperately needed in Philadelphia.

"It appears to me," Abigail Adams noted during a brief illness of the President, "that Union of the States, and consequently the permanency of the Government depend upon his life. . . ."

ANOTHER REVOLUTION

At the end of 1792, Washington was unanimously elected President for a second time. That winter, wild storms raced across the gray Atlantic, cutting the country off from Europe. For three months no ships could get through. Then, in April, came ominous news. King Louis XVI of France had been beheaded. The French nation, seething with revolution, was at war with Britain and Spain.

While serving there as American minister, Jefferson had been disturbed by the sullen and hungry faces everywhere in Paris, where one out of every five men was out of work. One afternoon in October, 1785, while walking in the country, the Virginian had met a French peasant woman.

"Wishing to know the conditions of the laboring poor," Jefferson wrote his friend Madison, "I entered into conversation with her. . . . She told me she was a day labourer, at 8 sous [8¢] the day; that often she could get no emploiment, and of course was without bread. . . .

"The property of this country is absolutely concentrated in a very few hands, having revenues of from half a million guineas a year downward," Jefferson continued. ". . . I asked myself what could be the reason that so many should be permitted to beg who are willing to work, in a country where there is a very considerable proportion of uncultivated lands? . . ."

In 1785, the government of France had been hovering on the brink of complete financial ruin. By 1786, France owed $600 million, almost half of which represented the cost of the fleets and armies she had sent across the Atlantic during the struggle for American independence. A wasteful and unjust system of government prevented France from paying this debt and forced her to borrow an additional $25 million each year.

Desperately casting about for more revenues, the King asked the wealthy nobility and clergy to contribute taxes. When they refused, the King called for a meeting of the ancient Estates General, an advisory body consisting of representatives of the three Estates of the Kingdom: the nobility, the clergy, and the merchants of the cities.

In May, 1789, just a few weeks after Washington had entered New York City for the triumphant beginning of his administration, the Estates General had sat down in Versailles for the first of a series of fateful meetings.

Against a decadent and bankrupt monarchy, power was easily seized. In a little more than a month the Third Estate transformed the Estates General into a French National Assembly. The Assembly represented particularly the new men of substance, the bourgeoisie: merchants, traders, manufacturers and bankers.

By summer, peasant uprisings had ended the King's authority in all the provinces. In October, the people of Paris marched on the palace at Versailles and brought Louis XVI and his family back to the city, virtual prisoners.

Meeting daily that fateful summer of 1789, the National Assembly abolished feudalism and drew up a "Declaration of the Rights of Man and of the Citizen," proclaiming that "Men are born and remain free and equal in rights," these rights of men being "liberty, property, security, and resistance to oppression." Religious toleration, freedom of speech, equal rights and liberty of the press were all affirmed.

In 1791, the National Assembly approved a new constitution, providing, like the American Constitution, for separation of powers — executive, legislative, and judicial, each to spring independently from the will of the people.

It seemed that a new day was dawning for mankind.

But more than a constitution, more than such forms of self-government were needed. Without experience in self-government and the arts of adjustment and compromise, the members of the first French Legislative Assembly soon found themselves hopelessly at odds with one another.

Meanwhile, the princes along France's borders were preparing large armies to come to the rescue of their fellow monarch. As Lafayette, at the head of the Assembly's defending forces, lost a series of battles to the armies of Austria and Prussia, the working people of Paris revolted, took over the government, and executed hundreds of nobles (among them the King and his family), clergymen, and their sympathizers.

With neither an orderly government nor fixed principles of justice, the reign of terror spread. Leaders of the revolution on Monday were suspected on Tuesday and beheaded on Wednesday. The humane invention of a certain Dr. Guillotin did the dirty work: an ax blade that dropped between two posts instantly snicked off the heads of each of 5,000 victims.

THE REPUBLICANS

The French Revolution became another means of separating those Americans who loved order first from those who loved liberty more. "Republican," the term by which the French revolutionists distinguished themselves, also became the badge of their American friends. As Anti-Federalists became Republicans, the Federalists applied the word as an epithet.

The arch-Federalists, fearing extension of voting privileges to ordinary workmen and backwoodsmen, pointed to the Paris terror as a horrible example of what might happen in America. "Our days are made heavy with the pressure of anxiety, and our nights restless with visions of horror," wrote the frightened Fisher Ames. "We listen to the clanck of chains, and overhear the whisper of assassins." The Republicans sympathized with the French people as fellow fighters against tyranny and oppression.

Washington's sympathies were divided. He also knew that it was his nation's interest to remain neutral, difficult as that course might be.

As the kings of Europe allied themselves against the menace of revolution, and as the people of France prepared to help other people overthrow their Kings, the United States found itself the only important trading neutral in the western world. The United States, too weak to defend her sailors against even the Barbary Pirates, now carried cargoes for all the warring nations of Europe.

The maintenance of neutrality was made even more difficult by the impulsive conduct of the Minister Plenipotentiary of the French Republic, Edmond Charles Genet. A converted aristocrat, the ardent revolutionary Genet arrived in Philadelphia early in 1793. Citizen Genet, as he called himself in the simple French republican revolutionary style, proceeded to recruit Americans for an expedition against Spanish Florida and Louisiana, to solicit funds for the arming of American ships and to commission American privateers. By such acts, Genet was involving America in a virtual war with Britain, Spain, and the rest of Europe. (To halt this activity, President Washington demanded Genet's recall. Before Genet could return to France, the revolutionary faction to which he belonged fell. Washington permitted him to remain in America, sparing him from certain death.)

If France's friends in America were embarrassed by Citizen Genet, England's friends were soon put in a similar plight.

On November 19, 1794, the American Envoy Extraordinary to Great Britain, John Jay, signed a Treaty of Amity, Commerce and Navigation with Great Britain. In this treaty Great Britain agreed to withdraw from Fort Miami, Detroit, Oswego, Niagara, Michilimakinac, in the northwest, positions which her troops had continued to occupy in violation of the Peace of 1783. (The Northwest Territory, the region bounded by the Great Lakes and the Ohio and Mississippi Rivers, had been taken from the British in 1779, by an expedition under George Rogers Clark.)

Connecticut Federalist and his wife. Oliver Ellsworth, U.S. Chief Justice (1796-99), believed that only the wealthy should have a vote.

Jay's treaty was very good, considering that it was made between a strong country and a weak one. But where the treaty spelled out this inequality between the countries, it touched a sensitive nerve. British trappers and traders, for instance, were given rights to the inland waters of the United States, yet Americans were denied similar rights in most of Canada; and southerners were ordered to pay the debts they owed Britons, but were given no credit for slaves that had been stolen by British raiders. Nor did the British promise to cease kidnaping American sailors from American ships.

While Washington worked tirelessly to keep the young nation out of war, his countrymen were becoming more divided. What was happening was that opposing state factions were finding allies in other states.

If Republicans ran the state, as in Virginia, then their western opponents became Federalists. In Federalist Connecticut and South Carolina, the westerners became Republicans. Different as they might be locally, the state parties joined together for national power. Aristocratic Virginia Republicans joined forces with the Tammany politicians of New York City. The arch-Federalists of Boston made common cause with the deer-slayers of the Shenandoah Valley. Republicans and Federalists had all kinds of Americans in their ranks, rich and poor, merchants and farmers, city dwellers and pioneers. What party a man belonged to depended more on where he happened to live than on what he believed.

But Washington did not understand this. He saw the parties as dedicated to opposing beliefs rather than as alliances of practical men for practical ends. Fearing factionalism, he designated a successor who would please neither party.

John Adams wasn't sure he wanted to be President. On the day after his inauguration, he wrote his wife that George Washington seemed to be saying: "Ay! I am fairly out, and you are fairly in! See which of us will be happiest!" Portrait by Gilbert Stuart, who put character on canvas.

THE DUKE OF BRAINTREE

John Adams was honest and forthright rather than clever and persuasive. He preferred saying what he thought, to soothing or flattering his hearers. He said that "the history of our Revolution will be one continued lie from one end to the other . . ." Of the Vice-Presidency he said: "My country has in its wisdom contrived for me the most insignificant office that ever the invention of man contrived or his imagination conceived."

The old patriot from Massachusetts was more concerned with principles than with men, "as disinterested as the Being Who made him," in the words of Thomas Jefferson. Intelligent and hard-working, he had been the most influential northern leader in the cause of independence. Like most of the rebels, he had opposed Great Britain in order to retain rights and liberties that Parliament was taking away. Having won the war and retained these rights, Adams was content. Attempts to enlarge these rights by, for instance, extending the vote to citizens who owned but small amounts of property, made him wary. He was unmoved by high-sounding phrases. The Declaration of Independence, in his view, breathed a dangerous spirit. How far were such ideas as "that all men are created equal" to be carried out? If all men believed themselves equal, might they not become intolerant of those with more property?

Shay's Rebellion and the events in France confirmed these views. Too much liberty made an end to order, and then nothing was safe.

But if he was opposed to Republicanism, Adams was equally opposed to the spirit of the party. If Madison feared Adams was a monarchist, the Federalist Hamilton found him cold and suspicious. Such was Adams, the man known in Massachusetts as "the Duke of Braintree."

MENACE FROM WITHOUT

As Adams took the oath of office, a great European coalition was falling before the turbulent armies of France. An unheard of draft law had subjected the entire French nation to military discipline, decreeing that "The young men shall go to battle; the married men shall forge arms and transport provisions; the women shall make tents and clothing, and shall serve in hospitals; the children shall turn old linen into lint; the aged shall betake themselves to the public places in order to arouse the courage of the warriors and preach hatred of kings and the unity of the Republic."

An age of polite wars of small professional armies had come to an end. The nation of revolution had become a nation in arms.

Between 1793 and 1797, a million French soldiers had subdued the armies of Austria, Prussia, Italy and Spain. Only England remained opposed to the French and to the brilliant young general, Napoleon Bonaparte.

In May, 1796, President Washington had received a report that two French agents had traveled through western Pennsylvania and Kentucky and down the Mississippi River to New Orleans. Western Americans were told that if they decided to secede from the United States they ought to look to France as "their natural ally and protector."

Trying to maintain Washington's policy of neutrality, President Adams sent a special mission to France. The result aroused American fears and hostility further. Talleyrand, the French Foreign Minister, had gained some insight into American politics during a recent sojourn to the states. He instructed his agents to insult the American diplomats, expecting this would embarrass the Adams Administration and help the American Republicans, whom he regarded as more friendly to France. The French officials' demand of a loan in return for leaving Americans at peace did not have the desired effect. Instead of embarrassing Adams, it dismayed Talleyrand by bringing the United States to the brink of war. The American diplomats, John Marshall, Elbridge Gerry and C. C. Pinckney, referred to the French officials as "X," "Y," and "Z," and the transaction became known as the *X Y Z Affair*.

Meanwhile, the French fleet was harassing American merchant vessels in the West Indies, seizing their cargoes and removing American seamen. The British, too, continued their interference with American shipping, and took American sailors from American vessels, claiming that they were deserters from the British Navy. The Insurance Company of North America estimated that in the last six months of 1798, America lost $280,000 to British ships and $260,000 to French privateers.

MENACE FROM WITHIN

The constant alarms caused by the prowling of foreign armed vessels off her shores, by the plotting of enemy agents within her borders, and the rudeness of the governments overseas, caused a jittery nation to pass four repressive measures. Even if the United States did not go to war, it seemed, the United States Constitution would be destroyed.

Madison had warned of the weaknesses of the Bill of Rights. Now a Sedition Act severely limited the freedoms of speech, press, and assembly. A Congressman was jailed for four months because of an attack on Adams' policies, and editors of opposition newspapers in Vermont and Pennsylvania suffered similar fates.

Other acts made it much more difficult for foreigners to become American citizens and subjected them to imprisonment or deportation at the will of the President. Such eminent men as the English scientists Cooper and Priestley, the French economist Du Pont, and the Swiss statesman Gallatin were attacked as spies and subversives.

These acts were parts of a six-fold plan of action devised by Alexander Hamilton to put down the Republicans and increase the power of the Federalists. The other parts of Hamilton's plan were: to cancel the treaty of alliance with France, to enlarge the army greatly, to build a navy to be administered by a Secretary of Navy, to enlarge the government's power of taxation, and to authorize the Government to borrow an additional $5 million.

Through both Congress and the Cabinet, Hamilton was now directing American affairs. He was able to do this because Adams was exerting no leadership himself.

In the first place, Adams tended to think of the President as an umpire rather than as a leader. Then, his narrow victory (he had defeated Jefferson in the election of 1796 by only three electoral votes) made his position weak. The feeling that he was merely Washington's successor had caused him to keep Washington's final Cabinet: Oliver Wolcott, Timothy Pickering, James McHenry, and Charles Lee.

Unfortunately, the first three men felt a deep obligation to Hamilton, who had recommended them to Washington. They looked to Hamilton rather than Adams for leadership. Since Adams had continued Washington's policy of putting issues to the vote of the Cabinet, Hamilton, through his influence on Pickering, Wolcott and McHenry, could control the Presidency.

Hamilton's program was designed not only to perpetuate the Federalist Party, but to make himself the first man in the nation. With little faith that the Constitution could survive the shock of foreign aggression, Hamilton expected that a great crisis would soon disrupt the Union. He was not a man to sit idle and be overridden by events. If a crisis came, he would be its master.

Hamilton had also been plotting with the Venezuelan, Miranda, for the liberation of the Spanish colonies in America. But the purpose of the enlarged army was neither this nor defense against the French. Hamilton planned to give commissions in his army only to the Federalists. He intended to use it against the Republicans.

VICTORY WITHOUT WAR

As Hamilton steadily maneuvered himself into the desired position, it seemed that his crisis was at last at hand. The legislatures of Kentucky and Virginia passed strong resolutions condemning the Alien and Sedition Acts.

The Kentucky Resolutions, written by

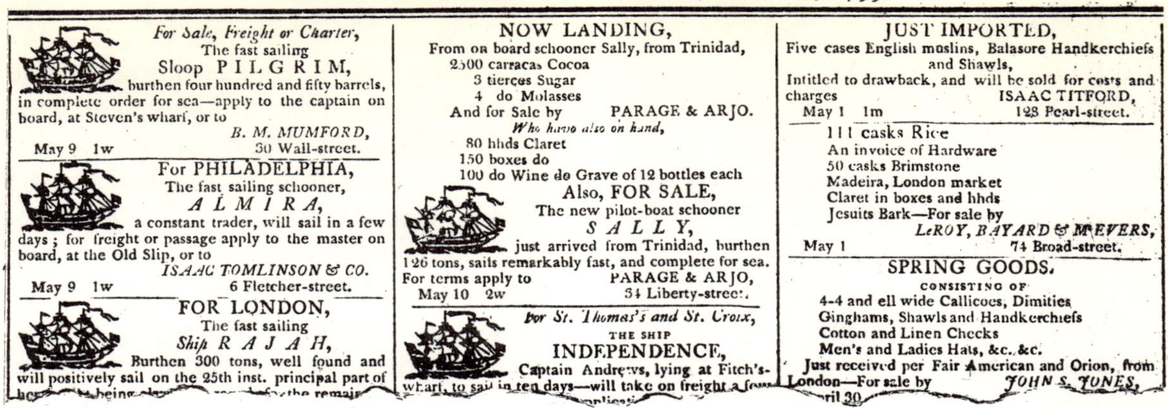
NEW-YORK, SATURDAY EVENING, MAY 11, 1799.

For Sale, Freight or Charter,
The fast sailing
Sloop PILGRIM,
burthen four hundred and fifty barrels, in complete order for sea—apply to the captain on board, at Steven's wharf, or to
B. M. MUMFORD,
May 9 1w 30 Wall-street.

For PHILADELPHIA,
The fast sailing schooner,
ALMIRA,
a constant trader, will sail in a few days; for freight or passage apply to the master on board, at the Old Slip, or to
ISAAC TOMLINSON & CO.
May 9 1w 6 Fletcher-street.

FOR LONDON,
The fast sailing
Ship RAJAH,
Burthen 300 tons, well found and will positively sail on the 25th inst. principal part of

NOW LANDING,
From on board schooner Sally, from Trinidad,
2500 carracas Cocoa
3 tierces Sugar
4 do Molasses
And for Sale by PARAGE & ARJO.
Who have also on hand,
80 hhds Claret
150 boxes do
100 do Wine de Grave of 12 bottles each

Also, FOR SALE,
The new pilot-boat schooner
SALLY,
just arrived from Trinidad, burthen 126 tons, sails remarkably fast, and complete for sea.
For terms apply to PARAGE & ARJO,
May 10 2w 34 Liberty-street.

For St. Thomas's and St. Croix,
THE SHIP
INDEPENDENCE,
Captain Andrews, lying at Fitch's-wharf, to sail in ten days—will take on freight a few

JUST IMPORTED,
Five cases English muslins, Balasore Handkerchiefs and Shawls,
Intitled to drawback, and will be sold for costs and charges ISAAC TITFORD,
May 1 1m 128 Pearl-street.

111 casks Rice
An invoice of Hardware
50 casks Brimstone
Madeira, London market
Claret in boxes and hhds
Jesuits Bark—For sale by
LeROY, BAYARD & M'EVERS,
May 1 74 Broad-street.

SPRING GOODS,
CONSISTING OF
4-4 and ell wide Callicoes, Dimities
Ginghams, Shawls and Handkerchiefs
Cotton and Linen Checks
Men's and Ladies Hats, &c. &c.
Just received per Fair American and Orion, from London—For sale by *JOHN S. JONES,*

the Vice President of the United States, Thomas Jefferson, maintained, "that the several states composing the United States of America, are not united on the principle of unlimited submission to their general government; nor was this general government the exclusive or final judge of the extent of the power delegated to itself . . .; but that as in all other cases of compact among parties having no common judge, *each party had an equal right to judge for itself . . .*"

It then went on to declare the Alien and Sedition Acts as void and of no force in the state of Kentucky.

The Virginia House of Delegates passed a similar resolution and raised the state's taxes by twenty-five per cent to purchase 5,000 stand of arms.

Hamilton suggested that Congress appoint a special committee to consider the Virginia resolutions for the "full evidence which they afford of a regular conspiracy to overturn the government." He also wanted the Alien and Sedition Acts strengthened and recruiting of the army speeded up.

But President Adams, at last aware of Hamilton's pretensions, refused to make any move toward giving him his army.

It was, finally, on the relations between France and the United States that the whole issue was to turn. If the United States became involved in a war with France, Adams would have to recruit Hamilton's army. As Adams wrote eleven years afterwards, the large army and the necessary taxes "would have raised a rebellion in every state in the Union, the very idea of the expense of it would have turned President, Senate, and the House out-of-doors."

Once Hamilton got his army, Adams said, it would take a second army to disband the first.

In 1799, the Government would have had to raise $11.5 million, double the entire Federal budget of 1796, just to pay for the Army and Navy! To raise just $8 million in 1798, Congress had passed taxes on land holdings, houses, and slaves (and even a Stamp Act!) and had had to put down an armed rebellion in three counties in Pennsylvania.

John Marshall of Virginia, one of the X Y Z Commissioners, had informed the President that the French Government, with Napoleon as dictator now, regretted the rude action of its representatives and would welcome a new American effort. While the extreme Federalists attacked him bitterly, Adams succeeded in coming to terms with the government of Napoleon.

With the threat of war with France ended, the schemes of Hamilton fell apart. The President, who had entered office fearing Republican excesses, had discovered a greater menace among the extremists of his own party.

"THE BEAUTY OF HER MOTION"

In 1796, a clever politician had succeeded in taking the state of Pennsylvania away from the Federalists. In the two previous elections, little-known party men had run as Presidential electors. In 1796, John Beckley succeeded in getting a number of the most distinguished gentlemen in Pennsylvania to run as Republican electors. He had had lists of the Republican electors printed and had distributed them all over the state a few days before the election. His calculation that many people would vote for electors they admired, rather than on the basis of party, proved correct.

In 1800, Aaron Burr, the Republican leader of New York, copied Beckley's tactics. He got influential New Yorkers such as George Clinton, Robert Livingston and General Gates to run for the New York State Assembly. With candidates like these, the Republicans won control of the state legislature, which, in turn, chose the state's Presidential electors. Burr's task was made easier by Hamilton, whose extreme policies and arrogance had driven some distinguished Federalists into the Republican camp.

Indeed, the policies of the Federalists, particularly of the followers of Hamilton, helped the Republicans in all the states.

Thomas Jefferson defeated John Adams by eight electoral votes. The Republican Presidential victory was viewed by many of both parties as a kind of second American revolution. But the victorious Jefferson came to the new city of Washington in a conciliatory spirit.

"Let us restore . . . that harmony and affection without which liberty and even life itself are but dreary things," Jefferson said. "And let us reflect that having banished from our land that religious intolerance under which mankind so long bled and suffered, we have yet gained little if we countenance a political intolerance as despotic, as wicked, and capable of as bitter and bloody persecutions . . . We have called by different names brethren of the same principle."

And to his friend John Dickinson he wrote: "The tough sides of our Argosy have been thoroughly tried. Her strength has stood the waves into which she was steered, with a view to sink her. We shall put her on her republican tack, and she will now show by the beauty of her motion the skill of her builders."

As Thomas Jefferson assumed the powers of the Presidency, it seemed that the winds of fate had suddenly shifted to part the storm clouds that had so long threatened the young nation.

American vessels suffered more depradations; but despite the loss of hundreds of ships and cargoes each year — even to the tiny navies of Denmark and Naples — trade (and smuggling) prospered.

President Thomas Jefferson in 1805: his red hair is turning white; the Declaration of Independence is 29 years in the past, along with his youth and the glorious uncertainties of Revolution. Portrait was painted by Rembrandt Peale.

Great Britain, cut off from Europe by France, paid high prices for American grain. France, which had taken Louisiana from weak Spain, suddenly agreed to sell this vast western Empire to the United States for $15 million.

Jefferson, who had opposed the National Bank as an unwarranted extension of Federal power, and who had written the Kentucky Resolutions protesting the Alien and Sedition Acts, now unhesitatingly authorized this purchase.

Thus Jefferson, as President, with the responsibility of doing what was best for the country, had used that same constitutional flexibility that had alarmed him when applied by others.

The purchase of Louisiana was a remarkable piece of luck. At one stroke the navigation of the Mississippi, and thus the allegiance of the Americans beyond the Alleghenies, was secured. The territory, comprising all the lands drained by all the rivers that flowed eastward into the Mississippi, doubled the size of the nation. The United States now stretched to distant and legendary western mountains. By peaceful purchase, Jefferson had gained more for America than Hamilton had dreamed to annex by conquest.

"We can no longer say there is nothing new under the sun," Jefferson wrote the scientist Priestley. "For this whole chapter in the history of man is new. The great extent of our republic is new. Its sparse habitation is new. . . ."

THE WAR OF 1812

The sea sustained the teeming coastal cities. Owners of ships calculated the profits of cargoes. Merchants in scarlet cloaks were followed by elegant Negro servants with Roman names. The newspapers published long lists of arrivals and departures. Sailors in broad-brimmed leather hats, short jackets and wide breeches, ship-builders, and shipfitters jammed streets, ropewalks, and sail lofts. Cartmen transported cargo from shipside to warehouse. Banks busily lent money against cargoes and for the exchange of credit.

The wealth and luxury of these eastern cities rested on a fragile base. It could only be maintained as long as those who controlled the seas, and foreign ports, permitted American ships to come and go. The warring European nations sank and captured American vessels to injure each other's trade. Jefferson and his successor, James Madison, sought to keep America out of war, and to retaliate against these attacks, by forbidding all shipping between America and the rest of the world. The embargo, and later non-intercourse acts directed at Britain and France, hurt America far more than they did Europe.

The attacks on American shipping and impressment of seamen, American as well as British from American ships, and the desire of Westerners to end British influence over the frontier Indians, led the United States to declare war on Britain on June 18, 1812. An American Army that expected to capture Canada met with a quick defeat. At sea, the solid victories of the *Constitution* over the *Guerrière,* and the capture of the *Macedonian* by the *United States* raised American hopes. But by 1813, the British Navy had pretty well bottled up the American fleet.

The climax came in 1814. With the exiling of Napoleon, the full power of Britain could now be exerted against the

United States. In August, the British won an easy victory at Bladensburg, Maryland and went on to Washington. There they burned the docks, ships, an arsenal, the Capitol, the White House, War Office, Treasury Building, and a bridge. The following month, the British were stopped before Baltimore when an all night bombardment failed to humble Fort McHenry. The sight of the American flag still flying over the fort on the morning of the fourteenth inspired a young lawyer, Francis Scott Key, to write "The Star-Spangled Banner."

Three days before the bombardment of Fort McHenry, a 31-year-old American commander won a decisive naval battle on a lake in New York State. Lake Champlain extends 107 miles south from Montreal, Canada. A British fleet, under Commander Downie, together with a British army, planned to gain control of the lake and, from there, move south against New York City and New England. The American Commander Thomas MacDonough, a veteran of a campaign against the Tripoli pirates, defeated the British fleet while General Macomb defeated the British Army at nearby Plattsburgh.

The defeats at Fort McHenry and Lake Champlain, and the loss of 1700 merchantmen to American privateers and men-of-war, discouraged the British and a peace was signed on December 24. Meanwhile, 26 New Englanders, meeting in Hartford, Connecticut, were considering seceding from the Union rather than facing further loss of trade. America, too, had lost some 1700 merchant vessels; and a British Expeditionary Force was landing in Louisiana. The two armies had no way of knowing that a peace treaty had been signed. The defeat of the British veterans five miles below New Orleans, gave Americans the feeling they had won the war after all; and the victory won for General Andrew Jackson the eternal gratitude of his countrymen.

THE MONROE DOCTRINE AND THE EXPERIMENT

Since 1810, South and Central American patriots had been struggling to free their countries from Spain and Portugal. By 1822, the forces of Simon Bolivar and Jose de San Martin seemed assured of success. And on September 27 of that year, Brazil broke away from Portugal.

When South and Central America achieved independence, only Russia (with Alaska and with ambitions in Oregon and California) and Great Britain would have substantial holdings in the Americas.

But in 1815, the Emperors of Russia and Austria, and the King of Prussia had agreed to support each other against any spread of republicanism. Subsequently, this program was endorsed by all the other rulers on the continent.

In 1822, at Verona, the allied kings forced a reactionary government on Spain. It was in the interest of the United States that the emerging nations of Latin America not be similarly repressed, with the establishment of Prussian, Austrian, or French, or the expansion of Russian, influence in the Western Hemisphere.

Primarily, this was a matter of American self-interest. Under Spain, or any other colonial power, Latin America would be closed to the merchant ships of the United States. On the other hand, independent South and Central American nations would welcome the products of the republic of the North.

After much deliberation, Secretary of

State John Quincy Adams and President James Monroe decided to assert that European powers should no longer consider the Americas for purposes of colonization. The principle was proclaimed in President Monroe's message to Congress, December 2, 1823. (From 1821 to 1824, while American exports to the rest of the world remained about the same, her exports to Latin America doubled.)

For thirty years, the British, opposed to outside interference with their trade with the new American nations, supported the Monroe Doctrine. By the 1850's, the United States was strong enough to defend the Americas herself.

Safe from foreign intervention, the United States was free to engage fully in the great experiment begun by the Declaration of Independence.

What an endlessly difficult experiment it was! Six years after the end of the War of 1812, nineteen years after the sunny optimism of his first year in office, Thomas Jefferson would write: "I regret that I am now to die in the belief, that the useless sacrifice of themselves by the generation of 1776, to acquire self-government and happiness to their country, is to be thrown away by the unwise and unworthy passions of their sons . . ."

What were these "unwise and unworthy passions"? What had happened to cause Jefferson to foresee failure and misery?

To answer these questions we must examine how the American people lived during the first half of the nineteenth century; how beliefs and fortunes were shaped by rivers, mountains, soil, climate, and just plain distance — the causes of great *sectional* interests in the North, West, and South.

THE NORTH: FACTORIES AND CORPORATIONS

THE OLD craft methods used in the pewterer's shop, shown above, were dying in the eighteenth century. In the early 1700s, the brothers Lombe had erected in England a factory building 500 feet long and six stories high in which, according to Daniel Defoe, "26,586 Wheels . . . work 73,726 yards of Silk Thread every time the Water Wheel goes round, which is three times in one minute." Such secret English machinery turned by water or steam made it possible for unskilled children and women to out-produce skilled craftsmen.

Bounties were offered to entice Englishmen to reveal industrial secrets. In 1790, Samuel Slater, an English textile worker, came to Providence, R. I., and built some spinning and weaving machinery from memory. The firm of Almy, Brown and Slater built plants in Pawtucket and Slatersville, R. I., in Amoskeag Falls, N. H., and in Oxford, Mass.

The bigger, better organized British factories were able to produce textiles cheaper than American plants. English cotton fabric, including the cost of transport across the ocean, undersold the native product.

The embargoes and the war had spurred development of American manufacturing. They prevented the entry of British goods, thus stopping the competition. And their interference with American trade was forcing men to find other ways of investing their money.

In 1814, while many of their fellow merchants were simply complaining, Francis Cabot Lowell and Patrick Tracy Jackson of Boston invested in a big textile factory in Waltham, Massachusetts. The machinery in the factory was based on sketches that Lowell had secretly made in Manchester, England.

The war against Britain ended in 1815. British and other foreign manufactures began once more to flood the United States. No longer protected against competition by embargoes and French and British edicts, American manufacturers were threatened with ruin. They induced Congress to erect another kind of protection. Duties raised the prices of foreign manufactures to the American level and provided the Federal Government with money. Under protection of tariffs, as such duties were called, American industry continued to prosper, and whole families began entering its service. For the two weeks ending November 28, 1828, for example, the Slater spinning mills in Pawtucket, Rhode Island, recorded the following earnings for the Howlands:

	days worked	am't earned
Willard	12	$10.00
Malvin	12	5.50
Munyan	12	1.33
John	12	1.17
Polly	12	4.00
Hannah	12	2.00
Lorinda	0	0
		$24.00

Against these earnings, they were charged 57¢ for pasturing their cow on company land and a rent of 96¢ for their quarters in the company village. They worked seventy hours during a six-day week.

Factories changed habits of living. More men worked closer together, and applied themselves to a single task. The Philadelphia cotton manufacturer, James Kempson, proudly told a British factory commission that none of his 400 employees was less than nine years of age, and that the work day varied from ten to fourteen hours, depending on the time of year. "Among our workmen there is no desire to have the hours of labor shortened," he explained, "since they see that it will necessarily be accompanied by a reduction of their wages."

In the factory, a manufacturing process was broken down into separate simple stages with the result that unskilled workers, tending machines, could greatly out-produce the finest craftsmen.

Probably the first machine-tools — precision machinery designed to make parts for other machines — were made by clock-makers and there were a lot of clock-makers in Connecticut. With these skilled craftsmen to draw on, Eli Whitney of Connecticut, in 1798 contracted to deliver 10,000 muskets to the United States Government in two years. To do this, Whitney built a factory in which new kinds of machines, which he designed, automatically made all the separate parts of muskets. By 1806, he had a factory equipped with power-driven machine tools that could manufacture muskets in quantity for less than they cost to make anywhere else in the world. And what was more remarkable, the parts for one Whitney musket would fit any other Whitney musket. Whitney could supply the army with interchangeable spare parts. This greatly simplified repairs and maintenance.

The British power spindle and power loom had replaced and multiplied the skills of spinners and weavers; Whitney's machine tools did the same to smiths and mechanics, the makers of machinery themselves. *Whitney's machines could make machines.* Now, it seemed, there was nothing the factory system could not accomplish.

UNREAL PEOPLE

Like the factory system, the corporation was a British invention. The London and Plymouth Companies that promoted the first settlements in Virginia and Massachusetts had been British corporations.

First of all, the corporation was a means by which a number of people could pool their capital for a single purpose. (Some sixty London merchants, courtiers, and tradesmen had put money into the London Company in order to finance the sending of settlers to Virginia.) In return for the money they put into the corporation, the investors received shares. For instance, it might be decided to sell 1,000 shares for $100, to raise a capital of $100,000. A man who invested $1,000 in the corporation would receive ten shares; a man who invested $500 would receive five shares. When the profits were divided up, the holder of ten shares would receive twice as big a portion of the profits as the holder of five shares. Corporations can also give shares to people in return for services of various kinds. Settlers in some of the early colonies, for example, were given shares in the colony's proceeds, although they had invested no money.

Because corporations own property, buy and sell, and engage in business, they inevitably must come into the law courts. The British courts and, following them, the American courts, decided that the corporation is, in effect, a kind of person. Thus, a corporation can be sued or can sue and can be punished or rewarded.

There are, however, important differences between a corporation and a *real* person. First, a corporation is composed of a number of people who can assign their rights to others (a shareholder can sell his shares, or leave them in his will to his heir). This means that the *real* people who make up the corporation are continually changing.

N° 101

Middlebury, Nov. 19, 1803.

Jonathan H. Hubbard of Windsor

is entitled to One Share, or one three-hundredth part of the Stock of CENTER TURNPIKE COMPANY, being N° 101; ſubject to the By-laws and Regulations of ſaid Company.

Daniel Chipman *Clerk.*

The first American corporations built turnpikes, bridges, and canals with exclusive rights of way. By 1821, Pennsylvania had authorized 141 turnpikes, and New York had 4000 miles of toll roads. One big east-west road, from Cumberland to Pittsburgh, was Federally financed.

Second, a corporation could only engage in the certain specific activities for which it was formed. The corporation received its life-charter from the Government and could only act in accordance with its charter.

Lowell and Jackson's Boston Manufacturing Company was chartered to build and operate a cotton manufacturing plant in Waltham. It could not build a canal.

Originally, corporations had depended on monopoly privileges. The Virginia Company had the exclusive right of settling its portion of North America. The Charles River Bridge Company was given the exclusive privilege of building a bridge over a river near Boston. The Supreme Court, in the Dartmouth College Case, ruled that no state could change a corporation charter, once it had granted it. If the charter gave a monopoly, the monopoly was perpetual.

Machinery and steam offered so many opportunities that monopolies were no longer needed to make investment attractive.

The Boston Manufacturing Company had no monopoly privilege. It was simply using the corporation as a means of pooling money. What made the corporation form desirable was that it limited the personal liability of the investors. The corporation could be sued, but not the people who owned it. If, for instance, the Boston Manufacturing Company had a million-dollar judgment entered against it for patent infringement and the company did not have a million dollars, it could go out of business. The holders of stock in the company would not have to make up the million dollars out of their own pockets.

MAKING MONEY

During the Administrations of Washington, Adams and Jefferson, what little gold or silver there was in the United States kept going out of the country to pay foreign debts. The shortage of cash was such that most business was carried on by a system of "book credit." A storekeeper, for instance, kept a book in which he wrote down the value of everything a farmer purchased from him. Against these purchases, he would credit the value of whatever produce — eggs, hams, bushels of wheat — the farmer sold him during the year. This balance might be carried on for years with never a penny changing hands.

Where a laborer was hired to build a railroad or a factory, book credit would not work. Laborers moved from place to place and had to purchase foods, clothes, and housing from strangers. They needed money.

We have already seen how many of the states printed pieces of paper that were used as money during the Revolution and how this paper money varied in value, depending on the confidence that it could be exchanged for something else of value.

In the early years of the Republic, most of the paper money was printed by private banks. The banks, by a number of devices, were able to greatly increase the amount of money in circulation.

For instance, nine merchants in Boston would obtain a charter to incorporate a bank. Each of the nine merchants would lend the bank $10,000 in the form of British pounds, or United States bonds or other forms of recognized money, or "specie." The total of $90,000 would then be lent to two of the merchants to buy three new sailing ships and cargoes of rum. Against this $90,000 loan, the two merchants would give the bank a note stating that they would repay the $90,000 at the end of one year, at ten per cent interest. (In other words, the

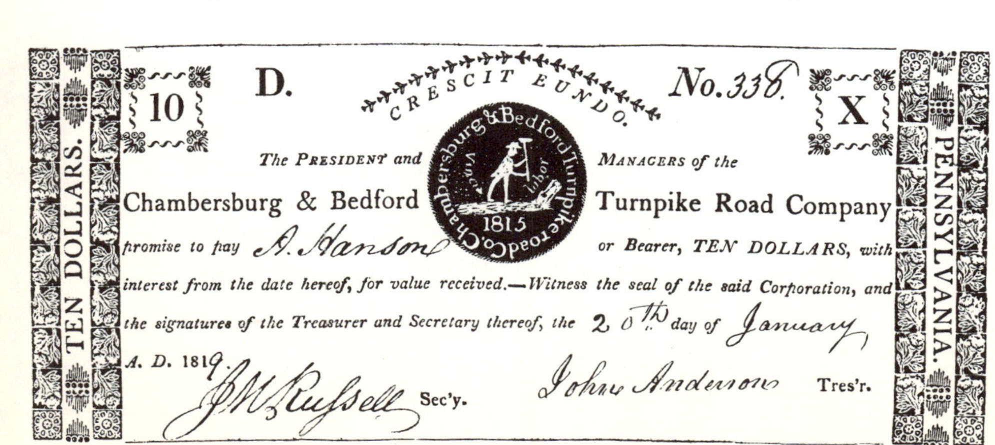

Turnpike companies, canal companies, and cotton mills all issued their own money. Anybody could issue money. Some was good; some wasn't.

bank would get back $99,000 in specie at the end of one year.)

The merchants' note would now be considered by the bank as capital against which paper money could be issued. Depending on the rules of the particular bank, $30,000, or $60,000, or even $90,000 in paper money would be printed. This money would be considered of real value because the note promised that the bank would have specie to exchange for it. A bank was thus able to make one dollar do the work of one-and-a-half, or even two dollars.

But everyone wanted to borrow the new bank note dollars from the banks — to buy new farms, horses, oxen, plows, shipments of goods, machinery, and factories. No matter how much money the banks printed, there wasn't enough.

To satisfy the demand, banks stepped up their printing of money, issuing three dollars, five dollars, ten dollars in bank notes to every one dollar of specie. Then men started banks with no specie at all, pretending to have borrowed specie that never had even existed! Such paper money was, of course, no more real than the gold at the end of the rainbow, but it passed for money as long as people believed it was secured by specie.

THE BUSINESS CYCLE

The northern states of the Union, where industry was concentrated, particularly became subject to violent business cycles. Periods of rising prices would be followed by periods of falling prices. As the amount of paper money increased, it would be easy to borrow, easy to get merchandise on credit. Prices would rise, there being more money in circulation relative to the amount of things to buy. As prices and sales went up, there was more work for everyone. Business was good and wages were high.

We have seen how a bank might print two or three dollars for every one dollar of specie. The system worked all right until heavy demands were made on specie. Merchants might suddenly need a lot of specie to pay foreign debts. If they found the banks slow in exchanging their dollars for specie, then others who did not need it right away, but who were worried by this slow payment, would demand it. As specie was withdrawn, the banks were left with less money to lend.

With money more difficult to borrow, the downward cycle would begin. Banks threatened with ruin, as demands were made on their dwindling supplies of specie, would be seeking to collect debts. As banks called in debts and refused to make loans, money grew scarce. As money became scarce, prices and wages went down. But while prices fell, sales fell, too, as merchants, worrying about their supplies of money, insisted on cash payments. With fewer sales, men would be thrown out of work. As business got worse, the banks, finding it more difficult to collect debts, would cause the money supply to grow even smaller.

The first such business crisis occurred in 1819. When the second came, in 1837, a New York mob broke open warehouses and helped itself to flour, sugar, and other foods. By January, 1838, one-third of the 200,000 wage earners in New York City were out of work, and not less than 10,000 were in "utter and hopeless distress." Soup kitchens were established to give the most destitute bread and a pint of soup a day. Twenty years later, during a third crisis, one out of every fourteen people in New York State had to be given some form of relief.

THE NORTH: GROWTH AND CHANGE

THE PROMOTERS of the seventeenth and eighteenth centuries, such as the Carters of Virginia and the Livingstons of New York, made their fortunes from land, buying it wholesale and selling it retail. As close relationships with royal governors had made possible wholesale purchases of land, influence over state legislatures now brought corporation charters for turnpikes, toll bridges, canals, and steamboat lines.

If factories and banks were needed, what was more natural than that the governments of New York, Massachusetts, Ohio, or Indiana should charter banking and factory corporations? What was more natural than that the states should give rights of way, even grants of land — that they should give exclusive rights to waterfalls and invest money in the enterprises themselves? Why should not the states encourage good citizens to perform essential functions?

Few articles could bear the cost of shipment by slow horse-drawn wagon, particularly over mountains. Away from rivers and seaports, there was little trade. But a new era of mechanical transportation was dawning. In 1807, Fulton and Livingston's Clermont *traveled up the Hudson from New York to Albany, against the current, at an average speed of five miles an hour. The trip took 32 hours.*

Nowhere else on earth could men build so freely.

CANALS

On July 4, 1817, the Governor of New York, DeWitt Clinton, shoveled up a spadeful of earth at a place near Albany. At 10 A.M., Wednesday, October 25, 1825, the waters of Lake Erie were let into the end of a canal at Buffalo, and the first barge began the 544-mile journey from the Great Lakes to New York City — from Buffalo to Albany on the Erie Canal, from Albany to New York City on the Hudson River.

The canal cut travel time between Albany and Buffalo from twenty to ten days. "A cent-and-a-half a mile for a mile-and-a-half an hour," but with inflation, the fare went up to 3¢ a mile. Freight charges fell from twenty-two dollars a ton to four dollars a ton. By 1826, Albany newspapers were announcing the

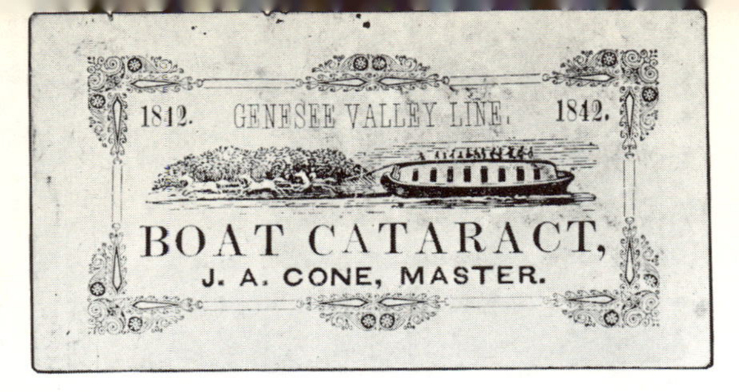

The Erie Canal, 500 miles long, was dug by ten thousand newly arrived immigrants, mostly Irish. They were paid 50 cents a day.

arrival of fifty barges daily, from the West. Travelers between New York and New Orleans began traveling by canal and coach to Pittsburgh, and down the Ohio and Mississippi by steamer.

The Erie was the longest and most successful of the 4,500 miles of canals built in the United States between 1790 and 1840. The heyday of the canal was brief. Another form of transportation, cheaper to build and swifter-moving, took its place.

RAILROADS

The first American steam locomotive to run on rails circled a half-mile track on the Hoboken, New Jersey estate of John Stevens in 1825. Newspaper stories of English railroad success encouraged more experiments. In 1829 and 1830, an English and an American engine operated over a few miles of track in Maryland. Baltimore sought to rival the Erie Canal with a railroad to the Ohio Valley. Railroads opened for business in Louisiana and New York in 1831. The first American railroad to carry passengers regularly was in Charleston, South Carolina. By its third year, 1833, service extended to Hamburg, S. C., 136 miles from Charleston. Tracks could be laid down for $10,000 a mile. The cost of digging a canal was $30,000 a mile. By 1840, there were more miles of railroad than of canals.

When the Boston-Worcester Railroad began operations in 1833, it charged six-and-a-quarter cents to carry a ton of freight one mile, or about one-third of the seventeen-and-a-half cents rate charged to carry the same amount of freight on the turnpike. As railroads improved, the cost of transport, particularly of such large bulky items as coal, iron ore, wheat, and other farm crops, shrank to one-twentieth of what it had been at the opening of the century. The cost of shipping by river also plummeted.

The effect of this lowering of transportation costs was to open up vast distant markets for the production of factories and farms. Traffic on the Erie Canal alone increased from 667,171 tons in 1837 to 1,635,089 in 1850 and 2,253,533 in 1860. No longer did inland farms have to restrict themselves to growing just for their own consumption; and the railroad was soon supplying country stores with the woolens, calicoes, clocks, and shoes of eastern factories.

In 1825, 16,500,000 yards of cloth were woven in New York homes. Thirty years later, home manufacture of textiles had fallen to less than a million yards.

More and more Americans were becoming accustomed to going outside of their homes to satisfy their wants—shopping, instead of making. The spinning wheel was disappearing from the American farm as the little truck garden was disappearing from the tailor's backyard.

The railroads followed the old paths through the Appalachian chain—Washington's route to Pittsburgh: and the Cumberland Gap to Memphis, Tennessee. Lines from Boston and other New England cities connected with Albany and the West. The railroads thus did for cities up and down the eastern seaboard

Grand Exhibition.

TRAVELLING MUSEUM.

The inhabitants of **are respectfully informed that the *American Travelling Museum* will arrive on** **and may be seen for** **and evening , at**
Admittance, **cents---Children under 12 years of age, half price.**

The *TRAVELLING MUSEUM* consists of two houses placed on wheels, so constructed that they may be placed contiguous to each other, and formed into a splendid and elegant room, which contains the following

CURIOSITIES AND WORKS OF NATURE AND ART:

A Mummy of an Indian Woman.

This great natural curiosity was discovered and taken from the interior of a cave in Warren County, Kentucky, where it probably had been secreted in its present state of preservation for 1000 years.
The *ALLIGATOR*, too terrible to describe, but well enough to be seen in conjunction with the *LOON* and other equatick Birds, &c. are attached to the exhibition—The *HEDGE-HOG FISH*, an animal not known to one tenth of the community—The *TIGER-CAT*, one of the rarest seen animals in the creation—The *MONKEY*, the sprightly creature of diversion; and last, though not least, the *EAGLE*, the bird that flourishes on our country's standard, marks its insignia, and rides triumphant over a host of enemies. Also, a *BULB*, or spongy substance, which grew on one of our forest trees, remarkably large, and bearing an exact likeness to a Turtle.

120 BIRDS, QUADRUPEDS, INSECTS, &c.

MUMMY. ***Wonderful* SEA LEOPARD.** **LOON.** **EAGLE.**

This very singular Curiosity was caught off the Cape of Good Hope, and brought to the United States.

A COSMORAMA,

Exhibiting a view of a superb and elegant painting, representing the *LAST SUPPER* of our Saviour with his Apostles. The painting, distinct from its elegance of execution, is well calculated to produce a salutary lesson, upon the mind, of youth particularly.

A PANORAMA,

Which exhibits a view of Mount Vesuvius in eruption by moonlight.

A variety of OPTICAL GLASSES will be exhibited, which never fail to amuse and divert the visitor.

TIGER CAT. **ALLIGATOR.** **HEDGE-HOG FISH.** **MONKEY.**

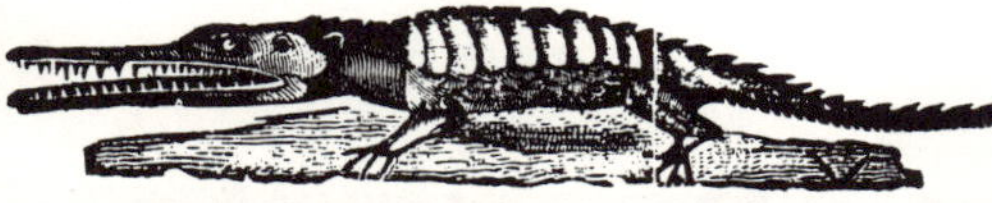

27 WAX FIGURES,

[illegible] Among them are the following eminent characters, viz: Gen. WASHINGTON, the saviour of his country; the founder of a great and rising republick. Gen. LAFAYETTE, the [illegible] Gen. ANDREW JACKSON, [illegible] SHAWIS CANAN, a celebrated Indian Chief. Mrs. NEWLIN, with her six children at one birth. MARAT, in the agonies of death, who was stabbed by Miss Charlotte Curday. Princess CHARLOTTE, daughter of George IV. WILLIAM PITT, Prime Minister of England. ALEXANDER, Emperor of Russia. NAPOLEON BONAPARTE. The Empress JOSEPHINE, and MARIA LOUISA, Ex-empress of France, and her son, the Ex-king of Rome. Also, several figures of those persons whose imprudent deportment has excited the attention and curiosity of the world; such as Hetereasa Howard, who murdered seventeen husbands, and destroyed sixteen, by pouring melted lead in their ears, while asleep. Mary Van Rambel, the famous fortune teller, who foretold the French Revolution 25 years before it came to pass. A PORTRAIT PAINTING of JOHN QUINCY ADAMS, President of the United States. Also, an exact likeness of Captain JAMES RILEY, who was wrecked on the coast of Barbary.

N. B. GOOD MUSICK.

Richard Oliphant, Fancy Job Pr. West Corner of South and Genesee-Streets, Auburn.

After photography and anesthesia, nothing seemed impossible, not even flying across the Atlantic.

what the Erie Canal had accomplished for the state of New York.

As the newly settled West became linked with the East, the older sections of the country found themselves exchanging their manufactures for food: the wheat, hogs, and cattle of the new states of Ohio, Iowa, Illinois, Indiana and Michigan. The western states became to the East what all America had been to England. Depot cities developed at the ends of canals, at the junctions of railroads and at inland river ports. Buffalo, Rochester, Pittsburgh, Cincinnati, Louisville, Cairo, St. Louis, and Memphis became like Philadelphia and Boston — new inland cities with their own merchants, traders, and cartmen, collectors of capital, factory builders, and risk-takers.

Nothing, it seemed, could stop ambitious Americans in their quest for wealth. European gold flowed westward across the Atlantic as Europeans sought to participate in America's unlimited opportunities. The more railroads, canals, and factories that were built, the more, it seemed, were needed. The needs of the railroads created new industries and refinements. There were new occupations — boiler-makers, gear-cutters, and makers of new kinds of automatic tools to shape gears, valves, and engine parts. And the knowledge needed to build and run railroads found application in many fields. From 1830 to 1850, as railroad mileage increased from twenty-three to 9021, iron production doubled and coal production increased ten times. Before people knew what was happening they were living in an age of iron and coal. (Time took on a new significance as trains came and went with clocklike precision; the time in one city had to be matched with the time in another city.)

Civilization had entered a new phase in which growth created more growth. Like the bird whose speed, once airborne, sustains its flight, the northern economy had "taken off." The rate of America's growth became the wonder of the world.

As steamships and railroads puffed up lonely rivers and paused at little towns and as new articles shone on the shelves of country stores, the optimism of the builders and investors began to be felt by almost everybody.

"The time will come when people will travel in stages moved by steam engines, from one city to another, almost as fast as birds fly, fifteen to twenty miles an hour," Oliver Evans had written at the turn of the century. "A carriage (steam) will set out from Washington in the morning, the passengers will breakfast at Baltimore, dine at Philadelphia, and sup in New York on the same day."

Only the wildest visionaries had believed Evans in 1800. By 1840, most Americans were ready to believe that anything was possible — and, most of all, that their lives would get better and better. If a railroad could take you from Boston to New York in less time than it had taken your father to get from Boston to Lexington, didn't that somehow promise to make the son a better man than the father?

BOUNDLESS OPTIMISM

In 1810, the total value of manufactures produced in the United States was about $200 million. In fifty years, the amount of manufacturing increased ten times, to $2 billion a year. There were 140,000 factories in the United States in 1860, employing a million men and a quarter of a million women. The cloth

Before the canal and railroads, Utica, N. Y. was a clearing in the forest. (The canal can be seen near the upper left.) In 1827, a traveller noted in another Erie Canal city that, "Everything in this bustling place appears to be in motion . . . huge pyramids of flour barrels, bales, and boxes (are) lying in the streets."

might not be as good as that made with care by the weaver at his loom, but it was good enough and sold for far less. Cloth sheeting sold for forty cents a yard in 1815. It sold for eight-and-a-half cents a yard in 1830.

One of the most interesting consequences of the factory system was the way it changed the people's outlook on nature. The new outlook was both a cause and consequence of the system. People began to feel that everything could be controlled by men.

Since earliest times, men had felt their smallness beside the mighty winds and tides of the natural world. Weak and defenseless against the shocks of earthquake and plagues, humanity had sought to bribe or entreat whatever hidden powers caused these cataclysms.

In the years following Columbus' return from the "Indies," a few men had grappled with nature with new hope. Columbus had demonstrated that there were, after all, things to be discovered. Perhaps the ancients of Greece and Rome hadn't known everything, after all.

The consequence of these investigations was that certain mathematical "laws" were found, in accordance with which certain natural motions could be described and even predicted. In 1609, for instance, the German, Johannes Kepler, had announced that the time it took each of the planets to revolve once around the sun was related to its distance from the sun.

When the English genius Sir Isaac Newton published his great work *The Principia* in 1687, he was so successful in describing all the known motions of things of earth and heaven that most of his readers made up their minds that all of nature would be found to obey certain simple mathematical principles.

If this faith in natural law gave men confidence to seek the "laws" of weaving and spinning, the discovery of such "laws" increased their confidence. Thus,

the success of their investigations convinced more and more people that nature could yield secrets beneficial to man. The feeling of optimism, of the unlimited possibilities of man's power, became as general in the America and Europe of the nineteenth century as had been the age-old feelings of insecurity and dread that it replaced. Whether they had heard of Sir Isaac Newton or not, a surprising number of people felt that they could do anything they set their minds to.

A most singular example of this optimism can be found in the career of Charles Goodyear. With no scientific training, with nothing but a dauntless belief that India rubber could somehow be made into a durable, waterproof substance that neither melted in summer nor became brittle in winter, he spent three years mixing raw rubber with cream cheese, ink, turpentine, acid, talcum powder — with anything that came to mind — until he found the secret of vul-

Police court: "With princely fortunes accumulating . . . and the stream of black poverty pouring in," The N. Y. Tribune warned, "contrasts . . . are springing up as hideous as . . . in the Old World." (The Tribune and other large-circulation penny papers became self-supporting as revenues, mostly from patent medicine ads, increased. They could even pay reporters to find news.)

canization. Similarly, the painter Samuel F. B. Morse, with no electrical knowledge, developed the electric telegraph, and a wealthy New Yorker named Asa Whitney offered to build a railroad across the continent in return for a strip of land thirty miles wide, running from Michigan to the Pacific.

This boundless optimism was particularly well-suited to the settling and development of what then seemed a boundless continent.

INDIVIDUALISM

Ever since the overthrow of feudalism and the Protestant break with the Catholic Church, money had been gradually replacing all other virtues. Reformer John Calvin, one of the principal formulators of the Protestant view of the universe, had taught that all men, before birth, were divided into the blessed, destined for heaven, and the damned. According to this theory of predestination, nothing a man could accomplish during his life on earth would move him one step nearer to either eternal reward or punishment. The aim of life, therefore, was not salvation, but the glorification of God. The world of strife and labor, dedicated to God, became sanctified. The means to worldly success, pursued for the sake of God, became sanctified.

Calvinism began as a rigid discipline. Every aspect of man's life was watched and ruled by the church, as in early Puritan Massachusetts. With time, the harsh discipline subsided, but the sanctification of worldly pursuits remained. Men felt justified in devoting themselves solely to the concerns of this world. If good deeds and self-sacrifice would carry one's soul no nearer heaven; worldly wealth, then, became a sign of God's felicity.

In the nineteenth century in the northern half of the United States, this Protestant ethic was reaching its fulfillment. With their corporations, their banks, factories, and railroads, men achieved the virtue that was wealth.

This triumph of Protestantism was a triumph of individualism. The essence of the Protestant revolt had been an insistence on a personal relationship between God and man. The individual conscience was the guide to action, rather than the word of the priest. The Bible, translated into German and English, printed in quantity on printing presses with movable type, had become open to all men. Like Christian in the story, *Pilgrim's Progress,* each man faced temptations alone, and alone worried over his salvation or misery.

In the feudal world, the lord was as a father to his serfs. It was a world in which the higher looked after the lower; in which honor, truth, and justice were sought as absolute virtues. The real world was heaven, unchanging and eternal. The world of nature, in which men lived, was an inferior place of sin and illusion, of transitory rewards unworthy of pursuit. Permanence was a virtue, change a vice. In the towns, the men of like trades organized guilds that presented fixed prices, set fixed conditions of work, and limited the numbers of practitioners.

With Protestantism and capitalism, all was unfixed. Change was introduced for the sake of earthly reward and justified out of a new faith in progress.

"We commenced building power looms to take the place of hand looms with all possible dispatch," an Amesbury, Massachusetts manufacturer recorded in 1821. "The saving in operating 60 looms by water instead of the old way, by hand, amounted to about $40 per day. Besides this saving we got rid of 60 weavers, the most of them men who in those bygone days were intemperate and exceedingly troublesome, and substituted for them 30 girls, who were easily managed and did more and better work."

The "we" in Mr. Aubin's statement is the new "we" of the manager: the man who tells weavers what to do, but does not weave himself. "We" could get rid of sixty weavers easier than "I" could dismiss one. And as time went on, managers would increasingly follow the wishes of men who seldom, if ever, came to the factory — corporate stockholders. The factory system had put the weaver to work at another man's loom. The corporation would set him before a loom owned by men he would never see.

A story was told of a farmer who had a request to make of a certain religious corporation. He had first called on the trustees individually. Each was friendly, one giving him "brandy, another beer, a third wine, a fourth Hollands." Next day, sitting together as a corporation, they refused his request. "Gentlemen," the farmer said, "I can compare you to nothing but the good cheer I received at your houses yesterday; taken separately, you are excellent, but mix you together and you are a mess for the d——l." As *Niles' Register,* the magazine in which this story appeared, commented:

"The conduct of corporate bodies sometimes would incline one to suspect that criminality is, with them, a matter of calculation rather than of conscience."

The factory system and the great construction projects created in the cities a huge new class of wage earners, often newly arrived immigrants from Ireland. Their meager style of living based on very low wages disturbed thoughtful Americans. A growing division between rich and poor was a refutation of the ideals of equality so boldly set forth in the Declaration of Independence. In Philadelphia, the rich businessman Mathew Carey wrote that in a certain part of his city, removed from the comforts of Chestnut Street, there could be found "fifty-five families, containing two hundred and fifty-three individuals huddled together in thirty tenements WITHOUT THE CONVENIENCE OF A PRIVY!!!!"

A Committee of the Massachusetts legislature found that corporations, unlike individual employees, "are not chastened and restrained in their dealings with the laborers by human sympathy...."

By forcing so many employees to work for low pay for as long as fourteen hours a day, the corporations not only oppressed "those whom they employ, but also . . . depress the condition and prolong the hours of labor of every branch of industrial pursuit."

As the personal relationship between employer and employee could not be maintained in a large factory owned by a soulless corporation, so the manufacturer and buyer were separated by the distance covered by railroads and steamships. There was no place in this new world, it seemed, for the restraints of human contact. Unseen customers became suckers to be cheated, as unknown workers became victims to be starved. A human world ruled by bonds of affection and respect seemed to be breaking up into a restless mass of individual atoms, subject, like Newton's atoms, only to the vast impersonal forces of a God who was a mathematician.

Where was America going? From his farm in Caroline County, Virginia, John Taylor saw the American democracy turning into a government of the rich. Every age had had its privileged orders who derived advantage from the power of making laws. The old robber orders, the priesthood and the nobility, had been overthrown in America. Now, paper money banking and the protective tariff (which kept the prices of manufacturers at the high American level) enabled a new financial aristocracy to rob the farmer and the mechanic of the products of their labor.

"Why should we be in such desperate haste to succeed and in such desperate enterprises?" a Concord, Massachusetts man named Henry D. Thoreau asked in 1845.

Thoreau, living in a small cabin he had made with his own hands, on an income of $23.44 a year, also noted: "Superfluous wealth can buy superfluities only. Money is not required to buy one necessary of the soul."

To Thoreau and his neighbor Ralph Waldo Emerson, man was the measure of all things. It seemed absurd that men could be fit into a factory routine or made to run to railroad stations to catch trains.

Emerson, writer and lecturer, had been born in a house in Concord, "by the rude bridge that arched the flood," where the opening shots of the revolution had been fired. There was more important work for Americans, he was sure, than accumulating wealth.

THE NORTH: THE NEW SOCIETY

THE OLD shapes and patterns of society melted with the growth of the factory system and the extension of the railroads. Far places became nearer at the same time that the familiar and near became transformed. Philadelphia might have been moved to within a few hours of New York, but to old citizens of New York, New York itself seemed farther away, a less comfortable and personal, more wild and reckless kind of place than it had once been.

Everything was changing. Once-prosperous handcraftsmen were being ground into poverty; boys were leaving farms to work in factories; new cities, along new railroads, were prospering; old towns, off the tracks, were dying. Rich new states were being settled west of the Appalachians. Some paper money was valuable, some was worthless, some was worth more one day than another. And the new faces! About 23,000 immigrants came to America in 1830. By 1840, it was 84,000 a year. By 1850, 369,980! They came from Ireland mostly, and Germany, and Great Britain.

Little English boys sang, "To the west, to the west, to the land of the free,

Where mighty Missouri rolls
down to the sea;
Where a man is a man if he's
willing to toil,
And the humblest may gather the
fruits of the soil. . . ."

In 1846, a potato blight caused a great

Steerage fare across the Atlantic was as little as ten dollars, but to afford even that, emigrants walked hundreds of miles to seaports, and slept in fields. In Liverpool, Limerick and Bremen, piles of hay for a penny a night were available while waiting for vessels to leave. In 1851, when these sketches appeared in The Illustrated London News, a record 221,000 Irishmen came to America.

Only the very wealthiest of emigrants had their goods brought to the quay by cart. Most even carried their heavy barrels of water through city streets and children dragged aboard the bales of straw on which they would sleep.

Steerage: each little partition, ten by five feet by less than three feet high, will be home to six, maybe ten people, for at least forty days. Some will die of sickness before the New World is reached, others will starve.

The lucky and the strong disembark in New York. Probably one tenth of all who sailed from Europe were buried beneath the ocean's waves.

famine in Ireland, already depressed by 200 years of English cruelty. In one poor cabin, a priest found "four or five unfortunate beings just risen from fever, crouched over a small pot of seaweed boiling on the fire, that one of them had crawled to the shore, to collect for their dinner." A third of the population, he thought, had already been carried away. The alternatives were death by starvation or typhus, or emigration to America.

In Germany, one traveler saw long files of carts "every mile, carrying the whole property of the poor wretches. . . . There they go slowly along; their miserable tumbrils — drawn by such starved drooping beasts, that your only wonder is, how they can possibly hope to reach Havre alive — piled with the scanty boxes containing their few effects, and on the top of all, the women and children, the sick and the bedridden, and all who are too exhausted with the journey to walk."

By 1844, they were leaving Bremen at the rate of 19,000 a year. Whole villages were selling their property for whatever they could get, a British writer noted, and setting out for America with their clergyman at their head. "The one great cause of this almost national movement," he noted, "is the desire for absolute political and religious freedom. . . ."

REALITY

Once in America, what did these immigrants do? The frontier, where the clearing of the forest went on, was strange to these newly-arrived Europeans, and they were unsuited to rough pioneering.

If he was a farmer, the immigrant rented or bought a farm that was already settled. Others found a new kind of American frontier in the big cities. If they had trades, they might find employment, or set up shop as tailors, stonecutters, blacksmiths, carpenters or shoemakers. If not, they would take any kind of a job, usually the hardest, while they struggled to learn a new language. The first American words they heard were: job, you, shovel, pay, dollars, cents, Sunday, boss, work, eat.

Brawny Irishmen dug out canals through marshlands, working all day hip-deep in water. They built railroads, bridges and roads. They could neither read nor write. They lived in houses made out of packing crates. They lived in shanties along the railroads that passed Thoreau's lake:

"I see in my daily walks human beings living in sties, and all winter with an open door, for the sake of light, without any . . . woodpile, and the forms of both old and young are permanently contracted by the long habit of shrinking from cold and misery, and the development of all their limbs and faculties is checked."

When he could find no work in New York, Abraham Kohn, a young emigrant from Bavaria, put a consignment of merchandise in a sack and went out to peddle to New England farmers:

"This, then," he wrote, "is the vaunted

luck of the immigrants from Bavaria! O misguided fools, led astray by avarice and cupidity! You have left your friends and acquaintances, your relatives and your parents . . . only to sell your wares in the wild places of America, in isolated farmhouses and tiny hamlets. . . ."

All these changes in the northern states — the flow of immigrants, the increase of paper money, the employment of women and children in factories, the decline in home handcrafts, and the extension of railroads — made new demands on government. Laws made for merchants and farmers could not always be applied to factory workers or manufacturing corporations. Even if the names of things: "merchants, manufacturers, mechanics," remained the same, the things themselves were different.

In Geneva, New York, for instance, as journeymen shoemakers were forced to accept the lower wages of more poorly paid immigrants, they formed an association, or union. When the union members refused to work for any shoe manufacturer who employed non-union help, they were arrested and charged with a conspiracy injurious to trade.

If the activities of the union succeeded, the public would have to pay more for shoes made by more highly paid labor. If the union failed, the families of the journeymen shoemakers would eat less. Besides, did the workman have any right to tell his employer whom he should hire? Where was the right in this case? Were the courts to protect the public, the shoemakers' families, the employers, or none of these?

In keeping with the Federalist ideal of alliance between merchants and government, Chief Justice Savage of the New York State Supreme Court ruled, "Combinations and confederacies to *enhance* or *reduce* the prices of labor, or of any articles of trade or commerce, are injurious. . . . Competition is the life of trade. If the defendants cannot make coarse boots for less than one dollar per pair, let them refuse to do so; but let them not . . . undertake to say that others shall not do the work for less price. . . ."

Writing in The New York Evening Post on June 2, 1836, the editor William Cullen Bryant slyly proposed that this principle be applied to bankers, owners of ships, butchers, insurance directors, and newspapers with their uniform rates, fees and prices.

"Or will it be allowed that the law would be unjust and oppressive if enforced against the opulent and prosperous, while it is contended that it is just and equitable when those who depend only on the labor of their hands are made its victims?"

The old battle between order and liberty, between property rights and human rights, had entered a new phase. The grounds had shifted; but the forces were the same. The struggle also spread into the area of paper money finance. Through their banks the big merchants controlled the supply of paper money. They could influence smaller merchants by granting or withholding loans. Many wage-earners suffered loss in earnings as the value of the paper money they received diminished. Some manufacturers, indeed, purposely bought up cheap money with which to pay their workers.

DEMOCRACY

In all countries, the rich and powerful have sought to increase their wealth and power at the expense of the poor and humble. The making of laws is nothing but a means of defining "good" and "bad." To the extent that what the government says is bad is not bad for all, government is an instrument of oppression.

". . . under pretense of governing," Jefferson had written, "they have divided their nations into two classes, wolves and sheep. . . This is the true picture of Europe."

Where any part of a nation had succeeded in drawing to itself all the powers and trappings of government, the only remedy of the oppressed had been violent rebellion.

Violence did not occur in the northern states of the Union in the years between 1810 and 1860 because the oppressed could use another weapon.

Their weapon was the ballot. In the years following Jefferson's accession to the Presidency, the right to vote was gradually extended throughout the North. Originally, only the owners of property had been permitted to vote. By 1830, only New Jersey and Rhode Island had heavy property qualifications on voting, and New York, Illinois, and Indiana permitted all white male citizens to vote. Vermont and Maine allowed all men to vote, white and black, and the remaining northern states merely required payment of a small poll tax.

The Germans brought the beer hall to American cities. Sunday had become a time for fun, soda water, fruit drinks, and ice cream.

That the extension of the suffrage threatened their hold on the government was clearly perceived by the Federalists. Universal suffrage, exclaimed Chancellor Kent in the New York Constitutional Convention of 1821, "has been regarded with terror, by the wise men of every age, because in every European republic . . . in which it has been tried, it has . . . been productive of corruption, injustice, violence, and tyranny . . ."

Was the country better off in the hands of men of property who were generally better educated? Would ordinary workers, dependent on other men for their wages, be free to make their own decisions? Would they be used by other men? Would the poor plunder the rich? If the men of property had been wolves, would the common people be wolves in turn?

That the fear of universal suffrage was not unfounded was proved by later events. Chancellor Kent had spoken in 1821. By 1838, the leaders of the Tammany Society, which controlled New York City through the allegiance of the voters of no property, were collecting $600,000 a year from gamblers and criminals in return for protecting them from the law. The year before, Samuel Swartwout, a Tammany politician and collector of the Port of New York, was found to have stolen a million dollars from government funds of which he was the custodian.

With the coming of universal suffrage, machines like Tammany seized control of all the big cities of the North.

Their power was based on real service to the poor and ignorant. Immigrants fresh off the boat found jobs through these political organizations. Tammany, and its counterparts in Boston, Philadelphia, Pittsburgh, and Cincinnati gave wood to the poor on cold winter days and proved a powerful friend when there was trouble with the law. The political machines, working through small local clubs in every part of their cities, provided the poor with the kind of lordly protection that the factory system was otherwise destroying. The local bosses knew their people by name. They kept them from starving, and they often kept them out of jail. If they asked for votes in return, it seemed a small price to pay.

But all that this proved was that a man of no property, if given power and responsibility, could resist temptation no better than any other man. Swarthwout was no better than the aristocrat Andrew Dexter, Jr., who, with a few friends, bought a New England bank with promises. With only a few hundred dollars in real money, the bank issued $800,000 in bank notes, none of which was ever redeemed.

REVOLUTION NUMBER 3

The important thing, the big question to be tested in the North during the first half of the nineteenth century, was: could the free institutions created by the Constitution survive the pressures of industrialism? Did the ideals of the Declaration of Independence, "life, liberty, and the pursuit of happiness," have any meaning in an America of steam engines, interchangeable parts, factory workers, millionaires, and uneducated immigrants? "The mobs of great cities," Jefferson had maintained, "add just so much to the support of pure government, as sores do to the strength of the human body. . . ." Certainly, by extending the vote to the ordinary workingman, and even to the immigrant, principles and traditions would be tested to the utmost.

The trials of the 1790s were nothing compared with what was now confronting the nation. Washington, Adams and Jefferson, whatever their differences, had worked within the aristocratic framework of a government subject to the influence of the small number of leading men in the several states. But following the conclusion of Monroe's second term of office, large numbers of voters newly admitted to the suffrage would, for the first time, participate in a Presidential election.

In 1824, 356,038 men had voted, or about one out of every seven white American men of voting age. More than 1,100,000 voted in 1828. The ship of

There was no such thing as the secret vote. To pass their marked paper ballots to opposing voters, Whig workers pretended to be Democrats and Democrats, Whigs. Sometimes, extra votes were hidden in trick ballot boxes. City "machines" organized squads of "repeaters" who voted many times at many polling places.

state had once and for all left the quiet harbor of Federalism to embark on the tempestuous ocean of popular democracy.

Washington had ridden to his inaugural in a coach and six, and Jefferson had walked to the capitol to take his oath in Republican simplicity. After Andrew Jackson's inaugural, the White House was filled with a noisy mob of farmers, fur trappers, workers, and tradesmen.

During the eight years of Jackson's Administration, new groups of Americans gained influence in the government. Ordinary newspapermen sat in Jackson's inner councils. The newly-rich land speculators of western states, the bosses of the northern states, and city political machines that had broken, or were seeking to break, the power of the old aristocracy, were welcomed in the White House. The western farmer, the small tradesman, the ordinary workingman, on whom the newer politicians depended for votes, began to have some attention paid to their demands. To the tune of "Yankee Doodle," they sang:

> "Mechanics, Carters, Laborers
> Must form a close connection
> And show the rich aristocrats
> Their powers, at this election . . .
> Yankee Doodle smoke 'em out,
> The proud, the banking faction.
> None but such as Hartford Feds
> Oppose the poor and Jackson."

THE WAR ON THE BANK

The first bank of the United States, erected by Alexander Hamilton in 1791, had gone out of business in 1811, with the expiration of its charter. A second Bank was chartered in 1816, with a capital of $35 million. Operating out of a main office in Philadelphia and with about twenty branches, at least one in almost every state, it exercised great control over the financial affairs of the nation. The effects of shifts in the supply of specie, for instance, (such as had brought on Shays' Rebellion) could be eased by the Bank, which thus curbed even the ups and downs of the great business cycles.

There were hundreds of different kinds of paper money circulating in the United States. They had been issued by local banks and even by factories and transportation companies. The second Bank controlled these currencies, and the many local institutions that issued them, by periodically (usually weekly) demanding specie from the banks of issue in return for its holdings of their notes.

This restrained local banks from overissue and, by controlling the price of money, placed the second Bank in the

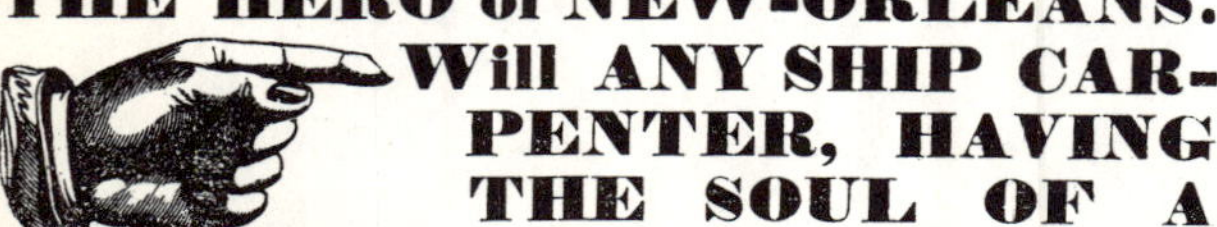

Andrew Jackson saw himself as the direct representative of the people, with a special duty to protect their liberties and rights. His beloved wife Rachel was dead; he had no children. Martin Van Buren said of him, "The people were his blood relations, the only blood relations he had."

middle of the age-old controversy between creditors and debtors.

The Bank also made commercial loans, which put it into competition with local banks. This prevented local banks from making their interest rates higher than the rates of the second Bank, and again involved the Bank in controversy.

The Bank's central control over specie, currency, and interest rates was bound to involve it in politics. The second Bank's charter was due to expire in 1836, but almost as soon as President Jackson assumed office, in 1829, Nicholas Biddle, the young president of the Bank, had begun urging that Jackson state his support for recharter.

Jackson delayed his decision. In 1832, his political opponents, Henry Clay and Daniel Webster, put a bill for recharter through Congress. Jackson's prompt veto of the bill gave Clay and Webster's new National Republican Party what they wanted. Recharter became a primary issue in the Presidential election of 1832.

This doomed the second Bank, for Jackson regarded his reelection as a mandate to kill it. As Jackson saw it, the Bank, whatever its merits (and he favored sound currency), had one fatal defect. It operated by favor of the United States Government, using Government money, and yet was a private corporation. (Only five of its twenty-five directors were appointed by the Government.) It thus could be looked on as an engine through which a small group of wealthy easterners, in Philadelphia, could greatly influence the Republic for their own benefit. Bank President Biddle meddled in politics, using the influence of the Bank to help Webster and Clay, but was foolish enough to state that "no officer of the Government, from the President downwards, has the least right, the least authority, the least pretense for interference in the concerns of the bank . . ."

In his assault on the Bank, President Jackson was joined by Wall Street financiers out to destroy the financial supremacy of Philadelphia, by local bankers from Mississippi to Maine, and by speculators, promoters, and farmers hungry for cheap and ready supplies of cash.

Determined to destroy the Bank even before its charter expired, Jackson took

More and more people were living in cities. From 1820 to 1850, the number of places with populations of more than 10,000 increased from 13 to 62. In 1820, not even one out of 20 Americans lived in cities. In 1850, 2,6000,00 out of a total population of 23,000,000, lived in cities. In the gaslit city, life raced on beyond the dark that put the countryside to sleep. At the faster pace, and with added hours of light, people could do so much more in a day that their lives seemed doubled. Crowding brought tenements with a whole family in one room for the poor; and "flats" in "Parisian buildings" for the well-to-do.

Manners were crude, but food was cheap, and good. The French showed how to eat vegetables. Germans brought cakes, sausages, and schnitzel. *Canals and steam developed a nation of travelers and a new kind of hotel. In 1829, Boston's Tremont House had tubes for hailing bellboys and — an unheard of luxury — gave each guest a cake of soap.*

out the Government's deposits. In doing so, he had arrayed against him all the influence the Bank could bring to bear. In the Congress, Webster and Clay fought for the Bank, but they had against them the clever and rapacious promoters of a dozen cities fighting for freedom from Government controls, and the brilliant Amos Kendall, who succeeded in presenting the struggle as between the poor farmer and laborer and the grasping Bank of the United States.

Almost every newspaper in the land reviled the President. But once Jackson's mind was made up, nothing could sway him. "I care nothing about clamors, sir, mark me! I do precisely what I think is just and right."

COMPETITION

The death of the Federalist Chief Justice Marshall removed an impediment to change. In Marshall's place, Jackson appointed his Attorney General. Roger B. Taney's decisions began to reflect a different attitude toward the forces in American society. Marshall had denied a state the right to change the charter of a corporation, even in the public interest. Taney reasserted the rights of the people in denying that the Charles River Bridge Company had the right to receive an exclusive monopoly from Massachusetts:

"... the object and end of all government is to promote the happiness and prosperity of the community by which it is established; and it can never be assumed, that the government intended to diminish its power of accomplishing the end for which it was created."

On the evening of June 13, 1836, 25,000 people crowded into City Hall Park in New York to protest Judge Edwards' fining of some striking journeymen tailors. In Congress, Representative Waddy Thompson of South Carolina mockingly reminded his northern colleagues that their wage slaves seemed as discontented and rebellious as the black slaves of the South were supposed to be.

The new spirit put an end to bargaining. The new system saved time, but it brought a lessened sense of self-importance as the customer bowed to impersonal printed price tags.

Unretouched Photograph

Judge Lemuel Shaw, some years after his decision in favor of the bootmakers. Knickerbockers, silk stockings, and wigs had been out of fashion since 1812. The silver snuff box had given way to the Havana cigar, and the cocked hat, to the "stovepipe."

Reply was made by the one labor leader who had been elected to serve in Congress — Ely Moore of New York City. Whenever the aristocracy moved to increase its own power, Moore warned, it first charged the people with revolutionary designs.

"Sir, can it be seriously and honestly believed," Moore asked, ". . . that the interest and safety of the State will be plotted against by three-fourths of the people composing the State? Where there is one instance where the rights of property have been violated by the people, or popular institutions, there are five thousand instances where the people have been plundered and beggared by the heartless cupidity of the privileged few. . . ."

There was a growing feeling that the journeymen tailors had been treated unjustly. A few weeks later, a jury refused to punish eight shoemakers who had walked out on an employer who had hired a man at less than union wages.

By 1842, even the courts had come to interpret the laws more in favor of the workingman. Arrested on the familiar charge of conspiracy, seven Boston bootmakers eventually found their case before Chief Justice Lemuel Shaw of Massachusetts.

"The case supposes," said Judge Shaw, "that these persons are . . . free to work for whom they please or not to work. . . . we cannot perceive, that it is criminal for men to agree together to exercise their own acknowledged rights . . . to subserve their own interests. . . ."

As the bonds between government and special small groups of citizens were broken, opportunities of all sorts were opened up to more and more people. The states passed laws so that anyone could form a corporation without applying for a special charter. If laboring men were free to fight for their rights, businessmen were freer to start new enterprises. Western bankers no longer felt at a disadvantage to eastern bankers. There seemed to be opportunity for everybody.

What was happening was very clearly seen by a newly arrived immigrant, the young German Carl Schurz:

". . . the first sight of this country fills one with dumb amazement," he wrote in 1852. "Here you see the principle of individual freedom carried to its ultimate consequences: voluntarily made laws treated with contempt. . . . On the one hand you see the great mass of laboring people in complete freedom striving for emancipation, and by their side the speculative spirit of capital plunging into unheard of enterprises. . . . All strength, all weakness, all that is good, all that is bad, is here in full view and in free activity. . . . He who wishes liberty must not be surprised if men do not appear better than they are. . . ."

THE WEST

JUST as the fate of great opposing nations is settled along a thin line where their armies meet in battle, so the destiny of America was decided along a thin, shifting line in the depths of the dark forest. The American nation evolved to the chopping sound of axes, the crackling and hacking away of branches, the odor of burning underbrush.

By 1800, moccasined Indians no longer walked the cobblestones of Boston; at midnight, Philadelphia glowed with street lamps; the old eastern seaboard was a world of newspapers, of investments, and interest rates, of books and Sunday church services. But a few hundred miles to the west, families lived in huts hastily woven of branches.

In the year 1770, Thomas Jefferson practiced law and attended fancy balls, and a lean and bearded youth stalked deer in a dark and pathless forest, eating raw meat to avoid the smoke that would put savage Shawnee Indians on his trail. Jefferson was in Williamsburg, Virginia. Daniel Boone was 200 miles west of Williamsburg in the Shenandoah Valley.

To travel west was to travel backward in time. Had Thomas Jefferson been able to return to the eastern Virginia of 1670, he would have found it as wild a place as the Shenandoah Valley of 1770.

As, in any one place, the stages of settlement from trapper to village succeeded each other in time; so at any one time they could be found side by side, succeeding each other in distance. A Concord, Massachusetts farmer would find farmers in Vermont living as his father had lived. Proceeding to Ohio, he would smell the same acid smoke of burning fields that his grandfather had smelled. America didn't have a *past* in the nineteenth century — it had a *West* instead.

THE TIDE

In the 170 years that passed between the arrival of the first permanent settlers in Virginia and the winning of the Revolutionary War, the American people had turned less than a hundred thousand square miles of wild forest into the kind of farm and village country in which they could feel safe.

In 1783, the people of the thirteen states formed a long narrow community 1200 miles long and averaging 75 miles wide. There was little settlement more than a day's walk from a river. Beyond the Appalachians were a few traders and trappers and 200,000 Indians. The powerful Iroquois Confederacy ranged from the western borders of North Carolina to Canada; the Shawnee inhabited the valley of the Ohio River; Cherokees, Creeks, Chickasaws, and Choctaws hunted and farmed from western Georgia through the lower Mississippi Valley to the Gulf Coast; and the Chippewas, Ottawas, and Hurons lived around the Great Lakes.

About 200,000 Americans were in motion in the years immediately following the end of the War for Independence. In the eighty years that followed, the tide of settlement swept past the Mississippi River. The turnpike, the canal, the steamboat, the railroad brought settlers into the western country at a prodigious rate and provided them with markets and manufactures.

By 1835, an area the size of Massachusetts was being converted to agriculture and settlement each year.

THE FRONTIERSMAN

The settlers' West was lonely. The women talked to themselves, then grew queer, believing after a while that the wished-for companion listened as they talked. There was the silence of the woods, the chattering of the birds, the heart-stopping fear when an acorn fell on the forest floor.

All the dangers of the West were magnified by isolation. If a man was trapped under a fallen tree, who would hear his cries for help? The relative of a sick woman would sometimes have to journey for four difficult days to summon the nearest nurse; and there were the rattlesnake, the water moccasin, and the copperhead.

Why then did men go into the forest, even taking their families with them, leaving behind the comforts of law and judges, of doctors, of neighbors, newspapers, of store-bought cotton cloth, rum, and oranges; to eat corn meal cracked on a stump instead of flour ground in a mill?

Many traveled to escape taxes, or in search of cheap land, or land they could grab free, beyond the reach of the law. Others went because the frontier world was more natural to them than the civilized world. America was breeding a race of forest-dwelling pioneers better suited to the wilderness than the village. What had begun as necessity had become a way of life.

Necessity was lack of funds. It was being desperate for a farm and having no money for cleared land. Just before the Seven Years' War, a thousand wagons were counted going through Hillsboro, North Carolina, southwest over the Catawba Path toward the Cherokee territory. Mostly Scotch-Irish — Scotch from northern Ireland — they passed Yadkin that had been wild thirty years before, heading for the wild Waxhaw region of the Carolinas, west of the settled plantation counties.

When such men had no money to buy land, they settled it, anyway. What right had those in safe eastern cities to titles to this forest? Was it not "against the laws of God and nature that so much land should be idle while so many Christians wanted it to labor on and to raise bread?" they asked.

To survive, a frontier family had to raise, hunt or trap food; build a house out of trees and whatever else was handy; find a supply of water; make all its clothing from hats to shoes.

Those who couldn't stand the hard work and the loneliness died or returned East to hire out as farmhands or clerks. Of those who did manage to stick it out, few gained more than barely sufficient food, clothing, and shelter.

Simple and spare as this frontier life was, it represented a very great achievement. In the forest, men and women had to maintain and build civilization with nothing but their own minds and hearts and hands.

But in learning that they could create life out of themselves, the pioneers learned that they could do without the common supports of civilization. Men of villages might pay taxes and tolerate unpleasant laws in return for the protection and justice of governors and courts. The frontiersman, requiring neither protection nor justice, was likely to consider laws and taxes as mere useless burdens. What need had he of courts or law? Insulted or injured, he resorted to force. Andrew Jackson was in three duels, issued challenges or was challenged to four others, and engaged in a wild shooting affray with the Benton brothers in the City Hotel in Nashville.

The frontiersman wanted nothing less than pure freedom with no constraints whatsoever. When he became a judge, he was likely to run his court in this fashion:

"If the court is right — and she think she air — why, then you air wrong, and she knows you is — shut up."

Such conditions, of course, had a special appeal to men threatened by laws of more settled places. The West was not without its escaped criminals and other men and women who would not dare return to certain villages and cities. "Let's all of us tell our real names," was a favorite joke amongst a gathering of Westerners.

"I CAN DO NO MORE THAN WEEP"

The advance of settlement meant the retreat of the Indian. The process had started along the Virginia coast. In 1647, following a massacre and a brief war, the Powhatan Indians had agreed to leave the peninsula between the York and James Rivers. In 1722, the six nations of the Iroquois had agreed to stay north of the Potomac River and west of the Alleghenies. Now the "long knife," as the Indian called the American, was west of the Alleghenies and crossing the Ohio River.

The "long-knife" hunters who shot deer, bear, and buffalo in the Indian hunting grounds of Indiana violated treaties. They had no more right to hunt in the Indian lands than they had to go east over the Appalachians and shoot sheep and cattle on Pennsylvania farms.

The treaty of Greenville, in 1795, by which the Indians of the Northwest Territory ceded a great deal of land to the United States, provided that no further treaties be binding unless representatives of *all* their tribes agreed. This was to prevent sachems (chiefs), who might be corrupted and bribed by whisky, from giving away lands.

In its efforts to obtain as much Indian land as possible, the United States Government ignored this treaty. President Jefferson told his Indian agent to tempt the chiefs into debt so that they would have to sell tribal lands:

"To promote this disposition to exchange lands which they have to spare and we want," Jefferson wrote in February, 1803, "for necessaries which we have to spare and they want, we shall push our trading-houses, and be glad to see the good and influential individuals among them in debt; because we observe that when these debts get beyond what the individuals can pay, they become willing to lop them off by a cession of lands."

The recipient of this letter was a thirty-year-old Virginian named William Henry Harrison, a descendant of Virginia's old Northern Neck landed aristocracy. As Governor of the Indiana Territory from 1800 to 1812, he induced the local Miami, Eel River, Wea, Piankashaw and Delaware Indians to sign away a great deal of fertile Indiana land.

Resolved to take steps before all their hunting grounds were lost, there arose among the Shawnee Indians two leaders.

Tecumseh and the Prophet proposed that all the Indians of the Northwest form a confederation which would have joint ownership of Indian lands. Where Tippecanoe Creek joins the Wabash, the two Shawnee leaders erected a village capital for the Confederacy. It was the spring of 1808.

"I told the redskins that the way they were in was not good, and that they ought to abandon it; that we ought to consider ourselves as one man," the Prophet told Governor Harrison a few months later on a visit to Vincennes, "but we ought to live agreeable to our several customs, — the red people after their mode, and the white people after theirs; particularly that they should not drink whisky; that it was not made for them, but the white people, who alone know how to use it; and that it is the cause of all the mischiefs which the Indians suffer. . . ."

In September, 1809, Governor Harrison summoned together the chiefs of the Miamis, Eel Rivers, Potawatomis and Kickapoos and obtained about three million acres of land in the heart of Indian country, and running for nearly a hundred miles up both banks of the Wabash River.

By 1810, Tecumseh had more than five thousand Indian warriors in his confederacy, including the powerful Hurons. The Confederacy declared the new cessions of territory void, as indeed they were.

Next year, Governor Harrison, with 800 men, marched on Tippecanoe. This was considered a particularly daring action since the Indian village was thought to be defended by 600 braves.

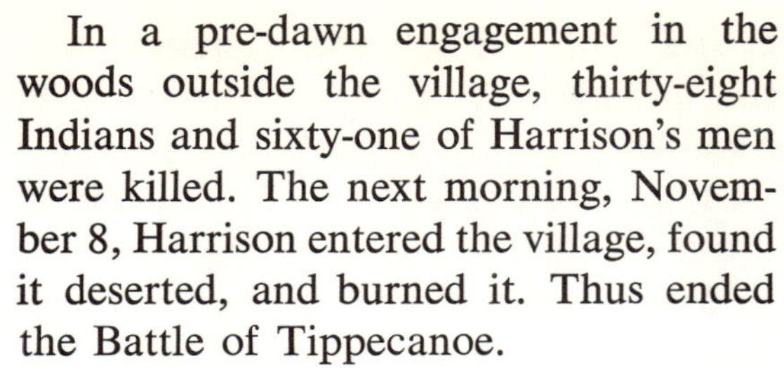

In a pre-dawn engagement in the woods outside the village, thirty-eight Indians and sixty-one of Harrison's men were killed. The next morning, November 8, Harrison entered the village, found it deserted, and burned it. Thus ended the Battle of Tippecanoe.

The population of Indiana, centered around Vincennes and on the Ohio River opposite Louisville, Kentucky, had grown from 2,500 to 25,000. Tecumseh was killed in a battle in 1813. Three years later, Indiana became the eighteenth state of the Union. That same year, 1816, the Indian leader Bill Weatherford, defeated in Georgia by Andrew Jackson said, "I have done the white people all the harm I could: if I had an army I would fight to the last; my warriors can no longer hear my voice; their homes are at Talladega, Tallushatches, Emuckfaw, and Tohopeka; I can do no more than weep."

THE MOVERS

In the Green River lands of Kentucky, a shot rang out and a farmer crumpled and fell. In Annapolis, to the east, men in wigs were inviting the states to send delegates to a convention to revise the Articles of Confederation. In Philadelphia, old Benjamin Franklin was wiping his bifocal glasses, perhaps at the very moment that a little boy, kneeling over his dying father on that Kentucky field, looked up to see an Indian. The buzzing sound of another bullet, another shot, and the Indian fell dead. The Indian had been shot by the little boy's older brother Mordecai.

Henceforth brother Mordecai would be a fanatic about Indians. He would hunt Indians whenever he had a chance, stalking them like deer.

The little boy grew to manhood. He had settled on a little place on the Big South Fork of Nolin's Creek, Kentucky, considerably westward of Green River, where he had seen his father die. He had become a middle-sized man, five-foot-nine, strong and stocky, with dark hair and eyes. He had become extraordinarily proficient with carpenter's tools. Thomas Lincoln was a fine cabinet-maker. He made beautiful corner-cupboards, but could not support a family without farming. His wife Nancy was slender. She had an angular, bony face with a high forehead, pointed chin, prominent cheek bones — a dark-skinned, dark-haired, gray-eyed woman.

Tom and Nancy lived with their little baby girl Sarah in a small one-room cabin constructed out of logs. There was one window. The door moved on leather hinges. The floor was dirt. Little Sarah was fed milk with corn bread crumbled in it — milk and mush. Tom and Nancy ate what Tom could shoot, and corn dodgers (little cakes made of corn meal, cold water and salt).

The Linkerns, as the family was called, had moved into the log cabin in the fall of 1808. It was the latest of a series of westward moves — from a hired man's cabin on a farm a few miles away; from a cabin near a courthouse in a village some fifty miles to the southeast. They had been married in Springfield, Washington County, Kentucky, forty miles farther east.

Tom Linkern's father, the farmer who had been shot by the Indian, was named Abraham. In the year 1782, Abraham Linkern had moved his family west from the Shenandoah Valley of Virginia into Kentucky where, according to his friend Daniel Boone, there were long valleys flowing with rich blue grass.

Abraham Linkern, or Lincoln, put in a claim for 2,000 acres of land on the Green River and began clearing land as had his father before him in the valley of the Shenandoah, and his grandfather in Pennsylvania. He came from a long line of forest-clearers, of tree-burners and stump-pullers, of men used to turning forest into farm land. He swung an ax as if it were part of his arm.

His son Tom Lincoln grew up in different places in Kentucky, hiring out to farmers, sometimes relatives, somehow learning carpentry and cabinet-making.

Tom and Nancy Lincoln's second child was born on February 12, 1809. They named the boy Abraham after his grandfather.

The land at South Fork was sticky clay, and stony. When little Abraham was three, the family moved about ten miles away to a farm on Knob Creek, in a valley surrounded by high hills.

The Lincolns and the people living around Knob Creek called themselves "pore" folks. They talked through their noses, pronouncing joints "jints"; cover, "civer"; creek, "crick." Their dogs "follered" coons; they "drapped" seeds at planting time; were bitten by "skeeters"; and watched the smoke disappear up the "chimbly" at night.

Before he was five, little Abe was doing errands around his father's farm, carrying water, filling the woodbox, cleaning ashes from the fireplace, hoeing weeds, picking berries. Once in a while he got to ride the horse hitched to the "bull-tongue" plow of wood shod with iron. He wore just a shirt, no pants.

Sometimes there was plenty to eat, a good crop of corn, potatoes or onions, wild turkey or partridge in the wood. Sometimes the pickings were lean. It all depended on the weather.

The Mississippi shifted channels and sandbars moved. Flimsy boilers blew up and vessels often caught fire, but in 1842, there were more steamers on the river than in the entire British empire.

"PORE" FOLKS

By 1816, when Abe Lincoln was seven years old, more than half of the people in Hardin County were colored. Well-to-do planters had been giving up worn-out Virginia plantations to move to Kentucky with their slaves. They would set slaves to clearing land or they would buy the cleared land of the settlers and float their tobacco down the Ohio.

The slave-owners built neither roads nor canals; little was done to encourage the small farmer to grow crops for market. Besides, the "pore" white had to do things for himself that the slave-owner made his slave do for him. It was discouraging for a man in dirty buckskin leggings to work all day behind the plow and look up to see a slave-owner on horseback, wearing shiny boots and dressed as if he were going to a wedding.

And if a man wanted to hire himself out he found himself bidding against hired-out slaves, and he had either to work for as little as the slave or not work at all. And with their wealth and their leisure the slave-owners could arrange everything to suit. The slave-owner was judge and legislator.

The "pore" white was by way of becoming a nobody in Kentucky. He could *feel* important, being a member of what he considered the "master" race. But if he wanted to rise in the world, he had to either buy slaves or get out of the country.

About thirty miles north of Knob Creek stood the town of Louisville on the Ohio River. On the far side of the Ohio River was the territory in which Congress, in 1787, had forbidden slavery. To the east of Louisville, up river a ways, was Ohio, bustling with settlers from Connecticut and Massachusetts.

Directly north of Louisville a new state had just been admitted to the Union. The state of Indiana, in accordance with the Ordinance of 1787, declared that "holding any part of the human creation in slavery, or involuntary servitude, can only originate in usurpation and tyranny."

In 1816, Thomas Lincoln heard that Indiana land could be bought from the Government for two dollars an acre — rich black land that yielded more corn per acre than Kentucky land. That fall he cut down trees, cut out logs and fastened them into a flatboat. Abe and his sister Sarah helped carry tables, chairs, carpenter's tools onto the flatboat. They also loaded ten barrels of whisky. Whisky was a kind of money in the West, as was anything that could be readily carried and traded. Tom Lincoln had sold his Knob Creek place for the whisky and twenty dollars in cash.

The farmer floated the raft down Knob Creek to Salt River and onto the Ohio, poled across to the Indiana side, and put in a claim for a quarter section, 160 acres of land, on Little Pigeon Creek. Then he walked back to get his family.

Cooking things, blankets, and the family Bible were packed in bags; the four Lincolns were loaded on two horses. They crossed rivers and creeks, going even deeper into the wilderness, the trees turning with fall, rabbits scampering through the dead leaves, squirrels scurrying overhead. At the claim there was only Little Pigeon Creek churning past their land, the trees throwing "shadders" on a carpet of brown leaves, and the cool smell of winter in the air.

Two trees about fourteen feet apart were used as the corner posts of a three-sided cabin, left open to the south. The sides and roof of this camp were covered with branches, dried grass and mud. A fire was kept burning in the open side night and day. The Lincolns slept in two corners of the shed, on blankets of bearskins, on piles of leaves.

Their food came out of the forest: nuts, berries, and game. A mile from the shed was a salt lick. Tom Lincoln would shoot deer as they bent their heads down to put their tongues on the salt. This provided the family with venison to eat, with buckskin for shirts, trousers, dresses, and moccasins.

The father chopped down trees and cut them for the fire. The children and their mother cleared the ground between the stumps for planting. All the next spring and summer, the air seemed alive with "skeeters." Sometimes the smoke of the fire would keep them away; sometimes it would blow into the shed, driving the Lincolns out. Sometimes the rain and snow would blow inside, turning the floor into mud, and they would shiver in wet blankets around the fire.

Their lives centered about the fire. All night and all day it crackled and blazed, roaring through blizzards and driving rain, crackling on dead limbs, dancing up branches of dried-out leaves, the green logs hissing and popping. Abe and Sarah fed that fire for a full year, and fetched water from a spring a mile away, and pulled up underbrush from between the stumps, and cut branches from fallen trees to stuff in the chinks of their shed or in the roof.

In 1817, eight-year-old Abe Lincoln used an ax for the first time, helping his father cut down trees and notch the ends of logs to build a cabin. For a few days Abe and his sister Sarah walked eighteen miles back and forth through the forest to school. School was a one-room shack with almost no books and little paper. It was called a "blab" school because instruction took the form of reading out loud and repeating. Tom Lincoln didn't see much use in having the children gone all day instead of helping out, but Nancy Hanks Lincoln wanted them "eddicated."

Late in the fall, Nancy Lincoln's tongue became coated with white and her insides burned. Full of fever, shivering with cold, she died of the "milk sick." Tom Lincoln sawed a log into planks, Abe whittled pinewood pegs.

When the coffin was finished, Nancy Hanks Lincoln was buried in the forest. Tom Lincoln made many coffins that winter for victims of the "milk sick."

Tom Lincoln went back to Kentucky and fetched a stepmother for the "young 'uns." Sarah Bush Johnston Lincoln also insisted that the boy be "eddicated," and so the boy grew up, helping his father, going to school when there was time, swinging an ax in the forest, chopping logs for firewood, splitting logs for rail fences and "puncheon" furniture, learning how to swing an ax to get the deepest bite in the tree.

THE SANGAMO

In 1829, Tom Lincoln was ready to move again. The farm on Pigeon Creek wasn't paying well, and it was said the land in the new state of Illinois, pronounced *E-la-noy* was better. They would move to Macon County, in the country the Indians had called *Sangamo,* meaning "the land of plenty to eat." The 80-acre farm (he had allowed a neighbor to buy the other 80 acres) on Little Pigeon Creek, at $2 an acre, had cost Tom Lincoln $160. He had struggled there for fourteen years. He had buried his wife and daughter there. Now he was selling the whole place for $125 cash, $35 less than he had paid for it.

The Sangamo was prairie land, all grass, growing six feet high and more. The grass grew so thick a tree couldn't get a start. Men, oxen, and wagons got lost in the grass. A man would walk off with a swishing sound. Then he would be gone and his companion would be all alone with a grass curtain all around.

The roots of the grass went deep and they were tough. There wasn't a plow that wouldn't break in the sod. But once you got the land stirred up, you could get fifty bushels of corn to the acre, or twenty-five bushels of wheat, or sixty bushels of oats. Any vegetable would grow in the rich black soil, and horses and cattle would shine with fat after grazing on the wild grass in spring. Six miles down the Sangamo River, Abe helped his father build a cabin and split logs for a rail fence. Unfortunately, at the end of 1830 a blizzard covered central Illinois with three feet of snow, cutting people off from each other. Families without firewood froze to death; others without cornmeal starved.

So, the next winter, the Lincolns moved a hundred miles southeast to Goose Nest Prairie in the southern part of Coles County.

A good many of the people of Illinois and Indiana had histories like the Lincolns. Some of the families of movers were led by men more inclined to look for better land to the west than to stay and struggle with what they had. Some of them really settled on poor land; others simply weren't good enough farmers. They could clear land and build cabins, but didn't attend to the weeding, the bug-picking and all the necessary daily chores. They let crops stand too long or didn't plant deep enough. For them, farming was satisfactory when relieved by hunting, but when more settlers made the game scarce, it was time to move on.

Serious farmers would stay and make good where the tough woodsmen who had really tamed the land failed.

In 1831, when he was twenty-two years old, Abraham Lincoln left his father's farm to make his own way in the world.

The young man stood six-foot-four inches in his stocking feet, could lift a

Raftsmen playing cards on the Mississippi; painting by George Caleb Bingham.

slippery 200-pound hog carcass clear off the ground, or hold a big ax out straight and steady by the end of the handle. At foot-racing, wrestling, pitching crow-bars, and jumping he was almost unbeatable.

The West had grown just about as fast and was equally vigorous. In one year, 1816, 16,000 wagons of movers had been counted proceeding west on the turnpike between Philadelphia and Lancaster.

A river of humanity crossed Pennsylvania on a road the British had built, during the Seven Years' War, to Ft. Duquesne (now called Pittsburgh). From Pittsburgh they floated down the Ohio River, whole families and groups of families on flatboats — chickens cackling from pens, cows hobbled and mournfully watching the river through big brown eyes, women stirring kettles over small fires. Whole towns and cities on rafts — rifles, plows, shovels and axes, pile of bedding, spinning wheels, chairs, mirrors stuffed in feather beds; books, and crockery in barrels. At night they would tie up along the shore and men with muskets or rifles would look out for Indians. Sundays, there would be religious services along the water, the Bible read beneath the open sky.

After 1828, they came on the Erie Canal by the thousands each month it was free of ice. Ohio, in 1830, had near a million population, more than all but three of the original states. In the ten years between 1820 and 1830, while Abe Lincoln was growing from a boy of eleven to a man of twenty-one, the population of Indiana doubled and the population of Illinois tripled.

By 1831, eleven states had been added to the original thirteen. Except for Vermont, split off from New York State, all had been created out of the territory west of the Appalachian Mountains. Of the 13 million people in the Union, more than 3½ million lived in the western states.

They came with money or whisky, bar

Dance in a country tavern. Lithograph by George Lehman, 1833-34.

iron or nails, anything valuable or small that could be traded for land. They came with their bare hands, with the mastery of trades — coopers, millwrights, shoemakers, printers, each with their hammers, their lasts, their iron wheels, their type molds and presses, aiming to set up shop. Some would fail and move on — further west or back east. Others would stay.

NEW SALEM

". . . I have always thought that one man of tolerable abilities may work great changes, and accomplish great affairs among mankind, if he first forms a good plan, and, cutting off all amusements, or other employments that would divert his attention, makes the execution of that same plan his sole study and business." So Benjamin Franklin had written in 1788.

In Illinois, Indiana, and Ohio, there were many men of tolerable qualities pursuing good plans. Into a curve in the Sangamon River in Illinois, in 1829, the Cameron and Rutledge families had packed a thousand wagonloads of gravel to make a power-dam. They built a mill and laid out a town on their land on the bluff above the bend in the river. They named it New Salem and sold lots. They put up a tavern with four rooms. Farmers came to have their grain turned into flour and to buy calico prints, sugar, salt, and hardware.

There were many such towns in Ohio and Indiana and Illinois. By 1831, a dozen families had bought lots and put up houses in New Salem. In that same year, a dozen families lived in another little town to the north on Lake Michigan. It was called Chicago.

Abraham Lincoln paddled down the Sangamon River in a canoe to take a job in a store that was opening in New Salem. He helped Denton Offut build his log-cabin store and when the goods arrived, he stacked them on the shelves and along the walls: salt, sugar, tea, coffee, butter, eggs, whisky, tobacco, crockery, calico prints, hats, gloves, shoes, ribbons, cordage, crackers, and hardware. All kinds of money came across the counter, from banks nobody had heard of, in Indiana, New York, Maryland. Abe Lincoln and the other clerk, Bill Green, had to ask, "What kind of money have you?" Lincoln told a story about a steamboat captain who offered wildcat money for firewood. The owner of the woodpile offered to trade cord-for-cord — a cord of wood for a cord of money.

BLACK HAWK

Said Black Hawk, chief of the Sac and Fox Indians: "My reason teaches me that land cannot be sold. The Great Spirit gave it to his children to live upon . . . Nothing can be sold but such things as can be carried away."

In 1832, enraged that settlers had taken his planting grounds, beaten squaws, and even plowed up an ancestral burial ground, the old man led 500 warriors across the Mississippi into Illinois. Regular army troops and volunteers followed Black Hawk into Wisconsin and, with the help of a Sioux war party, defeated him. Colonel Zachary Taylor of Virginia was one of the regular army officers who fought in the battle at the mouth of the Bad Axe River. In his command was a young lieutenant, a West Point graduate from the state of Missis-

Chief Black Hawk.

sippi named Jefferson Davis. When Black Hawk was taken prisoner, Lt. Davis escorted him to an army camp in St. Louis.

One of the companies of Illinois volunteers that served in this little war was led by Abraham Lincoln. As was the custom in volunteer companies, Lincoln was elected by his sixty-eight men. None had any military training. They quarreled with the regular army over the rations, but never got to fight any Indians.

Jefferson Davis always thought the real heroes of the war were "Black Hawk and his savages." It had taken 4,000 American soldiers and Indian allies to defeat 500 Indians encumbered with their families.

STEAMBOATS ON THE MISSISSIPPI

Early in January, 1812, a steamship arrived in New Orleans from Pittsburgh. It had been built by Livingston, Fulton, and the expert mechanic, Nicholas Roosevelt. In 1816, the stern paddle-wheeler, *Washington,* made two round trips between New Orleans and Louisville, Kentucky, cutting the traveling time upstream to a quarter of that required by poled barges or sail driven keel-boats.

By 1830, about 200 steamboats were operating on the Mississippi. The river was treacherous, with shifty sand-bars, submerged rocks, and a course that might change after a heavy rain. Boats with flimsy boilers, operating under full heads of steam, often blew up. Fires frequently spread from below deck to turn vessels into floating funeral pyres. Charles Dickens felt that a trip on a Mississippi steamer was about as safe as living in a gunpowder factory.

Since the average steamboat lasted less than two years, profits had to be quick and large. The *New Orleans,* which cost $40,000 to build, earned $20,000 the first year. The pressure to increase speed and lower rates, brought travel time and profits rapidly down. In 1814, it took five-and-a-half days to steam from New Orleans to Natchez. It took less than two days in 1834. In 1842, the year Dickens visited the Mississippi, there were more steamboats on the one river than in the entire British Empire.

CIVILIZATION

The people of Illinois and Missouri, sent Representatives and Senators to Washington, a month's journey to the east. They shipped pork, whisky, grain and cotton east, and livestock on the hoof; and bought clocks, plows, stoves, shoes and calicoes. A million dollars' worth of cattle were herded through the Cumberland Gap in one year; Cincinnati, Ohio, packing hams, bacon, and salt pork, was nicknamed "Porkopolis."

The Northwest was raising grain and cattle for the eastern states and Europe. It shipped horses, mules and corn to the southern cotton plantations, and fed the textile workers of Darbyshire and Lowell.

The Erie Canal brought the products of the East to Buffalo, on Lake Erie. From Buffalo, lake steamers shipped goods to Cleveland and Sandusky, whence they were carried by turnpike and canal down to Columbus on the Scioto River, or to Zanesville on the Muskingum, where they could be transferred to flatboats for shipment to the Ohio and the great valley of the Mississippi.

Traffic also went by lake steamer all the way from Buffalo to Chicago, with just a short portage north of Detroit. At Chicago, it was transferred to the Illinois

The growth of Chicago in just ten years: Above, 1830; right, 1840.

River, which flowed into the Mississippi. In 1831, a shipment could go from the East to St. Louis by Chicago for two-thirds of what it cost to ship by way of New Orleans. Warehouses were built in the little village by Lake Michigan. Chicago extended her wooden sidewalks over the marshes. Wood was collected for the stoking of the steamboats, pens were built for the collection of cattle and pork for shipment east. The manufacturing of wagons was begun; blacksmiths opened shops to hammer out iron wheel rims, to outfit the horses and wagons of farmers coming in to sell produce and buy hats, shoes, and calicoes. In 1845, 130 cattle were being slaughtered in Chicago every day for export to England, and trains of as many as 80 wagons were bringing in wheat from farms 250 miles away. Chicago began to look like a city.

New Salem grew, too. It had a sawmill, eventually, and fifteen houses, two doctors, two constables, a saloon, a church, and a Sunday school. A hundred people lived in New Salem in 1840. "Foxed pants," with buckskin sewed on the inner side, between ankle and knee, as protection against briers, were rarely seen now in New Salem. Indeed, some of the men wore "store" or "Sunday" clothes seven days a week, and it was not uncommon for a man to appear in a ruffled silk shirt, colored velvet vest, and watch chain with gold seals. Formerly consisting entirely of Southerners from Kentucky, Tennessee, Virginia, and the Carolinas, Illinois was now rapidly filling up with other folks. New Englanders were erecting towns in northern Illinois, and German and Irish immigrants flocked to the booming city of Chicago. Chicago's population grew from 15,000 to 110,000 between 1840 and 1860.

The movements of people brought about new trade routes — new turnpikes, new canals, new ferries, new places for putting in boats, landings along rivers (Cairo, Illinois, where the Ohio joins the Mississippi; Cleveland, Sandusky, Columbus, Zanesville, Cincinnati, Louisville and Indianapolis, and St. Louis); new trade routes helped the movement of people.

Springfield, Illinois, was the biggest town in Sangamon County when Lincoln moved there in 1837. It had a population of 1,500 and supplied 18,000 people living in and around it with tools and manufactures. It handled their grain, beef, pork, and other produce. Men changed from moccasins to rawhide boots before they set foot in Springfield, and women wore shoes.

But it was a long time before the streets were paved. There was a joke that what looked like a box in the middle of the street was really the Chenery House Bus up to its roof in mud.

Michigan entered the Union in 1837, Iowa in 1846, Wisconsin in 1848. In 1840, there were 30 miles of railroad in Ohio, 20 miles of railroad in Indiana, 24 miles in Illinois. In 1850, there were 575 miles of railroad in Ohio, 228 miles in Indiana, 111 in Illinois.

Men traveled the trains on matters of business. They kept appointments in Cincinnati and Chicago. They investigated the worth of real estate near Lake Michigan, calculated, carried spare shirts, collars, and socks in bags made of carpeting. Wheat, hogs, cattle, coal, and iron traveled the rails.

By 1860, Ohio and Illinois were first and second in the Union in miles of railroad track. The cities of the West were tied to each other and to the East by steel bands.

THE PRAIRIE, THE PLOW AND THE REAPER

The westward movement had been entirely through forest country, and the arts of settlement had been entirely involved with the woodlands — with the swinging of axes, the pulling of stumps and the arrangement of stumps into fences, or the splitting of rails into fences, the building of log-cabins, and the hunting of deer, squirrel, partridge and other game in the forest.

In Illinois, where Tom Lincoln finally settled, the great American forest came to an end. The Sangamon country was prairie land, covered with thick grass higher than a man.

Three hundred miles west of the Mississippi, from Iowa to Texas, the country was all prairie and plain. The grassland that reached into western Indiana and covered most of Illinois was part of an eastern extension of the great prairie, a bay of grass wandering in from Iowa.

The first pioneers to come upon this sea of grass shied away from it, fearing that if trees wouldn't grow in it, crops wouldn't either. They often came to conclusions in this way, jumping from one thing to another. They believed that if your ear itched, it meant somebody was talking about you. If the fire roared, there would be a quarrel in the family. If you fed gunpowder to a dog, it would make him fierce.

Then, when they did try to farm the prairie, the heavy, gooey sod broke their plows. Even an iron-shod plow did little good because the heavy soil stuck to it in big globs, and you had to keep stopping to scrape it off. But, it was worth sweating over because once the prairie land was broken up, it's astonishing fertility was revealed.

To make use of this fertility, the prairie farmers experimented with the shape of plows. The plow is essentially a wedge pulled through the soil to dig a shallow trench, or furrow. The side that throws up the soil is called the "moldboard"; the side that runs inside the trench, keeping the earth from falling back in, is called the "landside." (As early as 1793, Thomas Jefferson had experimented with the shapes of moldboards, finding which would throw the earth out of the trench most smoothly.) The prairie farmers felt that if they could just find the right shape of moldboard they could prevent the soil from sticking.

The problem was solved by a young blacksmith in Grand Detour, in the heart of the Illinois prairie country. John Deere noticed that steel saws polished themselves by their motion through the wood. It might not be the shape of the plow that made the soil stick to it, but the iron of which it was made. He hammered a steel saw into the shape of a plow and plowed ten straight furrows without stopping once. He was soon selling steel plows for ten dollars apiece as fast as he could make them. They were called "singing plows" because the steel vibrated and hummed as it cut through the thick soil. John Deere's plow broke the plains, but the amount of wheat a farmer could sow was limited by the amount he could reap.

Back in 1831, while Lincoln was helping Offut with his new store, a young Virginian had developed a machine that harvested oats six times as fast as a man could. The machine was of little use in Virginia, where farmers would rather use slaves than spend money on machines. But after the crash of 1837 had reduced his family to poverty, Cyrus McCormick went back to work on his reaper. He sold two reapers in 1841, seven in 1842, and eighty in the next two years. Two men using a reaper could do as much work as ten or twelve men with sickles, at a saving of more than 88¢ an acre.

In 1845, at the age of thirty-six, McCormick took a trip out west. One look at the waving fields of grain in Ohio, Indiana, and Illinois convinced him that he had found the perfect market for his invention. He started a factory in Chicago in 1847. In 1854, he made and sold 1,588 machines. He introduced time-payments, so that farmers could buy his machines over a period of years. If relatively few farmers, even on easy payment plans, could afford his machines, he still sold 23,000 in 1857, at a profit of more than a million and a quarter dollars.

THE END OF THE TRAIL

In the 1830's, the pioneers of the Northwest had entered the Illinois prairie. By 1857, the thrust of settlement had reached the edge of the woodlands 300 miles west of the Mississippi.

"They turned their faces to the west which they had for generations seen at sunset through traceries of the twigs and leafage of the primal forests, and finally stepped out into the open, where God had cleared the fields. . . ."

From Texas to Iowa, the long line of woodsmen hesitated. True, the prairie had been broken to the north, in Illinois, but there it was a kind of bay surrounded by the familiar forest, with sources of wood for cabins and fences and burning. Here, at the edge of the forest, it was like the ocean, endless and rolling. The woodsman didn't understand the prairie, or the arid plains beyond. He called the prairie squirrel a dog because he couldn't get used to the idea of a squirrel that lived in the ground. His ax was useless; there weren't enough streams to turn the mills he would need.

Rather than cope with this strange world, he traveled 2,000 miles across it to the familiar woods of Oregon.

The plains attracted many kinds of adventurers. In 1844, young Francis Parkman, to prepare for a career as an historian, went 1600 miles west of Boston to live among the Sioux.

Across the great open expanse owned by the mounted Indian, dry and treeless, with shallow rivers to be forded, strange ragged mountains to be pierced, men had to travel together. Guides were needed, and men had to organize to protect themselves from raw nature and hostile savages.

"For the Outfit and Organization," read a sheet of advice for such an expedition in 1843:

"100 men should be armed and equipped with a good rifle gun of large bore, carrying not less than 60 bullets to the pound — 4 pounds of powder, 12 of lead — (flint locks are to be preferred,) caps and flints in proportion — and [a] good knife and a small tomahawk. . . .

"It will be necessary in such a company, that they should be completely organized like a company of regular soldiers; and I would advise that they agree (after choosing their officers) that they . . . shall subject themselves to be governed by the rules and articles of war of the United States, so far as they shall apply . . . I would recommend that to 100 men, they elect one Captain, who should carry a spy glass, four Sergeants, and four Corporals — and there ought to be a Bugler to give the signals, and if one cannot be had, there should be a drum and fife. Guides and buffalo hunters will be required . . . to go hunting and shooting at pleasure. . . . Companies ought not to be less than fifty efficient fighting men, but 100 would be better; there are some Indians who are rather hostile, and they might attack a small party for plunder.

"One Who Intends to Emigrate."

THE GREAT AMERICAN DESERT

The country these men crossed had been more or less known for 300 years. In back of the tall grass prairie was a great barren plain marked down on maps as the *Great American Desert,* and beyond the desert were the Rocky Mountains. It was fixed in the minds of Americans, this Great American Desert, by the countless school maps on which it appeared, the speeches and newspaper stories in which it was mentioned.

Before 1542, the plains and the desert had been penetrated by the Spaniards de Vaca and Coronado. It was known that masses of buffalo roamed through the tall grass in herds miles wide, their motion shaking the ground like thunder.

As much as the strangeness of the plains, the westward movers were discouraged from settling them by the ferocity of the mounted Indians. The plains warrior riding bareback could put ten arrows in the air before the first reached its target, and he had mastered such difficult feats as "throwing himself entirely upon one side of his horse and discharging his arrows with great rapidity toward the opposite side from beneath the animal's neck while he is at full speed . . ."

The Sioux, Cheyenne, Comanche and other plains tribes had become the equals of the finest Tartar, Mongol, or Arab mounted warriors of the Old World. For 200 years they had kept the Spanish from coming north from Mexico.

The Texans, north of the Rio Grande, declared their independence of Mexico in 1836. But they, too, were confined, forced to remain in the woodlands in the eastern corner of their Republic until given a weapon with which they could successfully fight on horseback.

The muzzle-loaded rifle was useless in warfare against the mounted Indians because it could not be loaded on horseback. All the Indian had to do was run away until his enemy's rifle was discharged. Then the brave could turn on his pursuer and send a stream of arrows at him.

Sometime in 1839, a new weapon appeared in Texas. It was a pistol capable of firing six shots in rapid succession from the chambers of a revolving cylinder. Its ammunition consisted of newly developed cartridges that could be slipped fully loaded into the chamber and fired merely by the blow of a hammer. This remarkable pistol had been manufactured in Paterson, New Jersey, in accordance with the patent held by a young man named Sam Colt.

On June 8, 1844, Captain John C. Hays and fourteen of his Texas Rangers discovered seventy Comanches outside San Antonio. In a desperate battle, more than thirty Indians and a few Rangers were killed. ". . . the best-contested fight that ever took place in Texas," wrote the Texan Major Caperton, "and it showed that (the Rangers) could whip the Indians on horseback, . . . the pistols gave them the advantage . . ."

A CONTINENTAL UNION

Annexation of Texas, settlement of the Oregon boundary claim, war with Mexico, and the purchase of 45,535 square miles of desert brought the United States to its present continental boundaries. In 1848, two years after California was won from Mexico, gold was discovered at Sutter's Mill. Tens of thousands of men rushed westward by ship, around Cape Horn or across the Panama isthmus by railroad, and across plains and mountains by wagon train. A few found gold. It was easier, however, to make your fortune selling potatoes and eggs to miners for a dollar apiece. Almost overnight there was a big, lawless American city three thousand miles west of Baltimore — San Francisco.

In 1860, there were thirty-three states in the United States. A Union that had started with just thirteen states along a narrow strip of Atlantic Seaboard had been joined, in seventy-two years, by twenty more states. Here was something new in the world, a union of states taking to itself new states on a free and equal basis. A territory of a million square miles had grown to something over 3 million, and yet as it was settled there was no difficulty over administration, no weakening of the ties of government. The electric telegraph and the steam locomotive contributed to the administration of a continental territory. It was nevertheless clear that in permitting new self-governing states to freely join the older states, the Federal Constitution (adopting the policies of the old Confederation, as expressed in the Northwest Ordinance) had set in motion a system particularly well-adapted to the civilizing of a huge area.

In attacking the American forest, the European had struggled to convert it into the kinds of farms and towns he had known before. Penetrating deeper and deeper into the dark woods, generation after generation, he had been forced to throw aside beliefs and customs that did not fit this new environment.

In becoming a woodsman, a fur trapper, a pioneer, he became less of a European. Still, for almost 200 years, his farms and villages had all faced the European world he had left, and his rivers, all flowing into the Atlantic, tied him to an Atlantic community to which he sold his produce in return for the manufactures of Amsterdam, Liverpool, and Paris.

Across the Appalachian barrier, however, the rivers flowed west, away from the Atlantic. They made a single great drainage area almost as big as Europe. To the building up of this empire, the old eastern states could serve as Europe had once served them. They could supply skills and manufactures in return for the raw products of the soil. America looked westward to the valleys of Ohio and Mississippi. Having freed herself politically from the Old World, America might now not need Europe at all.

"BUT THE BASIN OF THE MISSISSIPPI IS *THE* BODY OF THE NATION," trumpeted an editorial in *Harper's Magazine* in 1863. "All the other parts are but members, important in themselves, yet more important in their relations to this. Exclusive of the Lake basin and of . . . Texas and New Mexico, . . . this basin contains about 1,250,000 square miles. In extent it is the second great valley of the world, being exceeded only by that of the Amazon. . . . It exceeds in extent the whole of Europe, exclusive of Russia, Norway and Sweden. . . . Latitude, elevation, and rainfall all combine to render every part of the Mississippi Valley capable of supporting a dense population. *As a dwelling place for civilized man it is by far the first upon our globe.*"

Or as Abraham Lincoln quoted an Irishman: "In this country one man is as good as another; and for the matter of that, very often a great deal better."

THE SOUTH

LIFE, the relationships between men, was transformed in the North by the factory system and the corporation. Masses of immigrants provided cheap labor, new words, and new dialects. Slavery and other forms of servitude proved neither practical nor profitable and were done away with. The vote was extended to the poorer classes of whites, and all became more dependent on buying and selling.

The South was not devoid of innovations; it was just that the effects were less. South Carolina and Maryland built the first operating steam railroads in the country, yet in 1860 the 15 slave states had only one-quarter of the 42,000 miles of track in the United States. In terms of square miles of settled land, the South was the most rapidly growing section of the country. The tempo of Southern life became faster, there were more plantations, planters, slaves, and crops every year; but industry grew far more slowly. With little foreign immigration, the character of the population remained unchanged. Far less than in the North were habits of life and thought transformed.

It was true in all the states at first, that they were dominated by a wealthy and educated minority. The rich merchants of Boston and Salem dominated Massachusetts in 1790 no less than did the planter aristocracy dominate Virginia. In the following years, there were struggles for political leadership: in Southern states as well as in northern.

The Southern states retained more of their aristocratic character because no new classes of manufacturers and financiers arose to challenge the old leadership. Also, the enumeration of slaves (five slaves were counted as three persons in apportioning Congressional representation) tended to give slave-holders an undue share of political power.

A Yankee from the Connecticut of 1800 would have been more at home in the Tennessee of 1860 than the Connecticut of 1860. In the South, old ways were perpetuated and new things stifled. The South was colonial America little affected by time.

THE GULF

In the beginning, the Negro slave had been looked upon as a kind of indentured servant, different only in that he was black and was indentured for life instead of for just a few years. In the early days of Virginia, black and white servants worked side by side in the fields, ate at the same table, slept in the same huts; and the black slave was protected by the same laws that protected the white servant. The courts had even recognized the right of a slave to protest against cruel treatment by his master.

Because of his greater resistance to malaria and lower cost, the Negro came to be preferred to the white servant for plantation labor, and eventually none but Negroes worked in the plantation fields. As master stood separated from servant by the gulf of race, the Negro slave came to be regarded as a mere property of the master, with no more legal or human rights than a cow.

Servant became synonymous with black and master became synonymous with white. White men, whatever their condition, came to look upon certain kinds of work as "black," or degrading. Labor was not respected, nor could there be pride in workmanship that itself was a sign of servitude.

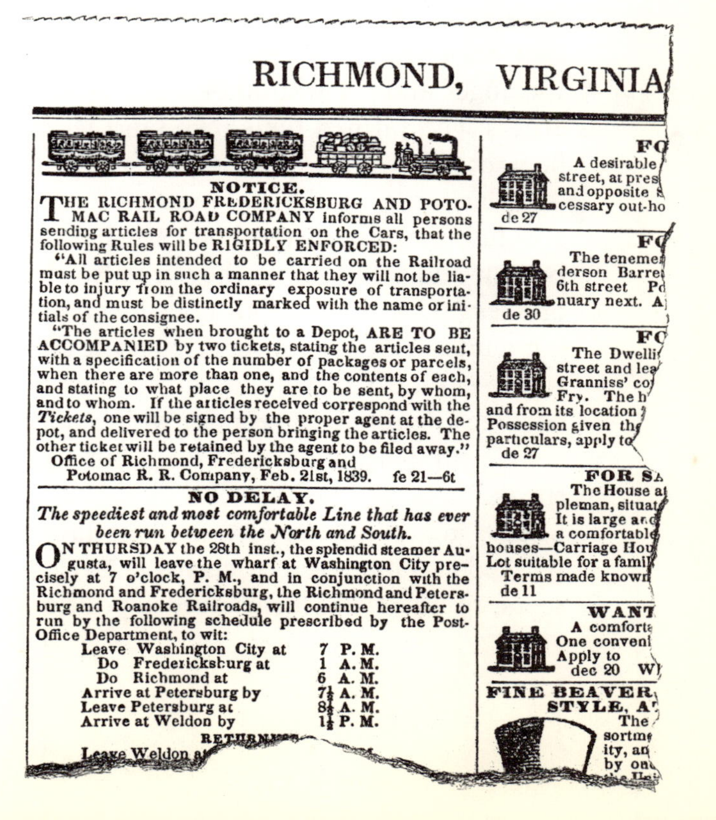

RICHMOND, VIRGINIA

NOTICE.

THE RICHMOND FREDERICKSBURG AND POTOMAC RAIL ROAD COMPANY informs all persons sending articles for transportation on the Cars, that the following Rules will be RIGIDLY ENFORCED:

"All articles intended to be carried on the Railroad must be put up in such a manner that they will not be liable to injury from the ordinary exposure of transportation, and must be distinctly marked with the name or initials of the consignee.

"The articles when brought to a Depot, ARE TO BE ACCOMPANIED by two tickets, stating the articles sent, with a specification of the number of packages or parcels, when there are more than one, and the contents of each, and stating to what place they are to be sent, by whom, and to whom. If the articles received correspond with the *Tickets*, one will be signed by the proper agent at the depot, and delivered to the person bringing the articles. The other ticket will be retained by the agent to be filed away."

Office of Richmond, Fredericksburg and Potomac R. R. Company, Feb. 21st, 1839. fe 21—6t

NO DELAY.

The speediest and most comfortable Line that has ever been run between the North and South.

ON THURSDAY the 28th inst., the splendid steamer Augusta, will leave the wharf at Washington City precisely at 7 o'clock, P. M., and in conjunction with the Richmond and Fredericksburg, the Richmond and Petersburg and Roanoke Railroads, will continue hereafter to run by the following schedule prescribed by the Post-Office Department, to wit:

Leave Washington City at 7 P. M.
Do Fredericksburg at 1 A. M.
Do Richmond at 6 A. M.
Arrive at Petersburg by 7½ A. M.
Leave Petersburg at 8½ A. M.
Arrive at Weldon by 1½ P. M.

RETURNING
Leave Weldon at

FO
A desirable
street, at pres
and opposite
cessary out-ho
de 27

FO
The teneme
derson Barre
6th street P
nuary next. A
de 30

FO
The Dwelli
street and lea
Granniss' co
Fry. The h
and from its location
Possession given th
particulars, apply to
de 27

FOR SA
The House at
pleman, situat
It is large and
a comfortable
houses—Carriage Hou
Lot suitable for a famil
Terms made known
de 11

WANT
A comforta
One conveni
Apply to
dec 20 W

FINE BEAVER,
STYLE, A
The
sortme
ity, an
by one

But the system degraded the master as well as the slave. As one Tennessee farmer noted, people who owned slaves were "always mad with them about something; half their time is spent in swearing and yelling at them." As Jefferson put it, "The whole commerce between master and slave is a perpetual exercise of the most boisterous passions. . . ."

THE LORDS OF THE LASH

Just to name Washington, Jefferson, Madison, and Monroe is to indicate the ability of the southern slave-holding aristocracy. Not only did Virginia produce four of the first five Presidents of the United States, but from the states of the South came a preponderance of the most distinguished leaders of the Continental Congress and of the Senate of the new Federal Government. From the plantation owners — not more than three per cent of the Southern white population — came almost all the leaders of the Southern states until 1865: governors, senators and congressmen. The slave-holders were often bitterly resented by the yeoman farmers of the South. The North Carolina born Hinton Rowan Helper voiced the anger and frustration of many Southerners who farmed their own land when he wrote:

"The lords of the lash are not only absolute masters of the blacks, who are bought and sold . . . but they are also the oracles and arbiters of all non-slaveholding whites. . . . Whenever it pleases, and to the extent it pleases, a slaveholder to become communicative, poor whites may hear with fear and trembling, but not speak."

The aristocrats, secure in their lands worked and managed by slaves and overseers, could devote themselves to politics. Able and industrious Southern representatives dominated the Federal Government for the first thirty years of its existence and thereafter exercised in national affairs an influence out of all proportion to their section's numbers.

THE NEW STAPLE

The price of tobacco declined. Before Washington was born, Robert Carter had complained that it cost him more to clothe and feed his slaves than they could earn on his plantations. Washington, the biggest slaveholder in Fairfax County, saw that his lands had been worn down by too many crops of tobacco in what he called the old "ruinous mode of farming." He tried to fight off the decline by growing wheat, milling flour, and netting fish.

Washington almost put Mt. Vernon on a paying basis. Virginians who did not experiment with their plantations found themselves running ever deeper into debt. Jefferson died penniless, after selling his library to pay some of what he owed. Madison died poor. Monroe spent his last years as a guest in the house of his son-in-law in New York City, after having been forced to give up the family residence.

Jefferson, Madison, and other thoughtful Southerners expected that slavery would die out as the good tobacco lands disappeared.

But the western lands kept the system going. As early as 1785, tobacco was being cultivated in Kentucky and shipped down the Ohio to the Mississippi and New Orleans.

Then an invention made practical the cultivation of a new and profitable staple product. The product was cotton. The invention was the cotton gin.

To appreciate what the cotton crop was to mean to the South, one must understand what had been happening in England since the time of the Seven Years' War.

Hargreaves, Cartwright, Arkwright, and others had designed machinery that could spin and weave cotton *by the hundreds of yards a day*. Chemical bleaching had been introduced, and printing presses that could make as much calico as 200 boys could have made before. British importation of cotton amounted to less than five million pounds in 1775. Ten years later, cotton imports exceeded 11 million pounds. In 1789, following the application of Watt's new steam engines to textile machinery, 32 million pounds of cotton came into Great Britain.

Cotton fabric, thousands of yards of fabric, miles of cloth, were woven in Lancashire and Yorkshire, England. The new and revolutionary means of manufacture made it possible to produce cloth for only a few cents a yard — cloth to clothe a world. English ships scoured the continents for cotton. Bales of the fluffy white fibers were loaded at Turkey and Brazil and unloaded at Liverpool. Cotton fabric was loaded at Liverpool and unloaded at Marseilles, at Naples, Kronstadt, Hamburg, Madras, Cairo, Hangchow. There was nothing like it in the world. Nowhere was there a fabric half so cheap, half as good, as English-manufactured cotton — calico, dimity, and muslin.

A new source of power, the steam engine, was applied. The mills of Lancashire worked night and day. In Wales, men dug deeper into the earth for coal to feed steam boilers to drive the jennies, frames and looms. The skies over Yorkshire became darkened in a new way — with the sooty black clouds of factory smoke. There didn't seem to be enough cotton in the world to feed the mills of England.

Some islands located just off the shores of Georgia and South Carolina were

Scene on New Orleans levee.

among the few places where a cotton with long white fibers or staples flourished. As much as two million pounds of Sea Island Cotton, as it came to be known, were exported, in 1791, by the two states.

Another kind of cotton grew wild along the hills a hundred miles inland, but its staples were so short that it didn't pay to remove the seeds entangled in the balls like burrs in a collie.

Seeing the market for Sea Island cotton, many Southerners sought better ways of removing the seeds from the short staple cotton. In 1793, at a Georgia plantation, a young visitor heard a discussion of this problem. Eli Whitney of Connecticut quickly devised a gadget in which a revolving cylinder with saw teeth drew the cotton through a screen so fine that it separated the seeds from the lint. One person, turning the little machine by hand, could remove as many seeds as fifty people without machines. A bigger model, powered by a horse on a treadmill, could clean from 300 to 1,000 pounds a day. A young Tennessee planter named Andrew Jackson was to note later that the new cotton engine, or "gin" as the Negroes called it, did the work of forty hands. He bought one.

THE FLUSH TIMES

With Whitney's invention, the story of the South becomes the story of cotton. — of the clearing of new lands by slave labor, the planting of cotton by slaves, the ginning of cotton, the shipment by riverboat to New Orleans, Charleston, Savannah, Mobile. In 1801, 40 million pounds of cotton were exported from the South. Thereafter, cotton exports doubled every ten years. By 1818, the bales shipped out by just two states, South Carolina and Georgia, were worth more than all the exports of all the rest of the states of the Union. In 1860, the South exported 1.2 *billion* pounds of cotton.

Whatever else he did for a living, the ambitious Southerner invested his earnings in land and slaves. (Andrew Jackson, when a young frontier lawyer, was always looking out for bargains such as "One fellow Daniel about 28 years old sawyer . . ." whom he bought for $250.)

Never was territory settled with greater speed than the great wilderness south of the Ohio and west of the Appalachians. Forests were cut and burned by the square mile, stumps pulled and blasted by the million. The new slaveholders were joined by planters from Virginia and the Carolinas, leaving the tired soil of the East for the fresh loam of Tennessee, Alabama and Mississippi. The old pioneers fled before this advancing army of planters and slaves. There was no joy in house-raisings to which planters, in white gloves, brought gangs of slaves. The planter offered more for cleared land than the farmer could afford to turn down, and outbid him for good new land. Negroes and masters disdained white men who worked with their hands. The pioneers had another reason for going — self-respect.

Cherokees, Choctaws, Creeks, Chickasaws were driven off ancestral hunting grounds in Georgia, Alabama, and Mississippi. Florida was purchased from Spain, and the whole vast fertile lowland plain of the Mississippi River, a kingdom of 880,000 square miles, stretching from North Carolina to the Red River country of Arkansas, and from the Ohio to the Gulf, awaited planting and development.

There was opportunity for all. Newly

established banks printed sheets of money as fast as the printing presses could turn them out and lent them at high rates of interest to anyone who wanted to buy land and slaves. A man could arrive in Alabama with nothing but the shirt on his back and a month later be in the middle of cane thicket directing his own gang of Negroes to the clearing of his land (all on credit, of course).

"The leading fiscal idea of [the] system was," one Southerner, the frontier lawyer Joseph G. Baldwin, noted, ". . . to make . . . the man that had *no* money a little richer . . . than the man that had a million. . . .

"In a new country," he also said, ". . . All have an even start and an equal chance."

Baldwin found the opportunities even greater for lawyers than for would-be planters. With so much land being quickly sold, and men buying and selling everything on credit, there were endless lawsuits.

"And such a criminal docket! What country could boast more largely of its crimes? What more splendid . . . felonies. What more terrific murders! What more gorgeous bank robberies. . . . And in INDIAN affairs! — the very mention is suggestive of the poetry of theft — the romance of a wild and weird larceny! . . . . Swindling Indians by the nation! Stealing their land by the township!"

(In 1826, Governor Troup of Georgia threatened civil war if the Federal Government tried to force him to keep a treaty with the Creek Indians.)

In 1811, Samuel Davis settled in Wilkinson County, Mississippi, twenty miles inland from the river. The Davises had moved west from Hardin County, Kentucky, not far from where Tom and Nancy Lincoln lived. The Davis family consisted of a wife, four girls, five boys, and about half a dozen slaves. The youngest child, the boy Jefferson, was three years old.

The family prospered. Samuel Davis, like many a pioneer, worked beside his Negroes in the fields. His oldest son, Joseph, became a lawyer. After taking in several "crops" of lawsuits, Joseph invested his money in slaves and in a fine piece of land directly on the Mississippi. His peninsula, jutting into a bend in the river, became known as Davis Bend.

Joseph made almost a million dollars and built a three-story mansion, Hurricane House, which had running water in the bathrooms, fed from an attic tank pumped full each morning by slaves. The house was fronted by a beautiful lawn, sloping down to the Mississippi River and planted with magnolias and camellias. To one side of the house stood the cotton gin and blacksmith shop, stout stables, barns, and smaller storage buildings. Farther away was the cluster of whitewashed slave cabins. Each had a vegetable garden and a chicken run.

The hundred or so Negroes at Hurricane apparently enjoyed a kind of self-rule devised by their master, who was a student of the English Socialist, Robert Owen. A Negro who shirked his job or stole was tried by fellow slaves who set the penalty for the offense.

Davis encouraged his slaves to be thrifty, resourceful, and inventive. They were allowed to raise their own vegetables and eggs to supplement their weekly rations or to sell in the market. Slaves could take jobs as long as they paid for the worth of regular field service out of their earnings. Two slave boys, Isiah and Thornton Montgomery, taught to read and write, grew up to serve Joseph Davis as clerk and secretary.

"Now what do I heah fo' him? He's intelligent and reli'ble — what'll you staht 'im at, sah? . . . Now, who'll say five hundred?" A slave auction in Virginia.

EASE AND ARROGANCE

At Harvard, in 1855, was William Henry Fitzhugh Lee of Virginia, known to his friends as "Roony" Lee. One of his classmates, the grandson of John Quincy Adams, observed that the tall, handsome, genial Southerner "had also the Virginian habit of command. . . . For a year, at least, Lee was the most popular and prominent young man in his class, but then seemed slowly to drop into the background. The habit of command was not enough, and the Virginian had little else. He was simple beyond analysis and helpless before the relative complexity of a school.

". . . the Southerner, with his slave-owning limitations, was as little fit to succeed in the struggle of modern life as though he were still a maker of stone axes, living in caves, . . . and that every quality in which he was strong, made him weaker . . . Roony Lee had changed little from the Virginian of a century before . . ."

The picture was exaggerated, but Henry Adams had caught an essential difference between Southern and Northern men. Slavery bred ease and arrogance in white men, whether propertied masters or improvident backwoodsmen.

The slave society had its own focus. In a world in which all slaves were black, all white men were privileged. The gulf that separated free men from slaves made the dirt farmer with his leaky cabin in the hills brother to the squire with his 5,000 acres in the valley.

A man didn't need money to be important. It was enough that his skin was white. Nor was there much of a chance to make money. The big plantations either made their own supplies or imported them from Europe or the North. Roads were built to move what the plantations grew. The rest of the country was left a wilderness where the yeoman farmer, cut off from markets, scraped out a living on land too poor to be wanted by a slave-owner.

From the beginning the owners of slaves had dominated the states of the South. As they consolidated their position, buying more plantations and more slaves to work for them, sending their sons abroad, or up north to college, smoking Havana cigars, racing thoroughbreds, importing books, harpsichords, fine clothes, painters and paintings, china, wines, and Chippendale furniture, and other refinements from the Old World, there arose throughout the South a small, powerful group of men, an aristocracy similar to the country gentry of England. They were very similar, indeed, to the gentry of the English County of Kent, the part of England from which a number of Virginians had emigrated. Kinship was carefully recorded, and every planter was the "cousin" of almost every other planter.

All hard labor and all personal service were performed by Negroes. The master could require the slave to work long hours, but he could not make him like it. Washington sold a strong field hand after despairing of getting him to work. In house service it was found that four slaves accomplished less, and needed more watching, than one paid servant in the North. When they weren't watched slaves stole anything they could carry. For 75¢ worth of cheap whisky, they gave peddlers expensive plumbing fixtures, parts of boilers and cotton gins.

The resentment was always there. A writer for a New York newspaper, Frederick Law Olmsted, noticed that the Negro oiling the wheels of a train in Richmond let the oil run on the ground. He watched an overseer ride amongst a gang repairing a road on a South Carolina plantation. As often as the overseer "visited one end of the line of operations," Olmsted noted, "the hands at the other end would discontinue their labor until he turned to ride towards them again."

SLAVE SALE

Unless he died when quite young, the chances were every slave would be sold: to provide some ready cash, or, on the death of the master, to settle his estate. A planter would die leaving slaves and land to five daughters. For each daughter

A quantity of old Rigging
2 lower Masts
3 Spars
2 Sails
1 Pump
1 Stove.
Conditions cash. Oct. 8

Washer and Ironer.
BY J. S. RIGGS, Jr.
TUESDAY, the 11th inst., at 11 o'clock, at the Exchange, will be sold,
EMMA, 38 years old, with her young child. She is represented as being a qualified Washer and Ironer, and is also a plain Cook. Warranted sound.
Conditions cash; purchaser to pay for bill of sale.
Oct. 7

An Uncommonly Likely Young Boy.
BY J. S. RIGGS, Jr.
On TUESDAY, the 11th inst., at 11 o'clock, at the Exchange, will be sold,
EDWARD, an uncomonly likely boy, about 15 years old, has been at the blacksmiths trade for several years past, and has quite a mechanical turn of mind, is sound and healthy, and sold as the property of an estate.
Conditions cash ; purchaser to pay for bill of sale.
Oct 6

STOCKS AND BONDS.
AT PRIVATE SALE.

to get her share, the slaves would be sold. When Thomas Jefferson died in 1824, all his hundred or more slaves were sold, except for five whom he set free. From Natchez, Mississippi, in December, 1801, Andrew Jackson, then in desperate financial circumstances, received a letter that read, "I will try to find a purchaser for your horses; as for Negroes, they are on great demand and will sell well."

When up for sale, a slave family would be separated. Mothers were separated from children, and husbands from wives unless some buyer could be persuaded otherwise. A New York Tribune correspondent recorded the following scene at a slave sale in Savannah, Georgia, in February, 1859. Speaking is the slave Elisha, chattel #5 in the catalogue of the trader, J. Bryan:

"Look at me, Mas'r; am prime rice planter; sho' you won't find a better man den me; no better on de whole plantation; not a bit old yet; do mo' work den ever; do carpenter work too, a little; better buy me, Mas'r; I'se de good sarvant, Mas'r. Molly, too, my wife, Sa, fus' rate rice hand; mos as good as me. Stan' out yer, Molly, and let the gen'l'm'n see . . . Show Mas'r your arm, Molly — good arm dat, Mas'r — she do a heap of work mo' with dat arm yet. Let good Mas'r see your teeth, Molly — see dat, Mas'r, teeth all regular, all good — she'm young gal yet. Come out yer, Israel, walk aroun' an' let the gen'lm see how spry you be." Then, pointing to the three-year-old girl who stood with her chubby hand to her mouth, holding on to her mother's dress and uncertain what to make of the strange scene, said: "Little Vardy's only a chile yet; make prime gal by-and-by. Better buy us, Mas'r, we'm fus' rate bargain . . ."

Mr. John Bryan, the Savannah slave trader, was the grandson of a prosperous Georgia planter and had been brought up in the family of John Randolph, the Virginia statesman. The representative of many a distinguished Southern family earned his living in the slave trade, buying and selling slaves on commission; speculating in slaves, buying them on his own account and selling them at a big profit in booming Mississippi and Alabama. The Business Mirror of the Lexington, Kentucky Directory for 1859-60, listed among the city's attorneys and bankers and other respectable professionals, four firms of slave dealers. There was big money in the trade. At least one trader, Louis D. DeSaussure, scion of a distinguished Charleston family, was known to clear $10,000 a year, more than the most prosperous South Carolina lawyer was making at that time. Traders boasted of making $30,000 in profit on one shipment of slaves.

THE VOLCANO

From 1840 to 1850, the number of slaves engaged in the raising of cotton increased from 800,000 to 1,800,000.

The price of cotton went down from thirty cents a pound to seven cents a pound. The old cotton states, Georgia and South Carolina, fell behind the new states of the West. Still the South boomed and prospered, wasting land to grow cheaper cotton. In Mississippi one day, Olmsted passed four or five large plantations on "hill-sides gullied like icebergs, stables and negro quarters all abandoned . . ."

But more great mansions lifted graceful white columns where there had been only wild grass, poplar thickets, and the calling of ducks. Like cotton itself, millionaires sprouted out of the Mississippi mud.

As this great prosperity sprang from the labor of slaves, the slave himself came more and more to be recognized as the basis of wealth in the South. He was a peculiarly valuable kind of property. By his work, the slave created wealth for his master. In having children, he created more slaves, to further increase his master's wealth. And the slave was as negotiable as cash money. (A loan of money made by Andrew Jackson was to be repaid by his brother-in-law, in the form of "one likely Country born Negro boy or girl . . .") He could be transported at little expense, for work or for sale, and there was always a ready market for him.

As the slave became the basis of wealth, ownership of slaves became the symbol of wealth. Although in Missouri, cotton flourished only in the southern counties, ". . . every decent Missouri family had at least one slave, and usually from two to four, as house servants."

The price of slaves rose steadily from about $200 to about $1200 for a good field hand. Specialized slaves such as blacksmiths, shoemakers or carpenters sold for more. Not the least factor in this rise in value was the law passed by Congress in 1808, forbidding the importation of slaves. This cutting off of the foreign source of supply insured that there would never be enough slaves to satisfy the growing demand.

As the slave rose steadily in value it became more and more apparent that he, rather than lands, or cotton, or sugar was the most desirable form of property. Slaves were seen to be an extraordinarily good investment. Widows were advised by Southern bankers to invest their cash in slaves as the best way to insure themselves of safe incomes. Slaves could be hired out to work for other people for $100 or $200 a year, up to twenty per cent of their cash value. In Charleston, Richmond, Mobile, New Orleans, and St. Louis, many elderly widows lived off such earnings.

More and more, trading in slaves became the principal business of the South. Slaves raised in Virginia and Maryland were shipped by road or boat, or marched in coffles (chain gangs) on the Wilderness Road through the Cumberland Gap to the frontier lands of Alabama and Mississippi. In January, 1832, Thomas Jefferson's grandson, Thomas Jefferson Randolph, told the Virginia House of Delegates:

". . . It is a practice, and an ever-increasing practice in parts of Virginia, to rear slaves for market. How can an honorable mind, a patriot, and a lover of his country, bear to see this ancient dominion, rendered illustrious by the noble devotion and patriotism of her sons in the cause of liberty, converted into one grand menagerie where men are to be reared for market . . . ?"

Slave traders scoured the older slave territories offering immediate cash for unneeded slaves, for old slaves, for boys and girls. Every city of consequence had its slave traders' jails, where Negroes were kept for sale, and its slave market, where almost daily the chanting of the auctioneers could be heard.

Land was cleared by slave labor and crops grown so that value could be obtained from the slaves while they themselves, through rising slave prices and by having children, were increasing in value. As the historian Frederic Bancroft pointed out to his readers:

"If the master could manage to live

from the labor of his Negroes, the equivalent of riches was only a matter of time. Ten young slaves . . . worth hardly $5,000 in 1840, might treble their number by 1855, when the value of the thirty of all ages was fully $20,000. . . . In two or three decades a small planter, starting in a fertile region with 15 or 20 young slaves, might, by industry, economy and purchasing girls and boys, easily become a 'large planter,' with a gang of 40 or 50 sturdy field hands and more than that many children . . ."

". . . So call and make your purchases [of slaves] to gather your crop," stated an ad in The Memphis Eagle and Enquirer — "and then call quick again and buy to make another crop. — By those means if you will keep up your purchases for ten years there is no telling how much you may be worth. This is the true Road to wealth. . . ."

Slaves came to be so valuable that many plantations were worked to rear slaves instead of slaves being purchased to work the plantation.

By 1850, transactions in slaves were taking place at the rate of 140,000 a year. This included 60,000 yearly hirings, at an average of $100 per hiring; 24,978 sales within the borders of the various states, at an average of $600; and 55,151 sales of slaves transported from one state to another, at an average of $800 per sale. The total amount of cash involved was almost $65 million.

Almost every Southerner who could afford them, owned slaves. A Negro Baptist minister in St. Louis, in 1836, owned 20 slaves. In 1860, 132 free "colored people" of Charleston owned 190 slaves. In the words of John Randolph of Roanoke, Virginia, slavery was "a volcano in full operation."

With such a great and profitable speculation in slaves, and the export of millions of bales of cotton, the South hardly bothered with other forms of trade or manufacture. As formerly it had exchanged its tobacco for English goods, it now became a market for Bibles, brooms, buckets, furniture, glassware, toys, clothing, medicine, pianos, and shoes made in the factories of Fall River, Hartford, Pittsburgh, Cincinnati, Chicago, New York, and a hundred other Northern cities.

"We go to the North for . . . all," complained Hinton Rowan Helper. "Instead of keeping our money in circulation at home, by patronizing our own mechanics, manufacturers, and laborers, we send it all away to the North, and there is remains; it never falls into our hands again."

And what money there was in the South did not circulate as it did in the North. Where laborers are not paid, money stays in the hands of the owners of labor. The South was always short of cash, not only for investment in railroads and other enterprises, but even for necessities. (George Washington's hired blacksmith had exchanged his work for butter, eggs, chickens or leather. When the master of Mt. Vernon wanted a boat, he swapped 1,536 pounds of pork for it. Slaves were used as money in Missouri for the purchase of land.)

The other states of the Union were racked by struggles for higher pay and better working conditions. From Illinois to New Hampshire, ordinary workingmen gradually won a voice in the government.

Where there was turbulence in the North, there was peace in the South. But

Fifty Dollars Reward,

Will be given for apprehending ISAAC, and delivering him to the Subscriber or the master of the Work House, on proof of his being harboured or employed by a white or free person of colour, or thirty dollars and all reasonable charges on his delivery. Isaac is nineteen years of age, about five feet, six inches high, very black, smooth skined and plausible; has a remarkable swelling on his breast, occasioned by a scald or burn when a child, is a good boat hand and i is supposed he is fishing and stops at Morris or Sulli vans Island. JOHN DOUGHERTY.

June 10 6—tf

the peace was the peace of despotism. The Cotton States remained tight little aristocracies where criticism was stifled and opportunity increasingly limited. The Reverend Daniel Worth of North Carolina was jailed for attacking slavery; Federal post offices were forbidden to deliver anti-slavery literature, and newspaper editors were shot for their opinions.

Cotton and slavery raised up an aristocracy and depressed the remaining ninety-seven per cent of the people, slaves and whites alike. The white farmer, forced back on inferior land, cut off from wild game as the forest was destroyed, was weakened by a dull diet of corn pone and razorback hog. He was prey to disease and kept down by a sparse educational system. At midcentury, the two Western towns of Natchez, Mississippi, and Springfield, Illinois, both had populations of about 19,000; 1,015 attended school in Natchez, as against 3,300 in Springfield. The public library in Springfield had 20,000 books. The library in Natchez had 2,000.

While the North was bursting into an industrial era unlike anything the world had ever seen, the South maintained a kind of racial feudalism. In defense of honor, back-country folk shot neighbors, and attorneys shot editors. The "po' " white farmer sipped from a jug on the porch while his wife planted corn, and on the plantations, the rich folk held tournaments like those they read about in novels by Sir Walter Scott.

The South had forced its people to choose. As slaves and their masters had moved into Hardin County, Kentucky, some families had bought slaves and some had headed north for the new state of Indiana, where, following the Ordinance of 1787, "holding any part of the human creation in slavery, or involuntary servitude" was seen as the product of "usurpation and tyranny."

The Davises had brought their slaves to Hardin County and then had moved with them to Mississippi. The Lincolns had sold their Kentucky farm for ten barrels of whisky and twenty dollars cash and had gone to Indiana.

KING COTTON

In 1830, while grass grew in the streets of Williamsburg and bear and deer wandered through abandoned Virginia plantations, large parts of Alabama and Mississippi became literally white with cotton: growing on square miles of fields, packed high on wharves, in press houses, in steamers and barges.

It might seem that the southern valley of the Mississippi provided almost limitless land for the planting of cotton. But as the cotton fields leaped across the Mississippi, even the annexation of Texas couldn't satisfy planters and slave traders hungry for new Alabamas.

Men like William Walker of Nashville, Tennessee, wanted to grab all the territory bordering on the Carribean Sea and the Gulf of Mexico for a great slave empire that would supply the world with cotton, coffee, sugar, and other staples.

The Kentucky Constitution of 1850 declared "the right of the owner of a slave to such slave, and its increase, is the same, and is as inviolable as the right of the owner of any property whatever."

"The world must have cotton and the world depends on [the American slave States] for it," one Southern statesman boasted. "Whatever they demand, that must be conceded them; whatever they want, they have but to . . . take it."

"Cotton is king . . ." James H. Hammond of South Carolina told the United States Senate in 1858.

AND THE PEOPLE: SIGHTS AND SOUNDS

"The pure contralto sings in the organ loft,
The carpenter dresses his plank, the tongue of his foreplane whistles its wild ascending lisp,
The married and unmarried children ride home to their Thanksgiving dinner,
The pilot seizes the king-pin, he heaves down with a strong arm,
The mate stands braced in the whale-boat, lance and harpoon are ready,
The duck-shooter walks by silent and cautious stretches,
The deacons are ordain'd with cross'd hands at the altar,
The spinning-girl retreats and advances to the hum of the big wheel,
The farmer stops by the bars as he walks on a First-day loafe and looks at the oats and rye,
The lunatic is carried at last to the asylum a confirm'd case,
(He will never sleep any more as he did in the cot in his mother's bed-room);
The jour printer with grey head and gaunt jaws works at his case,
He turns his quid of tobacco while his eyes blurr with the manuscript; . . .
The malform'd limbs are tied to the surgeon's table,
What is removed drops horribly in a pail;
The quadroon girl is sold at the auction-stand, the drunkard nods by the bar-room stove,
The machinist rolls up his sleeves, the policeman travels his beat, the gate-keeper marks who pass,
The young fellow drives the express-wagon (I love him, though I do not know him);

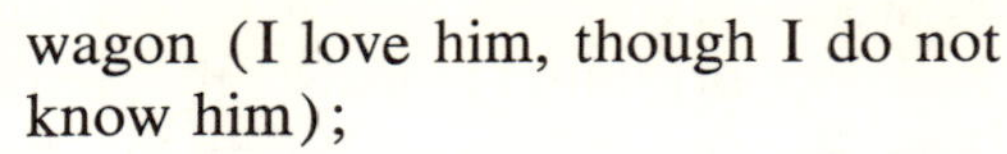

The half-breed straps on his light boots to compete in the race,
The western turkey-shooting draws old and young, some lean on their rifles, some sit on logs,
Out from the crowd steps the marks-man, takes his position, levels his piece;
The groups of newly-come immigrants cover the wharf or levee,
As the woolly-pates hoe in the sugar-field, the overseer views them from his saddle,

The bugle calls in the ball-room, the gentlemen run for their partners, the dancers bow to each other,
The youth lies awake in the cedar-roof'd garret and harks to the musical rain,
The Wolverine sets traps on the creek that helps fill the Huron,
The squaw wrapt in her yellow-hemm'd cloth is offering moccasins and bead-bags for sale,
The connoisseur peers along the exhi-bition-gallery with half-shut eyes bent sideways,
As the deck-hands make fast the steam-boat the plank is thrown for the shore-going passengers,
The young sister holds out the skein while the elder sister winds it off in a ball, and stops now and then for the knots,
The one-year wife is recovering and happy having a week ago borne her first child,
The clean-hair'd Yankee girl works with her sewing-machine or in the factory or mill,

The paving-man leans on his two-handed rammer, the reporter's lead flies swiftly over the note-book, the sign-painter is lettering with blue and gold,
The canal boy trots on the tow-path, the book-keeper counts at his desk, the shoemaker waxes his thread,
The conductor beats time for the band and all the performers follow him,
The child is baptized, the convert is making his first professions,
The regatta is spread on the bay, the race is begun (how the white sails sparkle!)
The drover watching his drove sings out to them that would stray,
The pedlar sweats with his pack on his back (the purchaser haggling about the odd cent);
The bride unrumples her white dress, the minute-hand of the clock moves slowly,
The opium-eater reclines with rigid head and just-open'd lips, . . .
The prostitute draggles her shawl, her bonnet bobs on her tipsy and pimpled neck,
The crowd laugh at her blackguard oaths, the men jeer and wink to each other,
(Miserable! I do not laugh at your oaths nor jeer you);
The President holding a cabinet council is surrounded by the great Secretaries,
On the piazza walk three matrons stately and friendly with twined arms,
The crew of the fish-smack pack repeated layers of halibut in the hold,
The Missourian crosses the plains toting his wares and his cattle,

As the fare-collector goes through the train he gives notice by the jingling of loose change,
The floor-men are laying the floor, the tinners are tinning the roof, the masons are calling for mortar,
In single file each shouldering his hod pass onward the laborers;
Seasons pursuing each other the indescribable crowd is gather'd, it is the fourth of the Seventh-month (what salutes of cannon and small arms)!
Seasons pursuing each other the plougher ploughs, the mower mows, and the winter-grain falls in the ground;
Off on the lakes the pike-fisher watches and waits by the hole in the frozen surface,
The stumps stand thick round the clearing, the squatter strikes deep with his axe,

Flatboatmen make fast towards dusk near the cotton-wood or pecan-trees,
Coon-seekers go through the regions of the Red river or through those drain'd by the Tennessee, or through those of the Arkansas,
Torches shine in the dark that hangs on the Chattahoochee or Altamahaw,
Patriarchs sit at supper with sons and grandsons and great-grandsons around them,
In walls of adobie, in canvas tents, rest hunters and trappers after their day's sport,
The city sleeps and the country sleeps,
The living sleep for their time, the dead sleep for their time,
The old husband sleeps by his wife and the young husband sleeps by his wife . . ."

WALT WHITMAN
from *Song of Myself*

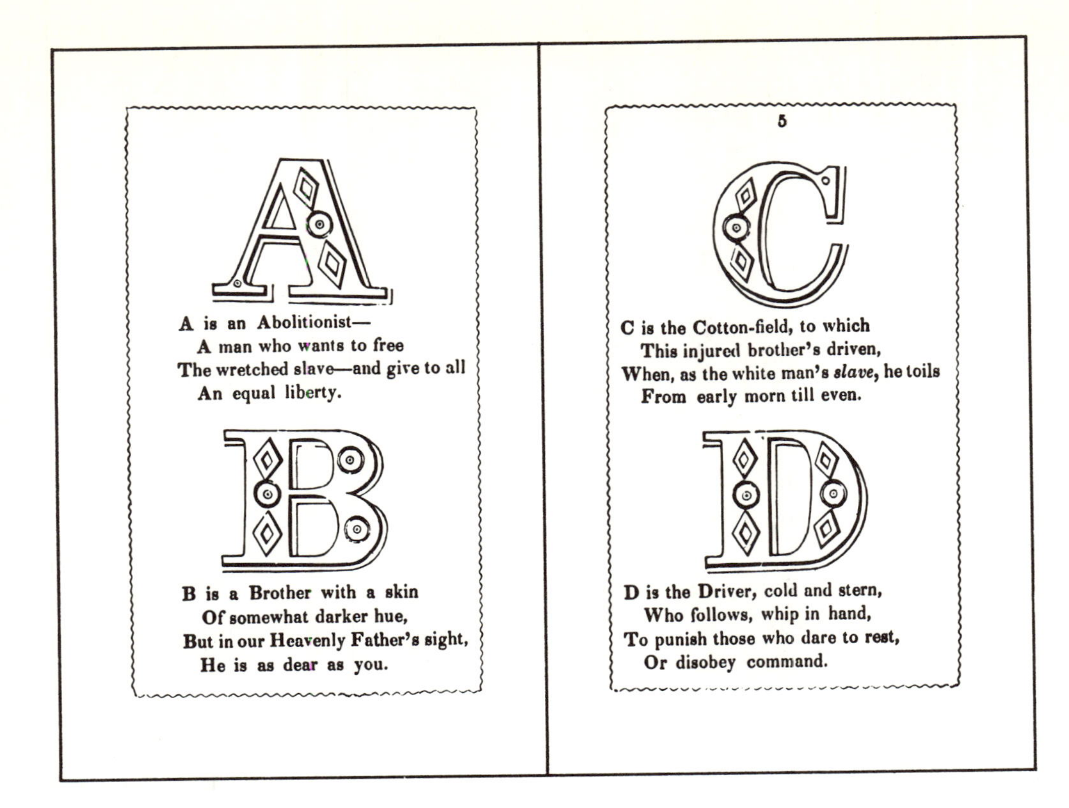

CRISIS

POLITICAL differences come down to differences in interest. A tariff is a government tax on imported articles. The manufacturer favors the tariff because it raises the prices of imports to as high as or higher than what he can sell his own manufactures for. The farmer objects to the tariff because it forces him to pay more for manufactures.

"Those who hold and those who are without property have ever formed distinct interests in society," James Madison wrote in 1787. "Those who are creditors and those who are debtors, fall under a like discrimination. A landed interest, a manufacturing interest, a mercantile interest, a moneyed interest, with many lesser interests, grow up of necessity in civilized nations, and divide them into different classes, actuated by different sentiments and views. *The regulation of these various and interfering interests forms the principal task of modern legislation . . .*"

A system of government resolves the clashes of interest by providing a means of settlement acceptable to all parties. The Congress, in framing laws, becomes a field for the trading of interests, for peaceful inquiry into the facts. Southern states had opposed Hamilton's assumption measure. Northern states had opposed moving the capital of the United States south. Southerners voted for Hamilton's measure in return for Northern agreement that the capital be moved to the Potomac River.

This is the business of government, the resolution of clashes of interest in an orderly manner. Wars and rebellions represent breakdowns in government. The War for Independence had been such a breakdown in the government of the British Empire, and the threat of a similar breakdown in the government of the Articles of Confederation brought about the formation of the Union.

During its first seventy-two years, through eighteen Presidential terms, the Union grew as no nation in history had ever grown before. It grew three times in size, eight times in population, leaped over three mountain ranges to the Pacific Ocean, added twenty states, and settled the great Ohio-Mississippi Valley. With the growth of factories in the North, of hundreds of thousands of prosperous Western farms, of Southwestern states white with cotton, new and stronger interests grew up in the land. To the chuff-chuffing of the steamboat, the clicking of iron wheels on iron rails, the pace quickened. As interests grew continental in scope, the clashes increased in power. The question was: could such great, continental interests be regulated? Were the principles of the Constitution applicable to a nation covering more than 3 million square miles and consisting of more than 31 million people?

THE IMPERFECT VISION

The first great political leader to come out of the West, Henry Clay, represented something new on the American scene. Born and educated in Virginia, he had moved across the mountains into Kentucky in 1797, when he was twenty years old. He opened a law office in the town of Lexington and quickly gained a reputation as an orator.

Tall and thin, with a light complexion and bright gray eyes, he swore freely, gambled heavily, and consumed large quantities of the newly invented corn, or bourbon, whisky. Not that the older Congressmen, those of the generation that had fought the Revolutionary War, had all been scholars and violinists; but Henry Clay was not apologetic about his habits. When a Boston lady asked Mrs. Clay if she minded her husband's gambling, she replied, "Oh, dear, no! He most always wins."

This was part of the feeling of the West that Henry Clay brought to Washington with him: that if it worked was the important test of a proposition.

As a Westerner, Henry Clay had a vision of America growing — America becoming. The American adventure had just begun. The old states along the Atlantic might look back to the glories of the War for Independence, but everything they had accomplished had just been preparation for settlement of the West.

Henry Clay wanted the Federal Government to finance the turnpikes and canals necessary to develop the West; the money was to come from tariffs and loans.

Henry Clay.

As "Harry of the West" saw it, everybody benefited from his "American System" — the West got transportation; Northern industry got tariffs to protect it; as Northern industry developed, farmers would find markets for their produce among the growing horde of factory workers and city dwellers; the expanded trade would benefit merchants; and bankers would be able to lend money to the Government at a good rate of interest.

Political independence might have been won in 1783. The American System would bring economic independence. Supplying her own manufactures, with her own markets for the products of her factories and farms, the United States would no longer be affected by Europe's struggles. Napoleons could come and go, England and France could fight whom they pleased. As the United States grew prosperous and self-sufficient, all the separate interests of America would be reconciled in the fulfillment of the nation's destiny.

Peace and prosperity in isolation! What more could any people want? This vision would haunt many generations of Americans.

The fulfillment of this vision depended, of course, on each of the various groups — farmers, manufacturers, and merchants — benefiting equally, or at least having the idea that they benefited equally.

Unfortunately, the system did not benefit the farmer. The growth of cities did not keep pace with the increasing size of his crops, and the tariff, by raising farm costs without raising farm income, reduced the farmer's earnings. The farmer who sold to foreign nations was particularly vexed. He was forced to accept low British prices, but was prevented from buying low-priced British goods.

CLASH OF INTERESTS

The financial panic of 1819 plunged the country into gloom. On May 22, 1820, John Quincy Adams, President Monroe's Secretary of State, had a conversation with John C. Calhoun of South Carolina. There were, Calhoun remarked, ". . . enormous numbers of persons utterly ruined; multitudes in deep distress . . ."

In the midst of the depression, Representative Baldwin proposed increasing the tariff. Pittsburgh, Henry Baldwin's home town, blamed its suffering on falling prices of the iron and glass it made. Duties on manufactured woolens and cottons would be raised one-third; on forged iron bars, the duty would rise from 75¢ to $1.25 per hundred pounds. On some other articles, the duties were doubled.

The measure passed the House of Representatives 91 to 78. New England was split on its votes, 18 to 17; New York, New Jersey, Pennsylvania, and Delaware voted 56 to 1 in favor of the tariff; and the Southern states voted 50 to 5 against it. Ohio, Indiana and Illinois favored the tariff 8 to 0; and Kentucky, Tennessee, and Louisiana opposed it 10 to 4. Except for divided New England, section lined up against section on this tariff issue — the Middle States and the Northwest on one side, the South and Southwest on the other.

The tariff was defeated in the Senate, and the issue was deferred to 1824. In the debates of that year Speaker Henry Clay led the tariff, or protectionist forces, and Daniel Webster of Massachusetts and George McDuffie of South Carolina led the opposition, or free trade forces. Webster represented the shipping and trading interests that dominated Massachusetts, now suffering from the decrease in foreign trade. McDuffie represented the victimized planters, whose cotton, tobacco, rice, and sugar accounted for two-thirds of the exports of the United States. Some planters were impatient. Representative John Randolph of Roanoke, Virginia, was an odd little rooster of a man. Opposed to the spread of slavery, he was at the same time an ardent advocate of the supreme rights of states which, he believed, were threatened by the tariff. "I consider the Constitution a dead letter," he shrieked during the debate. ". . . If, under a power to regulate trade, you prevent exportation; if with the most approved spring lancets, you draw the last drop of blood from our veins . . . the last shilling from our pockets, what are the checks of the Constitution to us? A fig for the Constitution! . . . There is no magic in this word *Union.*"

The 1824 bill passed the House by the very close vote of 107 to 102, the line-up in voting following the pattern of 1820. The debate went on as protective tariffs were voted in 1828 and 1832. The South grew bitter as the price of cotton fell from 30¢ a pound to 9¢ a pound, and as it appeared that the $16 million a year that the tariffs cost the South was going either into the pockets of northern manufacturers or the building of western roads.

A reporter for The Portland Daily Advertiser made hasty notes as Representative McDuffie addressed the House in 1833:

"Sir, (a thump on desk upon a quire of paper heavy enough to echo over the whole hall) sir, South Carolina is oppressed, (a thump.) A tyrant majority sucks her life blood from her, (a dreadful thump). Yes, sir, (a pause) yes, sir, a tyrant (a thump) majority unappeased, (arms aloft) unappeasable, (horrid scream) has persecuted and persecutes us, (a stamp on the floor.) We appeal to them, (low and quick) but we appeal in vain, (loud and quick). . . . They heap coals of fire on our heads (with immense rapidity) — they give us burden on burden; they tax us more and more (very rapid, slam-bang, slam — a hideous noise.) We turn to our brethren of the South, (slow with a solemn, thoughtful air.) We work with them; we fight with them; we vote with them; we petition with them; (common voice and manner) but the tyrant majority has no ears, no eyes, no form (quick) deaf, (long pause) sightless. (pause) inexorable, (slow, slow.) Despairing, (a thump) or resort to the rights (a pause) which God (a pause) and nature has given us, (thump, thump, thump) . . ."

NULLIFICATION

Late in November, 1832, a state convention in Charleston, South Carolina, had declared the tariffs of 1828 and 1832 void within the state after February 1, 1833. It further stated that should the Federal Government take any action except through the courts, to force payment of the tariff, "the people of this State will thenceforth hold themselves absolved from all further obligation to maintain or preserve their political connexion with the people of the other States, and will forewith proceed to organize a separate Government . . ."

In Washington, D.C., President Andrew Jackson penned a long and careful reply in which he said:

"I consider . . . the power to annul a law of the United States, assumed by one

State, *incompatible with the existence of the Union, contradicted expressly by the letter of the Constitution . . .*"

President Jackson moved in two directions at once: getting Congressional authorization to use force against South Carolina, and encouraging a lower, compromise tariff proposed by Senator Henry Clay. South Carolina expected that other Southern states would also nullify the tariff. They did not. Alone, facing invasion by the United States Army, the state legislature rescinded the proclamation. The threat of Federal power had brought South Carolina into line, but a direct confrontation had been avoided, and passage of the Clay tariff allowed South Carolina to claim victory of a sort.

John Randolph of Roanoke.

THE DEADLY DISEASE

Although the rivalry between North and South first became serious over the tariff question, the tariff was not the basic cause. The tariff was but a symptom, a surface outbreak. Just as to the eye of a trained physician a skin rash can indicate a deep-seated fever, so the uproar in 1833 expressed the deadly disease burning the vitals of the Republic.

The disease was slavery.

The Southern states were equal in population to those of the North and provided as much as two-thirds the total exports of the nation. That they were a minority in the Federal Government was due to the counting of slaves as equal only to three-fifths of a free man. Article I, Section 2, of the Constitution apportioned Congressmen (and electoral votes for President) and direct taxes "according to their respective Numbers, which shall be determined by adding to the *whole Number of free Persons . . . three-fifths of all other Persons.*"

All the perplexity of the authors of the Constitution with regard to slavery is held in this curious provision. If slaves were truly property, as their owners claimed, then surely they could be used as a basis for apportionment no more than land, buildings, ships, or any other property.

If they were persons, there was indeed justification for counting them. But as persons, were they not then among "WE THE PEOPLE of the United States," who were establishing the Constitution "in Order to form a more perfect Union, establish justice, insure domestic Tranquility, provide for the common defence, promote the general Welfare, and secure the Blessings of Liberty to ourselves and our posterity?"

Was a slave a person or property? The Constitution said he was three-fifths of a person. What is three-fifths of a person?

JOHN CALDWELL CALHOUN

Calhoun entered Congress in 1811, from the frontier region of South Carolina. At first he had been an ardent supporter of Henry Clay, favoring war in 1812 and the American System.

As he observed the workings of the system, he changed his views. "We are mere consumers, the serfs of the system," he complained in 1828. As he saw it, the South was an oppressed minority.

That minorities could be oppressed had been of great concern to Madison and the other authors of the Constitution. Madison had stated that it would be no wiser to permit a majority unlimited power than to allow an individual to be judge of his own cause. "If two individuals are under the bias of interest or enmity against a third, the rights of the latter could never be safely referred to the majority of the three."

Calhoun followed Jefferson's reasoning, as expressed in the Kentucky resolutions, that the Federal Government, as judge of the constitutionality of its own acts, was acting as a judge in its own cause. The only safeguard of minority interests, Calhoun concluded, was the people of a state meeting in convention — their ultimate recourse, nullification and secession.

Calhoun had served as John Quincy Adams' Vice President. In 1832, he resigned as Jackson's Vice President to fight the tariff on the floor of the Senate.

SOUTHERN TACTICS

The doctrines of nullification and secession were weapons of last resort against the growing power of the free population of the North. But the South could hope to achieve such influence that it would not have to employ its ultimate weapons. If the three-fifths rule doomed the Southerners to inferiority in the House of Representatives, it had no effect on the Upper House where each state had two Senators regardless of the numbers or conditions of its inhabitants. In 1812, the admission of Louisiana restored the balance between free and slave states. Thereafter, the South could hold the Senate simply by seeing to it that slave and free states were admitted to the Union in equal numbers. Between 1812 and 1819, two free states, Indiana and Illinois, and two slave states, Mississippi and Alabama, came into the Union. The Senatorial balance was preserved even while Northern votes in the House of Representatives increased to 123 as against 90 for the South.

And if the three-fifths rule deprived them of electoral votes for President,

John C. Calhoun.

they still had enough votes to swing elections to whichever of the two major parties they supported.

"A FIREBELL IN THE NIGHT"

By 1815, the great westward march had reached the Mississippi River, and trees were starting to go down west of Illinois, Kentucky, Tennessee, and Alabama. Pioneer families pushed their wagons into Iowa, and slaves were marched in ragged lines across Illinois to a place called Missouri.

In 1818, the application of Missouri for admission to the Union presented the country with a grave problem. The Ordinance of 1787 had set the Ohio River as a clear dividing line between the free and slave portions of the original territory of the Union. West of the Mississippi River, no such line had been laid down.

Slaveholders had already established themselves in Missouri when it asked for statehood in 1819. Should Missouri be admitted to the Union as a slave state? Did Congress have any right to say whether there ought or ought not to be slavery in Missouri or in any part of the Louisiana Territory?

The struggle began in the House of Representatives on February 13, 1819, when Tallmadge of New York proposed that Missouri prohibit the introduction of more slaves and agree to gradually free the slaves already within her borders. The arguments became bitter. Finally, Cobb of Georgia declared:

"You have kindled a fire which all the waters of the ocean cannot put out, which seas of blood can only extinguish."

Tallmadge's and other measures dealing with slavery in the Territory were defeated in the Senate, where some Northern Senators voted with the South.

This was a gray and stormy year in the history of the Republic. Troubled with a depression that had ruined banks, lowered crop prices and thrown thousands out of work, the people were now agitated by the Missouri question. There were mass meetings. The legislatures of New York, Pennsylvania, New Jersey, Ohio, and even of the slave state of Delaware passed resolutions against the further introduction of slaves into the Territories and against the admission of new slave states. Southerners protested that the denial of slavery unfairly excluded southern planters from American Territories.

To Speaker Henry Clay, presiding over the House of Representatives, all the agitation over Missouri, the question of slavery or non-slavery, seemed a dangerous distraction. It turned the nation away from consideration of tariffs, the building of roads, and other essentials of his American system. Here was arguing, agitating, feelings inflamed, when all sections should be working together for the benefit of all.

The controversy was settled by a compromise put forward by Henry Clay and by Senator Thomas of Illinois. Missouri was admitted as a slave state and Maine was admitted as a free state, preserving the balance. A dividing line was drawn across the Louisiana Territory, westward from the southern boundary of Missouri. States carved out of the Territory south of the line would be admitted as slave states — north of the line, as free states. Since there was six times as much Territory north of the line as south of it, the North felt it had the better of the bargain.

Jefferson, an old man of seventy-seven, felt that Congress had no right to legislate slavery. Writing to Senator Holmes of Massachusetts, he remarked that he had long since ceased paying attention to public affairs. "But this momentous question, like a firebell in the night, awakened and filled me with terror. I considered it at once as the knell of the Union. It is hushed, indeed, for the moment. But this is a reprieve only. . . . A geographical line, coinciding with a marked principle . . . once conceived and held up to the angry passions of men, will never be obliterated; and every new irritation will mark it deeper and deeper. . . . I regret that I am now to die in the belief, that the useless sacrifice of themselves by the generation of 1776, to acquire self-government and happiness to their country, is to be thrown away by the unwise and unworthy passions of their sons . . ."

ABOLITION

Slavery had long troubled men's hearts. In 1688, four Mennonites had admonished their fellows in Germantown, Pennsylvania, against what they called "the traffic in men-body." Pointing out how the Mennonites themselves had, while at sea, feared enslavement by Turkish pirates, they said:

"Ah! do consider well this thing, you who do it, if you would be done at this manner — . . . . have these poor negers not as much right to fight for their freedom, as you have to keep them slaves."

And the slave-owner Jefferson had written: ". . . all men are created equal."

In 1790, there had been 40,196 slaves in the Northern states. New York, with 21,324 slaves, had more slaves than Kentucky, Tennessee, or Delaware. But by the time of the Missouri Compromise, slavery was dead or dying in all the old states north of the Delaware River.

That the Northern states outlawed slavery was not due to superior virtue. There were doubtless as many Southerners as Northerners offended by slavery. But where climate and a natural river transportation system made production of slave-grown staples easy and profitable in the South, slave labor had been found useless in the shipyards, factories, shops and on the sailing vessels of the North. A slave cannot be forced to exercise the skill or care necessary to operate a lathe or weaving frame.

Where Northern opponents of slavery had been able to move their states toward abolition, Southern opponents of slavery met with increasing difficulty. For a while, as old lands wore out and new lands were hard to get to, the colonization movement had sympathy throughout Virginia, Maryland, Delaware, and the Carolinas. But the invention of the cotton gin and the opening of the West changed all that. As slaves doubled in value and thousands of ambitious men erected sumptuous plantations in Alabama and Mississippi, those who preached against slavery seemed increasingly dangerous.

Some were merely ostracized, their lectures unattended and their messages refused by newspapers. The Reverend George Bourne was tried for heresy by his church in Virginia. Others were threatened with physical harm. Despairing of reforming their native states, Southern opponents of slavery either quit agitating or emigrated north. The preachers Gideon Blackburn, John Rankin, and David Nelson all moved from Kentucky to Ohio or Illinois. James Lemon, a close friend of Jefferson's, moved from Virginia to found the first anti-slavery church near Collinsville, Illinois, in 1809.

A slaveholder who freed his slaves was giving up wealth. He was sacrificing the

THE MINUTES

OF THE

KENTUCKY ABOLITION SOCIETY,

MET AT GEORGE SMITH'S, IN FRANKLIN COUNTY,

On the 20th of October, 1813.

Members present.—David Barrow, William Morris, George Smith, Lewis Martin, James Martin, Enoch Smith, John Ward and Charles Crabb.

1st. After pray[illegible] unanimously elected [illegible]

others, is doing as we would be done by. But when we take a view of things at present, as they really are, this appears to be the age of selfishness: nothing is so much pursued w[illegible] ardor as the [illegible] vain world[illegible]

During the War of 1812, this broadside warned, "The Almighty Sovereign of the Universe has decreed, that moral evil shall be cured by physical; and often our own follies are made to correct us. . . ."

ease and comforts enjoyed by his wife and children, and was exchanging leisure for uncertainty and toil. Only men of great courage and resourcefulness dared so to throw their fortunes to the winds. A few bold men sent their liberated slaves north of the Ohio. A few others supported the American Society for the Colonization of the Free People of Color in the United States and, from 1816 to 1836, sent 4000 former slaves to Liberia in Africa. During the same period, the number of slaves in the United States increased by a million. Even those who felt that slavery was evil usually doubted that white men and former slaves could live peacefully together. ". . . we have the wolf by the ears and we can neither hold him nor let him go," Jefferson wrote at the time of the Missouri question. "Justice is in one scale, and self-preservation in the other."

By 1833, after much soul-searching, a number of men had become convinced that only by outlawing slavery could the evil be ended. Their new doctrine, abolition, called for the forced freeing of slaves, an end to colonization, and the granting of full civil liberties to the freed slaves.

Meeting in a Philadelphia house, forty men and women, including a number of former slave-owners, formed the American Anti-Slavery Society, and called on the people of the free states to remove slavery "by moral and political action, as prescribed in the Constitution of the United States. . . . With entire confidence in the over-ruling justice of God, we plant ourselves upon the Declaration of our Independence and the truths of Divine Revelation. . . . We shall organize anti-slavery societies, if possible, in every city, town, and village in the land."

As a radical doctrine, harsh, uncompromising, and immoderate, preaching new laws and new interpretations of laws and changes in the settled ideas and opinions on which society rested, abolition aroused great opposition in all the Northern states, even in Boston, where Garrison and other abolitionists were bullied and beaten.

In Cincinnati, in 1836, the mayor and leading citizens warned a publisher against continuing his abolitionist paper, The Philanthropist. A mob then attacked the paper's offices and threw the printing press into the river.

The home of the New York abolitionist Lewis Tappan was plundered, his furniture carried into the street, broken up and burned. Minister David Nelson had to hide with his children in an Ohio wood while armed men hunted them. Pennsylvania Hall in Philadelphia was burned down when a mob attacked a female anti-slavery convention.

In Alton, Illinois, Elijah P. Lovejoy, a young Presbyterian minister, attempted to continue the abolitionist activities for which he had been driven across the Mississippi from St. Louis. Three times, mobs threw the press and type from which he printed The Alton Observer into the river. The fourth time, they killed him, a willing martyr:

". . . the contest has commenced here, and here it must be finished. . . . If I fall, my grave shall be made in Alton."

Thoughout the North, people were becoming disgusted with these scenes of violence. They did not have to agree with the abolitionist doctrines, to agree that the abolitionists had a right to speak. As the abolitionist Edward Beecher remarked, "Ten thousand presses had he employed them all, could never have done what the simple tale of [Lovejoy's] death will do."

By 1838, the year of Lovejoy's murder, abolitionists were beginning to get a fair hearing. The American Anti-Slavery Society sold almost 8,000 books and 61,000 pamphlets, folders and prints. A monthly magazine, Human Rights, had 189,000 subscribers. The weekly Emancipator reached 217,000 homes, and a children's magazine, The Slave's Friend, sold more than 131,000 copies. One in twenty Northerners was an abolitionist in 1838.

EXPERIMENT IN CINCINNATI

The colonization policy had been based on the belief that Negroes were inherently inferior and would, if freed, create a permanent problem. Nor was this belief confined to the South. The escaped slave Frederick Douglass noted, "Prejudice against free colored people has shown itself nowhere so invincible as among mechanics of the North." Abolition insisted that the Negro was potentially every bit as good as the white man. Belief in Negro inferiority could excuse slavery; belief in Negro equality condemned slavery.

To prove what the Negro could accomplish, if given the opportunity, became the task of a class of unusual theology students in Cincinnati.

In 1833, Cincinnati, separated from the slave state of Kentucky by the winding Ohio River, contained 2,500 of Ohio's 7,500 free Negroes. Many were emancipated slaves who had bought their freedom from their masters; many were sending money south to buy freedom for relatives still in bondage. Under the leadership of the Reverend Theodore Weld, fifty-three graduate students at Lane Seminary established a lyceum for Negroes. They gave nightly lectures on grammar, geography, arithmetic, and science, and mingled freely with their pupils, encouraging them and giving advice on all the problems of living as free men and women.

When the faculty threatened them with dismissal, Weld and his followers deserted to Oberlin College. Affirming their devotion to the cause of abolition, they told the Lane faculty that they could not be intimidated.

"Slavery," they said, "in this land of liberty and light . . . its days are numbered and well-nigh finished. . . . The nation is shaking off its slumbers to sleep no more."

Convinced that the inferiority of the slave was caused by his condition rather than by any natural weakness, the Lane Seminarians carried their message

THE LIBERATOR.

WILLIAM LLOYD GARRISON AND ISAAC KNAPP, PUBLISHERS.

VOL. I.] BOSTON, MASSACHUSETTS.] OUR COUNTRY IS THE WORLD—OUR COUNTRYMEN ARE MANKIND. [SATURDAY, JANUARY 1, 1831. [NO. 1.

of Universal Emancipation at Baltimore, in September, 1829. My conscience is now satisfied.

I am aware, that many object to the severity of my language; but is there not cause for severity? I *will be* as harsh as truth, and as uncompromising as justice. On this subject, I do not wish to think, or speak, or write, with moderation. No! no! Tell a man whose house is on fire, to give a moderate alarm; tell him to moderately rescue his wife from the hands of the ravisher; tell the mother to gradually extricate her babe from the fire into which it has fallen;—but urge me not to use moderation in a cause like the present. I am in earnest—I will not equivocate—I will not excuse—I will not retreat a single inch—AND I WILL BE HEARD. The apathy of the people is enough to make every statue leap from its pedestal, and to hasten the resurrection of the dead.

It is pretended, that I am retarding the

DISTRICT OF COLUMBIA.

What do many of the professed enemies of slavery mean, by heaping all their reproaches upon the south, and asserting that the crime of oppression is not national? What power but Congress—and Congress by the authority of the American people—has jurisdiction over the District of Columbia? That district is rotten with the plague, and stinks in the nostrils of the world. Though it is the Seat of our National Government,—open to the daily inspection of foreign ambassadors,—and ostensibly opulent with the congregated wisdom, virtue and intelligence of the land,—yet a fouler spot scarcely exists on

William Lloyd Garrison was 26 when he printed the first issue of his paper in a Boston boarding house. Twenty years later, Georgia was offering $5000 to anyone who would bring him in for trial for inciting a slave rebellion.

through Ohio, Pennsylvania, and Illinois, preaching it from pulpits, lighting fires of abolitionism wherever they went.

THE FUGITIVES

The country became more and more divided into two camps. But if all abolitionists were north of the Ohio River, or 36°30′; and all slave-owners south of it, it might seem that they could forever live side by side in peace. With all their books, tracts, speeches, and meetings, the abolitionists could not free a single slave in Virginia. Nor could a single slave holder bring his slaves into Ohio.

Unfortunately, slaves escaped. What happened when a slave made his way across the Ohio? In Kentucky, he was property. In Ohio, he was a man. The authors of the Constitution, foreseeing this difficulty, had provided that "No person, held to service or labor in one State, under the laws thereof, escaping into another, shall, in consequence of any law or regulation therein, be discharged from such service or labor, but shall be delivered up on claim of the party to whom such service or labor may be due."

The law was on the side of the slave holder. Wherever he went within the United States, the slave must be returned to his master. But there was a further difficulty. For as on one side of the river the slave was property, and on the other side he was a man;- so on one side of the river the slave had no legal rights, and on the other side he *had* legal rights.

In 1793, Congress passed a law setting forth the procedure whereby a fugitive slave was to be recovered. The slave-owner or his agent was given the power to arrest an escaped slave on sight — *anywhere in the United States.* After his arrest, the slave was to be taken to a justice who was empowered to issue a certificate transferring the slave back to his owner. Evidence was to be taken from the slave-owner or his agent, but not from the accused slave.

Since the victim of arrest was not permitted to testify, this meant, with regard to Federal law, that some of the free men of the free states (Negroes) were not as free as other free men of the free states (whites.)

The Federal Government, as the government of all the states, could take no position relating to slavery that did not resolve itself into some such contradiction. A ruling treating the United States as a slave nation must offend the rights of free men just as a ruling treating the United States as a free nation must offend the rights of slave-holders.

The principle behind the Union itself was not proof against men's convictions on slavery. In 1842, the masthead of The Liberator read: "A repeal of the Union between Northern liberty and Southern slavery is essential to the abolition of the one and the preservation of the other." And not a few Southerners wondered if they might not gain more than they lost as members of a separate union of slave states. Jefferson Davis of Mississippi told the Senate:

"If folly and fanaticism and pride and hate and corruption of the day are to destroy the peace and prosperity of the Union, let the sections part like the patriarchs of old . . ."

This courageous woman liberated more than 300 slaves. Harriet Tubman escaped from a Maryland plantation in 1849, and almost immediately returned South as a "conductor" of the underground railway. Aided by an infallible memory for geographic detail, she conducted 20 large raids. She would spur on faint-hearted followers at pistol point. With a price of $40,000 on her head, she stole her aged parents from Maryland and brought them north with a stolen horse and wagon when they insisted on taking their feather bed and a hen coop full of chickens. During the 1850's, Harriet Tubman and other "conductors" and "engineers" led about 75,000 slaves to the free states and Canada.

Daguerreotype portrait of John Quincy Adams.

JOHN QUINCY ADAMS AND THE GAG RULE

John Quincy Adams left the White House in 1829, defeated by Andrew Jackson. In 1831, sixty-four, he entered the House of Representatives. On January 4, 1836, he presented to Congress a petition "of Albert Pabodie and one hundred and fifty-three inhabitants of Millbury, in the County of Worcester and Commonwealth of Massachusetts, praying for the abolition of slavery and the slave-trade in the District of Columbia."

As Adams wrote in his diary, "... after stating the contents of the petition . . . [I] said it was my intention to move that . . . it should be laid on the table."

He continued his account of the incident, "I was instantly interrupted by my next neighbor, John M. Patton, who enquired whether the petition had been received; to which the Speaker answered that it had not; whereupon Thomas Glascock, a new member from Georgia, moved that it be not received, . . ."

A debate followed, with no decision. Four months later, a committee of Congress presented a resolution that all petitions or papers on slavery in future be quietly "laid upon the table, and that no further action whatever shall be had thereon." The resolution passed 117 to 68 and thus, in the Congress of the United States, a decree of silence was imposed on the subject of slavery.

Adams could not be cowed by Southern threats of secession. ". . . if the dissolution of the Union should result from the slave question," he noted in his diary, "it is as obvious as anything that can be foreseen of futurity, that it must shortly afterwards be followed by the universal emancipation of the slaves. . . . Slavery is the great and foul stain upon the North American Union."

Year after year, the Congressman from Massachusetts presented anti-slavery petitions only to have them tabled without discussion. As the new states north of the Ohio River grew in importance, the "gag" majority dwindled. Finally, in 1844, Adams succeeded in killing the "Gag Rule," 108 to 80. In December, 1844, anti-slavery petitions were received and referred to the Committee on the District of Columbia. John Quincy Adams was almost seventy-eight years of age. In his diary he made this notation:

"Blessed, forever blessed, be the name of God!"

THE SECOND CONVULSION

Outside of the regulation of fugitives, the Federal Government's concern with slavery was confined to the organization of lands outside the states — that is, to the District of Columbia and the territories.

The pursuit, the rescue, the hiding, and capture of fugitive slaves formed the constant day-to-day struggle between the sections. The great convulsions came when the country expanded into the territories.

The first convulsion, as we have seen, occurred in 1820, with the attempt to establish slavery throughout the Louisiana Territory. With only the Arkansas Territory left to them by the Compromise of 1820, the slave-owners sought new lands to the south and west.

If the settlement of the West was a race between North and South to add territory to their respective systems, then the South was more successful than the North. Except for Oregon, Northern expansion had all been confined to territory that had been in the Union in 1783, while Southern planters had crossed the Mississippi River, invaded Mexico, and, in 1836, set up the independent Republic of Texas.

When Texas joined the Union in 1845, the Southern interests had added nine states, with a total territory of 679,176 square miles as against six Northern states, with 234,953 square miles.

Annexation of Texas was followed by a war with Mexico, which many Northerners resented as being only for the purpose of increasing the amount of land open to slavery. While a series of victories added almost a million square miles of Western territory, Whig Congressmen accused President Polk of "unnecessarily and unconstitutionally" commencing the war. Abraham Lincoln, a Whig Congressman from Illinois, demanded that Polk prove his claim that the Mexicans had provoked the war. A

Free Soil Democratic Congressman from Pennsylvania, David Wilmot, sought to ban slavery from the territories won from Mexico. The Senate, where the South and North were equally represented (Iowa and Wisconsin, added to the free states, restored the balance) kept defeating Wilmot's provisos, with the result that no action toward organizing the new areas was taken. A special situation in California forced a decision.

California could not wait while Congress settled on a territorial policy. The discovery of gold in 1848 had brought a tremendous increase in population. Seamen of a dozen nations had deserted their ships in San Francisco harbor to search the hills for gold. Missouri farmers and Georgia crackers had wandered west. Adventurers from eastern America and European cities had shipped to Panama, crossed the isthmus, and sailed north in the rush for quick wealth. In rough, strange little places with such names as Dry Diggings, Hangtown, Poker Flat and Skunk Gulch, Yankee sailors, London cockneys, and Mississippi riverboat gamblers rubbed elbows with Mexican peons and "heathen Chinee."

Too many people had come too fast, and among them were more than the usual number of desperadoes, cut-throats, and card sharks. What one man found in the ground, another would seize by murder or guile. President Zachary Taylor, aware of the desperate need for government, suggested that California apply directly for statehood. If it came before Congress with a state constitution this would, he hoped, avoid the kind of entanglement in the slavery issue that would occur if it applied for a territorial government.

But the crisis could not be avoided. The 1849 Congress was presented with a California State Constitution that forbid slavery. Southerners knew that, of the territory taken from Mexico, only California was not too dry for cotton. Against the territory north of the Missouri Compromise line, the South had a treaty giving the U.S.A. the right to carve five states out of Texas. California, then, looked like the state that could tip the balance. "If you seek to drive us from California," Robert Toombs of Georgia announced, "I am for disunion."

An old man of seventy-two helped end the crisis. Henry Clay, who had resolved the troubles of 1819 and 1832, re-entered the Senate in December, 1849. Working with Senator Stephen A. Douglas of

Clay and Webster in 1850. Two years later both were dead and, Calhoun having preceded them to the grave, an era was ended. These representatives of the North, South, and West had become central figures in the Government; but they possessed more regard for Union than some of their successors.

Unretouched Photograph

Congressmen at work.

Illinois, Clay proposed the following compromise. The North was offered admission of California as a free state and an ending of the slave trade in the District of Columbia. The South was offered a strong fugitive slave law and the division of the remaining Mexican land into the territories of New Mexico and Utah without mention of slavery.

The proposals were attacked by men representing the extremes of Northern and Southern opinion. Abolitionists called fugitive slave laws compacts with the devil. Senator Jefferson Davis of Mississippi pleaded that the Missouri Compromise line be extended to the Pacific, opening part of California to slavery. Calhoun, sixty-seven years old and desperately ill, sent a speech to the Senate demanding that slavery be permitted in all the newly acquired territory and an end to discussion of the issue.

"If you of the North will not do this," he concluded, "then let our Southern States separate and depart in peace."

Daniel Webster supported Clay's proposals. Putting preservation of the Union above personal popularity, he agreed that without Northern cooperation in catching and returning slaves, the Union could not last. With regard to opening up the rest of the Mexican Territory to slavery, Webster saw that insufficient rainfall denied the area to cotton growing. Where nature outlawed slavery, human argument was irrelevant.

After much debate, the various acts of the Compromise of 1850 were passed, and the Union was preserved.

THE SQUATTERS

The Compromise was a truce, not a settlement. The new fugitive slave law was respected no more than the old, and Southern leaders plotted to maintain their hold over the Union.

In May, 1854, the Democratic Senator from Illinois, Stephen A. Douglas, with the help and encouragement of the Democratic President, Franklin Pierce, repealed the Missouri Compromise, opening up about half a million square miles of Louisiana Territory to slavery.

Iowa, directly north of Missouri, had entered the Union as a free state in 1846, and the territory north of Iowa and west to the Missouri River had been organized into the free Territory of Minnesota. Now all the land remaining in Louisiana was divided into two territories: Kansas, south of the Fortieth Parallel, and Nebraska, north of it, "it being the true intent and meaning of this act not to legislate slavery into any Territory or State, nor to exclude it therefrom, but to leave the people thereof perfectly free to form and regulate their domestic institutions in their own way, subject only to the Constitution of the United States . . ."

Passage of this act was made possible first, by the determination of the South and its skill at parliamentary maneuver; second, by the indecision of many people of the North and West; third, by the desire of many Westerners to hasten the settlement of the Kansas and Nebraska Territories, particularly to the end of constructing a transcontinental railroad.

The indecision of the North came from a growing fear of the tendencies of the abolitionists. The same fierce intolerance of slavery that led many abolitionists to despise the Constitution, led them to uphold other radical doctrines such as the right of women to vote, and the rights of the working people to shorter hours and better working conditions.

The principle expounded by Douglas, that of letting the people of a territory themselves determine whether or not to permit slavery, became known as "Squatter Sovereignty." What recommended it to Douglas was that the violence of feelings, North and South, threatened disunion whichever side the Federal Government took on the issue of slavery. Squatter Sovereignty, by leaving the decision to the people of the territory, removed the Federal Government from the controversy. As a practical matter, Douglas felt that he had made but an empty concession to the slave holders since cotton could never flourish in Kansas or Nebraska.

But Douglas had failed to appreciate that the source of conflict resided in the feelings of the people. Changing the method of handling the differences between North and South left these strong feelings unchanged.

Southerners and Northerners poured into Kansas, hungry for vacant land. They came from neighboring Missouri, intent on winning the territory to their way of life. Equally determined to make Kansas free, families raced from Ohio, Indiana, Illinois, and New England.

In throwing the decision back to the people, the Government had given up its role as the settler of interests. It had ceased to be a government.

The Kansas-Nebraska Bill, said Senator Charles Sumner of Massachusetts, ". . . puts Freedom and Slavery face to face and bids them grapple."

Less than a year after passage of the bill, Kansas had a population of 8,500, including 242 slaves, and had two constitutions, two governments, and two governors, one pro and one anti-slavery, neither of which could receive recognition in Washington.

"Get ready, arm yourself," called out the slavery leader, Senator David Atchison of Missouri; "for if they abolitionize Kansas you lose $150 million of your property." Meanwhile, the Emigrant Aid Society, in New England, was providing money, supplies and weapons to abolitionists willing to settle in Kansas. Among them were five young men named Brown, from Ohio. In October, 1855, they were joined, at Osawatomie, Kansas, by their father, a grizzled lean old man. "I am here," John Brown declared, "to promote the killing of American slavery."

Early in 1856, some pro-slavery ruffians raided the town of Lawrence, burned down the hotel, and wrecked two abolitionist newspapers. On the night of May 24, without warning, John Brown and seven followers, four of them his sons, killed five Southerners living along Pottawatomie Creek.

These were the first blows in an undeclared war that soon gave the territory the name of "Bleeding Kansas."

THE PROPAGANDA WAR

Uncle Tom's Cabin first appeared in the abolitionist National Era, where it ran as a serial from June, 1851, to April, 1852. The author, Harriet Beecher Stowe, had been in Cincinnati during the pioneering days of the Lane Seminary. She had helped fugitive slaves in that city on the Ohio. She had heard from the slaves and from her brothers, who traveled through the South, tales of life on the plantations. The Compromise Act of 1850 incited her into writing the book.

A very gifted writer, Mrs. Stowe was able to fill the pages of *Uncle Tom's Cabin* with living, breathing people. She introduced a host of characters into American folklore: Topsy, Uncle Tom, Little Eva, Simon Legree, and Miss Ophelia.

Mrs. Stowe, writing in Brunswick, Maine, with the fires of abolition burning in her heart could not help presenting the Southern slave-owners as warm human beings, as sensitive to human suffering as other men. Her success in this demonstrated that the evils of slavery came out of the system itself rather than out of personal malice. The Southerner was caught in a dreadful web that forced him to impose great suffering on the Negro, whether he wanted to or not. Over and over again, the book struck at the one outrage peculiar to slavery — the forced, unpredictable separation of families.

Violence in the Senate. A young South Carolina Congressman, Preston Brooks, clubs Charles Sumner of Massachusetts to unconsciousness.

On the other side, there were men in the South who saw in slavery an answer to the social ills of the North and of other "free" societies. Rejecting the Declaration of Independence as a mere justification for separation from England, they referred back to the family, with the natural authority of the father, as the model of government.

The evils which they saw in the North — wages forced down to starvation levels, gang fights in cities between natives and immigrants, riots, strikes, and crime waves — all came, they insisted, from a breakdown in the ancient family relationship. The freedom preached in the North was not freedom of slaves from masters, but freedom of masters to not care for their slaves.

As George Fitzhugh of Virginia said to the employers of the North: "You, with the command over labor which your capital gives you, are a slave owner — a master without the obligations of a master. They who work for you, who create your income, are slaves without the rights of slaves. Slaves without a master!"

Reformers in the new industrialized societies, Fitzhugh predicted, would eventually come to his way of thinking. In insisting on the rights of workmen to their jobs, and to more of a share in the proceeds of their work, were they not asking that masters recognize the right of slaves to be cared for? Were not Socialism and Communism, the new theories of these new worlds of factories and steam engines and telegraphs, but new words for slavery?

Mrs. Stowe believed that advancing civilization would live down slavery. Fitzhugh believed that advancing civilization would live down freedom. "One set of ideas will govern and control after a while the civilized world," Fitzhugh wrote. "Slavery will everywhere be abolished or everywhere be re-instituted."

SECOND CLASS CITIZENS

As the slave of the army surgeon, Dr. John Emerson, Dred Scott had gone to Fort Snelling, Wisconsin Territory, and had lived in the free state of Illinois. In 1846, after Dr. Emerson had brought him back to Missouri, Dred Scott sued for his freedom. Scott claimed he was no longer a slave because he had lived in a territory from which slavery had been prohibited by the Missouri Compromise, and in a state where slavery was against state law.

The case was brought to the Supreme Court with the help of Dr. Emerson's widow, who had married an abolitionist Congressman from Massachusetts. It was a test case, to get some decisions from the Supreme Court on the constitutionality of laws regarding slavery in states and territories. Whatever the decision of the Supreme Court, Dred Scott's owners were determined to set him free.

Chief Justice Taney and the majority of the Supreme Court ruled that it was against the principles of the Constitution for the United States Government to deny slavery in any territory. They also stated that free Negroes could not become citizens of the United States.

In effect, the Court created two classes of citizens — citizens of the states, merely, and citizens of the United States. As citizens of the states, merely, the free Negroes would not be recognized in Federal Courts as anything but property.

"We think [Negroes] . . . are not included, and were not intended to be included, under the word 'citizens' in the Constitution," said the Court, "and can, therefore, claim none of the rights and privileges which that instrument provides for and secures to citizens of the United States."

The Court also decided that neither "slaves nor their descendants . . . free or not . . ." were "intended to be included in the general words used in" the Declaration of Independence.

The Supreme Court had taken a long step toward reinstituting slavery in every state in the Union.

BREAKDOWN OF THE PARTIES

To the upholder of slavery, the purpose of the Constitution was to preserve the situation as it existed in 1787. To the abolitionist, the Constitution was an engine of change and progress. So deeply held were these different beliefs after 1850, that men of either side would disobey laws and court decisions and believe themselves good citizens in so disobeying.

"How does it become a man to behave toward this American government to-

Dred Scott.

day?" Thoreau asked in Massachusetts. "I answer, that . . . I cannot for an instant recognize that political organization as *my* government which is the *slave's* government also."

To keep voters from breaking away, the parties sought to please all factions. The Whigs had to conciliate Cotton and Conscience Whigs, and the Democrats feared offending the planters in the South and the Northerners who favored giving free Western farms to small, independent farmers.

This was an impossible task. Following the Kansas-Nebraska Act, the national parties began seriously breaking up. In 1854, groups of Free Soil Democrats and Conscience Whigs met in all the Northern states to nominate candidates to Congress pledged against extension of slavery to the Territories, and in favor of giving 160 acres of Government land to every settler. They began calling themselves Republicans, after the party founded by Thomas Jefferson, the author of the Declaration of Independence.

Two years later, the Republicans nominated John C. Fremont for the Presidency of the United States. Fremont received one out of every three votes. This was not enough to win the election, but the Republicans carried eleven states: New Hampshire, Massachusetts, Rhode Island, Connecticut, New York, Vermont, Ohio, Maine, Michigan, Iowa, and Wisconsin. A strange and ominous phenomenon had appeared on the American scene — a political party based on one section of the country only.

The rise of the Republicans forced northern Whigs, friendly to slavery, into the Democratic Party. In the South, Whigs and Democrats combined around the banner of slavery. With the Whigs gone, another new party tried to build power on reconciling the sections. The American Party, which nominated President Millard Fillmore in 1856, appealed to all those who resented the incursions of immigrants whether as laborers in the cities or as hard-working farmers on the Western prairie.

Since 1849, more than a million immigrants had been arriving in America every three years. In 1850, one out of every eight white Americans was of foreign birth. By pledging itself to restrict immigration, to limit office to native-born Americans, and to make it much more difficult for immigrants to become citizens, the American Party sought support in the North and West. In the South, to which few immigrants came, the American Party sought to lure the Cotton Whigs by pledging non-interference of the Federal Government in the affairs of the states.

With a platform opposing new immigrants, Douglas' repeal of the Missouri Compromise, and abolitionism, the American Party polled almost 900,000 votes, or about one vote out of every four-and-one-half votes cast.

"THESE PRINCIPLES CANNOT STAND TOGETHER"

Among the Republicans who campaigned for John C. Fremont was a former Whig Congressman from Illinois named Abraham Lincoln.

Lincoln's opposition to the Mexican War had been very unpopular. At the end of his term in Congress, he had stood aside to permit the nomination of another man, just as another former Congressman had stood aside in 1846 to let Lincoln run. Discouraged as to his political future, Lincoln had stayed in Illinois, building up a prosperous law practice with his partner, William Herndon. They defended railroads and manufacturers in suits over rights of way and patents.

The tall thin man in the stovepipe hat was a well known figure in county court houses throughout the state of Illinois. "Ain't you glad to see me?" he would greet the other lawyers. "Ain't you glad I come?" He knew lots of funny stories; maybe he made them up. He had a way of explaining things so that anybody could understand.

During the Fremont Campaign, when he was asked his opinion of the American Party, he told about asking an Irishman why he had not been born in America. "Faith," Pat had replied, "I wanted to, but me mother wouldn't let me."

Southern Illinois was a kind of peninsula of free soil bordered by the slave states of Kentucky and Missouri; no other free state faced so much of the frontier of the slave empire.

Southern Illinois was full of slave catchers and stories of slave runaways and the chasing and capture of slaves. Following the circuit court around the state of Illinois, Lincoln met abolitionists, masters of slaves and their agents, keepers of depots on the Underground Railway, and professional catchers, paid $100 for each slave returned. Abraham Lincoln knew men who talked of buying and selling slaves as they talked of buying and selling cattle. Abraham Lincoln knew men who said that the Constitution of the United States, which permitted slavery, was an invention of the devil.

Lincoln puzzled over a matter a long time, as if in his head there was some kind of courtroom in which two lawyers argued the case exhaustively, arguing it up and arguing it down, testing the rightness and wrongness of each way of looking at the matter. "He can sit and think without food or rest longer than any man I ever saw," said Lincoln's law partner Herndon.

"There are few things wholly evil or wholly good," Lincoln said. "Almost everything, especially of government policy, is an inseparable compound of the two; . . . so that our best judgment of the preponderance between them is continually demanded."

His friend Josh Speed once said Lincoln had a quick mind.

"No, you are mistaken," Lincoln replied. "I am slow to learn and slow to forget. My mind is like a piece of steel — very hard to scratch anything on it, and almost impossible after you get it there to rub it out."

He would make notes as he puzzled over the rightness and wrongness of slavery:

"If A can prove, however conclusively, that he may, of right enslave B, why may not B snatch the same argument, and prove equally that he may enslave A? You say A is white and B is black. It is color, then; the lighter having the right

TO THE ANTI-SLAVERY ELECTORS OF CONNECTICUT.

CIRCULAR.

A number of the friends of distinct nominations for the time being, having held a meeting in Hartford, August 27th, for the purpose of making out an

ELECTORAL TICKET,

for the coming Presidential Canvass, the following persons were selected, viz:

BENEDICT BULL, Litchfield Co.
LEWIS BEERS, 2d., Fairfield "
LEVI YALE, 2d, New-Haven, "
SAMUEL DEMING, Hartford, "
F. A. PERKINS, New-London, "
ELISHA STEARNS, Tolland, "
GEORGE SHARPE, Windham, "
GEORGE READ, Middlesex, "

The undersigned were appointed a Committee to print and circulate the above Ticket, recommending it to the Anti-Slavery Electors in the coming Election. This they do by this Circular.

The above gentlemen having given full proof of their sound Anti-Slavery principles, we are fully confident will not give their votes for either of the persons now in nomination by the Democratic and Whig parties for President and Vice President of the United States, pledged as they are to the support of the horrible system of American Slavery, but will cast their suffrages for none but such as are in favor of the immediate abolition of Slavery, and the enfranchisement of all their fellow-citizens in their natural and political rights.

And now, brethren, do not all our professions and principles as abolitionists, the dictates of an enlightened conscience, and the fear of an impartial God, bind and obligate us to give our preference to the above, rather than to a *pro-slavery Ticket?* Let our votes at the polls say, YES. Signed in behalf of the meeting,

JOHN C. LEWIS, HARLOW ISBELL, J. G. BALDWIN, D. PLUMB, *Committee.*

Hartford, August 27, 1840.

to enslave the darker? Take care. By this rule, you are to be slave to the first man you meet with a fairer skin than your own. You do not mean color exactly? You mean whites are intellectually the superiors of the blacks, and therefore have the right to enslave them? Take care again. By this rule you are to be slave to the first man you meet with an intellect superior to your own . . ."

Even if there could be no reasonable basis for slavery, it was still necessary to determine whether the United States Constitution permitted its existence, even its propagation.

"Most governments," Lincoln wrote, "have been based, practically, on the denial of the equal rights of men . . . ours began by affirming those rights. They said, some men are too ignorant and vicious to share in government. Possibly so, said we; and, by your system, you would always keep them ignorant and vicious. We proposed to give all a chance; and we expected the weak to grow stronger, the ignorant wiser, and all better and happier together . . ."

In 1856, Republican Congressmen were pledged to oppose extension of slavery into territories. The position of the party was that slavery be contained, that it be allowed to exist where it was, but that it spread no further.

". . . if the safeguards of liberty are broken down, as it is now attempted," Lincoln saw, "when they have made *things* of all the free Negroes; how long, think you, before they begin to make *things* of poor white men?" he asked.

The Constitution was a system of laws, an instrument of government. But to find what the United States had been formed for, the spirit that moved it, one had to go back to the Declaration of Independence. The Declaration was to the Constitution what the soul is to the body.

Lincoln saw that what was fundamentally at stake was the spirit of the Declaration of Independence. If the United States had been formed to promote its noble sentiments, then no laws creating or protecting slavery could be legal.

Slavery would not be safe, Lincoln saw, until the spirit of the Declaration was destroyed. That was why "it is assailed and sneered at and construed, and hawked at and torn, till, if its framers could rise from their graves, they could not at all recognize it."

The framers of the Declaration, Lincoln asserted, "meant to set up a standard maxim for free society, which should be familiar to all, and revered by all. . . . The assertion that 'all men are created equal' was . . . meant . . . to be — as, thank God, it is now proving itself — a stumbling-block to all those who in after times might seek to turn a free people back into the hateful paths of despotism. They knew the proneness of prosperity to breed tyrants, . . ."

"Little by little, but steadily as man's march to the grave, we have been giving up the old, for the new faith. Nearly eighty years ago we began by declaring that all men are created equal; but now from that beginning we have run down to the other declaration, that for SOME men to enslave others is a 'sacred right of self-government.' These principles can not stand together."

Lincoln had predicted that the Kansas-Nebraska Act would cause violence: 200 men and women were shot and murdered in Kansas and Missouri. Lincoln had warned that the free Negro would not be safe in the North; the Dred Scott decision denied free Negroes United States citizenship.

As events followed his predictions,

Lincoln's influence grew. Through the spring of 1858, Lincoln worked on a speech that he would deliver before a convention of Republicans who were planning to nominate him to run for the United States Senate. Since he would be running against Senator Stephen A. Douglas, he aimed to attack Douglas' Kansas-Nebraska Act. He wanted to show what he thought was bad about the act, but, more than that, he was determined to put down exactly how he and many other Americans in the Northwestern United States felt about the slavery issue; and about what it was leading to.

He wrote the speech and rewrote it, trying to make each word as clear and sharp as if it were engraved on steel. He read the speech to his law partner. Herndon said it would make Lincoln President of the United States. He read it to some of his political friends in Springfield, and they said it would lose him votes, that it was a mistake, that it was "ahead of its time."

"If we could first know where we are, and whither we are tending," Lincoln said, "we could better judge what to do, and how to do it. We are now far into the fifth year since a policy was initiated with the avowed object and confident promise of putting an end to slavery agitation. Under the operation of that policy, that agitation has not only not ceased, but has constantly augmented. In my opinion, it will not cease until a crisis shall have been reached and passed. 'A house divided against itself cannot stand.' I believe this government cannot endure half slave and half free. I do not expect the Union to be dissolved; I do not expect the house to fall; but I do expect it will cease to be divided. It will become all one thing or all the other."

THE GREAT DEBATES

Stephen A. Douglas, Democratic Senator from the state of Illinois, was esteemed, through the 1850's, as the greatest man in the West. A small, organ-voiced man, a magnetic and spellbinding orator, "the Little Giant" was looked upon as the heir of Henry Clay and a leading contender for the Presidency. It was to further his ambitions and the settlement of the West, to which he believed his destiny was tied, that he had sponsored the principle of Squatter Sovereignty and the Kansas-Nebraska Act.

Lincoln challenged "the Little Giant" to a series of debates to be held in seven different towns in Illinois: Ottawa, Freeport, Jonesboro, Charleston, Galesburg, Quincy, and Alton, from August 15 to October 15. Douglas accepted.

That "a house divided against itself" could not stand, Douglas said, was "a slander upon the immortal framers of our Constitution . . . our government can endure forever, divided into free and slave States as our fathers made it — each State having the right to prohibit, abolish or sustain slavery, just as it pleases. This government was made upon the great basis of the sovereignty of the States, the right of each State to regulate its own domestic institutions . . ."

Lincoln expounded the principles of the Declaration of Independence and of moral law as above any laws of the states or decisions of the Supreme Court.

"The real issue in this controversy," he said, ". . . is the sentiment on the part of one class that looks upon the institution of slavery as a wrong, and of another class that does not look upon it as a wrong. . . . It is the eternal struggle between these two principles — right and wrong — throughout the world. They are the two principles that have stood face to face from the beginning of time; and will ever continue to struggle. The one is the common right of humanity, and the other the divine right of kings . . ."

More than a Senate seat was at stake. Both men were looking two years ahead to their chances of receiving their parties' nominations for the Presidency. In this greater contest Lincoln had the advantage. Douglas, as a Democrat, had to appeal to the South as well as the North. Lincoln as a Republican, had only to appeal to the North.

Squatter Sovereignty and states' rights gave Douglas a means of avoiding the moral issue. As long as "the people" were to decide on whether or not they wanted slavery, Douglas wouldn't have to say whether he was for it or against it.

Very clearly, Lincoln saw that such straddling could be carried too far. Where the South had been pleased with Squatter Sovereignty as a means of getting slavery into territories from which the Missouri Compromise had excluded it, it might now resent "Squatter Sovereignty" as a means of keeping slavery out of a territory to which the Dred Scott decision had now admitted it.

During the second debate, in Freeport, Illinois, Lincoln proposed this question:

"Can the people of a United States Territory, in any lawful way, against the wish of any citizen of the United States, exclude slavery from its limits prior to the formation of a State constitution?"

"It matters not," Senator Douglas replied, "what way the Supreme Court may hereafter decide as to the abstract question whether slavery may or may not go into a Territory under the Constitution, the people have the lawful means to introduce or exclude it as they please . . ."

Douglas' favoring of Squatter Sovereignty now angered Southerners, who saw in it a threat to the Dred Scott decision's affirmation of their right to take slaves into the territories.

Douglas won the seat in the Senate, but his "Freeport Doctrine" split the Democratic Party.

"IT IS NOW NO CHILD'S PLAY"

All over the United States, now, people were reading the words of the tall lawyer from Springfield, Illinois:

"All I ask for the Negro is that if you do not like him, let him alone. If God gave him but little, that little let him enjoy."

"In the right to eat the bread, without the leave of anybody else, which his own hand earns, he is my equal and the equal of Judge Douglas, and the equal of every living man."

In the North and South, people read these statements with growing feelings of wonder and fear. These were not ordinary politicians' words, trying to sound like more than they were. They were simple and clear and hard as sentences out of the Bible.

"What constitutes the bulwark of our liberty and independence? It is not our frowning battlements, our bristling seacoasts . . . or the strength of our gallant army . . .

"Our reliance is in the love of liberty which God has planted in our bosoms. Our defense is in the preservation of the spirit which prizes liberty as the heritage of *all men, in all lands everywhere*. Destroy this spirit and you have planted the seeds of despotism around your own doors. Familiarize yourself with the chains of bondage, and you are preparing your own limbs to wear them."

James Buchanan.

Some, reading these words, were reminded of things half-forgotten, as if there were more important concerns, after all, than making a living, keeping a job, buying the land on the other side of the creek. Others, reading them, vowed never to live in a land where their author would be President.

"Free Society! We sicken of the name. What is it but a conglomeration of greasy mechanics, filthy operatives, small-fisted farmers, and moon-struck theorists?" so said The Muskogee (Alabama) Herald.

"Free society in Western Europe is a failure . . . it betrays premonitory symptoms of failure even in America," wrote George Fitzhugh of Port Royal, Virginia. To a Northern abolitionist he wrote, "I am quite as intent on abolishing Free Society, as you are on abolishing slavery."

For some time, Senator Jefferson Davis of Mississippi had been saying, "Slave property is the only private property in the United States specifically recognized in the Constitution and protected by it."

Now Senator Wigfall of Texas said, "I am a plain, blunt-spoken man. We say that man had a right to property in man. We say that slaves are our *property*. We say that it is the duty of every government to protect its property everywhere. If you wish to settle this matter, declare that slaves *are* property, and like all other property entitled to be protected in every quarter of the globe, on land and sea. Say that to us and then the difficulty is settled."

Lincoln noted:

". . . it is now no child's play to save the principles of Jefferson from total overthrow in this nation."

In the White House, President Buchanan, a tired old man of sixty-eight, felt immeasurably sad. The whole country, it seemed, was going insane. What had happened to the forbearance and respect which men of opposing views once had held for each other?

Buchanan felt that slavery was morally wrong, but would not break the Union because of his feelings. What had happened to Americans that they would destroy the best government the world had ever seen? Was self-government an impossible ideal?

All patriotism had vanished. There were principles that had suddenly become more important to many Americans than the preservation of the Union.

"I FOUGHT FOR THE POOR AND I SAY I WAS RIGHT"

On Monday morning, October 17, 1859, the telegraph brought ominous news. Harper's Ferry attacked! A small town, just 40 miles west of Washington,

On his way to be hanged, John Brown handed another prisoner a scrap of paper which read: "I, John Brown, am now quite certain that the crimes of this guilty land will never be purged away but with blood. I had, as I now think, vainly flattered myself that without much bloodshed it might be done."

held by a band of armed abolitionists from the North! The U. S. Government armory seized! Rifles being given out to slaves to rise in rebellion against their masters!

John Brown and twenty-one followers had captured Colonel Lewis Washington, a great grand-nephew of General George Washington, given rifles to his slaves, and set them over him as a guard. Several people in Harper's Ferry were killed by Brown and his men, among them the mayor and a free Negro named Shepherd Heyward who had failed to halt while on his way to work.

But the slaves refused to heed the call to arms, and the rebellion was easily put down by a detachment of marines commanded by Colonel Robert E. Lee. On October 31, a grand jury found John Brown guilty of treason against the state of Virginia, of inciting slave rebellion, and of murder.

Certain abolitionists in the North had given old Brown the money for his expedition—for rifles, pikes, and wagons. They had called the projected raid a "speculation in wool." Now, shocked and confused by Brown's indictment for murder, one of the abolitionist backers, Gerrit Smith, had to be confined to the New York Asylum for the Insane.

In Boston, Caleb Cushing declared that Virginia must be secured against future raids from the North. "If not," he said, "then I say it is right . . . of the Southern states to separate from the Northern states."

John Brown said, "One man and God can overturn the universe." His grave and dignified conduct, while on trial for his life, drew praise from all.

Governor Wise of Virginia said, "Brown is a bundle of the best nerves I ever saw. . . . He is a man of clear head, of courage, fortitude. He is a fanatic, vain and garrulous, but firm and truthful and intelligent."

When the judge sentenced the old man, Brown said, "Had I taken up arms in behalf of the rich, the powerful, the intelligent, the so-called great . . . Every man in this Court would have deemed it an act worthy of reward rather than of punishment. But the Court acknowledges the validity of the law of God. I see a book kissed here which is the Bible, and which teaches me all things that I would have men do unto me, so must I do unto them. I endeavored to act up to that instruction. I fought for the poor; and I say I was right . . ."

"THE DIE IS CAST"

The Democratic Party broke apart in Charleston early in May, 1860. At separate conventions in June, Northern Democrats nominated Stephen Douglas, and Southern Democrats nominated John Breckenridge of Kentucky.

In the middle of May, the Republicans, in Chicago, nominated Abraham Lincoln. "We defy the whole slave power and the whole vassalage of hell," said Carl Schurz of Missouri.

There was more talk in the South of leaving the Union in the event the abolitionist Abraham Lincoln was elected. Candidate Breckenridge proposed that the states of the Northwest also secede from the Union and form a nation of their own. He suggested that New England and the middle states form one Republic, California and the far Western states another, and the Southern states another. Each of the new, smaller nations would have its own army, trade regulations, and laws. They would exchange ambassadors, and make treaties with one another as did the nations of Europe.

Alexander Stephens of Georgia, a ninety-pound wisp of a man, said:

"Men will be cutting one another's throats in a little while. In twelve months we shall be in a war, the bloodiest in history. . . . Because there are not virtue and patriotism and sense enough left in the country to avoid it."

The nation was like a man on a sunny beach who sees, across the blue water, a great storm approaching. In the distance the sky is black with clouds mounting toward the sun. The wild tossing of waves can be dimly seen; yet the observer stands transfixed, watching with horror, helpless, knowing he is to be engulfed, perhaps destroyed, and that there is nothing he can do.

The South was muttering that it would leave the Union if Lincoln was elected, and the split in the Democratic Party made his election inevitable. Of the 4,600,000 votes cast that November, Lincoln received 1,800,000, far less than half, yet sufficient to insure his election. He carried all the states of the North except New Jersey, and all the Northwest, and California and Oregon. Of his portion of votes, only 26,000 were in southern states, and of these, 17,000 were in the state of Missouri.

Mrs. James Chesnut, wife of Senator James Chesnut of South Carolina, was traveling on a train on November 7. A man in her coach received a telegram with news of Lincoln's victory, and everyone, she noted in her diary, became very excited. "Everybody was talking at the same time — One, a little more moved than the others, stood up — saying despondently — 'The die is cast — No more vain regrets . . . The stake is life or death'."

In the South, there were many men who wondered if the Union could not be held together. Jefferson Davis warned that states would not be permitted peaceably to leave the Union. And in the North, many thought that the South was justified, that the North had violated the Constitution in not obeying the Fugitive Slave Laws.

In the mountains of Virginia, in the backlands of Tennessee and Kentucky there were farmers who put Union above slavery.

The South Carolina Legislature voted to raise and equip 10,000 soldiers. Louisiana and Georgia voted money for arms and troops.

At a party in Washington on the evening of December 20, President Buchanan, hearing a commotion in the hall, asked a lady if there was a fire.

Investigating, the lady found Representative Keitt of South Carolina leaping up and down and shouting, "Thank God! Thank God!"

"Have you lost your mind, sir?" the lady asked. "The President hears you and wants to know what is the matter."

"Oh," the Congressman exclaimed. "South Carolina has seceded. I feel like a boy let out of school."

When this news was reported to the President, he gasped, turned pale and sank back into his chair.

South Carolina had its own flag, its own army, its own post offices. In The Charleston Mercury, stories from Philadelphia were headed *Foreign News*. Six more states seceded from the Union: Georgia, Florida, Alabama, Mississippi, Louisiana, and Texas. "Let the erring sisters depart in peace," wrote Horace Greeley, the editor of The New York Tribune.

In Washington, President Buchanan would neither agree that states had a right to secede nor that he had a right to use force to prevent them.

"Our Union rests upon public opinion," he said, "and can never be cemented by the blood of its citizens shed in civil war."

But he decided that it was his duty to protect Federal property. He shipped 250 reinforcements to Fort Sumter, Charleston Harbor. On January 5, the merchant steamer *Star of the West* was fired on as she approached the fort. She retired, with the reinforcements, and Buchanan decided to leave the problem to the incoming President.

Committees sought to reconcile North and South. Thirty-three Congressmen drew up proposals. Thirteen Senators, led by John J. Crittenden of Kentucky, sought to restore the Compromises of the past, to put up a continental dividing line at 36° 30′, to renounce the Dred Scott decision. Would Republicans concede the South right to slaves in return for Southern agreement not to extend slavery beyond a fixed line?

When he was asked to quiet the fears and suspicions of the South, Lincoln refused. He had already made his stand clear, he insisted. Anyone who wanted his opinion on slavery had only to read the many speeches he had made.

He had made his detestation of slavery quite clear, but he had also stated that he had "no purpose either, directly or indirectly, to interfere with . . . slavery in the States where it exists . . ." And with regard to the right of secession, he had also been quite emphatic. On the day John Brown was hanged, Lincoln had told southern sympathizers in Kansas that John Brown "has just been hanged for treason against the State of Virginia; and we cannot object, though he agreed with us in calling slavery wrong. No, if you undertake to destroy the Union contrary to law, if you commit treason against the United States, our duty will be to deal with you as John Brown has been dealt with. We shall try to do our duty."

He advised friends that he would rather be hanged than buy a peaceful inauguration by making bargains with the South.

On February 4, in Montgomery, Alabama, the seven seceding states founded a new nation, the Confederate States of America, elected Jefferson Davis President and Alexander Stephens Vice-President and adopted a Constitution almost exactly, word-for-word, like the U. S. Constitution.

"Revolutions are much easier started than controlled," Vice-President Stephens warned his fellow citizens of the Confederate States of America.

In Boston, the Abolitionist Wendell Phillips snarled:

"Let the South march off, with flags and trumpets, and we will speed the parting guest. . . . All hail, disunion!"

Arsenals, post offices, and ships were taken over by the Confederate States of America. Buchanan proclaimed a Fast Day and told his friends he was the last President of the U. S. A.

Meanwhile, Abraham Lincoln and his wife packed suits, dresses, shoes, combs, and brushes. The contents of drawers and closets in the Springfield house were packed in trunks marked "A. Lincoln, The White House, Washington, D. C."

Perhaps, Lincoln thought, he hadn't made his idea of the nature of the Federal Government clear enough. Did he believe that differences between the states and the Federal Government were to be settled by the states, or that the Supreme Court was the final arbiter? At Indianapolis, on his way to Washington, he carefully gave his views. The states, he said, were just subdivisions of the nation. They were to the Federal Government, what the counties were to the states. Nor was there any ultimate protection for minorities beyond the checks provided in the Constitution itself:

"If the minority will not acquiesce," he said at his inaugural in Washington, "the majority must, or the Government must cease . . . Government is acquiescence on one side or the other."

He also held that "the Union of these States is perpetual . . . It is safe to assert that no Government proper ever had a provision in its organic law for its own termination . . ."

"You have no oath registered in heaven to destroy the Government," Lincoln told the South, "while I shall have the most solemn one to 'preserve, protect, and defend' it."

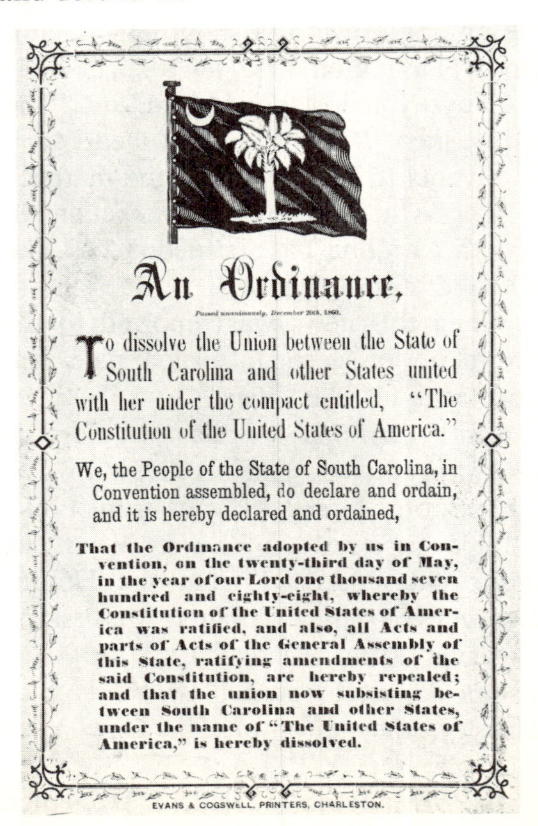

An Ordinance,

Passed unanimously, December 20th, 1860.

To dissolve the Union between the State of South Carolina and other States united with her under the compact entitled, "The Constitution of the United States of America."

We, the People of the State of South Carolina, in Convention assembled, do declare and ordain, and it is hereby declared and ordained,

That the Ordinance adopted by us in Convention, on the twenty-third day of May, in the year of our Lord one thousand seven hundred and eighty-eight, whereby the Constitution of the United States of America was ratified, and also, all Acts and parts of Acts of the General Assembly of this State, ratifying amendments of the said Constitution, are hereby repealed; and that the union now subsisting between South Carolina and other States, under the name of "The United States of America," is hereby dissolved.

EVANS & COGSWELL, PRINTERS, CHARLESTON.

It seemed impossible that 3550 miles of coastline could be closed off, but by 1864, 500 Federal vessels stood off the Confederacy. Flour was $300 a barrel! Old General in Chief Winfield Scott outlined Northern strategy: blockade, division of the Confederacy by capture of the Mississippi, and invasion. Few others in Washington, in April, 1861, foresaw how long and hard was the task ahead.

END OF INNOCENCE

OF THE fifteen slave states, seven had seceded. If the remaining eight also left, the free North would be almost pinched in two where Ohio stood between Kentucky and Canada, and the Union would be lost. But how could the seven seceders be restored without losing all eight of the other slave states? And what could be done anyway, when the North was full of people willing to let the "sisters depart in peace?"

Even before his inauguration, Lincoln had been in touch with friends in Kentucky, Missouri, Tennessee and the other still-loyal slave states. He was getting reports on how their people felt; on what was likely to make them jump one way or the other; on who favored secession and who did not. In Washington he waited more than a month, outwardly doing nothing, while those most anxious to save the Union called him weak and foolish.

Meanwhile the Confederate government sent commissioners to Washington to obtain recognition of their new nation and make plans to get foreign support. The manufacture of cotton cloth was England's biggest industry, and three quarters of the cotton woven on English looms came from the South. In Charleston, in April, 1861, W. H. Russel, correspondent of The London Times, was told: "Why, sir, we have only to shut off your supply of cotton for a few weeks, and we can create a revolution in Great Britain . . . we know that England must recognize us."

The Federal Government retained control over two small pieces of property in the Confederacy: Fort Pickens, Florida, and Fort Sumter, South Carolina. Lincoln sent reinforcements to Fort Pickens and decided to ship supplies to Fort Sumter, whose small eighty-one-man garrison was almost out of food. On April 8, the Confederate government in Montgomery was notified of this intention. On April 11, the CSA demanded the immediate evacuation of the fort. The following morning, three men rowed across Charleston Harbor to hand Major Anderson, Fort Sumter's commander, the following message:

April 12, 1861, 3:30 A.M.

"Sir:

By authority of Brigadier General Beauregard, commanding the provisional forces of the Confederate States, we have the honor to notify you that he will open the fire of his batteries on Fort Sumter in one hour from this time."

The Union troops in the fort waited until daylight to return the Confederate fire. Then, after breakfast, Captain Abner Doubleday divided his company into three details and went to work:

"In aiming the first gun fired against the Rebellion," he wrote afterward, "I had no feeling of self-reproach, for I fully believed that the contest had been inevitable. My first shot bounded off from the sloping roof of the battery opposite . . ."

After thirty-four hours of sustained bombardment, and down to its last four barrels of powder, the fort surrendered.

"I COULD SCARCELY BELIEVE MY SENSES"

Now that the stars and stripes had been fired on, sympathy with secession had plainly become sympathy with treason. Had Lincoln wished to turn northern opinion firmly against the Confederacy, Beauregard had obliged him.

With the North aroused, Lincoln ordered the people of the seven seceded states to disperse and return peacefully to their homes, and he issued a call for 75,000 three-month volunteers.

To most Southerners, Lincoln's order was the first sign that the North would seriously oppose secession. When it "was read on the bulletin boards of the telegraph offices," one young Carolinian wrote, "crowds perused the document with laughter.

"At the first whisper of war . . . a hundred youths . . . drew up a muster-roll, inscribed their names for twelve months' service, and began drilling in a concert hall . . ."

North Carolina, Tennessee, Arkansas, Virginia, Kentucky, Maryland, and Missouri refused to furnish volunteers to the Federal Government, and the first four seceded, bringing an additional 3¾ million people into the Confederacy. Lincoln's response was to call for forty regiments of three-year volunteers and to add 27,000 men to the regular Army and 18,000 to the Navy. To the "squeaking of fifes, the clangor of drums, the shout and hurrah of citizens," the volunteers came to camp in gaudy militia uniforms.

A Virginia lady "heard distinctly the drums beating in Washington. As I looked at the Capitol in the distance, I could scarcely believe my senses. That Capitol of which I had always been so proud! Can it be possible that it is no longer *our* Capitol?"

Secession confronted many men with difficult decisions. Lincoln had had "to choose whether, using only the existing means . . . which Congress had provided, [he] should let the Government fall at once into ruin, or whether, availing [himself] of the broader powers conferred by the Constitution . . . [he] would make an effort to save it . . ." Governor Sam Houston of Texas refused to join the Confederacy and was removed from office. Of the West Point graduates serving in the regular Army, 330 came from seceded states, and 168 of them resigned their commissions to go south. Among them was Colonel Robert E. Lee, who had written that slavery was "a moral & political evil in any Country"; but who declined command of the enlarging Federal Army to fight for his native Virginia. When another Virginian, old granite-face Admiral David Farragut was offered command of the Rebel navy, he vehemently declined. Then he packed up and went north. He had exchanged the comforts of his home in Virginia for a small cottage in Hastings-on-Hudson, New York.

"BALLOTS ARE THE RIGHTFUL AND PEACEFUL SUCCESSORS OF BULLETS"

On the 4th of July, President Lincoln convened a special session of Congress in order to obtain authority for the extraordinary actions he had taken. The issue raised by secession, he told the Congress, "embraces more than the fate of these United States. It presents to the whole family of man the question whether a constitutional republic or democracy — a government of the people by the same people — can or cannot maintain its territorial integrity against its own domestic foes. It presents the question whether discontented individuals, too few in number to control administration according to organic laws . . . can . . . put an end to free government upon the earth. It forces us to ask: Is there in all Republics this inherent and fatal weakness? Must a government, of necessity, be too strong for the liberties of its own people, or too weak to maintain its own existence? . . .

"Our popular government has often been called an experiment. Two points in it our people have already settled — the successful establishing and the successful administering of it. One still remains — its successful maintenance against a formidable internal attempt to overthrow it. It is now for them to demonstrate to the world that those who can fairly carry an election can also suppress a rebellion; that ballots are the rightful and peaceful successors of bullets; and that when ballots have fairly and constitutionally decided, there can be no successful appeal back to bullets . . ."

NEUTRAL STATES AND UN-NEUTRAL MEN

With 800,000 square miles of territory, with 12 million in population, the Confederacy was formidable indeed. If the 3 million people in Maryland, Kentucky, and Missouri were added to the South, its population would equal that of the North, Washington, D. C. would be isolated, and the Union irretrievably destroyed.

Maryland requested each belligerent, North and South, to respect her property. With pro-secession governors and legislatures, Kentucky proclaimed neutrality

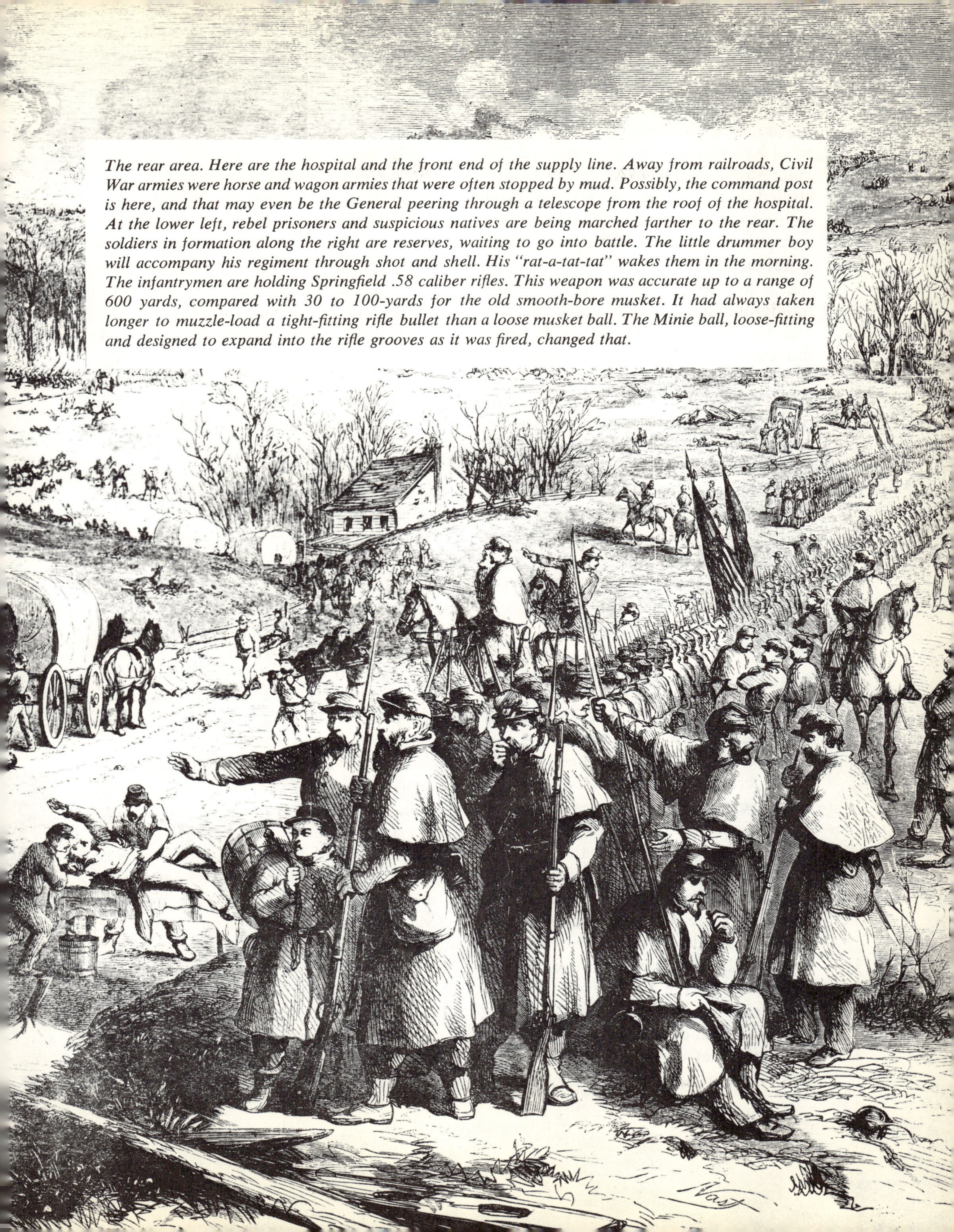

The rear area. Here are the hospital and the front end of the supply line. Away from railroads, Civil War armies were horse and wagon armies that were often stopped by mud. Possibly, the command post is here, and that may even be the General peering through a telescope from the roof of the hospital. At the lower left, rebel prisoners and suspicious natives are being marched farther to the rear. The soldiers in formation along the right are reserves, waiting to go into battle. The little drummer boy will accompany his regiment through shot and shell. His "rat-a-tat-tat" wakes them in the morning. The infantrymen are holding Springfield .58 caliber rifles. This weapon was accurate up to a range of 600 yards, compared with 30 to 100-yards for the old smooth-bore musket. It had always taken longer to muzzle-load a tight-fitting rifle bullet than a loose musket ball. The Minie ball, loose-fitting and designed to expand into the rifle grooves as it was fired, changed that.

and Missouri slid into a kind of internal civil war. Lincoln was cautious; Jefferson Davis, bold. Lincoln shipped rifles to loyal Kentuckians in boxes marked "circular saws," and Federal troops demonstrated on the far side of the Ohio. Davis refused to respect Maryland property and sent an army into Kentucky. Both states came out for the North. An uprising, composed mostly of loyal German immigrants in St. Louis, made Missouri safe for the Union. In none of the states did the people unanimously favor one side. The Illinois and New Jersey Legislatures issued pro-Confederate proclamations, and Louisiana loyalists hid in the swamps to escape Confederate service. Union sentiment was strong in the mountain regions of North Carolina, Alabama, and Tennessee, and the Virginia mountaineers seceded from their state to form West Virginia. At one time or another, 300,000 white men from Confederate States served in the Union Army.

THE FACTS OF WAR

From the beginning both sides understood that for the North to win the war, it would have to invade and conquer the Confederacy. The Confederacy, on the other hand, like the colonies during the Revolution, had merely to maintain its independence until the North grew tired or other nations came to its aid.

A second Confederate advantage was that it had interior lines of communications. It could shuttle troops from one threatened point to another over shorter distances than the attackers would have to travel.

This second advantage was partly offset by the fact that the North had three miles of railroad track to every mile in the South. The North also had greater manufacturing resources and manpower. In fact, Southerners conceded that they could be neither a commercial nor "extensively a manufacturing people. . . . Negroes should never be brought into habitual contact with white men, beyond those to whom they owe obedience . . ."

Less than 10 per cent of the manufactures of the country in 1860 had been turned out by the states that joined the Confederacy. They mined only 3 per cent of the nation's iron ore, and rolled only about 6 per cent of the iron processed in the nation's mills.

For the rest, geography and the spirit of the contestants would dictate the progress of the war. Slantwise, running from southwest to northeast was the Appalachian chain of mountains. Extending down to the northeastern corner of Alabama they shielded all the old states of the South from Western invasion. East of the Appalachians the two enemy capitals, Washington and Richmond, were barely a hundred miles apart. Both cities had to be defended at all costs — Washington, because its capture would give the rebels the prestige they needed to bring other nations to their side; Richmond, because the loss of the Tredegar Works would deprive the South of its single big rolling mill, the only one capable of casting heavy guns. The vital importance of these capitals would force each side to keep armies between them and the enemy. It meant that about 10,000 square miles of Maryland and eastern Virginia, between the mountains and Chesapeake Bay, would become a bloody battleground any time one of the armies crossed the Potomac River. It also meant that the lush Shenandoah Valley, running for 150 miles through the mountains, would play a singular role. Opening onto the Potomac, it was a protected food-filled pathway from the heart of Virginia to the Union frontier. Through gaps in the Blue Ridge Mountains, the valley's eastern wall, any invader on the eastern plain could be threatened.

THE EASTERN CAMPAIGNS

The first army to cross the Potomac was a Northern force under General Irvin McDowell, in July, 1861. Winfield Scott's warnings that the raw Union recruits were ill-prepared for an offensive expedition had been submerged in the clamor of Northern newspapers for a quick capture of Richmond. There was also a worry that recruiting would suffer should the three-month men be sent home without a battle.

The Union Army met defeat at Bull Run Creek, just east of the Manassas Gap of the Shenandoah Valley. The defeat left the Confederate army cocky and overconfident.

In Richmond, a veteran of the fight noted contemptuously:

". . . a great number of officers in ex-

Professional soldiers believed that charging infantrymen could overwhelm a defending line — in the era of muskets, only the final 15 seconds of a charge had been dangerous. It was different now that a man faced a rifle that had him in range for a minute and a half and that, with Minie balls, could fire five rounds. This charge of Pickett's Brigade, July 2, 1863, on Cemetery Hill, near Gettysburg, Pennsylvania, was the last serious Confederate threat to the Union.

pensive uniforms strutted about on 'sick leave.' Many of them had never been in the army at all . . ."

In Washington, Lincoln signed a bill for 500,000 volunteers and appointed a new commander-in-chief.

The war ground on and there was sadness, now, when a volunteer left home. There were widows and orphans, and Western Union messenger boys twisting their caps in the doorway while a painful message was read. And at the front, before a battle, men were pinning little slips of paper to their coats. On these slips of paper their names were written, so that if they fell, their bodies would be identified. They had seen the face of war, and the *hurrah* of it had withered in their throats.

"We had not reached the enemy's fortifications," a minister wrote after one day's fighting, "but only that fatal crest where we had seen five lines cut to earth as by a sword swoop of fire. We had that costly honor which sometimes falls to the reserve — to go in when all is havoc and confusion, through storm and slaughter, to cover the broken and depleted ranks of comrades and take the battle from their hands. Thus we had replaced the gallant few still struggling on the crest, and we received that withering fire which nothing could withstand by throwing ourselves flat in a slight hollow of the ground within pistol shot of the enemy's works; and, mingled with the dead and dying that strewed the field, we returned the fire till it reddened into night and at last fell away through darkness into silence.

"But out of that silence from the battle's crash and roar rose new sounds more appalling still — rose or fell, you knew not which, or whether from the earth or air: a strange ventriloquism, of which

you could not locate the source, a smothered moan that seemed to come from distances beyond reach of the natural sense, a wail as far and deep and wide as if a thousand discords were flowing together into a keynote weird, unearthly, terrible to hear and bear, yet startling with its nearness. The writhing concord was broken by cries for help, pierced by shrieks of paroxysm. Some begged for a drop of water. Some called on God for pity, and some on friendly hands to finish what the enemy had so horribly begun. Some with delirious, dreamy voices murmured loved names, as if the dearest were bending over them. Some gathered their last strength to fire a musket so as to call attention to them where they lay helpless and deserted. And underneath, all the time, came that deep bass note from closed lips too hopeless or too heroic to articulate their agony."

Behind the front, the great sudden need for war supplies was creating the usual temptations. Northerners and Southerners used political influence to

Above, Sherman's men destroy tracks and enemy supplies in Jackson, Mississippi, during the Vicksburg campaign. William Tecumseh Sherman, a tall, ruddy-bearded Westerner saw, as did General Grant, that in an era of citizen soldiers, there would be Confederate armies as long as there were men determined to fight and sources of arms. Grant and Sherman also understood the military value of railroads. 20,000 men, moved 80 miles a day by railroad, were as good as 80,000 men who could march only 20 miles a day. And the railroad was as good a supply route as a river.

get fat war contracts. Ruthless men made fortunes reselling to the Federal Government guns and other supplies that the Government itself had previously auctioned off as old and useless. Other contractors sold overcoats made of "shoddy" shop sweepings glued and rolled into a kind of felt. In the South, blockade-breaking corporations, with fleets of fast, gray side-wheel steamers, grew so rich and powerful that the Confederate government itself was forced to pay whatever outrageous prices they demanded.

Meanwhile, all through 1862 and 1863, Lincoln kept trying to find a general who could defeat the Confederates in Virginia and capture Richmond. Handsome George McClellan, appointed after Bull Run, was too cautious. But none of his successors — Pope, Burnside, Hooker or Meade — seemed any match for the opposition. Lincoln was forced to be his own general-in-chief. The Federal Army of the Potomac did well only on defense. It stopped one Confederate invasion at Antietam, Maryland, and a second at Gettysburg, Pennsylvania.

In the spring of 1862, during McClellan's invasion of Virginia, the Confederate commander Joseph E. Johnston had been wounded, and President Davis' military adviser, General Robert E. Lee, had taken over the Army of Northern Virginia. It was Lee's military genius, and that of General Thomas "Stonewall" Jackson, one of his subordinates, that was baffling the Northern armies.

Lee had the ability, unmatched by any

DESERTER!

Descriptive List of Substitute Deserter.

	ENLISTED	WHERE	DESERTED	WHERE
JOSEPH BROOKS,	**Sept. 29th.**	**at Troy.**	**Oct. 1st, 1863.**	**at Troy, N.Y.**

Said Deserter has blue eyes, dark hair, dark complexion and pock marked; is 5 feet 5 1-2 inches high--by occupation a *Boatman*.
He has 2 sailor marks on the right arm, one of which is a cross; on the left arm is a full length figure of a female, marked with blue and red ink. He is a little round shouldered, has a downcast look; wore when he deserted a dark blue flannel sack coat, light blue pants, army forage cap, army shirt--gray knit, coarse boots.

THIRTY DOLLARS REWARD

Will be paid for the arrest and delivery of this Deserter at my office.
CHARLES HUGHES,
Troy, N. Y., Oct. 2d, 1863.
Capt. and Provost Marshal, 15th Dist. N. Y.

of the Federal commanders he faced, to keep in mind the general layout of the land and the various movements of large bodies of troops. He could work with a map and with information brought to him by messengers. A man like the Federal's "Fighting Joe" Hooker, on the other hand, was a fine commander in the field, but he could understand nothing beyond the range of his eyes and ears. "Stonewall" Jackson, a master of surprise and speed, fought six battles in the Shenandoah Valley in the course of one eleven-week campaign. He defeated, in detail, Federal forces three times as large as his own.

All this time the soldiers were learning and improving. Men in Federal blue and Confederate gray were starting to dig in whenever they camped. They were learning how to use the swells and hollows of the ground, when to crawl and when to run, how to build up firing lines along the ridges at the sides of roads. The Union Army had plenty of mechanics and mathematicians. Its engineers were building bridges and roads faster than anyone had thought possible. Its artillery was becoming deadly accurate. In long range duels it silenced Confederate artillery, and, wheeled quickly into action, it worked from the front lines against enemy infantry. Loaded with two special anti-personnel charges, grape and canister, cannons mowed closely-packed men down like scythes.

In April, 1862, as the one-year enlistments ran out, the Confederacy, fearful of recruiting the many Negroes in its midst, was forced to pass a draft law. By midsummer there were 340,000 Southerners in arms. With an effective population three times as large to draw on, the North could still rely on voluntary enlistments. "We are coming Father Abraham, three hundred thousand more." There were 673,000 men wearing Federal blue.

A GENERAL IS FOUND

Northern men enlisted with their neighbors in companies and regiments, and they usually elected their company officers. These lieutenants and captains, in turn, elected the majors and lieutenant colonels. Regimental commanders were appointed by Governors, and generals were named by the President with the advice of Governors and other politicians.

In Springfield, Illinois, Governor Richard Yates knew that the temporary mustering officer at the reception center was a lot better qualified for command than most. Sam Grant was a West Point graduate who had seen service in the Mexican War. He was thirty-nine years old in 1861, a slight, stoop-shouldered man with curly brownish hair and clear blue eyes. He had a kind of defeated look to him, and there was a story that he had left the army because of some trouble in Oregon. When Fort Sumter was fired upon, he had been clerking in a store in Galena, working for his two younger brothers.

Governor Yates made Grant colonel of a wild volunteer outfit that nobody had been able to control. In just a few days, the disheveled little man in worn civilian coat and old felt hat had somehow quieted them down. On September 4, 1861, Grant was a general in command of a small Federal Army in Cairo, Illinois, at the junction of the Ohio and Mississippi Rivers. There he became acquainted with Flag Officer Andrew H. Foote who was readying some new ironclad navy gunboats for service on the Western waters.

Through Kentucky, the Tennessee and Cumberland Rivers empty into the Ohio. Both rivers wind hundreds of miles southward and eastward across the

Opposing front line soldiers are drawn together by the hardships they share. "Johnny Reb" and "Billy Yank" also had a common language. Men on outpost duty frequently let each other chop wood for campfires. Often, they swapped Confederate tobacco for Yankee coffee, salt, or flour.

main east-west routes of the Confederacy. The Cumberland traverses a good part of northern Tennessee. The Tennessee penetrates to Mississippi and Alabama, in the heart of the Confederacy. Aware of the dangerous access these rivers gave to their territory, the Confederates had put a fort on each, just south of the Kentucky-Tennessee border. In February, 1862, Grant and Foote captured both forts. The Rebels had to retreat from Kentucky and western Tennessee. Foote's gunboats cruised into Alabama, and Confederate General Albert Sidney Johnston began calling in troops all the way from Florida and Texas to halt any army that would follow the boats down the river.

Halleck, the commander in the West, sent Grant down the Tennessee to destroy the main east-west Confederate railway, the Memphis and Charleston. On April 6, 1862, at Pittsburgh Landing, near a little church called Shiloh, Grant's army was surprised by Johnston. The fight went on for two days at close quarters. With incredible bravery, Federals and Confederates stood their ground. Of some 100,000 men engaged, each side lost about 12,000. One Confederate brigade of 2,750 lost 1,800 men in the first day's fighting and finally left the battlefield with 58 men. The long casualty lists in the newspapers chilled many a heart.

Grant was criticized for allowing the enemy to surprise him. But Lincoln noted that after the surprise the General had stayed and fought and that it had been the Confederates who had retreated. This was just the opposite of what usually happened after eastern battles. And Lincoln also liked the tone of Grant's message to the commander of one of the forts he had captured in Tennessee:

"... No terms except an unconditional and immediate surrender can be accepted. I propose to move immediately upon your work.

Your obedient servant,
U. S. Grant"

Halleck was called to Washington as General-in-Chief, and Grant came into the command of the armies of the Tennessee and the Mississippi.

In April, 1862, Admiral Farragut, restored to active duty in the Union Navy, had captured New Orleans, the biggest city in the South. Then a Federal Army under Gen. N. P. Banks had marched upriver as far as Baton Rouge, and Federal gunboats had worked down from Memphis. The Mississippi was cleared of all Confederate resistance except for a stretch of a couple of hundred twisting miles between Port Hudson, north of Baton Rouge, and Vicksburg, Mississippi. If these two strong points were reduced, the entire Mississippi could be patrolled by Federal gunboats. The

March 1864. The war-haunted face of Ulysses S. Grant as he appeared in Washington to confer with Lincoln. Behind him were Shiloh, Vicksburg, and Chattanooga; before him was the most terrible campaign of the war. In Grant's view, the Civil War was visited on the country as a punishment for the Mexican War, which he believed to have been unjust. Grant disliked Abolitionists; yet, when losing his Missouri farm and in need of cash, he freed his one slave. After half an hour with the General, Lincoln gave him command of the Union Army.

Unretouched Photograph

Confederacy would be split in two and the northern states of the Ohio Valley would regain their outlet to the sea.

Grant began operating against Vicksburg in December, using Memphis as a base. Finally, in May, he was able to take an army across the river below Vicksburg, on a fleet of boats that had run past the powerful Rebel batteries.

In charge of the Confederates in Vicksburg was the Pennsylvanian, General John Pemberton. Both he and Grant had served under Winfield Scott in the campaign on Mexico City. In Mexico, Scott, like Cortez, had left his seaside base and marched his army inland to live off the fertile valley of Mexico. Grant did the same thing in fertile Mississippi, striking quickly inland with but five days' rations. For six days, his army moved through Mississippi, a self-contained unit, while Pemberton wasted precious time trying to cut the non-existent supply line in Grant's rear.

Seventeen days after the landing, Jackson, the state capital, was a ruin, the railroad supplying Vicksburg had been destroyed, Pemberton and his army were shut up in the city, under siege, and Grant had a secure new supply line from a tributary of the Mississippi north of Vicksburg. His men had marched 130 miles, split the Rebel forces in Mississippi, and won five battles.

The city surrendered on July 4, after a painful six weeks' siege. Banks captured Port Hudson five days later and, in President Lincoln's words, "The Father of Waters once more flows unvexed to the sea."

Grant paroled Pemberton's 20,000 men on their word not to again take up arms against the United States. In August, a Peace Party, strongly supported by paroled Vicksburg prisoners, carried several counties in Alabama. In Columbia, South Carolina, a Confederate officer observed, "The tone of the people is lost; it is no longer a reproach to be known as a deserter . . ."

In October, Grant was given command of all the Western armies, except that occupying New Orleans, and he went up to Chattanooga where a Union Army under General Rosencrans was besieged. Grant opened up a new line of supply, brought in Sherman's army and had 20,000 men from Washington shipped west by railroad. In two days of fighting the besiegers were defeated, to retreat south into Georgia. "God bless you all," Lincoln telegraphed, and Congress promoted Ulysses Simpson Grant to Lieutenant General.

THE WILDERNESS

Subject to Grant's orders was a Union Army of 970,000 men in seventeen different commands. Up to now, the campaigns in the East and West had proceeded separately according to the whims of their commanders and Lincoln's urging that Lee be defeated.

Grant proposed to use the entire Army in one gigantic, coordinated campaign to crush the Confederacy. The capture of Chattanooga, and Bragg's defeat, had opened the gateway to Georgia, the fertile breadbasket of the Confederacy. Grant ordered Sherman, to whom he had turned over the Western armies, to invade Georgia. Meanwhile, Grant would move the Army of the Potomac south against Lee. His campaign would keep Lee from sending help to the West, while Sherman's campaign would keep the Westerners from reinforcing Lee; and while Grant was hammering away at the Army of Northern Virginia, Sherman would be reducing all the country in

Lee's rear. As Lincoln put it, "Those not skinning can hold the leg."

Lee had become a master of defensive warfare. His men, who called him the "King of Spades," dug trenches, sharpened poles and fastened them into impenetrable hedgehogs, and waited to slaughter whatever Federals dared attack. Lee's army was dug in some sixty miles northwest of Richmond, behind the Rapidan River, with a mountain protecting its left. Directly to its right was the Wilderness, a wild tangle of second-growth forest filled with "a dense undergrowth of scraggy pines, dwarfed oaks and laurel bushes . . . while in the low points are sluggish streams and dank marshes choked with alders, twined closely with luxuriant tangled and prickly vines . . ."

The Wilderness stretched fourteen miles from east to west and ten miles from north to south, and was crossed by very few roads. It was a jungle in which men could hardly maneuver, in which a strange invading army would be at the mercy of natives who knew the ground, in which artillery would be useless, in which numbers counted for little. Lee had chewed up a Union Army under Hooker in the Wilderness in 1863, and wounded men had burned to death as the dry forest floor caught fire.

Grant had two choices. He could move on Lee's left, using the Orange and Alexandria railway as a base, in which case Lee could watch his moves through forty miles of open country; or he could move on Lee's right, through the Wilderness, using the Potomac and Rappahannock Rivers for supplies. If he moved on Lee's left, his supply line would be open to attack from the gaps in the Shenandoah; if he moved the other way, his supply lines would be safe. Once through the Wilderness, he would be in a position to threaten Lee's supply lines.

During the night of May 3, five bridges were laid across the Rapidan. There was the tramping of feet on wooden pontoon bridges, the clatter of hoofbeats, the rumble of artillery caissons. The Army of the Potomac, 119,000 strong, entered the Wilderness: an army of old-timers, three-year men who had somehow been induced to re-enlist, of new volunteers, and mean-looking draft-substitutes, from the cities, who would only behave as soldiers under iron discipline.

On the morning of May 4, signalers on Clark's mountain began wig-wagging, and Lee's men moved east to the Wilderness — 64,000 lean and confident veterans.

In two days of fighting, the Federals lost 15,000 men. On the night of May 7, to Lee's astonishment, the Union troops moved south, deeper into the Wilderness. For twelve days, they assaulted Lee's strong position around a place called Spotsylvania Courthouse, hammering, slugging, without let-up, suffering 18,000 casualties. Then they slipped south again, finally clear of the Wilderness, making Lee follow as they threatened to get in between him and Richmond. June 3, three Union corps stormed another powerful Confederate position at Cold Harbor, south of Spotsylvania, and in one hour, lost 7,000 men.

Never had there been fighting such as this. In one month Grant lost about half the big army he had taken into Virginia. Northern newspapers called Grant a butcher. Mothers implored Lincoln to put a stop to the slaughter; no cause was worth 2,000 men a day. Greeley cried for peace on any terms. Prospects for Lincoln's re-election were dimmer than ever.

But Grant had just begun to fight. He sent General Philip H. Sheridan with 30,000 cavalrymen, armed with new repeating breech-loading rifles, to ravage the farms in the Shenandoah Valley, so that Lee would never again be able to send men through it to threaten Washington.

As for Lee, 25,000 of his men were dead, wounded, prisoners, or missing. "We must destroy the Federal Army before they get to the James River," Lee told one of his generals. "If they get there it will become a siege and then merely a question of time."

Before Lee knew what had happened, Grant's army was across the James in front of Petersburg, a railway-junction city in the rear of Richmond. But the Federals, battle-weary, with too many casualties, hesitated, and the chance to take the city by surprise was gone. Both sides prepared for a long siege.

"The war is a failure!" Northern newspapers declared, agreeing with the Democratic candidate, George McClellan. Greeley begged Lincoln to let some other Republican run for President.

On August 23, Lincoln asked the members of his Cabinet to put their signatures to a paper so folded that none of them could read what they were signing. The members of the Cabinet had unknowingly assented to Lincoln's possibly taking extraordinary dictatorial steps. As the President had noted in the document, ". . . it seems exceedingly probable that this administration will not be re-elected. Then it will be my duty to so coöperate with the President-elect as to save the Union between the election and the inauguration as he will have secured his election on such ground that he cannot possibly save it afterward."

All through the war party politics was a major vexation. Lincoln could neither stifle all dissent, nor leave it unregulated. Stephen A. Douglas had done his best, before his death to rally northern Democrats to the cause of Union. But a minority in the party, adhering to the Jeffersonian states rights tradition or opposed to abolition, remained friendly to the South. In the early difficult months of the war, when the Union hung on the verge of a complete break-up, outspoken Copperheads, as disloyal Northerners were called, had been imprisoned without benefit of trial. Eventually more than 15,000 men languished in jails, deprived of the constitutional guarantee of *habeas corpus*. "Must I shoot a simple-minded soldier boy who deserts while I must not touch a hair of the wily agitator who induced him to desert?" Lincoln asked.

After Gettysburg and Vicksburg, with the worst of the danger past, the Copperheads were let out of jail. But free expression could never flourish in the midst of war. Copperhead papers were banned from college libraries and Harvard students were not allowed to wear Democratic badges. The pro-slavery president of Dartmouth was forced to resign, and an Ohio college even refused to allow a senior to give a talk on the suppression of civil liberties.

Few Presidents have been abused as Lincoln was all through the war. Newspapers called him a "half-witted usurper," and worse. Republicans called him a "dictator," "coward," "utterly foolish"; and a reporter observed, in Washington, an "absence of personal loyalty to the President . . . he has no admirers."

The most eminent American historian of the time declared Lincoln, "ignorant, self-willed . . ."

BUMMERS, HAIRPINS, AND PROPHETS

But while Grant had been slugging through Virginia, Sherman had been moving on Atlanta. On September 2, he sent a message to Lincoln:

"Atlanta is ours, and fairly won."

The fall of this industrial and rail center ended stories that the war was a failure. The Democratic candidate, General McClellan, promised to finish the war if elected. With the votes of Sherman's furloughed men, and with another army preventing fraud at the New York City polls, Lincoln and his running mate, Andrew Johnson of Tennessee, were elected.

On November 12, Sherman began a campaign of such audacity that it even worried Grant. After burning Atlanta, Sherman's army, cut off from all Union sources of supply, began a march eastward to the sea.

The men marched in four columns, about fifteen miles apart. The army was like a great caterpillar worm, sixty miles wide, and as it moved it devoured wheat and beef and chickens and corn. It destroyed barns and silos full of grain so that after it had passed there was nothing left to eat.

"Georgians be firm!" the leaders of the state announced. "Never before have you had so good a chance to destroy the enemy; remove all food from the invader's path; destroy the roads, rise in arms. Death is preferable to the loss of liberty."

But the men who might have risen in arms were in the trenches in front of Petersburg or following General Hood through the mountains to the north, or buried at Gettysburg, Antietam, Chattanooga, and the Wilderness.

Sherman's army made ten miles a day. "Fancy a ragged man, blackened by smoke, mounted on a scrawny mule without a saddle, with a gun, a knapsack, a butcher knife and a plug hat, stealing his way far out on the flanks of the column," wrote a northern captain. ". . . Think how you would admire him if you were a lone woman, far from help, when he blandly inquired where you kept your valuables . . . when he pried open your chests with his bayonet or knocked to pieces your tables, pianos and chairs, tore your bed clothing in three inch strips . . ."

Such men became known as "Sherman's bummers."

The army pried up railroad tracks and bent them around trees into "Sherman's hairpins." It left the blackened chimneys of burned down houses: "Sherman's monuments." Bands of slaves followed the army, waving their hands and singing hosanna and jubilee: "Sherman's prophets." On December 10, Sherman, bum-

Connor's Farm, Appomattox Courthouse, April 9, 1865. On the field stands all that remains of the Army of Northern Virginia. General Lee is announcing Grant's generous terms of surrender.

mers, prophets, and all were in Savannah. Two months later, they were in Columbia, South Carolina.

A MEETING AT A FARMHOUSE

Richmond was swollen with refugees. Ruined aristocrats lived in crowded rooms, their supply of coal piled in one corner; slaves were getting "uppity"; and mistresses of plantations sewed canvas boots for a living. The Confederate government authorized the recruiting of 300,000 Negroes. On enlisting, slaves would be given their freedom. But if freedom is considered a reward for slaves "then slavery is originally, radically, incurably wrong and sinful, and the sum of barbarism," said The Richmond Examiner.

On February 23, 1865, General Joseph E. Johnston was put in command of the Confederate Army of the Tennessee, in North Carolina. The one hope left to the Confederacy was that Lee join Johnston and smash Sherman before Sherman joined up with Grant. First Grant's army had to be weakened so that Richmond and Petersburg could be held with fewer men. This Lee was unable to accomplish. When the Federals cut the railway feeding Petersburg from the west, Lee had to leave the cities.

The race started on the night of April 3. Lee with 30,000 ragged, hungry men, 1,000 horses and 200 artillery pieces hurried westward. Grant followed along, his men on forced marches, making forty-two miles in twenty-four hours, scarcely believing that Lee finally was on the run. Grant kept to the south between Lee and Johnston. On April 6, General Ewell and the Confederate rear guard, were captured.

The next day Grant sent Lee a note inviting surrender, but Lee decided to cut through the Union lines. What was the Army of Northern Virginia fighting for?

"There has been no country for a year or more," one of his officers told Lee. "You are the country for these men . . ."

On the morning of Sunday, April 9, what was left of the Army of Northern Virginia ran into the Federal cavalry in the fields beside Appomattox Court House. The Confederates fired. There was the whish-whishing flutter of shells in the air. Explosions. The Federal cavalry wheeled aside to reveal long lines of blue-coated infantry marching into view. There was the grim pause as men prepare for battle on an open field. A horseman galloped out from the Confederate lines, a white flag at the end of a staff.

Grant and Lee met at the house of a Mr. McLean, Lee in a handsome gray full-dress uniform, polished boots, and a gold-mounted sword, Grant ill-shaven in an old private's coat, his three stars pinned to the shoulders. They reminisced about the old Army. When it came time to write the terms, Grant permitted every Confederate soldier who claimed to own a horse or mule to take one home. Grant also put in the surrender terms that Confederates who signed parole and went home were "not to be disturbed by the United States authority so long as they observe their paroles and the laws in force where they reside."

This would prevent any of them from being jailed or hanged, as certain politicians were threatening.

Lee left Grant a little before four in the afternoon. They shook hands. One of Grant's aides noticed that as Lee strolled away, the gray-bearded Virginian "gazed sadly in the direction of the valley beyond, where his army lay — now an army of prisoners. He thrice smote the palm of his left hand slowly with his right fist in an absent sort of way . . ."

Johnston surrendered to Sherman on April 26. Altogether, some 2½ million men had fought, and half a million had died.

"WITH MALICE TOWARD NONE"

At his second inaugural, Lincoln proposed that "With malice toward none, with charity for all, with firmness in the right as God gives us to see the right, let us strive on to finish the work we are in, to bind up the nation's wounds . . ." Louisiana, Arkansas, and Tennessee had been occupied; Lincoln had sought to ease their way back into the Union.

Republicans in Congress were insisting that, in rebelling, states had ceased to exist and could now be treated as territories subject to Congressional authority. Lincoln disagreed, and restored the states to the Union as soon as 10% of the number of their voters in the 1860 election had taken oaths of allegiance, agreed to the Emancipation Proclamation, and established a new state government. As the end of the war approached, Lincoln became more and more concerned that the defeated states not be treated in a manner that would deepen, rather than heal, the bitterness between the sections. At the end of March he went down to Virginia to confer with Grant and Sherman on the terms to be offered the Confederate armies. At a conference aboard Lincoln's yacht, Admiral Porter noted that the President "was wrought up to a high state of excitement. He wanted peace on almost any terms. . . ."

On April 14, five days after Lee's surrender, Lincoln expressed concern over the "feeling of hate and vindictiveness" possessed by certain Congressional leaders. That evening he was assassinated, and Andrew Johnson assumed the task of reconstructing the South.

On December 18, 1865, the 13th Amendment was added to the Constitution:

"Section 1. Neither slavery nor involuntary servitude, except as punishment for crime whereof the party shall have been duly convicted, shall exist within the United States, or any place subject to their jurisdiction. . . ."

THE RESTORATION OF PEACE

In 1865, the question was: what kind of nation is the United States now? Some things had been settled. The Federal Government was supreme over the states. The "right" of secession did not exist. Mr. Calhoun's "concurrent majority" did not exist. It was also clear that the right of a man to own another man was no longer to be recognized in the United States, that the workman must be paid wages for his work, and that master and servant were thereafter to be bound only by money. If a worker was to be free to live and work as he pleased, the employer was to be free not to regard himself as responsible for him in any way.

Faith in individualism seemed justified. Men went westward to settle Ohio, Indiana, and Illinois, intent only on making their way in the world, and they found that in building farms and enriching themselves they also benefited their nation. And did not the successful Rhode Island cotton mills make profits that might otherwise be lining the pockets of Englishmen? No matter what kind of success a man achieved, he seemed also to be helping his country.

Not only had the outcome of the war firmly established that the ways of the North would be firmly those of the entire nation, but the stimulus of the war itself — fat war contracts, the need for manufacturing quickly great quantities of arms and ammunition, of soldiers' hats, boots, knapsacks — had speeded up development, particularly in the North. Also, the prosecution of the war had enlarged the powers of the Federal Government, and war-time Congresses, released from Southern competition and restraint, had passed a Homestead Act, providing for gifts and very low cost sales of public lands to individual settlers, had set aside other public lands for the support of state universities, and had given land to a company that would build a transcontinental railroad. Thus the war strengthened those very tendencies in the Northern and Western states that had helped bring it about.

In the South, the accustomed bonds of society had been shattered by Government edict. In the rest of the country, it seemed as if men had grown bolder and

A 14-year-old newsboy on the Grand Trunk Railway. Partly deafened by an angry trainman, he yet views the future with confidence. The year is 1861. The boy is Thomas Alva Edison.

more careless during the years of war. The South, in defending its institutions, had said *Yes* to the ancient question, "Am I my brother's keeper?" but had put its own peculiar meaning to the word "keeper." The Northerner denied that he was his "brother's keeper." Now the rule was "every man for himself and the devil take the hindmost."

Individualism, the freedom of man from man, was the new order. And in the absence of the old restraints of custom, violence held sway.

"GOVERNMENT IS UNDERGOING A STRAIN"

If the Constitution is compared to a tree planted in Philadelphia in 1787 and nurtured through the administrations of 15 Presidents, the Civil War can be likened to a thunderbolt that has riven the tree. Split, but still erect, a great white wound exposed to the elements, the Constitution-tree may wither and die. If it survives, the storm scars will never disappear.

Without Southern representation, the Congress had become a regional body. The influence of Northern business men, no longer restrained by the agricultural South, was supreme. "The close of the war with our resources unimpaired," Senator John Sherman told his brother, the general, "gives a [higher] scope to the ideas of leading capitalists . . . They talk of millions as confidently as formerly of thousands."

Wartime Government purchases had stimulated industry, and policies made necessary by war had tended to favor manufacturers over farmers. High wartime taxes, for instance, had increased the prices of American manufactures. To protect high-priced American products against foreign competition, high tariffs had been levied. Would Northern industrialists yield to others the power to lower tariffs and to build rival railroads to the Pacific?

Civil War had twisted and distorted the delicate fabric of the Constitution. It had brought an increase in executive power. The non-participation of the South gave Congress an unusual unity and strength. Lincoln had had to fight Congress over the direction of the war, even over the designation of commanding officers, despite his clear constitutional responsibility as Commander in Chief.

As they clashed over the conduct of the war, executive and legislature disputed the peace. The division was deepened by the circumstance that on the shape of the peace depended the composition, and future policies, of the Congress. At his last Cabinet meeting, President Lincoln had expressed satisfaction that the war had ended while Congress was recessed. "If we are wise," he had said, ". . . we shall reanimate the Southern States and get their governments into successful operation . . . before Congress comes together in December."

In sum, the great constitutional crisis had not been healed at Appomattox. A hot war between North and South was replaced by a cold war between President and legislature.

Mingled with these constitutional questions were the great issues of the war itself. The war had not been fought simply to keep things as they had been before the war. What the North looked forward to in 1865 was not a restoration of the South to the Union, but a Reconstruction.

Unretouched Photograph

"The . . . dispute, having been decided against us, it is the part of wisdom to acquiesce," said Robert E. Lee in August, 1865. The nation remained divided, but men yearned for reconciliation. In Massachusetts, Charles Francis Adams declared that if Lee had "been technically a renegade to his flag," he had very respectable company, "William of Orange . . . Oliver Cromwell . . . and George Washington. . . ."

Fundamental to the whole problem of Reconstruction was the circumstance that the fate of one group of Americans was in the hands of another group of Americans. In seceding, Southerners had deprived themselves of Federal representation. But this lack of representation, Lincoln saw, threatened the basic principle of government by consent of the governed. Lincoln wanted the Southern states quickly restored to Congress so that they could take part in the deliberations over Reconstruction.

But speedy restoration would leave southern states in the hands of the planter aristocracy. In Congress were men who feared that the continued influence of old Southern leaders would prevent certain necessary reforms. Indeed it would signify, to these men, defeat of the objects for which the war had been fought.

Most extreme in their desire to reform the South was a small group of Republican radicals. Leaders of this faction in the Senate were Ben Wade of Ohio and Charles Sumner of Massachusetts. The leading radical in the House was Thaddeus Stevens of Pennsylvania.

Thaddeus Stevens believed in the equality of men as proclaimed in the Declaration of Independence and was convinced that the war had been fought on that issue. Born with a club foot, he had become an accomplished horseman and swimmer. Handsome and dashing, he had struggled upward from poverty in Vermont to prominence in his adopted Lancaster, Pennsylvania. From 1849 to 1853, he had served in Congress as a Whig. He was a Republican when he returned to Congress in 1859. Bold, ruthless, witty, and tenacious, he worked to bring equality to Negroes. Because his aim was noble, he believed any means was justified in accomplishing it. He was an old man in 1865, sickly and set in his ways.

In Stevens' path stood the office of the Presidency and its incumbent, Andrew Johnson. Not even Lincoln had traveled a longer road to the Presidency than Andrew Johnson. As a poor boy in Raleigh, North Carolina, he had received his education in a tailor shop, listening to men hired to read newspapers and books while the tailors sewed. He taught himself to read and became apprenticed to a tailor. After he had opened his own tailor shop in Greenville, Tennessee, his young wife taught him to write and do sums. Never deserting his origins, he remained a spokesman for the laborers and small farmers of Tennessee. When his state seceded, Senator Andrew Johnson was the only Southerner to remain in either house of Congress. During the war, he served as military governor of Tennessee. He was named Lincoln's running mate in 1864 by the National Union Convention, a war-time coalition of Republicans and Northern, pro-war Democrats. The radicals were pleased when Johnson succeeded Lincoln to office. They looked upon him as a renegade Southerner who would hate the South with a renegade's hate. Johnson shared the radicals' distrust of the planter aristocrats, but he was not prepared to revolutionize the South.

Acting according to his understanding of the Constitution, Johnson imposed on the South a Reconstruction program slightly harsher than Lincoln's. His exclusion of all rebels worth more than $20,000 from political rights deprived at least 100,000 Southerners of citizenship. Johnson's purpose was to destroy the influence of the Southerners responsible for rebellion. (The measure, however, slowed economic recovery and a return to normal business relations with the North.)

Johnson's program was not disliked by the majority of Senators and Representatives, but his position was weak. As a Democrat put into office by Republicans he was trusted by neither party. And tactless, he acted without consulting leaders of the recessed Congress. "Better call an extra session than allow many to think the executive was approaching usurpation," Thaddeus Stevens warned. Other legislators who might have supported Johnson's program opposed what they conceived to be an encroachment on their jurisdiction.

Nor did the Reconstructed states help the cause of moderation. Their situation was difficult. Many Negroes, newly freed and uneducated, wandered about the countryside or flocked to the cities. They wandered because "freedom" meant that they didn't have to stay on the plantation. They went to the cities where Federal troops were stationed because they believed that the Federal Government was about to give them farm land and mules.

Lincoln and Johnson had urged that Reconstructed states permit at least educated Negroes to vote. But the states reacted to the disorder by passing laws that all but returned the Negro to slavery. The so-called Black Code of Louisiana required that all farm laborers work on a yearly contract basis. The laborer was forbidden to "leave his place of employment" and was to be fined two dollars a day for "all absence from home without leave." Mississippi permitted the indenture of Negro orphans to their former masters and Alabama allowed freedmen to testify in court only in cases involving other freedmen.

President Andrew Johnson.

The radicals, strengthened by Johnson's tactlessness and the Southern Black Codes, were soon to prove irresistible. On December 18, 1865, Thaddeus Stevens told the reconvened House that "The future condition of the conquered power depends on the will of the conqueror. Southerners and Democrats," he warned, would "at the very next election take possession of the White House and the halls of Congress." Only Negro suffrage, which would create Republican majorities in the South, could prevent this.

With this vision of perpetual Republican supremacy, Stevens harnessed the powerful commercial interests of the North to his idealistic dream. A Congressional Joint Committee on Reconstruction was formed. Dominated by radicals, it became the center of Federal power.

President Johnson lost all influence over Reconstruction as representatives from Southern states were refused recognition and Congress passed the Joint Committee's measures over his veto. "An aristocracy based on nearly two billion and a half of national securities has risen in the Northern States to assume that political control which . . . formerly [belonged] to the slave oligarchy," President Johnson told newsmen in the summer of 1866.

The President was a skilled stump speaker. At the end of August he set out on a tour of Northern cities to take his fight to the people. He addressed more than a million Americans with little effect. The fall elections strengthened the radicals in Congress. "We are living in a revolutionary period," Secretary of the Navy Gideon Welles noted in his diary in January, 1867, "and the character of the government is undergoing a strain which may transform it into a different character."

The new Congress divided all the South except Tennessee into military districts and made approval of the 14th Amendment a condition for readmission to the Union. Elections held in the presence of Federal troops put Republican legislatures and governors into Southern state houses. With justice the South could ask why it was expected to permit its Negroes to vote when only three Northern states (two, Maine and Vermont, with very few Negroes) permitted their own Negroes to vote.

Meanwhile, large masses of ill-informed, easily influenced voters swarmed to the Southern polls. The Southern states came to resemble Northern cities where great numbers of similarly ill-informed immigrants voted as soon as they left the docks.

South Carolina, Louisiana, and Virginia had legislatures as corrupt as those in New York and Pennsylvania. The South Carolina state house was equipped with gold cuspidors at least as outrageously expensive as any in the new court house in New York's Municipal Park. But the new Southern legislatures, run by Northern adventurers, or carpetbaggers, and local Negroes and scalawags, did introduce public school systems. In the words of James Russell Lowell, the South was being "transplanted . . . into the nineteenth century."

"My brother Henry," wrote Harriet Beecher Stowe from her new Florida home, ". . . takes the ground that it is unwise and impolitic to endeavor to force Negro suffrage at the point of a bayonet." The author of *Uncle Tom's Cabin* agreed with her brother.

Nor was Thaddeus Stevens satisfied. The 14th Amendment, which reversed the Dred Scott decision and forbad states to limit the rights of citizens, had not gone far enough. He had dreamed since youth, he said, that when "any fortunate chance broke up for a while the foundations of our institutions," they could be recast so "as to have freed from them every vestige of human oppression . . .

"This bright dream has vanished . . . I find that we shall be obliged to be content with patching up the worst portions of the ancient edifice. . . ."

Noting the President's futile struggle against the radicals, General Sherman compared him to King Lear, "roaring at the wild storm, bareheaded and helpless." Johnson, he said, "attempts to govern after he has lost the means to govern."

The radicals had been seeking grounds to impeach the President since 1866. Democratic gains in the elections of 1867 pointed to a possible Democratic President and Congress in 1868. (A factor in Democratic victories in Ohio, Minnesota, and Kansas was opposition to Negro suffrage.)

Fearing defeat, the radicals impeached President Johnson in February, 1868. He was charged with violating the Tenure of Office Act. This radical act, which forbad the President to dismiss anyone appointed with Senatorial approval, without its approval, was clearly illegal. If Johnson were convicted, the radical Ben Wade, President *pro tem* of the Senate, would become President.

Johnson had disregarded the Tenure of Office Act by firing Secretary of War Stanton. After a three-months trial, the Senate came one vote short of the two-thirds vote needed to convict. Had the President been convicted, the Government of the United States would have been permanently twisted into its post-war shape. Congress would have remained supreme and the President would have become its minister, instead of an independent executive.

Three months later, old Stevens was dead and buried in a Negro cemetery in Lancaster. His epitaph:

"I repose in this quiet and secluded spot
not from any natural preference for solitude,
but finding other cemeteries
limited by charter as to race,
I have chosen this that I might illustrate in death
the principles which I advocated through a long life,
Equality of man before his Creator."

THE NEW SOUTH

Beneath all the strains of Reconstruction, life went on. People must eat and clothe themselves. There were fields to be planted, houses to be rebuilt, new factories and stores to put in operation. Old Confederate General Pendleton, in tattered shirt and patched pants, plowed his Virginia land himself, walking like a field hand behind a mule.

William Tison, a former South Carolina state legislator, spent the autumn of 1866 with his wife and eight children living in two rooms unprotected from the weather. Destitute, with no clothing but what they wore, they had only the corn wasting in the fields, and no meat but what they could shoot.

The big plantations were useless without slaves to work them, worse than useless where there were large taxes to pay and no way of raising crops. Some were abandoned. Land worth eighteen dollars an acre in 1860 was sold for three dollars an acre in 1865 to farmers who had once been pushed off to the poorer soil of the pine barrens. Plantations that weren't sold piecemeal were often broken up into sections and rented to former slaves. The plantation owner provided his tenants with tools and seed, and often directed them in their work. Hard-working and thrifty Negroes could sometimes save enough, after a few years of sharecropping, to buy farms of their own. At its best, this rental system served as a training station for the slave with no experience in managing for himself. At its worst, with the landowner taking as much as two-thirds of the crops and keeping his tenants in debt, sharecropping became a means of perpetuating a state uncomfortably close to slavery.

Immersed in hard everyday tasks, men tended to forget the ideals that had driven them apart. In the business world there are neither Democrats nor Repub-

Freedom meant wages and picking things out at the store.

licans, Northerners or Southerners — there are only buyers and sellers. As they had once supported movements toward appeasement of the South, Northern businessmen were anxious to heal the breach. They wanted cotton for their mills. They wanted customers for their cloth, manufactured shoes, clocks, furniture and high silk hats.

For their part, Southerners were waking up to the fact that while they had been preoccupied with slaves and plantations, other Americans had found other paths to wealth.

The Nashville Banner recalled that for fifty of the eighty-four years of national history the South had dominated the Federal Government:

"What have we to show for this power?" . . . the newspaper asked. "A few tumble-down buildings and a gigantic poverty . . . The village of Kickapoo, in Wisconsin, got an appropriation of two hundred thousand dollars five years after its original settlement." Of the $103 million spent on public works between 1865 and 1873, less than $10 million went to the South. The old foes of Government encouragement of industry were preparing to board the gravy train. Attitudes were changing.

Phosphate dug out of the ground near Charleston, S. C., increased cotton yield by as much as five times. The South began supplying itself with many things after the war. Birmingham, Alabama, developed into the second biggest iron-producing region in the country, and Southern mills wove a great deal more Southern cotton than ever before. Cigarette manufacture, that would become a major industry, began modestly in North Carolina in the middle 1870's.

"If the Old South had a contempt for the worker," stated one Southern educator, "the New South has a greater contempt for the . . . idler."

All through the region men were seeking ways to recover their fortunes.

THE NEW WEST

From the edges of the eastern timber to the high Sierras that shield the green valleys of California and Oregon, the Great Plains comprise about half of the area of the continental United States. The plains are high, seldom less than 500 feet above sea level, and devoid of trees, except for some scattered "islands" of forest.

The "prairie plains," a narrow strip west of the timber's edge, comprise the most fertile large area of land in the world. But as one proceeds westward, there is less rainfall. West of the ninety-eighth meridian the rainfall is insufficient for normal agriculture. There are hundreds of thousands of square miles of grasslands. Further west are the sands of the true desert where the cactus grows.

The region west of the ninety-eighth parallel typifies the new America that emerged from the war. The war had destroyed old restraints and set the nation, and individual men, on a new course. The plains destroyed old customs and made men over.

At first, the plains had repelled men accustomed to the forest. The great open spaces had been bewildering, if not frightening. Without trees, with only unbroken mile after mile of gently rolling plain, with great vistas across which a storm could be seen coming for half a day and where the shadows of a cloud would darken the color of a row of hills, men felt small and alone.

The plains appear strange and empty to the traveler on foot. But place him on

Since the 1840's, buffalo had been shot by the hundred thousands each year, many just for the meat their tongues provided. One hundred-thousand skins were shipped through St. Louis in 1848. When railroads penetrated the plains, the slaughter increased. Of the perhaps 60,000,000 bison that existed at the beginning of the century, less than a thousand remained in 1895.

a horse, and a change begins. The great high grassy plains were the natural home of the horse and of cattle.

So emerged the Western cowboy, rider over a range a thousand miles long. As the plains resembled the sea, the man on a horse resembled the ship at sea, a law unto himself, neither protected nor restrained by the bonds of society — individual in an age of individuals.

Abilene, Kansas, in 1867 was a small, unlively place consisting of about one dozen log huts. But in that year J. G. McCoy, an enterprising Chicago businessman, built some stockpens in Abilene. He knew that the north-south cattle trail came close to the east-west railroad line at Abilene. 35,000 cattle were brought into Abilene in 1867. Four years later, the number was 700,000. As the railroads brought range-fattened steer to the cities of the East, men made fabulous profits. A $5 steer was worth $45 in four years of eating free grass. In 1883, twenty cattle corporations, backed by $12 million Eastern dollars, were formed in Wyoming alone.

VIOLENCE

On the plains, the absence of restraints was physical. There were no neighbors to witness a robbery of cattle, no police with jurisdiction. In the rest of the nation it was a state of mind. On dusty plain or in plush city office, Americans pursued their own ends until stopped by force. It was an era of violence.

The owners of railroads charged as much for freight as they could get. Acting through newly formed Granger Clubs, farmers took over state legislatures and passed laws regulating railroad rates. When the railroads disobeyed these laws, the farmers boarded trains and, at gunpoint, forced trainmen to transport their produce.

Congress sought to reform the South with guns. The South's answer was the secret night-riding Ku Klux Klan. Hooded ex-Confederate officers terrorized those Negroes and whites who cooperated with the forces of Reconstruction.

Business methods were ruthless and unrestrained. Competing railroads secretly returned to some valued customers a portion of what they paid for freight. Such secret rebates, in turn, became a means by which certain companies obtained an advantage over competitors. John D. Rockefeller, a young Ohio oil refiner, was able to sell oil cheaper than his rivals because of rebates he received from the Pennsylvania Railroad.

Corruption itself knew no bounds. The Congress gave thousands of square miles of western land to a trans-continental railroad company, and Congressmen, Cabinet members, and even the Vice President of the United States accepted stock in the company that built the railroad.

Congress had authorized an income tax during the war, in 1862. It was discontinued in 1872. Mark Twain told how a tax agent showed him how to dodge his income tax payments, how he swore to lies and frauds "until my soul was coated inches and inches thick with perjury and my self-respect gone forever and ever."

But what of it? "It is nothing more than thousands of the richest and proudest and most respected, honored and courted men in America do every year."

THE ECONOMIC EXPLOSION

In a frenzy of energy the ruthless, hard-driving Civil War generation built up America in the years following 1865.

Between the huge land grants to railroads and the Homestead Act, settlement proceeded at a prodigious rate. At least a million acres of prairie succumbed to the plow each year after the war. Five million acres of green prairie disappeared in 1871, fenced off by barbed wire, a new invention that kept cattle off farmland at a low cost. During the final burst of settlement, America had more people living under pioneer conditions than ever before.

From 1860 to 1880, the number of miles of railroad track in the United States more than tripled, and the entire continent was spanned. The America that produced \$860 million worth of manufactures in 1859, was producing at

Jay Gould and his partner Jim Fisk purposely caused bank panics by removing big deposits.

In 1865, a record 41,000,000 acres of land was given to railroads.

the rate of $1,080,000,000 in 1869 and near double that in 1879. New mineral lodes were located, new machines and methods were developed, factories and mills increased production to meet the needs of an expanding, hard-working, closer-knit population.

That the railroads and telegraph were knitting an entire continent into one large market and trading area, bringing Georgia within range of Ohio furniture factories, Montana wool into New Hampshire mills, and bringing Chicago investors into Wall Street, was the principal cause of the economic explosion.

What canals and turnpikes had once done for states, what rivers did for valleys, the railroad was doing for a continent.

THE FOURTH CONVULSION

While the railroads and the pressures of business were drawing the nation together, the hatreds and idealism of the Civil War were keeping people apart.

In 1876, the Civil War was eleven years in the past. But was the United States at peace or still suppressing rebellion? As long as Federal troops occupied portions of the country, lending some states the appearance of conquered provinces, one could not be certain.

If the troops were removed, would the South accept the results of a national election, or would it again seek to withdraw from the Union? And would the North, for that matter, which had been using the power of the Federal Government to enforce its wishes, ever peacefully give up that power? Would the Republican Party, the instrument of Northern supremacy, yield the Government, and the Army, to another party?

In none of its first three victories had the Republican Party won a majority of the votes of the whole country. Lincoln's 1860 election had resulted from a split in the Democratic Party, and in 1864, the Southern states had been in rebellion. In 1868, with only six of the eleven states of the former Confederacy voting, the Democratic candidate, Seymour, had received only five per cent less votes than General Grant. The General won a more substantial victory in 1872, but the Democratic parties in the Southern states continued to make gains. With each election, more Southern Democratic Senators and Representatives appeared in Washington. Democratic governors were winning elections; Negro voters were being wooed away from the Republicans, or frightened from voting, with a diminishing of the strengths of the carpetbag legislatures.

When the 1876 election returns were in, it appeared that a coalition of Democrats and reform Republicans had elected Samuel Tilden of New York President of the United States. The election was, however, extremely close, and the Republicans, through their control of Florida, Louisiana, and South Carolina, were able to cast enough doubt on the verdict to force the Democrats to bargain with them.

On the one hand, with their armies

In 1876, the Republican South Carolina legislature was fighting for its life against a rival Democratic legisature. When Reconstruction ended, Southern Negroes lost political power.

occupying three states, the Republicans felt they could control enough Southern votes to guarantee the election. On the other hand, Democrats in all parts of the country were threatening violent action to obtain what they were certain they had won at the polls. If fanatics of both parties were ready to begin another Civil War, there were many on both sides who sought a return to normal conditions. Many Northern Republicans felt that business opportunities in the South were hampered by the continued military occupation. Many Southern Democrats were hungry for the Federal financial assistance that Republican Congresses had been denying them. They wanted a Southern trans-continental railroad and a national program of flood control over the waters of the Mississippi.

The Compromise of 1877 was the last of the big sectional bargains. The Democrats agreed to the election of the Republican Rutherford B. Hayes. The Republicans agreed to withdraw the armies of occupation and to support Government aid to the South.

In effect, the North had given up its radical ideals in return for southern allegiance. If the South had won a victory in that it would manage its "domestic" affairs without outside interference, slavery, at least, had been done away with. If now the Negro would lose many of the rights granted him by the Thirteenth, Fourteenth, and Fifteenth Amendments, he was at least free to undertake the long hard road of self-improvement.

Some Negroes had fled the renewed oppression. 25,000 had migrated to Kansas. For those who remained, the educator Booker T. Washington predicted a different kind of exodus "from ignorance, vice, and lack of thrift."

THE NEW NATION

WITH peace between the sections at last restored and immigrants arriving in unheard of numbers, the nation could concentrate its energies on other things. The Republicans were still inclined, every four years, to dust off the passions of the Civil War and wave the "Bloody Shirt." Yet steadily, the bitterness of the past receded into the background. The Republican Garfield captured the White House in 1880 without resort to armed force, and, with Grover Cleveland, the Democratic Party returned to power in 1884.

Probably 2 million of the 10 million men who voted in the election of 1884 had arrived in the United States after the Civil War, and of the natives who voted, there were many who had not even been born when Fort Sumter was fired upon. A new generation was growing up to whom the Civil War was nothing but history and a line of middle-aged men carrying flags on Memorial Day.

Partly, the country was willing to accept a peaceful transition of power from party to party, because politics no longer occupied the center of the stage. Business was the main concern — the building up and development of national markets. To do this required "administrative rulers, generals, diplomatists . . . of the finest gifts." It was not surprising that the business world attracted the most able men. Boys whose fathers had dreamed of becoming President of the United States, dreamed of becoming presidents of railroads. Charles Francis Adams, son of the wartime minister to Great Britain, grandson and great-grandson of Presidents, became President of the Union Pacific Railroad. Convicted murderers, gamblers, liquor wholesalers, and ex-prizefighters took over political machines.

With its able men, vast resources, and driving energy, the business interest was easily able to dominate the Government in Washington. The Republican Party had brought a return to Federalism, vaster in scale than anything that Washington or Hamilton had dreamed of. It was Henry Clay's American system multiplied by a thousand. From 1865 to 1871, Republican Congresses had given 68 million acres of public land to railroad builders. Protection of industry by high tariffs; protection of bankers by deflation that increased the value of money, favoring creditors over debtors; the sanctification of the rights of corporations — these were the policies of the Government.

CENTENNIAL

1876 was a big year in the history of the Republic. A full century had passed since the Declaration of Independence. The new peace between North and South seemed fulfilled when, on July 4, 1876, Richard Henry Lee of Virginia came to Philadelphia to read aloud the words of Jefferson's stirring document.

Thirty-seven other nations exhibited at the 1876 world's fair. Americans and foreigners alike were astonished at the changes taking place in the young country. The German visitor Friedrich Goldschmidt noted, "the constant effort to remove purely mechanical work from the human hand and to apply it only where artistic shapes and forms are required. . . . Think of our nailsmiths! How soul destroying . . . is the work, and how little, perhaps 100 nails a day, can be manufactured by one worker. In America there are no more nailsmiths; the nail there is manufactured by the machine . . .

"The tour through the main building . . . has shown us that in many other branches American industry is also superior to ours. In a short time it has risen to a height of which those in Europe had no idea . . ."

On his tour through the exhibition, Goldschmidt may have noticed a curious wooden box. Alexander Graham Bell brought his telephone to Philadelphia and went into business the following year. It took a while for people to get used to the new gadget. "The dignity of talking consists in having a listener," said Popular Science Monthly, "and there seems a kind of absurdity in addressing a piece of iron." Twenty-three years later, more than a million telephones were in use in the United States.

Some ten million people thronged through the fair grounds in Philadelphia. While they contemplated marvels of refinement and civilization, General George Armstrong Custer and 200 cavalrymen were being massacred by Sioux Indians in the Dakota Territory two thousand miles to the west.

NATIONAL MARKETS

Men thought in terms of thousands of miles where formerly they had thought in terms of hundreds. They spent millions where they had spent thousands. They shipped carloads of produce, shoes or hardware where formerly they had shipped crates. With such a vast virgin field of operations, new inventions and new adaptations of old inventions could be turned into wealth with unprecedented speed. The refrigerator railroad car, for instance, was nothing but a railroad car with frames to hold ice. Yet the shrewd men who realized that cooling would enable them to cut freight costs by shipping only the saleable parts of the steer, founded great fortunes. Two cars of cold beef were worth as much as three cars of live steers on the hoof. Freight costs per pound of meat were slashed, and Chicago beef sold in New York and Boston for less than the meat of local slaughterers.

The result, inevitably, was the replacement of local slaughterers by Swift and Armour and their refrigerator cars. Thus another result of the new national markets emerges — concentration of processing or manufacturing as big, efficient operations make use of new developments to undersell smaller, local concerns. As the packing house replaced the local slaughterer, the furniture factory replaced the cabinet maker and the clothing manufacturer, the tailor.

CONCENTRATION

Not only was more business being done than ever before, and at a faster rate due to swift communications, but a handful of giant corporations seemed to be gradually taking over in all the various fields of business.

The atmosphere of the country was particularly favorable to the formation of giant combinations, or trusts. The states, their authority weakened by the Civil War, could exact little control over the great corporations that appeared in their midst. The Fifth Amendment had prohibited the Federal Government from depriving persons of property without due process of law. The Fourteenth Amendment applied the prohibition to states. In 1886, the Supreme Court would affirm that corporations were among the persons protected from the states. The states, however, were not protected from big corporations. Corporations spent great sums of money on bribing state legislators.

The result was the creation of trusts in many different industries. Instead of cutthroat competition, price wars and struggles over markets, there was cooperation, the designation of fixed territories in the national market, and fixed prices.

There were advantages and disadvantages to this development. On the one hand, such concentrations of wealth and power could be dangerous to the nation. It was pointed out that the sugar trust, for instance, could "close every refinery at will, . . . artificially limit the production of refined sugar, enhance the price to enrich themselves . . . at the public expense, and depress the price when necessary to crush out a foolhardy rival."

On the other hand, a well-managed trust could effect certain economies and create conditions for orderly growth. The public was not always victimized. The Michigan Salt Association, for instance, actually brought down the price of salt by preventing dealers from hoarding.

THE PROMOTERS

Andrew Carnegie came from Scotland in 1848. He went to work as a bobbin boy in a cotton mill, at a salary of $1.20 a week. The following year, at fourteen, he became a Western Union messenger, at a salary of $2.50 a week. At that time, telegraph messages were recorded on tape. With his alert mind, young Carnegie soon became one of two or three Americans capable of receiving Morse code by the sound of the clicks. He became an operator at $4.00 a week. In 1853, one of his customers, Tom Scott of the Pennsylvania Railroad, hired Andrew as his private secretary and telegraph operator. In 1865, he succeeded Scott as superintendent of the western division of the Pennsylvania Railroad. He had had ample opportunity to learn the business possibilities of the region between the Alleghenies and Chicago, that was to become the heartland of American industry. He also had been in a position to do favors, for which he would be amply repaid. On top of a salary of $2,400, he was soon earning almost $50,000 a year from his interests in an oil company, an iron foundry, and an express company.

In 1872, he saw a Bessemer converter in full blast. His railroad career had taught him all the disadvantages of iron rails that had to be constantly replaced, of iron bridges that buckled under strain or rusted into disuse. Foreseeing a tremendous market for a steel competitive in price with iron, he immediately set about going in the steel business.

Up to this time, iron and steel had been businesses of foundrymen — craftsmen who understood the arts and vagaries of their metals. Carnegie based his steel business on his knowledge of markets—on the uses of steel rather than on knowing how to make it. The Edgar Thomson Steel Works, which he built outside Pittsburgh on the banks of the Monongahela River, made a forty-two per cent profit in 1877. In 1880, Carnegie's steel plants netted him $1,625,000.

"The old nations of the earth creep on at a snail's pace," he said, "the Republic thunders past with the rush of the express."

A number of men began producing steel in the United States by the new cheap methods developed by the Englishman Bessemer and the American Kelly. In 1870, 30,500 tons of Bessemer steel rails were made in the United States. Ten years later, production was thirty times that; and in 1890, the figure was staggering. In that time iron as a material for railroad tracks almost disappeared. Steel replaced all other substances for bridges, had begun to revolutionize architecture, and had become the basic industry of the United States.

Steel cable made the Brooklyn Bridge possible. The four great supporting cables were spun out of over thirteen thousand separate wires. The 1595-foot center span was by far the longest in the world in 1883 when the bridge was completed.

Carnegie demonstrated that more money was to be made in turning out huge quantities of steel at a low profit per unit than in manufacturing less steel at a higher profit per unit. He seized on new methods and new ideas as opportunities for profit, rather than as threats to his business.

General George A. Custer

The oil industry, like steel, also came to be controlled by a few giant corporations. In 1863, a young Cleveland produce merchant named John Davison Rockefeller had opened an oil refinery in what was then the center of the petroleum industry. Seven years later he and his partners established the Standard Oil Company of Ohio. With tenacious attention to detail and ruthless efficiency, the Rockefeller group quickly extended its control over many competitors.

By 1878, Standard Oil of Ohio was

turning out more than ninety per cent of the oil of the United States. Soon after, the separate oil companies that Rockefeller and his associates controlled were combined into a new kind of super-company called a "trust." While seeming to operate as before, as separate corporations, they had really surrendered control to a group of nine trustees. As a committee of the House of Representatives reported, "This form of combination was obviously devised for the purpose of relieving the trusts and trustees from the charge of any breach of the conspiracy laws of the various States . . ."

In 1892, an Ohio Court ruled against the trust, saying, "A society in which a few men are the employers and a great body are merely employees or servants is not the most desirable in a republic; and it should be as much the policy of the laws to multiply the numbers engaged in independent pursuits, or in the profits of production, as to cheapen the price to the consumer."

But the courts insisted that corporations were persons, and the Constitution provided, "The citizen of each State shall be entitled to all Privileges and Immunities of Citizens in the several States." All the states, therefore, had to accept what any other state would permit its corporations to do. In 1889, New Jersey passed a special law permitting holding companies. A holding company holds stock in other companies. By controlling other companies through stock ownership, it becomes a trust. New Jersey made a great deal of extra revenue. After the adverse ruling in 1892, the Standard Oil Company of Ohio became

Oil in Pennsylvania was near the surface. Indians discovered it, floating on pools of water. At first, it was sold as medicine. "Seneca oil" was supposed to cure everything from stomach-ache to rheumatism. The high price of New Bedford whale oil sent men looking for cheap substitutes. Kerosene, distilled from coal, came into use about 1855, but it had an unpleasant odor. Meanwhile, another kind of kerosene, distilled from "Seneca oil" was found to be better. Shortly before the Civil War, a railroad conductor named Edwin Drake worked out a way of sinking and joining iron pipe in the ground so that wells could be drilled through sand and water to where the oil was. On August 28, 1859, his crew struck oil at a depth of 70 feet. The boom was on, and lamps like this (left) became popular. Plentiful supplies of cheap kerosene blighted the whaling industry, and whaling men came to Pennsylvania from New Bedford, exchanging harpoons for drilling rigs and charges of nitroglycerine. The explosive, lowered in the well, increased the flow of oil by crushing the rock in which the oil was trapped. What was left of the crude oil, after kerosene was distilled off, was sold as a lubricant. As the ad at the right shows, the manufacturers of other lubricants (from animal and vegetable greases) were worried about the new competition.

TAKE ONE.

Offices of Frazer Lubricator Co.,
No. 73 MURRAY ST., NEW YORK.
31 Superior Street, CHICAGO,

TRADE MARK.

FARMERS AND TRUCKMEN

who use Axle Grease are not aware of the vast amount of injury to their wagons and trucks caused by the use of Grease made from Petroleum or Paraffine Oils. It is generally known that Benzine or Kerosene Oil will, in a few minutes, penetrate and loosen a nut on a rusty bolt, thus showing its powerful effect on iron. The same injurious effect is produced on wood, the spokes in the hub becoming loose and the strength of the wood greatly impaired. But this is not all. There is used in refining and whitening an acid which is still more destructive, and which inevitably eats into and destroys the iron of the axles and boxes. This destruction, though slow on solid iron, is certain, and from these two causes combined, the destruction of wagons, trucks and threshing machines throughout the United States is immense. These Petroleum Greases, whether yellow, black or light colored, are all of the same general character.

the Standard Oil Company of New Jersey. It operated exactly as before, only now it was safe from Ohio law. Against the corporation, the individual state was powerless.

Rockefeller compared his giant organization to the American Beauty rose, which "can be produced in its splendor and fragrance only by sacrificing the early buds which grow up around it."

A NEW FORM OF TYRANNY

While industry expanded and trade accelerated and boomed, many people were gradually becoming aware that all was not well in their world.

Children provided a substantial portion of labor. This was bad for the children, and kept wages down. In 1890, it is estimated, about 750,000 boys and girls under the age of sixteen worked up to 12 hours a day in the breaker rooms of coal mines, tending bobbins in cotton mills, in glass factories and foundries, and as Western Union messengers. Another million or so picked berries or cotton, and did other farm work. Only one state, Connecticut, had a law making school attendance compulsory. Most children between the ages of 8 and 14 went to school for only three months a year.

In the cities, a new kind of building made it possible to crowd more people into a small space than ever before. The five- or six-story double tenement consisted of perhaps eighty small, mostly unventilated rooms opening onto narrow, evil-smelling hallways. From 1879 to 1888, the number of slum dwellers in New York City alone rose from half a million to a million. These slum dwellers, many of them immigrants who could hardly speak English, found themselves in a new kind of American frontier. As earlier immigrants had sacrificed to gain farms of their own, these newer Americans struggled and scraped to break out of the tenements to the more pleasant parts of the city.

James Bryce, a distinguished English visitor, noticed, "The power of groups of men organized by incorporation . . . or of small knots of rich men acting in combination, has developed with unexpected strength in unexpected ways, overshadowing individuals and even communities, and showing that the very freedom of association which men sought to secure by law when they were threatened with the violence of potentates may, under the shelter of the law, ripen into a new form of tyranny."

With the interests of their stockholders paramount, and with an unshakable conviction of their absolute rights to manage their railroads and factories exactly as they pleased, the new captains of industry sought to maintain their profits before all else. During the hard times following the crash of 1873, for instance, William H. Vanderbilt cut wages on the New York Central Line while maintaining his dividends at eight per cent. He could have saved more money by lowering the dividend rate to six per cent than by cutting the salaries of brakemen who were already hard-pressed to feed families on forty-one dollars a month.

But that a cut in wages hurt a brakeman's family far more than a two per cent cut in dividends would hurt a shareholder, would have simply seemed to Vanderbilt as beside the point. Businesses were run for profits, not to feed the families of switchmen and conductors.

A NEW FORM OF REVOLT

As businesses outgrew state boundaries, the organizations of the laborers they employed became nationwide. During the depression years following 1873, the Brotherhood of Locomotive Engineers organized two successful strikes that forced the New Jersey Central and Grand Trunk (between Detroit and Montreal) Railroad Lines, to reinstate workers and restore cuts in pay. By 1877, the union had more than 50,000 members—conductors and trackmen, as well as engineers. In July of that year, a ten per cent wage cut on all lines east of the Mississippi resulted in a strike that paralyzed every railroad east of the Mississippi and north of the Potomac. The number of railroad men who prevented freight trains from leaving terminals, or walked out on their jobs, was far greater than the membership of the Brotherhood, and the strike even spread to two lines west of the Mississippi where wage cuts had not yet been made.

With no savings to fall back on, the strikers feared starvation if they did not win quickly. Desperation led to violence. Nine persons were killed during rioting in Baltimore. In Pittsburgh, a pitched battle took place between an armed mob and soldiers who came to the assistance of local police. Following the retreat of the United States Army across the Allegheny River, law and order vanished in Pittsburgh. Stores were sacked, and at the Union Depot of the Pennsylvania Railroad, locomotives and freight cars were set on fire and destroyed before a larger contingent of the United States Army was able to force its way into the city. In Chicago, St. Louis, Buffalo, San Francisco, Toledo, and in many smaller

The Erie strike at Susquehanna, Pennsylvania. Strikers stop an express train.

cities and towns there was rioting and bloodshed.

The general public was horrified. Their peaceful country had suddenly been revealed to them as torn between powerful contending forces. If many feared a return of mob violence, they were also, for the first time, aware of how many of their countrymen were desperately underpaid or out of work.

Meanwhile a new nationwide labor movement gained many followers. Quoting Edmund Burke: "When bad men combine, the good must associate, else they will fall, one by one, an unpitied sacrifice in a contemptible struggle," the Knights of Labor asserted that ". . . individual and moral worth, not wealth, [are] the true standard of individual and national greatness," and demanded an eight-hour day, the creation of bureaus of labor statistics, the abolition of laws favoring capital over labor, the prohibition of child labor, equal pay for women and men for equal work, and a graduated tax on incomes and inheritances. They also had their own form of protectionism. They wanted immigration

Many children under 16 worked in the breaker rooms of coal mines, in cotton mills, glass factories, and foundries, and on farms. In 1890, only one state, Connecticut, had a law making school attendance compulsory.

limited so they would not have to compete with lower-paid immigrant workers.

With Grand Master Workman Terence V. Powderly traveling all over the country, membership by 1885 had reached 104,000. The Knights also sought to establish cooperative institutions for the benefit of members. By 1886, they had organized over a hundred such ventures, among them a coal mine that sold coal to members at a reduced price. As groups of members opened shoe factories, printing plants, and plumbing shops, it was found that instead of making "every man his own master," the cooperatives were tending to make some men into masters, who acted very much like other masters in the same businesses. In other words, the pressures of the business world, the need for holding down prices to meet competition, were what divided laborers from bosses and not any natural difference between "good men" and "bad men."

A financial panic in 1884 resulted in a new wave of unemployment, and by 1887, the ranks of the Knights of Labor were swollen by 600,000 members. At first the huge membership, comprising, with families, about five per cent of the total population, was able effectively and with public sympathy to employ such peaceful procedures as buyers' strikes against difficult employers. A boycott of all jewelry stores that handled watches using Dueber Watch Case Company cases, for instance, forced that company to rehire employees it had fired because of membership in the Knights of Labor.

But the organization had grown too fast. It could not coordinate the activities of its members nor was it any better prepared than the Brotherhoods to sustain a long strike. It quickly declined after the failure of a strike against the Texas and Pacific Railroad.

COLLECTIVE BARGAINING

Where the Knights of Labor failed, another, more modest labor organization was having better success. The Knights had sought to recruit all working men in all industries into one big union. The American Federation of Labor, as the other organization came to be called, kept the men of different skills apart, even in the same industry. Under the leadership of Samuel Gompers of the cigar-makers union, several of these unions of skilled workmen had begun acting cooperatively through the Federation of Organized Trades and Labor Unions of the United States of America and Canada. Gompers had become convinced that labor ought to aim for a steady, long-term, orderly improvement. He saw that although wages were often much too low and working conditions bad, the thing to aim for was not simply to raise wages or to force bosses to rehire men, but to change the relationship between the boss and his employees so that wages could not be cut nor men arbitrarily dismissed in the first place. Where the Knights of Labor aimed to reconstruct society, the American Federation of Labor came to regard as its goal the trade agreement, in which the employer accepted the policy of negotiating wages and conditions of work with the union (collective bargaining).

THE POOR FARMER

Like the workingman, the farmer felt left out of the country's material advance. While industrial profits climbed, farm profits fell. The measure of control over railroad fares that his Granger societies had won did not seem to markedly improve his position. He borrowed money for seed and equipment. If he had a good crop, it seemed he could not buy quite as much with his profits as he had expected. If he had a bad crop, he was in trouble with the bank. This large economic problem often simply magnified a personal problem — insufficient capital. Free or cheap land (paid for by annual installments) attracted ambitious young farmers who possessed neither sufficient implements nor animals to make the land yield a living. (Others made the mistake of settling land on the Western plains that was little better than a desert, that would never support a family without irrigation.)

The conflict between Western settler and Eastern financier, over money values, was as old as America. The farmers of western Massachusetts had fought to

To match the organized power of railroads and manufacturers, Grangers pooled their purchasing power, bought grain elevators, and even operated farm machinery factories. They also sought to free themselves from bankers by buying only for cash. This proved a boon to the new mail order houses.

pay debts in paper money. Now farmers in Kansas agitated for the printing of paper money, or greenbacks. The Greenback movement was the historic struggle between debtor and creditor, between those who want cheap money, and those who like expensive money. But now it was national in scope.

In the election of 1878, an alliance of farmers and workingmen gained more than a million votes for their Greenback-Labor Party and sent fourteen Representatives to Congress.

With the breaking up of many large plantations and diversification of agriculture, the South had increasingly come to resemble the West. Southerners joined Westerners in the Greenback movement. From both sections there also came complaints over the high tariff policy of the Republicans. This again, was nothing but the renewal of an historic grievance. It was John Randolph all over again, the complaint of the agrarian who pays for protection but gets nothing for it.

If the South was beginning to sound like the West, the West was beginning to talk the language of John Taylor of Caroline. The Ohioan S. S. Cox jokingly recommended that Congress tax sunshine as a competitor of Pennsylvania coal. A national agricultural interest was becoming as real as a national business interest, as a national labor interest.

THE NEGRO UNDERGROUND

Kept out of labor unions, hated even by the downtrodden and rebellious poor whites of the South, mostly deprived of the vote, the Negro existed almost outside the history of the time. Everything seemed against him. Three amendments had been passed to insure his rights as an American citizen, but the courts almost consistently recognized all sorts of limits on their application. Dissenting from a Supreme Court decision in favor of segregation, Justice John M. Harlan noted that "Our Constitution is color-blind, and neither knows nor tolerates classes among citizens." Discriminatory laws were defended as resulting from Negro inferiority. But in 1880 the Court pointed out how such discrimination is itself a cause of inferiority: "The very fact that colored people are singled out and expressly denied by a statute all right to participate in the administration of the law, as jurors . . . is practically a brand upon them, affixed by law; an assertion of their inferiority, and a stimulant to . . . race prejudice . . ."

When Southern leaders met in Atlanta in 1895 to discuss the special problems of their region, the Negro educator Booker T. Washington said, "To those of the white race who look to the incoming of those of foreign birth . . . for the prosperity of the South . . . I would repeat what I say to my own race, 'Cast down your bucket where you are.' Cast it down among the 8 million Negroes whose habits you know. . . .

"No race that has anything to contribute to the markets of the world is long . . . ostracized. . . . The opportunity to earn a dollar in a factory just now is worth infinitely more than the opportunity to spend a dollar in an opera house."

To some Negroes this sounded like a weak-kneed acceptance of Jim Crow discrimination, but Washington knew that economic opportunity was the necessary first step to other opportunities. And if Southern whites applauded the educator's seeming docility, they overlooked two words in his statement. Washington had agreed to exclusion from the opera house "just now." He hadn't said Negroes would always be content with second-class citizenship.

THE POPULAR PRESS

While employed on a German-language paper in St. Louis, the immigrant Joseph Pulitzer discerned that public schools were producing millions of literate persons who were not newspaper readers.

In 1878, Pulitzer purchased The St. Louis Post-Dispatch and set to work to change it into something that would appeal to the working people of the city.

Sentences were shortened, headlines made larger, and more space devoted to murders, fires, and other sensations. Circulation soared as the newspaper became easier to read and harder to resist.

In 1883, Pulitzer was ready to apply what he had learned to the biggest newspaper market in the country. He bought The New York World from Jay Gould, dedicating it to the "cause of people rather than that of purse-potentates, . . ." The paper advocated popular measures like income, luxury, and inheritance taxes, tariff and civil service reform. It featured death and blood and with picture cartoons, comic strips and Sunday features, circulation rocketed from 15,000 to 1 million.

Yet at the same time the aspirations of the people were gaining a new voice, the press was becoming increasingly beholden to business. At the beginning of Pulitzer's career, the major part of a newspaper's revenue came from circulation. By 1890, the main source of revenue was advertising. Harper's Magazine had once refused to sell its back page to a sewing machine company. Its October, 1888 issue contained fifty-four pages

In 1884, Democrat Grover Cleveland became President. His Republican opponent, James G. Blaine, had an interest in a railroad that received Government help. Years of power left Republicans open to charges of corruption.

of ads. The October, 1898 issue had eighty-three pages of ads.

Indeed, advertising was becoming a major force in the land, not only in newspapers of large circulation and in national magazines, but painted on the sides of buildings and almost anything else that was handy. Of a soap company campaign, Bret Harte wrote in 1876:

"One Sabbath morn, as heavenward
White Mountain tourists slowly
spurred,
On every rock, to their dismay,
They read the legend all the way —
SAPOLIO."

Anti-saloon "besieging wagon" shows that the reform impulse was not dead. On another front, President Hayes began Civil Service exams.

Bret Harte, who wrote short stories and novels, and advertisements only in fun, was able to keep himself in comfort by obtaining Government jobs. From 1878 to 1885, he was U.S. consul in Germany and in Scotland. Herman Melville, the author of *Moby Dick,* supported his family on the slim salary of a customs house clerk. Most poets, painters, and composers could only keep from starving by spending most of their time at other occupations.

Yet many a city-dwelling American yearned for something beyond utility to fill his increasing leisure time. Teams of traveling lecturers set up "Chautauqua" camps in many communities, and offered lectures by many of the leading thinkers and writers of the time. Rudyard Kipling, recalling four days as a Chautauqua lecturer in 1889, wrote that ". . . the curse of America (is) sheer hopeless, well-ordered boredom . . . The other races are still shuffling for their three meals a day. America's got 'em and now she doesn't know what she wants but is dimly realizing that extension lectures, hardwood floors, natural gas and trolley-cars don't fill the bill. . . ."

THE TARIFF AND THE LOBBYISTS

The direction the nation was tending to move was made crystal clear to the dispossessed farmer and laborer in the agitation that took place over the high tariff.

If the tariff provided the Government with needed revenues, then its defenders could claim that it benefited all Americans by relieving them of other forms of taxation. But the Government had more money than it needed.

Neither President Arthur nor President Cleveland was able to bring about a reduction in the tariff. Cleveland devoted his entire message to Congress in December, 1887, to the need of reducing the tariff, and the only result was that he lost the Presidential election the following year to Benjamin Harrison. Two years later Congress passed the highest tariff ever.

The new tariff was named after the new Chairman of the House Ways and Means Committee. William McKinley, an Ohio Congressman believed the high tariff was the foundation of American prosperity. The McKinley Bill dropped all pretense of tariffs being needed for revenue by giving the President the power to adjust tariffs downward as a means of inducing other countries to lower their tariffs against American goods. As an example of how the tariff was used to favor certain American industries, the McKinley Bill put inedible raw sugar on the free list and placed a prohibitive duty on edible raw sugar. Thus, the kind of raw sugar that the consumer could have put in his coffee was made hopelessly high in price while the raw sugar that was needed by the refiner, and which was useless to the consumer, was kept low in price. The president of the sugar trust admitted that the McKinley Bill enabled his trust to make a profit of $25 million in three years.

The various trusts and manufacturers dependent on high tariffs very skillfully defended their interests in Washington. They sent numbers of high-priced lawyers to testify before committees of Congress and employed other gentlemen to persuade the lawmakers by other means. During Arthur's Administration, these industrial pleaders became established in the District of Columbia as permanent ambassadors of the various trusts. Lobbying, as this kind of special pleading was called, had become big business in Washington.

In between testifying before committees, the lobbyists sent Congressmen reports on the benefits the nation derived from protecting particular industries. They entertained lavishly and sought in other ways to befriend Senators and Representatives.

"I do not feel there is anything in my connection with the Senate to interfere with my buying or selling (sugar) stock when I please . . ." said Senator Matthew S. Quay of Pennsylvania. The Senate, the members of which were elected by state legislatures (themselves subject to corporation pressures) seemed particularly influenced. So successful were the lobbyists that after Cleveland's re-election in 1892 on an anti-protection platform, and after the financial disasters of 1893, the Wilson-Gorman Act of 1894 provided duties almost as high as the McKinley Bill. "Is this to be a government by a self-taxing people or a government of taxation by trust and monopolies?" asked Congressman W. L. Wilson, of West Virginia (whose tariff cuts had all been raised by a Senate Committee).

The Australian secret ballot would, it was hoped, make voters more independent.

THE PEOPLE'S PARTY

To arouse people to battle for their interests, the Farmers' Alliance Lecture Bureau sent speakers through the agrarian states of the South and West. The most popular of these fiery speakers, a thirty-six-year-old lady lawyer named Mrs. Mary E. Lease, made 160 speeches in 1890:

"What you farmers need to do is raise less corn and more HELL," she would say. "We wiped out slavery and by our tariff laws and national banks began a system of white wage slavery worse than the first . . ."

Despairing of relief from either of the two major parties, members of the Farmers' Alliance, Grangers, Greenbackers, and Knights of Labor joined forces in Nebraska in 1890, and captured a majority of the State Senate and half the lower house. Similar groups met with success in Kansas, Minnesota, and South Dakota. Farmers' Alliances captured the Democratic Party organization in the four Southern states of Florida, Georgia, North and South Carolina. Eight Farmers' Alliance men went to Washington in 1890, seven to the House and one as U. S. Senator from Kansas.

In 1891, 1,400 delegates assembled in Cincinnati to found the People's Party.

To vote for a Person, mark a Cross X in the Square at the right of the name.

GOVERNOR, ...	Vote for ONE.	
JOHN BLACKMER—of Springfield	Prohibition	
JOHN Q. A. BRACKETT—of Arlington	Republican	X
WILLIAM E. RUSSELL—of Cambridge	Democratic	

LIEUTENANT-GOVERNOR, ...	Vote for ONE.	
JOHN W. CORCORAN—of Clinton	Democratic	
WILLIAM H. HAILE—of Springfield	Republican	X
BENJAMIN F. STURTEVANT—of Boston	Prohibition	

In 1892, the party nominated the old Greenbacker James B. Weaver for President. The party proclaimed that:

"The fruits of the toil of millions are boldly stolen to build up colossal fortunes for a few, unprecedented in the history of mankind; and the possessors of these, in turn, despise the Republic and endanger liberty. From the same prolific womb of governmental injustice we breed the two great classes—tramps and millionaires."

Convinced that the evils of society stemmed from some simple cause, the party favored "free silver," a graduated income tax, Government ownership of railways, telegraphs and telephones, a shorter work day for urban workers, and popular election of United States Senators. The People's Party, or Populist Party as it came to be known, was against Eastern bankers, "undesirable" (non-Protestant) immigration, and against the rights of the Negro in the South. Some Southern Populists sought to win Negroes to their cause. In 1892, scrawny, red-haired Tom Watson was telling Georgians that "the accident of color can make no difference in the interest of farmers, croppers, and laborers." But what sounded like appeals to the Negro somehow turned out to be a way of using him. The Populists polled a million votes, elected 5 U. S. Senators, 10 Congressmen, and 1,500 state officers and legislators. What was more surprising, the Populists won 22 of the 444 electoral votes. As the first new party to obtain electoral votes since 1860, it undoubtedly threatened the existing order.

WILLIAM JENNINGS BRYAN

The Populist Party had, of course, drawn recruits from both the Democrats and the Republicans. But even among those who had remained faithful to the older parties, there was much discontent. Men who did not wish to defeat their parties from without, had to try to reform them from within.

Through two terms in Congress, the Nebraskan Democrat William Jennings Bryan had come to feel that his party did not protect the interests of the common man against the large corporations. In March, 1892, in Congress, he made a noteworthy speech in which he blamed falling farm prices on the tariff. Another young Congressman told Bryan that, in his opinion, falling prices were due to the rise in the value of gold. After considerable study of the currency, Bryan became convinced of this. Inflation, rather than lowering the tariff, he decided, would solve the farmer's problem.

Unquestionably there was a shortage of money. At the end of the Civil War, the Government had begun withdrawing

[November 30, 1889.

THE KODAK.

PRICE, $25.00.

ANYBODY can use the Kodak. The operation of making a picture consists simply of pressing a button. One hundred instantaneous pictures are made without reloading. No dark room or chemicals are necessary. A division of labor is offered, whereby all the work of finishing the pictures is done at the factory, where the camera can be sent to be reloaded. The operator need not learn anything about photography. He can "*press the button*"—*we do the rest.*

Send for copy of Kodak Primer, with sample photograph.

The Eastman Dry Plate and Film Co.,
ROCHESTER, N. Y.

Overhead electric and telephone wires in lower New York City in 1883. Another development, the safety elevator, meant that buildings could be made taller. People were coming to accept invention as part of the natural order, and that new devices could be produced by systematic search.

"Greenbacks" from circulation, with the result that the number of dollars circulating per person had fallen from about $32 in 1865 to about $16 in 1878. In 1892, there was still only $24 circulating per person. Retail prices (including farm prices) had consequently fallen, so that in 1879, 93¢ would have bought as much as $2.24 in 1865. Meanwhile, with the discovery of silver in Nevada and Colorado, silver production had climbed from $156,800 in 1860 to $30 million in 1875 and $57 million in 1890. Only a small fraction of this was being bought by the Government for coinage.

Bryan favored the "free and unlimited coinage of silver" at the ratio of sixteen ounces of silver to one ounce of gold. But there was so much silver coming from the new mines that one ounce of gold was worth about thirty-two ounces of silver. This meant that a silver dollar sixteen times as heavy as a gold dollar would be really worth only half as much as the gold dollar. Since a law authorizing such coinage would artificially make silver worth more than it should in relation to gold, it would artificially make gold worth less in relation to silver. Bryan favored "free silver" because, like many Westerners, he viewed gold as the metal of Eastern bankers, merchants, and manufacturers who had too long imposed high tariffs and low prices on the West. "Free silver" was the engine of equalization that would cheapen the gold the East gained from the rest of the country. It would raise the value of Western produce at the expense of the East.

Up and down the land traveled Bryan from 1892 to 1896, preaching "free silver" to small gatherings of Nebraska farmers, Kansas storekeepers, and Montana stockmen. He kept trying out different phrases in different places—"cross of gold," "the pioneers who rear their children near to Nature's heart."

JOHN P. ALTGELD AND THE PULLMAN STRIKE

John P. Altgeld, a self-made millionaire and former judge, had been elected Democratic-Populist Governor of Illinois in 1892. Six years earlier, as a justice on the Cook County Superior Court, he had criticized the prevailing spirit of government. In a time of violent labor disputes he found the policy known as "laissez faire," a French term meaning *leave alone,* and referring to government leaving business alone, both immoral and unwise. It was foolish to hold, he said, "that the state as the embodiment of society, has no power to prevent or to remove those conditions which, if left to themselves, would lead to its own overthrow."

As a matter of fact, the term *laissez faire* was extremely misleading. A government that protected industry with high tariffs, or that gave railroads land, was not leaving business alone. In practice, *laissez faire* meant helping business, but leaving alone farmers and laborers.

The financial Panic of 1893 brought the same rise in unemployment and cuts in pay that had followed the panics of 1873 and 1884, and the same stirrings of unrest among the working men.

Starting with $40,000 and the belief that Americans would pay for comfort in railroad travel, George Pullman had in thirty years built up one of the largest and most prosperous businesses in the state of Illinois. The Pullman Palace Car Company plant was ten miles south of Chicago. There, at a place called Hyde Park, Pullman built luxurious sleeping cars, diners, and lounge cars, and maintained a model town for his employees.

Living conditions in the town of Pullman were in many ways more pleasant than what the workmen and their families would otherwise have known. Streets were wider and cleaner, lawns were neater, and company physicians and company medicines succeeded in lowering the death rate to about one-third of what it was among other workingmen and their families. On the other hand, the town did belong to George M. Pullman, lock, stock, and barrel. No resident of Pullman could buy his home nor could he have any say in the government of the town, and rents were somewhat higher than those charged elsewhere. Had Pullman built his town out of a sense of charity or business? Probably it was a mixture of the two.

The depression found Mr. Pullman with $4 million in reserve capital and $26 million in undivided earnings, and the problem of maintaining his business against a decline in orders. His first moves were to cut his labor force from 5,800 to 2,000 and to cut twenty-five per cent from the wages of those he kept on. Next, taking orders at a loss of $300 per car, he was able to build up production to the point where he could rehire more than half of the men he had fired.

In May, 1894, shortly after this restoration, a delegation of three employees reminded Mr. Pullman that he had not reduced rents on his houses when he had reduced wages. Mr. Pullman's reply was that "none of the reasons urged as justifying wage reduction by it as an employer can be considered by the company, as a landlord."

He also discharged the three members of the delegation. It happened that the delegation was composed of members of a local of the American Railway Union, an organization that Mr. Pullman was not anxious to have in his plant.

Governor John P. Altgeld.

The American Railway Union at this time had more members than any other Union in the United States. Founded in 1890 by Eugene Victor Debs, a former secretary of the Brotherhood of Locomotive Firemen, it had enlisted 150,000 white employees of railways and related industries in one year.

On May 11, 1894, after Pullman's refusal to reinstate the three workmen, a strike was called. Pullman closed the doors of his plant, expressing delight that he no longer had to keep making cars at a loss. The American Railway Union then requested that its members not run trains in which Pullman cars were hooked. So that the Federal Government would not be forced to intrude, the Union particularly asked that Pullman cars be left off mail trains.

Switchmen on various lines leading into Chicago were discharged for refusing to attach Pullman cars to trains. The strike spread until twenty-four railroads were tied up. What had begun as a local dispute between a manufacturer and his employees had become a nationwide strike crippling the movement of passengers and freight through half the United States.

With the mayors of Chicago, Detroit, and fifty lesser cities begging him to arbitrate, Pullman stood firm. In this, he was encouraged by the General Managers Association, representing the twenty-four railroads. Meanwhile, Governor Altgeld was besieged by requests that he apply for Federal aid in preventing outbreaks such as had terrified Baltimore and Pittsburgh during the dark days of 1877. Altgeld declined, confident that he had the situation well in hand.

The twenty-four railroads then applied directly to the Federal Government for help in insuring mail delivery. President Cleveland's Attorney-General, Richard Olney, a former lawyer for one of the members of the General Managers Association, was sympathetic to their cause, and 3,600 special deputies were recruited by the U. S. Marshal in Chicago. With the appearance of the special deputies, fighting, looting, and tearing up of railway tracks and destruction of railroad cars began. There was now an excuse for calling in Federal troops. They arrived on the scene July 3, 1894.

On July 2, a Federal Court had issued a special order, or injunction, forbidding Debs, his fellow strike leaders, and "all other persons whomsoever" from interfering with the operation of the railroads. Two weeks later, Debs and three others were arrested and jailed for disobeying the injunction. This demoralized the strikers, and the strike ended on July 20.

Two things about these events enraged Altgeld. In the first place, the Federal troops had come into his state without his bidding.

"If any assistance were needed," he had written President Cleveland on July 5, "the State stood ready to furnish a hundred men for every one man required. . . . To absolutely ignore a local government . . . when [it] . . . is amply able to enforce the law, . . . is in violation of the basic principle of our institutions."

In the second place, he regarded the special court order by which the strike had been broken, as illegal:

"The judge issues an ukase (decree) which he calls an injunction," Altgeld said, "forbidding whatever he pleases and what the law does not forbid, . . . and he deprives men of the right of trial by jury when the law guarantees this right, . . . throwing men into prison, not for violating a law, but for being guilty of contempt of court in disregarding one of these injunctions."

What was happening was clearly summarized by the Governor in his annual message to the legislature in 1895:

"Combinations of capital against the public and against labor have succeeded, no matter by what means, and the men who accomplished it are now patriots; while combinations among laborers for self-protection have failed, and the men who advocate it are enemies of society (i.e. 'anarchists')."

In reply to Altgeld, President Cleveland had curtly asserted his right to order the Army where it was needed to quell violence. The newspapers took Cleveland's side, The Chicago Tribune going so far as to call Altgeld a "lying, hypo-

A dynamite bomb explodes among Chicago police. The terrible Haymarket affair.

critical, demagogical, sniveling Governor" who "does not want the laws enforced. He is a sympathizer with riot, with violence, with lawlessness, and with anarchy . . ."

But a Federal commission appointed to study the strike agreed with Altgeld that Federal troops had not been needed. The Superintendent of Mails testified that at no time, during the strike, had the mails been delayed more than nine hours. Carroll D. Wright, the chairman of the investigating committee, told a Boston newspaper editor that "the burning of the mass of cars . . . was instigated by the railway managers themselves as the surest way to bring the Federal troops and defeat the strike."

ALTGELD AND THE ANARCHISTS

In June of 1893, Illinois' Governor Altgeld pardoned three anarchists who had been sentenced seven years before for killing and injuring a great number of Chicago policemen with a bomb thrown in a place called Haymarket Square. Of the eight well-known anarchists arrested for the dastardly deed only three, Samuel Fielden, Michael Schwab, and Oscar W. Neebe, remained in custody of the law. Four had been hanged and one had committed suicide.

Almost immediately after his election, Altgeld had been asked to release the anarchists. He had not done so until, after a thorough study of the records of the trial, he had become convinced an injustice had been done. The release of the anarchists brought upon his head a terrible storm of abuse. It was not just that he had reversed a popular decision of the courts. In reversing it, he threw a harsh light on the exact methods by which injustice had been done.

In January, 1893, he had told the graduating class of the University of Illinois that justice, far from being firm and absolute, was "a struggling toward the right." Judges take their human failings with them to the bench, he explained.

In releasing Schwab and Fielden, Altgeld seemed to be illustrating his lecture to the graduates of the state university. First of all, Altgeld showed that the jury selected to try the anarchists had been picked only from amongst men who the bailiff believed "would hang the defendants." Then he went on to criticize the judge, for his conduct of the trial.

"No matter what the defendants were charged with," Altgeld declared, "they were entitled to a fair trial, and no greater danger could possibly threaten our institutions than to have the courts of justice run wild or give way to popular clamor . . ."

The record showed "that every ruling throughout the long trial on any contested point was in favor of the state; and further, that page after page on the record contains insinuating remarks of the judge, made in the hearing of the jury, and with the evident intent of bringing the jury to his way of thinking."

Yet "the state has never discovered who it was that threw the bomb that killed the policemen, and the evidence does not show any connection whatever between the defendants and the man who did throw it."

The hard times following the Panic of 1893 were to help Altgeld more than the vicious attacks of newspapers and the mocking nickname, John "Pardon" Altgeld, would hurt him.

FREE SILVER AGAINST THE GOLD STANDARD

The Panic of 1893, the third such disaster within a period of twenty years, had been taken by many as final evidence that something was basically wrong with the institutions of the country. The farmers, who even in so-called good times resented repaying the banks dollars more valuable than the banks had loaned them, saw their incomes shrivel to almost nothing with each financial convulsion.

Through the West and the South, men of Populist sympathies had been winning Democratic primaries and becoming Democratic candidates. The Democrats who assembled in Chicago in 1896, after three years of depression, were a far different group from those who had nominated Cleveland in 1892. Cleveland was now repudiated, and the convention specifically denounced "arbitrary interference by Federal authorities in local affairs as a violation of the Constitution of the United States . . ." and especially objected to "government by injunction as a new and highly dangerous form of oppression by which Federal judges, in contempt of the laws of the states and rights of the citizens, become at once legislators, judges, and executives; . . ."

Had he not been born in Germany, Altgeld might have been nominated for the Presidency. As it was, there were no outstanding contenders when William Jennings Bryan, confident and handsome, mounted the rostrum to address his fellow delegates.

During a bitter fight over the "unlimited" coinage of silver, the defeated Cleveland Democrats had argued that disturbances to the money of the country would hurt business.

In the course of his fifteen-minute speech, Bryan turned to the defenders of the gold standard:

"We say to you that you have made the definition of a business man too limited in its application. The man who is employed for wages is as much a business man as his employer; the attorney in a country town is as much a business man as the corporation counsel in a great metropolis; the merchant at the crossroads store is as much a business man as the merchant of New York; the farmer who goes forth in the morning and toils all day, who begins in the spring and toils all summer, and who by the application of brain and muscle to the natural resources of the country creates wealth, is as much a business man as the man who goes upon the Board of Trade and bets upon the price of grain; the miners who go down a thousand feet into the earth, or climb two thousand feet upon the cliffs, and bring forth from their hiding places the precious metals to be poured into the channels of trade are as much business men as the few financial magnates who, in a back room, corner the money of the world."

Bryan was saying things that many hardworking people had been thinking, with increasing dismay. The doubts, the uncertainties, the disappointments of the immediate past seemed to roll away as he hearkened his audience back to the great traditions of their party — to Andrew Jackson who, in destroying "the bank conspiracy . . . saved America"; to Thomas Jefferson who held that "the issue of money is a function of government, and that the banks ought to go out of the governing business"; to all who put human rights before property rights.

"You come to tell us," Bryan said, "that the great cities are in favor of the gold standard; we reply that the great cities rest upon our broad and fertile prairies. Burn down your cities and leave our farms, and your cities will spring up again as if by magic; but destroy our farms and grass will grow in the streets of every city in the country. . . . we will answer their demand for a gold standard by saying to them: You shall not press down upon the brow of labor this crown of thorns, you shall not crucify mankind upon a cross of gold."

The silver delegates and Populist-Democrats, aroused to a frenzy of enthusiasm, bestowed the nomination on the thirty-six-year-old Nebraskan. Bryan's nomination confronted the Populists with a dilemma. If they named a candidate of their own, they would rob Bryan, and free silver, of any chance of victory. If they went along with Bryan, they would lose their identity and with it, any hope for an income tax, Government ownership of railroads, and other reforms. They followed Bryan and were destroyed.

The Republicans had nominated William McKinley and pledged themselves to sound money and the gold standard (an international system that fixed the worths of different currencies in terms of gold). It was unfortunate that "free silver" became the main issue of the campaign, because it tended to disguise the other important differences between the parties — over the tariff, Federal use of injunctions, the need to regulate trusts and pools, and the Government's general encouragement of industry and banking at the expense of the working people.

In defending the gold standard against

free silver, the Republicans could pose as defenders of faith, honor and justice.

"Messrs. Bryan, Altgeld, Debs, Coxey," said a young Republican politician named Theodore Roosevelt, ". . . are strikingly like the leaders of the Terror of France in mental and moral attitude."

Marcus Hanna, McKinley's manager, raised more than $3 million for campaign expenses, partly by assessing leading banks one quarter of one per cent of their capital and surplus. He obtained free private trains from the managers of railroads, and mobilized 1,400 expert speakers to address groups all over the country on the dangers of free silver.

Following McKinley's election, the free silver issue floated out of sight. Discoveries of gold in Australia, the Alaskan Klondike, and Africa, and a new process of extracting the precious metal, increased the world's gold supply. The effect was the same as if more silver had been coined. Money became less valuable, prices went up, and debtors were no longer forced to give bankers better dollars than they had borrowed.

Yet nothing, really, was settled. The trusts were as influential as ever, and farmers and laborers remained without a voice in government. The unions were demoralized by the Pullman victory. Debs was in jail. The tariff was as high as ever. Indeed, the new President had been the author of the highest tariff ever passed. Would there be still more crises like those of 1873 and 1893? Had all the sufferings of strikers, the meetings of Grangers, the plans of Farmers' Alliances, the passion of the Populists, gone for nought?

"Applause lasts but a little while," Altgeld had remarked during the jubilation over Bryan's "Cross-of-Gold" speech. "The road to justice is not a path of glory; it is stony and long and lonely, filled with pain and martyrdom."

Pioneers without trees. They made houses of sod and, with barbed wire fences, deprived cattlemen of the plains. These Nebraskans were not interested in the gold standard.

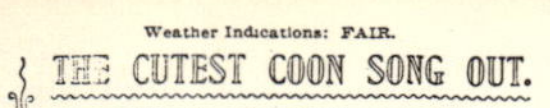

Weather Indications: FAIR.

THE CUTEST COON SONG OUT.

"Hush, My Little Coon."

Complete with Words and Music in Sheet Form with Next Sunday's World.

Beautiful Art Magazine!

"Circulation Books Open to All." "Circulation Books Open to All."

Weather Indications: FAIR.

Spring Dress Fashions.

Real Samples of Real Goods.

Reproduced in Colors from Originals.

Unique and Valuable to Every Woman.

With the Sunday World!

VOL. XXXVIII. NO. 13,345. (Copyright, 1898, by the Press Publishing Company, New York World.) NEW YORK, FRIDAY, MARCH 4, 1898. PRICE ONE CENT in Greater New York and Jersey City. TWO CENTS outside of Greater New York and Jersey City and on trains.

CROKER AND MAYOR HAVE A QUARREL.

Angry Words Heard in the Main Parlor of the Democratic Club.

VAN WYCK WAS STUBBORN

Declared Plainly He Would Not Do Something the King Demanded.

LEFT ROOM IN WROTHY MOOD.

It Overheard by Several Members, One of Whom Gives the Details of It to The World.

SPECULATION AS TO OUTCOME.

Tammany Leaders Discuss an Order Giving John F. Carroll Charge of Patronage.

...e ironclad hand of friendship be... Richard Croker and Mayor Robert ...an Wyck has been subjected to a ...s strain. The two men had a dis... ...ment at the Democratic Club a ...ago Wednesday night, which was ...d by five or six members.

...st night Croker and the Mayor, ...g to the story of one of the wit... ...f the happening, were sitting to... ...n the large parlor of the club. ...roker was doing most of the talk... ...was early in the evening, and ...ors were comparatively empty. ...Croker was speaking earnestly ...yor suddenly interrupted, saying ...e that could be heard all over ...:

..."t do anything I can't stand ...

...kept on talking, until Van... ...ke in again, saying with loud ...

"...use talking more about it." ...t paying any attention to the ...ion, Croker kept on speaking. ...an Wyck fidgeted in his chair. ...he jumped up, saying: ...ave said enough. It is no use." ...another word more the Mayor ...t of the parlor and through... ...f the club...

SPEAKER THOMAS B. REED OPPOSING MEASURES OF SAFETY.

The Autocratic Ruler of the House Stubbornly Fights All Necessary Naval Preparations.

(Special to The World.)

WASHINGTON, March 3. — The most determined foe to every measure of prudence or precaution, the most stubborn obstacle opposing every preparation for war in the whole country is the Speaker of the House of Representatives, Thomas B. Reed.

He guesses that the Maine was blown up by accident. He guesses that there is nothing to fight about, even if the Maine was blown up by design. He does not see why the United States should bother about the butcheries of Cubans. He does not think much of the Cubans anyhow.

When Mr. Reed is not ruling the House of Representatives with an iron hand he is discharging his duties to the big insurance companies which employ him at a large annual salary to act as referee for them. His employers pay his salary right along, whether he is acting as Speaker of the House or as referee for the life-insurance combine.

JAPAN WANTS LIST OF HER DEAD.

She Will Look First to the United States for Payment in Case There Is Indemnity.

(Special to The World.)

WASHINGTON, March 3.—The Japanese Minister, Toru Hoshi called today at the State Department and asked that his Government be given a list of the Japanese upon the Maine at the time she was destroyed.

Inquiry at the Japanese Legation drew forth the following explanation:

"The only purpose of the Japanese Government in seeking to ascertain the names and character of the Japanese on board the Maine when the disaster occurred was that a record might be made. This legation has at present no accurate list of the men who were killed. It is understood that there were seven Japanese on board the Maine at the time. The purpose of the inquiry was not to make a demand for indemnity at this time.

"If the United States collects indemnity for the loss of the sailors on board the Maine, it is confidently expected that the families of the men will be properly dealt with, and Japan has no fear that the United States will not deal fairly with her subjects temporarily in the service of the United States.

"It is admitted that these Japanese subjects were landsmen of the United ...

LONG'S SHIPS SAILED WITHOUT MUNITIONS.

Secretary of Navy Sent Pacific Squadron Away Short of Powder and Shot.

FLEET IS NOW NEAR SPAIN'S ASIATIC ISLANDS

Bureau of Ordnance of the Navy Recommended Full Supplies—He Saw No Need of Them.

ADMIRAL DEWEY'S SHIPS NOW 4,000 MILES FROM SUPPLIES

The Magnificent Fleet of Admiral Sicard at Key West also Unequipped but Soon Will Be.

HURRY ORDERS SENT OUT AFTER THE WORLD'S PUBLICATION.

(Special to The World.)

WASHINGTON, March 3. — The World's exclusive publication on Tuesday of the fact that the magnificent squadron of over twenty United States fighting ships, now under Admiral Sicard in the Gulf, had not ammunition enough on board to last ten hours' active fighting may have been one of the causes of the extraordinary activity since in the Ordnance Department of the Navy.

Of the three great first-class battle-ships now at Key West, the Iowa, Indiana and Massachusetts, only one has on board enough projectiles for her big guns to last one day's bombardment.

This statement, telegraphed exclusively to The World, was read with amazement ...

TORPEDO BLEW UP THE MAINE, HIGH SPANISH OFFICER SAYS.

If His Story Is True It Verifies The World Correspondent's Earliest News.

NO MINE LAID IN HARBOR AT HAVANA.

Only Experiment in That Line Made by Weyler at Chorrero.

GIVEN UP BECAUSE OF DANGER TO SHIPPING.

Ton of Saluting Powder in Reserve Magazine Set Off by Initial Explosion.

TELLTALE ROPE FOUND GIVES ADDED PROOF.

Two Boats and Three or Four Common Watermen Might Have Done the Work.

THE DARK NIGHT MADE THEIR HIDEOUS TASK EASY.

Tourists in Havana Arrange to Pay Honor to the American Martyrs Buried There.

(Copyright, 1898, by the Press Publishing Company, New York World.)

(Special from a World Staff Correspondent, sent from Havana to Key West by the World Despatch Boat.)

On Board the World Despatch Boat Confidence, Havana, Cuba, March 3.

A high Spanish naval authority thinks a big torpedo, towed by ...

WORLD POWER

THE GREATER the population and extent of a nation, the more groups there will be with the same interests. Such webs of common interest bring together people divided on other issues. The Maine farmer, for instance, opposes the Maine manufacturer on the tariff question, but votes with him on bringing a railroad to Bangor. Such crossing-over of relationships, binding different people together on different issues, is the cement of Union. It was a breakdown of such crosslinks that brought on the Civil War.

There were Americans, in the 1890's, who saw in the agitations over silver, wages, and working conditions a similar breaking down of crosslinks. On the one hand there were the insurgent trusts, the concentration of great portions of the nation's wealth into the hands of a few individuals; on the other hand were the millions of ordinary working people. The have-nots on Western farms were separated geographically from the bankers of the East. And workmen in the cities were losing faith that the American system allowed for improvement of their condition.

Great numbers of discontented Americans cast about for some simple remedy. Free silver — the "single tax" (based on the proposition that the rise in the price of land, and rents, that accompanied growth of population and commerce, was the means by which the people were robbed of the fruits of honest toil) gained millions of adherents overnight; and, in jail, Eugene Victor Debs, president of the American Railway Union, read some books by a German named Karl Marx and became convinced that there could be no justice unless the Government itself owned all the factories, railroads, mines, and electrical and telephone systems in the nation.

It is likely that the increase in tension, the Populist's transformation of the Democratic Party and the violence of the Presidential campaign of 1896, were caused as much by the loss of an old link between Americans as by depression and other forces of division.

The old link lost was the frontier. As an historian noted in 1893:

"In a recent bulletin of the Superintendent of the Census for 1890 appear these significant words: . . . at present the

The finest moment in his life — Theodore Roosevelt at the top of the hill near San Juan, that he captured from the Spanish just eight days after his arrival in Cuba. He is surrounded by the cowboys of his "Rough Rider" regiment. A week later, Santiago fell and the war, in effect, was over. As John Hay later said, it had been "a splendid little war."

unsettled area has been so broken into by isolated bodies of settlement that there can hardly be said to be a frontier line. . . . This brief official statement marks the closing of a great historic movement. . . ."

The passing of the frontier meant the passing of an emotion all Americans had shared — a feeling of growth, a pride in that growth, and the hunch that if things got too bad, one could always move west and start all over.

THE "SPLENDID LITTLE WAR"

A people too deeply divided to find ways of compromising might seize on some substitute for the frontier. There were other adventures a whole nation might share. "Whether they will or no," a scholarly naval officer noted, "Americans must now begin to look outward. . . ."

They looked at Cuba.

The largest island in the Caribbean had inspired many an American dream. There had been much interest in Cuba in 1814, when Andrew Jackson invaded Florida. In the years before the Civil War, Southern filibusterers had hoped to make it part of the expanding cotton kingdom. Several insurrections had offered opportunities for American intervention. President Grant had come close to annexing Cuba. By 1894, American trade with the island had reached $100 million a year. A fierce rebellion, which began in 1895, reduced trade to almost nothing. Americans were aroused by stories of Spanish cruelty. Again, there was talk of American intervention.

William McKinley, who had become President in 1897, believed that America needed foreign markets, but he abhorred war. "If I can go out of office with the knowledge that I have done all in my power to avert this terrible calamity I shall be the happiest man in the world," he told Grover Cleveland on the night before his inauguration. But to the post of Assistant Secretary of the Navy he appointed a gentleman who, a year before, had told a friend, "This country needs a war."

Theodore Roosevelt possessed a mystical yearning for war for a *righteous* cause, and for demonstrations of national virility. Yet it is also true that many a thoughtful American was becoming aware of the nation's need to change its attitude toward the world.

First of all, as the chief of the bureau of foreign commerce noted in 1896, the U. S. could "no longer afford to disregard international rivalries, now that we ourselves have become a competitor in the world-wide struggle for trade."

Of course, the United States had long been a competitor for world trade. (In protecting her interests, she had sent an expedition to Tripoli in 1804 and another to Syria in 1858, and had intervened in Mexico and various Spanish colonies no less than thirty times, in Nicaragua and Panama six times, in Samoa and Hawaii four times, in Chile three, in Paraguay twice, and had more than once warned Japan, China, and various settlements along the eastern coasts of Asia. Marines had landed in Tientsin and Korea, American ships had bombarded Greytown, Nicaragua, and Quallah Battoo, Sumatra. In the words of the historian Albert Bushnell Hart, twenty-five cases of armed intervention in the years 1836-1861 indicated that "the United States was rapidly becoming the policeman of the Americas and the terror of the Orient." American fleets had expressed the sympathy of Americans for Rumanian, Armenian, and

Greek rebellions. As a Republican disturber of the peace, the nation had been friendly toward the Hungarian Kossuth and French and German rebels in 1848, when all Europe seemed at the edge of revolution.

But the struggle was becoming more intense. During the last half of the nineteenth century, Africa had been carved into European colonies; Germany had claimed what few Pacific Islands remained unoccupied by other naval powers, and Japan had begun removing raw materials from a portion of northern China. The quest for colonies and privileges became more intense as frontiers all over the world disappeared. The American Admiral Mahan wrote, "Within, the home market is secured; but outside, beyond the broad seas, there are the markets of the world, that can be entered or controlled only by a vigorous contest, . . ." His words interested men in many lands.

If there were no peoples left, any place, to be conquered and used, more powerful nations would seek to take colonies away from those too weak to hold them.

The weakest major colonial power during the closing years of the nineteenth century was Spain. Between April 21 and August 12, 1898, the new steel United States Navy destroyed two Spanish fleets, in the Bays of Santiago and Manila, losing just one man; and 17,000 enthusiastic and poorly trained American troops helped the Cuban revolutionaries to victory over the Spanish forces.

Meanwhile, during the height of "the Little War," Congress voted the annexation of the Hawaiian Islands. The Spanish secession of Guam and the sale of the Philippines for $20 million gave the United States a formidable group of possessions in the Pacific. The annexation of Puerto Rico and a Cuban grant of a naval station made the Caribbean an

"American lake." In less than four months, the United States had manifestly become a world power.

THE TRANSFORMATION OF THE PRESIDENCY

McKinley, as he feared, had become an imperialist. The Cubans were given their independence only in exchange for a naval station, and their economy was dominated by the National City Bank of New York. The Philippines continued their struggle for independence against their new American masters. One hundred twenty-three years after the battle of Lexington, an American Army spent three years subduing rebellious colonial subjects.

From 1900 to 1914, American investments abroad increased from the millions to the billions. Empire was expensive. Army and Navy expenditures almost doubled following the Spanish-American War. The Federal budget in 1910 was almost twice the amount it was in 1897. The 16th Amendment, legalizing the income tax, opened up a new source of revenue. The amendment, ratified in 1913, was necessary because the Supreme Court had ruled an 1894 income tax unconstitutional (Federal income taxes had been collected from 1862 to 1872). At first, only incomes above $5000 were taxed, which left out most of the population. The tax rate was very low. Incomes of $100,000 were taxed 2.5%. In 1914, individual income taxes brought the Government $41 million. (By 1954, individual income taxes had soared to $33 *billion* and an income of $100,000 was taxed 66.8%. The lowest income tax rate was 8%, and it was paid on $1,000.)

But if superior power enabled the United States to seize portions of territory in various parts of the world, her kind of civilization brought some benefits. Yellow fever and malaria were practically wiped out in Cuba, Puerto Rico, the Canal Zone, and America's other tropical possessions. Typhus and other scourges were brought under control. The people of Puerto Rico and the Philippines were given systems of free public schools. Hookworm, too, was eradicated from Puerto Rico (and at home the debilitating disease, which was found in almost half of all the children examined in the Southern states between 1910 and 1913, was conquered by the Rockefeller Sanitary Commission).

The price of world power was continual vigilance. Everything that happened on every sea, on every continent, affected a power with possessions extending halfway around the globe. In 1899, when it appeared that a weak and poorly-governed China would, like Africa, be carved up by the great powers, Secretary of State John Hay tried to get other nations to agree that no arrangements would exclude the United States, or anyone else, from trade. The following year, American forces joined those of five other nations in suppressing an anti-foreign uprising in Peking.

The supreme responsibility of the President in foreign affairs made him vastly more powerful now that the United States had become a great power in a world in which great powers rubbed shoulders.

Shortly after McKinley began his second term of office, he was assassinated. When, on September 14, 1901, his Vice President was sworn in, the United States had a President who would not hesitate to use these extended powers. The new President was Theodore Roosevelt.

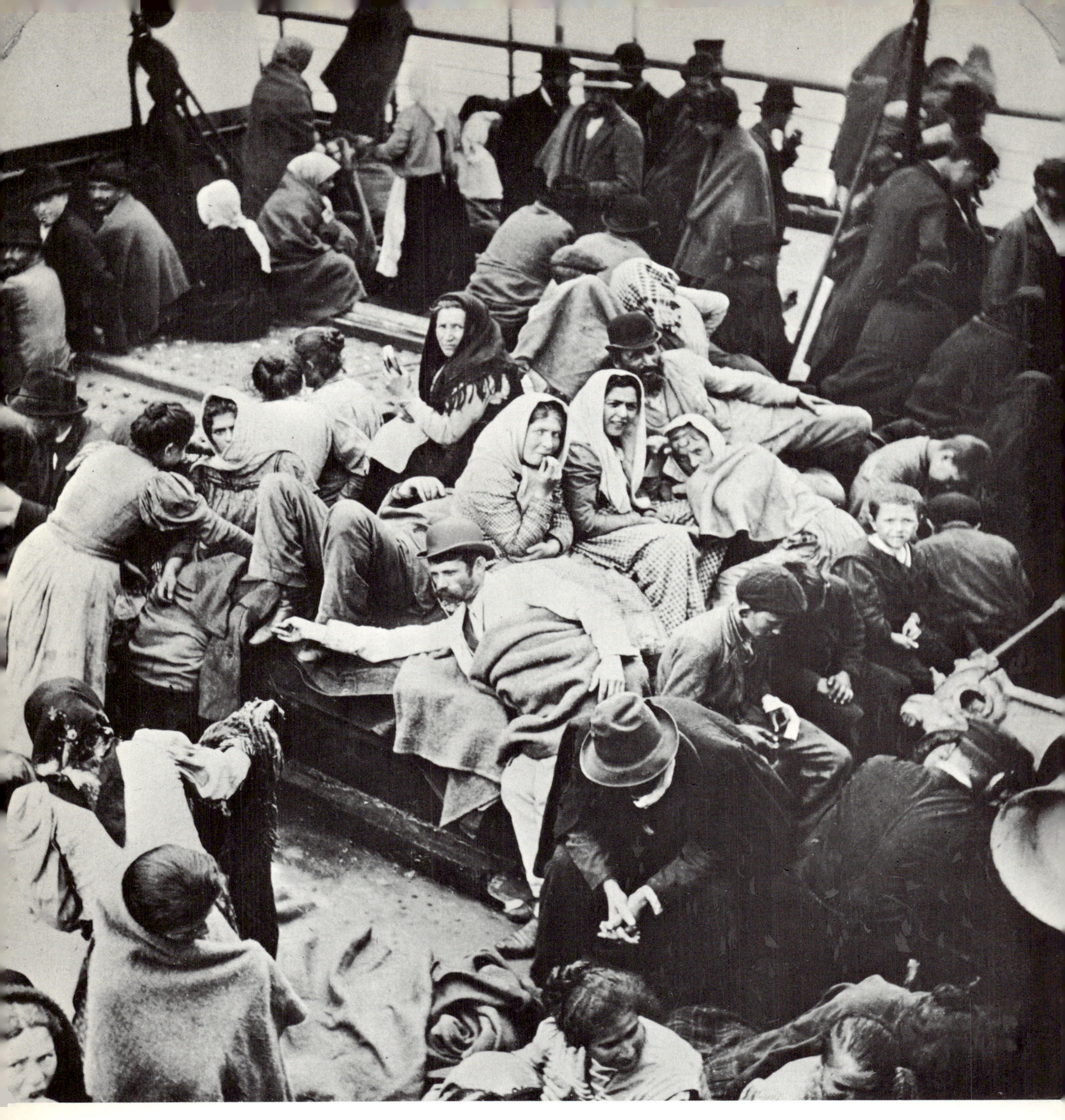

In 1896, for the first time, there were more immigrants from southern and eastern Europe than from its north and west. Eleven million came in 12 years, starting in 1903, but there were so many Americans that the proportion of foreign-born to native-born remained one out of seven, as it had been since earliest times. The Western frontier was gone, but there are other frontiers. For these new Americans, as for most of their predecessors, the frontier was the city.

THE NEW FREEDOM

Eugene V. Debs.

THERE was a growing sense of America as a nation amongst nations. When Colombia proved reluctant to accept American terms for an isthmian canal, a deal was made with Panama, after Panama was encouraged to seek independence from Colombia. Roosevelt also enlarged the Monroe Doctrine, asserting the interest of the United States in any dispute between Latin America and a non-American power; he corresponded with Kings and Prime Ministers and, in 1905, brought Russian and Japanese statesmen to New Hampshire to settle a war. At home, too, the President distinguished a national interest from the special interests of citizens. Water and other resources were protected. Millions of acres were taken off the market so that their value to the nation as a whole could be assessed, and laws were passed to prevent the destruction of forests.

The fifty years since the Civil War had seen the growth of giant combinations—railroad mergers and trusts. With tremendous resources at their disposal, with millions of employees, the policies of these great organizations affected the welfare of the entire nation. Yet they were largely beyond the jurisdiction of state law, and no Federal legislation had been able to curb them. President Roosevelt rightly termed them "subjects without rulers."

As if to serve notice that no person or institution could any longer regard itself as unaccountable to the Government, President Roosevelt moved against the most powerful private citizen in the country.

The Congress had, in 1890, passed the Sherman Anti-Trust Act. This vaguely worded law, which put the Federal Government on record as opposed to "every combination . . . in restraint of trade" had thus far restrained only combinations of laboring men.

But in February, 1902, the Department of Justice brought suit against the Northern Securities Company, a holding company formed by J. P. Morgan to combine two big competing Western railroads.

Finding himself prosecuted for violating the Sherman Act, the banker came down to Washington. "If we have done anything wrong," Morgan told the President, "send your man to my man and they can fix it up." He meant that Roosevelt should send the Attorney General of

Foreign investors, disliking the tricks of men like Fisk and Gould, provided John Pierpont Morgan with money to buy control of properties. Eventually, Morgan began assembling trusts; competition, like buccaneering, hurt dividends. Morgan lived, and acted, like a king.

the United States up to New York to see Morgan's lawyer. As Roosevelt later remarked, Morgan "could not help regarding me as a big rival operator . . ."

In another demonstration of Federal authority, the President ended the greatest coal strike in the nation's history. He put great pressure on the mine owners to agree to arbitration of their dispute with the United Mine Workers. If persuasion failed, he was resolved to run the coal mines with soldiers.

The United Mine Workers had been formed in 1890, mostly out of old Knights of Labor locals. It was an industrial union, open to all coal mine workers, no matter what their skills. Such industrial organization had failed elsewhere, but the UMW, led by John Mitchell, grew in strength. In 1902 it struck for a 20% wage increase, a nine-hour day, payment by honest weight, and recognition. Mitchell agreed to abide by the decision of impartial arbitrators who would determine whether the "average annual wages received by anthracite mine workers are sufficient to enable them to live, maintain and educate their families in a manner conformable to established American standards. . . ." George F. Baer, head of the mine operators committee, replied that, "Anthracite mining is a business, and not a religious, sentimental, or academic proposition."

Roosevelt also made skillful use of the press. Congress passed legislation for a Bureau of Corporations two days after the President told reporters of a Rockefeller telegram to six Senators, opposing the Bureau.

"Neither this people nor any other free people will permanently tolerate the use of the vast power conferred by vast wealth without lodging somewhere in the Government the still higher power of seeing that this power is used for and not against the interests of the people as a whole," Roosevelt said in 1905. To cope with "Big Business," it seemed, there was a need for "Big Government."

But how was the Government to act? Should all big combinations be broken apart, whether they benefited the nation or not? Could the nation retain the benefits of, say, a unified oil industry and yet escape such dangers as monoply-created high prices?

Equally serious was the fact that as "Big Business" grew bigger and profits mounted, too many Americans felt they were not sharing sufficiently in this growth. Two-thirds of American workingmen were receiving less than $12.50 a week in wages, eighty per cent of the people barely subsisted, and it was estimated that 1% of American families owned more than half of the nation's wealth.

There was wild talk in the air. If the owners of industry insisted on keeping all the profits themselves, perhaps the men whose labor helped make the profits ought to take the plants away from their owners and run them for themselves. In the Presidential campaign of 1908, Eugene V. Debs, the Socialist candidate, running on a platform of government ownership of railroads, utilities, mines and many heavy industries, polled almost half a million votes out of a total of 15 million. Unless something was done to curb "Big Business," would not the American people take radical steps? Was it not the role of government to end abuses before this happened?

Roosevelt left the White House, in 1909, to his chosen successor, William Howard Taft. But his concern for these problems remained. Taft proved politically inept. He prosecuted trusts and tried to lower the tariff. Yet, while offending those he opposed, he won no support. As a New York Times reporter put it, Taft's "bump of politics" was "a deep hole." Roosevelt, convinced that Taft had allied himself with Big Business, fought for the 1912 Republican nomination. When he failed, he joined other reformers and accepted the nomination of a new Progressive Party.

What had become of the America they had been brought up to believe in? The journalist Lincoln Steffens (here with lawyer Clarence Darrow) found that cities and states were often run by obscure bosses who told elected officials what to do. Theodore Roosevelt enjoyed such exposés, but later, as President, compared their authors to the man in Pilgrim's Progress *"who could look no way but downward with the muckrake in his hands." Steffens and his kind became known as "muckrakers."*

He believed "in shaping the ends of government to protect property as well as human welfare," Theodore Roosevelt said in 1910. "Normally, and in the long run, the ends are the same; but whenever the alternative must be faced, I am for men and not for property. . . ."

Robert M. La Follette, Governor of the Wisconsin of the Wisconsin Idea.

THE LABORATORIES

The Federal Government, giving life to the ideas of the Declaration of Independence, had brought freedom to slaves within all the states. It had encouraged, over the long run, the spread of equality of opportunity and of the voting privilege. States that sought to check the spread of these principles eventually found themselves in trouble. The effort of Rhode Island, for instance, to keep most of its citizens from voting had resulted, in 1842, in an armed rebellion and the defeat of the old, repressive regime.

But whenever the Federal Government lingered behind the needs of the people, states could take the lead. The Supreme Court, for instance, had shown that it did not know how most Americans lived when it declared various state laws establishing eight-hour work days as "unwarrantable interference with the right of both the employer and employee in making contracts"; and in declaring, in 1905, that a New York State law establishing a ten-hour day for bakers was illegal interference with the rights of individuals, both employers and employees, to make contracts regarding labor . . . "and, as such, reached and passed the limit of the police power."

The State of Wisconsin set up a series of special commissions to regulate railways, public utilities and industry. The commissions had power to examine company books, to regulate rates, and to enforce laws that defined working conditions and hours of work. Another commission tried to arrive at a just method of taxation that neither favored the rich nor discouraged enterprise. A direct primary law permitted citizens to participate in the nomination of candidates to public office. A workman's compensation act sustained injured workers. A state insurance system was set up, and a board of economic affairs sought to develop the wealth of the state with due regard for the conservation of resources.

The powers of the state were greatly increased by these reforms, which owed much to the planning, able administrators, and consultants contributed by the University of Wisconsin (state colleges founded on gifts of public land, under the Morrill Act, 1862, were playing an ever greater part in the intellectual life of the nation).

The Wisconsin Idea, and the reforms of other states, demonstrated some of the ways in which democratic government could cope with the problems of an industrial society. The states were laboratories for a multitude of experiments.

"...SERVANTS OF CORPORATIONS"

Reforms were necessary if the American people were to retain their freedom amongst the new giants in their midst. But how were the great corporations and trusts to be controlled? Roosevelt proposed that the trusts be kept as they were, but be forced by the Federal Government to act in the public interest. His "New Nationalism" called for special commissions with strong powers. Woodrow Wilson, the Democratic candidate in 1912, advocated other methods.

Wilson agreed with Roosevelt on the need for reform, but he did not believe any men could be trusted with the powers of the proposed commissions. He wanted new laws, spelling out what the trusts could not do, rather than men with new powers.

"Our life has broken away from the past," Wilson said. ". . . We have come upon a very different age from any that preceded us . . . we do not . . . carry on any of the operations of manufacturer, sale, transportation, or communication as men used to carry them on. There is a sense in which in our day the individual has been submerged. In most parts of our country men work, not for themselves, not as partners in the old way in which they used to work, but generally as employees — in a higher or lower grade — of great corporations. There was a time when corporations played a very minor part in our business affairs, but now they play the chief part, and most men are the servants of corporations.

"You know what happens when you are the servant of a corporation. . . . If the corporation is doing the things that it ought not to do, you really have no voice in the matter and must obey the orders, . . . Your individuality is swallowed up in the individuality and purpose of a great organization.

"It is true that, while most men are thus submerged in the corporation, a few, a very few, are exalted to a power which as individuals they could never have wielded. Through the great organizations of which they are the heads, a few are enabled to play a part unprecedented by anything in history . . . in the determination of the happiness of great numbers of people. . . .

"Today, the everyday relationships of men are largely with great impersonal concerns, with organizations, not with other individual men. . . . The employer is generally, in our day, . . . not an individual, but a powerful group; and yet the workingman when dealing with his employer is still, under an existing law, an individual. . . .

"We are all caught in a great economic system which is heartless . . ."

The pressure for reform had split the Republican Party between Taft and Roosevelt, just as slavery had divided the Democrats in 1860. The results were similar — victory for the unbroken party. But popular support for reform could not be doubted. Of the 15 million votes cast in the election, 10 million had gone to Wilson and the Progressive Republican Theodore Roosevelt.

REFORM TRIUMPHANT

In February, 1912, toward the end of Taft's Administration, a subcommittee of the House of Representatives Committee on Banking and Currency had begun an investigation. There was a widespread feeling that vast hidden forces were at work in America.

The committee, headed by Congressman Arsene P. Pujo of Louisiana, was able to show that the directors of five New York City banks — Morgan and Company, the First National Bank, the National City Bank, the Bankers Trust Company, Guaranty Trust Company (the latter two controlled by Morgan and Company) — held "one hundred and eighteen directorships in 34 banks and trust companies . . . Thirty in 10 insurance companies . . . one hundred and five in 32 transportation systems having a total mileage . . . of 150,200 . . . Sixty-three in 24 producing and trading corporations . . . In all, directorships in corporations having aggregate resources or capitalization of $22,245,-000,000 . . ." (or between one-third and one-half of the total resources of the United States).

Among the large individual enterprises in this empire were the Atchison, Topeka & Santa Fe Railway; the Chesapeake and Ohio Railway; the New York, New Haven & Hartford Railroad; the New York Central Lines; the Southern Pacific; the Union Pacific; the Northern Pacific; the American Can Company; the General Electric Company; the International Harvester Company; the Pullman Company; the United States Steel Corporation; the Equitable Life Assurance Society; the American Telephone & Telegraph Company; the Consolidated Gas Company of New York; the Western Union Telegraph Company; and the companies that owned and transported 88% of all anthracite coal deposits in Pennsylvania.

As a congressional commission was to announce two years later:

"The final control of American industry rests . . . in the hands of a small number of wealthy and powerful financiers. . . . A careful and conservative study shows that the corporations controlled by six financial groups . . . employ 2,651,684 wage earners. . . . The lives of millions of wage earners are therefore subject to the dictation of a relatively small number of men. These industrial dictators for the most part are totally ignorant of every aspect of the industries which they control except the finances . . ."

To deal with such situations, Congress, in the fall of 1914, created a Federal Trade Commission and passed the Clayton Anti-Trust Act. The Federal Trade Commission was empowered to prevent ". . . unfair methods of competition in commerce." The Clayton Act specifically outlawed a number of practices that big businesses had used against small competitors. It sought to prevent the future growth of trusts by limiting the degree to which corporations could buy stock in other corporations and to dissolve such huge power pyramids as those delineated by the Pujo Committee.

The Federal Trade Commission and the Clayton Act set forth new rules under which the game of free competition would be played, and made the Government the umpire of the game. The campaign of 1912 had clarified many of the problems of control of industry. Roosevelt had emphasized the need for control and Wilson the need for restraint on whatever control was needed. The New Freedom and the New Nationalism both tended to similar measures. Both grew from the belief, stated by Wilson during the campaign, that "America is not now, and cannot in the future be, a place for unrestricted individual enterprise."

During the first two years of Wilson's Administration it seemed as if many injustices of the past were to be redressed. Acts to prevent the labor of children under fourteen and to regulate stock issues failed, but the Federal Reserve System set up a central banking system with regional banks closely attuned to the needs of the different sections of the country; the tariff was finally lowered; appropriations were made to help farmers improve the growing, storage, marketing and financing of crops; and the adoption of the Seventeenth Amendment provided for the popular election of Senators (who no longer would be appointed by corrupt state legislatures in the pay of powerful corporations).

Two generations of unrest, the feelings of a nation gone wrong, had found a voice, and a single will. A government that had fostered "Big Business" with tariffs and land gifts began to encourage small enterprise.

As president of Princeton and Governor of New Jersey, Woodrow Wilson had, over strong objections, reformed a university and a state. He once said, "I am sorry for those who disagree with me, because I know they are wrong." To this confidence was coupled a political scientist's knowledge of the possibilities of the Presidency.

THE AUTOMOBILE

YOUNG Henry Ford was not the first to conceive of a self-powered vehicle. In 1858, five years before he was born, a steam bus had operated briefly in London.

The internal combustion gas-burning engine, which was developed in Europe while Americans were occupied with the resolution of the Civil War, stimulated development of a self-moving vehicle. It promised more power per pound than existing steam engines.

Ford's peculiar vision was not the automobile, but that such a machine would replace the horse. In 1893, after he had become chief engineer for the Edison Illuminating Company in Detroit, Ford spent as much time as he could in his company machine shop, making parts for a gasoline engine. Evenings, he would work over a bench he had set up in the woodshed in back of his house.

Detroit made carriages, railroad cars, stoves, machinery parts. As chief engineer of the Edison Illuminating Company, Ford met many mechanics. As he worked in the shed on Bagley Avenue, Henry Ford was able to find other mechanics who would help him, who understood carriage construction and the transmission of power from engine to wheels, and who had built gasoline engines. Somehow, he could get them to make things that had never been made in exactly the same way before — new things, that would work.

In May, 1896, what Henry Ford called his quadricycle was ready for a trial run. If the automobile was to replace the horse, it had to be low in price. In keeping with this aim, the quadricycle was small and, at 500 pounds, the lightest man-carrying automobile anyone had ever made. The little car was sturdy and simple as well. If the automobile was to replace the horse, it could not be so complicated or delicate that only a mechanic could handle it. Henry Ford knew

Most roads were at least better than this.

what he wanted — lightness, strength, dependability.

Suddenly, everyone was manufacturing automobiles. In 1904, there were 178 different automobile makers in the United States. The largest Detroit factories — the Cadillac, Packard, Wayne, Olds, Ford, and Northern had national reputations.

Almost everybody believed that the future of the automobile industry was in big, expensive machines. As they saw it, there were only a limited number of people who could afford cars or who had any use for them. There were but a few hundreds of miles of road in the whole country on which an automobile could travel all the year round.

What Henry Ford saw was something quite different. For instance, roads would be improved when more cars created the need. To Ford's business associates, a lower-priced car, with smaller profit per car, simply meant less total profits. A hundred cheap cars might not yield as big a profit as fifty expensive cars.

Henry Ford began with the idea that a lower-priced car would sell better. He saw that as more cars were produced, better methods could be used to produce them, which would bring the cost down even further. If he made enough cars, it would pay him to buy machinery to make parts. If he made his own parts, they would fit together better than the parts he bought from outside machine shops. If they fit better, it would take less time to assemble a car. If it took less time to assemble a car, the labor cost would be less and the car could be sold for less. What Henry Ford saw was that if he sold more cars he could lower their price. It was a remarkable vision.

From 1903 to 1906, Ford sold between one to two thousand cars a year, little runabouts for eight or nine hundred dollars; and a few big "touring cars" at $2,000. The quarrel within the company — high-priced "touring cars" versus "runabouts" — continued, but work on the little car never really stopped. There was endless experimenting. The engine was moved out from under the seat. An electric generator was built into the motor so that the car no longer needed a dry cell to furnish sparks for the engine.

The engine itself was changed — and the brakes, the transmission, the wheels, the springs. What Ford sought was a single design of car he could concentrate on. Big savings resulted from making great numbers of the same parts. Better to sell a single kind of car than six different models. In the year 1906-1907, Model N was ready. A handsome little car with nickel-plated lamps and a four-cylinder motor capable of forty-five miles an hour, it sold for $600. That year Ford sold more than five times as many cars as he had sold the year before. He was approaching his ideal car. He had assembled a remarkable team of mechanics and metal experts. Together, they had discovered a number of ways to drastically cut down the number of hours of work needed to assemble a car. Now all that remained was to construct a plant in which these discoveries could be applied to the fullest. Ground was broken outside Detroit, at a place called Highland Park.

THE MOVING ASSEMBLY LINE

In 1913, it was found that 12½ man hours of work (fifty men working for a quarter of an hour, for example) went into the assembly of each Model T chassis. By the end of 1914, this had been reduced to one and one-half man hours.

At the Highland Park plant, a great conveyor system moved the thousands of parts so that the automobile flowed together. Axles were assembled along the lines that met the lines on which the car frames were assembled. At another point, newly assembled and painted wheels joined the line, to be fastened to the ends of the axles. Every part of the Ford car flowed through the great factory at a rate carefully regulated to the speed of the laborers along the line. It is true that no single one of the elements in this vast process was original with the Ford Motor Company. Eli Whitney had manufactured muskets with standardized parts a hundred years before. The big Cincinnati butchers had been swinging hogs to the workers along moving overhead chains since the time of the Civil War. Frederick W. Taylor had been studying and improving work-motions since 1885.

What was new was the application of these principles on so vast a scale and with the aim of lowering prices.

MODEL T

The Model T was perfected while the Highland Park plant was being built. The first year it sold for $850. In 1909, to help pay the cost of the move to Highland

Each improvement at Highland Park built automobile creation into the plant machinery and took it out of the hands and nerves of men. As Ford grew older, he spent more and more time finding and preserving evidences of the manual skills his genius was destroying.

The increase in automobile use was due partly to the discovery of huge amounts of oil in Texas. Spindletop, the first Texan well, brought in by Anthony F. Lucas on January 10, 1901, produced more oil than the Standard Oil Company of New Jersey.

Park, the price was raised to $950. In its first year of operation, the Highland Park plant turned out 34,528 Model T's, which sold for $680 each. Below are the figures for the next six years:

	Number of cars	Price of one basic roadster
1911-12	78,440	$590
1912-13	168,304	525
1913-14	248,307	500
1914-15	221,805	440
1915-16	472,360	390
1916-17	730,041	345

The Model T Ford was, by all accounts, a most unusual car. Its inventor had sought a machine that would take the place of the horse, and he seemed to have created something that was almost half animal. As one admiring owner wrote:

". . . even when the car was in a state known as neutral, it trembled with a deep imperative and tended to inch forward. . . . In this respect it was like a horse, rolling the bit on its tongue, and country people brought to it the same technique they used with draft animals.

"Its most remarkable quality was its rate of acceleration. In its palmy days the Model T could take off faster than anything on the road. . . . To get under way, you simply hooked the third finger of the right hand around a lever on the steering column, pulled down hard, and shoved your left foot forcibly against the low-speed pedal . . . the car responded by lunging forward with a roar. After a few seconds of this turmoil you took your toe off the pedal, eased up a mite on the throttle, and the car . . . catapulted directly into high with a series of ugly jerks and was off on its glorious errand . . ."

THE NEW WORLD OF PLENTY

In its first seven years, the Highland Park Plant turned out 2 million Model T's. Between 1918 and 1927, the Ford Motor Company sold all the cars it could make — more than 15 million. During many of those years, more than half of all the cars on America's roads were Model T Fords.

Henry Ford's "more cars, lower prices" cycle was beginning to have important effects on the nation as a whole. The industries that provided the materials and fuel for cars — steel, rubber, and petroleum — grew also, and as roads were improved and the new means of transportation spread into areas distant from rivers and railroads, the pace of all business quickened. In his early years, Ford had frequently told his workmen that he aimed to make a car they could afford to buy. As the motor car created jobs and produced wealth, it was, in effect, providing the money with which more people could buy motor cars.

The Ford system upset almost all the rules by which men had previously managed businesses. Everything Ford did was aimed at increasing production without increasing labor. Machinery was discarded as soon as more efficient machinery could be obtained, even if it had been used but a few months. When you were producing thousands of automobiles a day, the most expensive machinery could cost no more than a few cents per car. The labor the new machinery saved would invariably be greater than what the machinery cost.

The wages of the workman were less important than the amount of work he did. The historic system of paying wages "by the day" had little meaning in an institution where the amount of work per day was constantly changing. Ford's plant was constantly being improved so that less and less hours of work were required to manufacture a car, with the result that each man in the plant was producing more cars. Increasing the pay of a man in this kind of situation did not necessarily mean that the cost of what he made was increased. Indeed, if the speed of production could be increased fast enough, the cost of the cars could be lowered while the wages of the men were raised.

In 1914, the Ford Motor Company doubled the pay of its employees. Men who had been getting $2.40 for a nine-hour day were paid $5 for an eight-hour day. To an astonished world, it seemed as if a new economic era might be dawning: a world of plenty instead of want; a world in which production, rather than sales, would be the problem of business; a world in which the more you paid your workers, the greater your profits would be. The profits were enormous, more than $2 million a month; and overshadowing even this was the hint that old ways of thinking about work might be obsolete.

December 17, 1903, Kitty Hawk, N.C. Inside the fragile machine is Orville Wright, a 32-year-old bicycle mechanic from Dayton, Ohio. Watching is his younger brother, Wilbur. Men were slow in understanding the implications of controlled, powered flight but, its advent marked a turning point in history. All lands are shores of the world-ocean of air, open equally to peaceful commerce or destruction. Some kind of world order had become inevitable.

"PEACE WITHOUT VICTORY"

To EVERYONE'S surprise, Europe went to war in 1914. It began when the Austro-Hungarian empire invaded the Balkan kingdom of Serbia and soon brought the "Central Powers": Germany, Austro-Hungary, and Turkey into collision with the "Triple Entente": England, France, and Russia, later joined by Japan and Italy.

The decay of the Turkish Empire at the eastern end of the Mediterranean Sea had left several small, weak, independent principalities on the Balkan Peninsula, between Austro-Hungary and Russia. Behind Russia stood Great Britain. Behind Austro-Hungary stood Germany, building a railway reaching to Persia. Domination of the Balkans would give the Central Powers control of the whole route of a railway that would short-circuit the Suez Canal, opening a path to India and a whole section of the world from which Great Britain and France derived wealth and power. At stake were the possessions, trading interests and "spheres of influence" of the *Entente* all over the world.

England and Germany, the leaders of each coalition of warring powers, were the sources of the two largest groups of American immigrants. On August 19, two weeks after England entered the war, Wilson asked that his countrymen remain neutral in thought as well as deed. (But in 1913, in a little-noticed article in a British magazine, an American diplomat, worried by signs of war, had warned, "Unperceived by many Americans, the European balance of power is a political necessity which can alone sanction on the Western Hemisphere the continuance of an economic development unhandicapped by the burden of extensive armaments . . . If it then neglects to observe that the interests of . . . nations crushed are likewise its own, America will be guilty of political blindness which it will later rue.")

Neutral feelings largely vanished on May 7, 1915, when 114 Americans perished in the sinking of the liner *Lusitania* by a German submarine. The *Lusitania* had been carrying munitions as well as passengers, and the German Government had warned Americans not to use the ship, but Americans were outraged that the ship had been torpedoed before the passengers had been given a chance to board lifeboats. Wilson's note to the German Government was so strongly worded that William Jennings Bryan, dedicated to peace and neutrality, resigned his post as Secretary of State. After the *Lusitania* sank, publishers noticed that headlines telling of Allied victories sold more newspapers than announcements of German successes.

The United States was also drawn closer to the *Entente* by certain facts of geography. As inland nations, the Central Powers were more effectively blockaded than their enemies. As it was possible for the United States to trade only with the *Entente,* it was inevitable that they grow closer in sympathy.

OCEAN STEAMSHIPS.

CUNARD

EUROPE VIA LIVERPOOL

LUSITANIA

Fastest and Largest Steamer now in Atlantic Service Sails SATURDAY, MAY 1, 10 A. M.

Transylvania, Fri., May 7, 5 P.M.
Orduna, - - Tues., May 18, 10 A.M.
Tuscania, - - Fri., May 21, 5 P.M.
LUSITANIA, Sat., May 29, 10 A.M.
Transylvania, Fri., June 4, 5 P.M.

Gibraltar–Genoa–Naples–Piraeus
S.S. Carpathia, Thur., May 13, Noon

ROUND THE WORLD TOURS
Through bookings to all principal Ports of the World.
Company's Office. 21-24 State St., N. Y.

NOTICE!

TRAVELLERS intending to embark on the Atlantic voyage are reminded that a state of war exists between Germany and her allies and Great Britain and her allies; that the zone of war includes the waters adjacent to the British Isles; that, in accordance with formal notice given by the Imperial German Government, vessels flying the flag of Great Britain, or of any of her allies, are liable to destruction in those waters and that travellers sailing in the war zone on ships of Great Britain or her allies do so at their own risk.

IMPERIAL GERMAN EMBASSY

WASHINGTON, D. C., APRIL 22, 1915.

American Line
AMERICAN STEAMERS

In May, 1915, one hundred-fourteen Americans perished in the sinking of the Lusitania *by a German submarine. Outraged Americans felt that no one had a right to deny them the sea.*

Trade between the United States and the *Entente* grew apace — especially after Germany, in response to Wilson's protest, stopped sinking merchant ships without warning. By the end of 1915, American food, iron, steel, explosives, and weapons were flowing across the Atlantic in such volume that Britain and France were running out of gold to pay for them. Billions of dollars' worth of securities in American corporations flowed westward to the United States as France and England turned investments in American industry into needed cash.

When England and France ran out of cash, Wilson allowed them to borrow money from American banks. Secretary of State Bryan warned that loans must tie America even closer to the Allies. But Wilson was sympathetic to England and France. Also, he did not wish to face the unemployment and depression that must follow a drop in war production. America became, for the first time, a creditor of Europe.

Meanwhile, Wilson, who as a boy in Confederate Georgia had seen the ugliness of war, was learning that Europe's statesmen would suffer millions of men to be killed rather than lose anything of the empires for which they fought. To his amazement, they considered his high-minded efforts toward peace only as aids in defeating their enemies. How did it happen, Wilson wondered, that supposedly civilized men acted as suspicious and vengeful as Dakota Sioux? Wilson decided the system was at fault. He planned to reform the whole world.

AMERICA GOES TO WAR

Theodore Roosevelt rejoined his old party in 1916 to campaign for the Republican candidate Charles Evans Hughes. With both major parties united, the election would be close. The Republicans promised a "stronger" foreign policy. Wilson, to appeal to pacifists and neutralists, whose votes might swing the election, campaigned with the slogan, "He kept us out of war." Meanwhile, the Navy ordered destroyers. Young men drilled in Officers' Training Camps.

On January 22, 1917, President Wilson told the United States Senate that he had been giving a great deal of thought "in regard to the duty of our Government in days to come when it will be necessary to lay afresh and upon a new plan the foundations of peace among the nations . . ."

He called for a peace settlement that would include the New World as well as the Old, and would be guaranteed by the organized force of mankind, "so much greater than the force of any nation now engaged . . . that . . . no probable combination of nations could . . . withstand it. . . .

"The question upon which the whole future peace and policy of the whole world depends is this: Is the present war a struggle for a just and secure peace, or only for a new balance of power? If it be only a struggle for a new balance of power, who will guarantee, who can guarantee the stable equilibrium of the new arrangement?

". . . it must be a peace without victory . . . . Victory would mean . . . a victor's terms imposed upon the vanquished. It would be accepted in humiliation . . . and would leave a sting, a resentment . . . upon which terms of peace would rest . . . as upon quicksand. . . .

"The equality of nations upon which peace must be founded if it is to last must be an equality of rights; the guarantees exchanged must neither recognize nor implying a difference between big nations and small, between those that are powerful and those that are weak. . . . Equality of territory or of resources there of course cannot be; . . . But no one asks or expects anything more than an equality of rights. . . .

"And there is a deeper thing involved than even equality of right among organized nations. No peace can last, or ought to last, which does not recognize and accept the principle that governments derive all their just powers from the consent of the governed, and that no right anywhere exists to hand peoples about from sovereignty to sovereignty as if they were property . . ."

Wilson was addressing not just the Senate, but the whole world. The time had come, he was saying, for a new way of life among nations. The American experience, he believed, provided the basis for a new era. The principles that maintained peace among 100 million people in forty-eight states could maintain peace among the nations of the world. Wilson was saying that the time had come to extend the Declaration of Independence to all mankind. What he did not say was how the United States was to make the rest of the world follow these principles. In the past, peace terms had always been made by victors. But the only way the United States could become a victor was by entering the war. Could America, could any people, fight a war, become victors, and deny themselves victory, as Wilson asked?

As a neutral, the United States would have little influence on the peace. As a victor, she might very well fail to act temperately. Did Wilson perceive that the heart of his dream was pierced with irony?

A week later, Germany announced a resumption of "unrestricted submarine warfare." Knowing this would bring America into the war, the German Government was gambling that it could end the conflict before American military force would have any effect.

The Germans thought they could end the war quickly because Russia was collapsing. Once Russia was out of the war, millions of additional German troops from the eastern front would be freed for western service against France, England and Italy.

In March, 1917, the workers of the two biggest cities in Russia went on strike. Rioters in Petrograd and Moscow were joined by the Russian soldiers sent against them. At the front, army discipline broke down. Consumed by revolution, Imperial Russia ceased to be a force in the war.

On the night of April 1, Frank Cobb of The New York World found the President worried and restless. He was about to send a war message to Congress, and he was torn between his hopes that victory would bring a better world, and fears that war itself might deprive America of her ideals. "Once lead this people into war," he said (remembering perhaps the South of the 1870's), "and they'll forget there ever was such a thing as tolerance. To fight you must be brutal and ruthless, and the spirit of ruthless brutality will enter into the very fibre of our national life . . ."

The next day Wilson read his war message to Congress. The United States declared war on Germany to make "the world safe for Democracy," and the President wondered how safe democracy would be at home.

Twenty-six million men between 18 and 45 registered for military service. The draft was an improvement over the

Civil War system. Substitutes could no longer be hired, nor was there any way of purchasing exemption. Before the war was over, three and a half million men were drafted. Industry, too, was mobilized. The Government ran the railroads, controlled production and prices of food, coal, petroleum, iron ore and other metals, and coordinated construction and production. As in 1861, the United States Government had to become a centralized dictatorship.

"LAFAYETTE, WE ARE HERE"

The war was moving to a great climax. In April, the month the United States entered the war, almost a million tons of allied shipping were sunk by German submarines. All through the summer of 1917, ships were being sent to the bottom at a rate that exceeded the building of new ships. The ability of America to ship sufficient troops to Europe was in doubt. In Russia, the first revolutionary government had sought to continue the war. In November, 1917, the Bolshevik Party, led by Vladimir I. Ulyanov (Lenin) seized control of the revolution. The Germans had sent the exile Lenin to Russia with the understanding that he would use his influence to make peace with Germany. This the Bolsheviks did in March, 1918.

As trains crossed Germany night and day, rushing men and munitions to the western front, it became plain that the fate of the war would be decided by the American troops. The convoy system, in which ships crossed the ocean in fleets protected by fast destroyers, greatly reduced losses at sea. Less than three months after America declared war, a convoy landed 14,500 soldiers at the port of St. Nazaire. The AEF, the American Expeditionary Force, was under the command of General John J. "Blackjack" Pershing. As the first members of the AEF planted their feet on French soil, Colonel Charles E. Stanton, one of Pershing's aides, said, "Lafayette, we are here." He was acknowledging an old debt. All that fall, winter, and spring doughboys had been arriving in shiploads, to travel through France in little boxcars built to hold forty men or eight horses, to march across soft French fields, lined by poplars against the sky.

These Americans only dimly understood Europe. Their school geographies had told them that in France, "Education is not universal, but the better classes were refined and cultivated," and that the people of Prussia "are intelligent." In general, they had been taught that Europeans were rather quaint and behind the times. The poorly educated tend to look down on, and deride, people whose language or customs differ from their own. (And the sons of immigrants, who tended to mark their parents' poor English as a sign of inferiority, transferred that inferiority to all foreigners.) This attitude would not always engender friendship, even among allies.

The warfare that millions of young Americans were preparing themselves for was not unlike the siege of Petersburg at the end of the Civil War. The invention of the machine gun, capable of firing hundreds of bullets a minute, made movement dangerous and defense secure. Every machine gun emplacement was a strong point, and every advance on it became a siege.

World War I was a war of sieges. Battlefields became lines of opposing trenches and barbed wire.

In the great battles of the war, such as at Verdun, advances of but a few miles

While returning soldiers were joyfully greeted at victory parades, other Americans at the Peace Conference took long midnight walks, nervously puffed at cigarettes, and wondered how they would ever shake off regrets of a golden opportunity lost.

had been paid for by hundreds of thousands of lives. In three years of such battles, England, France, and Germany, had each lost an entire generation of young men. Altogether, it proved to be the bloodiest and costliest war that had ever taken place.

The English and French commanders, feeling the press of time, wished to feed the American soldiers into their own armies. Such an arrangement, they felt, would give the Americans the benefit of their experienced leadership. It was, they were certain, the fastest way to bring their new allies into effective combat.

General Pershing felt otherwise. In the first place, he was not at all convinced that the British and the French Armies had been fighting the war in the right way, nor did he want American troops to become mere parts of other armies. General Pershing and his staff felt certain that, despite the machine gun, properly-trained troops could advance without taking impossible losses. Accordingly, the AEF was trained as an offensive-minded army. American soldiers were taught to crawl forward, to use every slight rise in ground for protection as they moved toward the enemy, and to employ the machine gun to cover advancing troops.

The German offensive began in May. A weakness developed in the eastern end of the Allied position near a place called Chateau-Thierry. The American Second and Third Divisions stopped the German advance.

To the west, the German Army ground forward. It was stopped finally, just forty miles from Paris.

An Allied offensive was now mounted in which the Americans had to advance through a great forest at the eastern edge of the front. The forty-seven-day Battle of Argonne Forest was a bitter affair. It was very much like General Grant's Wilderness campaign, but much bigger in scale.

The number of American troops engaged was twelve times the number that fought under General Grant. They fired ten times as many guns, a hundred times as many rounds of ammunition, and suffered four times as many casualties. The weight of the ammunition expended was greater than that fired by the Union forces during the entire Civil War.

But if war had grown bigger, fewer soldiers died of disease. As recently as the Spanish-American War, five times as many men had succumbed to microorganisms as to shot and shell. In 1917 and 1918, only half as many soldiers died of disease as from wounds.

One by one, Germany's allies had left the war during the long fall of 1918 and finally, on November 11, after a revolution had forced the Kaiser Wilhelm II from his throne, Germany signed an armistice.

At war's end, 2 million American soldiers and marines were in France, over a million of whom had seen action. They held one-fifth of the western front, which stretched about six hundred miles from the English Channel to the border of Switzerland.

VICTORY WITHOUT PEACE

America had come into the war last of all the great powers and suffered a fraction of the casualties and none of the physical damage of England and France. Yet Wilson's Fourteen Points, announced January 8, 1918, had been accepted as the basis of the peace.

The Fourteen Points were a precise program for the future of the world. To the proposals made in his January, 1917 speech, Wilson had added a plea for an end to secret agreements between nations. The fourteenth and most important point advocated "A general association of nations . . . formed under specific covenants for the purpose of affording mutual guarantees of political independence and territorial integrity to great and small states alike."

To insure the adoption of the Fourteen Points, Wilson had decided to attend the Versailles Peace Conference. He arrived in France in December, 1918, the first

Wilson in 1920, ailing and disappointed.

American President to set foot on European soil. He was greeting by a tremendous display of adulation. People everywhere, even of the defeated nations, believed in Wilson. They believed that the United States had fought to free men everywhere, and opposed only oppressive, unrepresentative governments. They expected a new kind of peace that would create a new era.

But the other statesmen at the bargaining table did not share these beliefs, and they knew that Wilson's position at home was weak. During the 1918 Congressional campaign, the President had urged the election of Democratic Congressmen to insure the success of his peace program. The implication that Republicans were disloyal strengthened political opposition to Wilson's foreign policy and resulted in the election of Republican majorities to both houses of Congress.

As Wilson left for Europe, ex-President Roosevelt had declared, "Our Allies and our enemies and Mr. Wilson himself should all understand that Mr. Wilson has no authority whatever to speak for the American people at this time. His leadership has just been emphatically repudiated by them . . ."

The treaty that came out of Versailles was a caricature of the Fourteen Points. Self-determination, for instance, was applied only to the peoples of the conquered lands. Czechs and Slovaks, who had been subjects of Austro-Hungary, were given their independence; but the Irish were kept tied to Great Britain. What had been intended as a principle of universal right had become a means of depriving defeated enemies of their territory. Of other provisions of the treaty, the British economist John M. Keynes wrote, "Reparation was their main excursion into the economic field, and they settled it as a problem of theology, of politics, of electoral chicane, from every point of view except that of the economic future of the States whose destiny they were handling."

In yielding to this corruption of his principles, Wilson was able to obtain agreement to the formation of a League of Nations and to some sort of international supervision over the colonies and territories taken from Germany and Turkey, all of which ended up as parts of the British, French, or Japanese empires.

To be binding on the United States, the Versailles Treaty would have to be approved by a two-thirds vote of the now Republican Senate. A small group of powerful Senators, led by Henry Cabot Lodge of Massachusetts, opposed the Treaty and the League of Nations. And the President refused any compromise. Wilson expected to once more exercise the arts of legislative leadership to gain approval of his measures.

As in the past, he took his plea to the people. He made forty speeches during September, 1919, hurrying from one city to the next, always fearful that he was not doing quite enough. Perhaps he sensed that the people, this time, were not listening. September 25, unable to stand the strain, he collapsed.

Following the Senate's rejection of his treaty, the weakened man seemed to withdraw further into himself. He spent the final eighteen months of his term obscure from public view, an invalid confined to a few upper rooms in the White House, attended only by his wife and a few of his closest associates. He was certain that within twenty-five years, the world would be consumed by another, even more terrible war. There had been victory, but there would be no lasting peace.

11:59 A.M., September 16, 1920. Thirty-eight people were killed on Wall Street when a wagon filled with dynamite and iron exploded. One of many meaningless violent events that followed the war.

THE NEW ERA

WHILE American soldiers and sailors came back to their home towns, hung up their uniforms and adjusted to the softer tides of peace, men were killing one another in Russia. Gradually the Bolsheviks were bringing the largest country in the world under their control. The Japanese proceeded to extend their influence in Manchuria, in northern China, where, despite the "Open Door" policy, the United States Government had agreed Japan *did* have special interests.

The first year after the war was a year of unrest. Factories were retooling from war production. Michigan plants that had been turning out airplane engines were going back to making automobiles. But while everything was being readjusted, who would buy steel from the steel mills? Would there be jobs enough for the millions of men home from the war? And if there were jobs, what rights would a worker have? President Wilson's National War Labor Board had encouraged collective bargaining and broadened union recognition. Union membership had increased 25%. The war ended and the Federal Government withdrew from the scene. A strengthened labor movement, determined to increase its power, faced industrial leaders determined to treat labor as they had before the war. At some time or other, during 1919, 4 million men were out on strike. (Among them 1100 Boston policemen who lost their jobs when the Governor of Massachusetts brought in the militia. Admired for this action, Governor Coolidge became the 1920 Republican candidate for Vice President.)

Basically, the men were striking for union recognition and the right of collective bargaining. But the issues were higher pay and an eight-hour day. Prices of manufactured goods kept rising and workers demanded higher pay to keep up with the increased cost of living. Industrial leaders convinced the public that the increased prices were caused by the union demands. And they were further able to discredit the unions by charging them with revolutionary intentions. (In a few cases, strikers really did have revolutionary intentions. Among the Industrial Workers of the World were Communists who talked about setting up workers' soviets after the Russian pattern. And the I.W.W. did start some strikes.)

But the continual strikes, a series of explosions, the discovery in the New York Post Office of thirty-six bombs wrapped in plain brown paper and addressed to such prominent Americans as J. P. Morgan, John D. Rockefeller, to Cabinet members and other high government officials, and the unsettled mood of the American people led to a series of violent measures.

In a matter of weeks "Reds" replaced Germans as America's number one villains. Woodrow Wilson's Attorney General, A. Mitchell Palmer, rounded up alien members of the Communist Party for wholesale deportation. On New Year's Day, 1920, Federal agents, police and voluntary aides, without search warrants, invaded the headquarters of the Communist parties in various cities, seized everything and arrested everybody in sight. On this and succeeding nights other Communists were arrested in their homes. Altogether, about 6,000 men were bundled off to jail. In Detroit, a hundred men were herded into a bull pen measuring twenty-four by thirty feet, and kept there a week. In Hartford, Connecticut, authorities even arrested those who came to visit the men and women captured in the raids.

As during John Adams' Administration, a foreign revolution had alarmed many holders of property. In 1917, the United States had entered the greatest war in history, confident that the spread of her free institutions would create a new and better world. In 1920, she was fearfully depriving people of their constitutional liberties.

"... A QUESTION OF PROXIMITY AND DEGREE"

Appointed to the Supreme Court by Roosevelt in 1902, Oliver Wendell Holmes had long demonstrated a concern for human rights as opposed to property rights and a belief that laws were made for men, rather than the other way around. As such, he was in frequent disagreement with the rest of the Court. The war was violently opposed by many American Socialists, and others of pacifist inclinations, and Holmes, grievously wounded in the Civil War, found himself ruling on the torments of a later generation, fighting an even more violent war.

He conceded that war might justify restrictions on the liberties guaranteed by the Constitution, even freedom of speech, and that "the character of every act depends on the circumstances in which it is done. The most stringent protection of free speech would not protect a man in falsely shouting fire in a theatre and causing a panic. . . . The question in every case is whether the words used are used in such circumstances and are of such nature as to create a clear and present danger . . . It is a question of proximity and degree."

But such limitations were justified only by the gravest of circumstances. In another opinion in 1919, Holmes said that "when men have realized that time has upset many fighting faiths, they may come to believe even more than they believe the very foundations of their own conduct that the ultimate good desired is better reached by free trade in ideas — that the best test of truth is the power of the thought to get itself accepted in the competition of the market, and that truth is the only ground upon which their wishes safely can be carried out. That at any rate is the theory of our Constitution. It is an experiment, as all life is an experiment. Every year if not every day we have to wager our salvation upon some prophecy based upon imperfect knowledge. . . . Only the emergency that makes it immediately dangerous to leave the correction of evil counsels to time warrants making any exception to the sweeping command, 'Congress shall make no law . . . abridging the freedom of speech' . . ."

But when was the emergency to be judged "immediately dangerous"? In an opinion in 1927, Justice Brandeis (joined by Holmes) clarified this point: ". . . no danger flowing from speech can be deemed clear and present, unless the incidence of the evil apprehended is so imminent that it may befall before there is opportunity for full discussion. If there be time to expose through discussion the falsehood and fallacies, to avert the evil through the processes of education, the remedy to be applied is more speech, not enforced silence . . ."

Oliver Wendell Holmes at 35.

PROHIBITION

Final expressions of the Populist spirit of reform were the Eighteenth and Nineteenth Amendments. The former prohibited the sale of intoxicating beverages; the latter gave women the right to vote in national elections. (Women had been voting in many Western states for some years.)

The passage of the Eighteenth Amendment had been forwarded by the idealism and spirit of sacrifice with which many Americans had entered the war. Advocates of reform habitually say, "There ought to be a law." Prohibition was to show that sometimes there oughtn't. (Congress passed the Volstead Act to provide for the enforcement of the Pro-

Al Capone, millionaire bootlegger

hibition Amendment. From 1921 to 1923, 4,000 special agents made 65,760 arrests. For every violator who was caught, a dozen went undetected.)

If the corner saloon was closed, secret drinking establishments called "speak-easies" did a booming business in every city in the country. Newspapers freely reported the antics of comedians and singers who performed in the "speaks." You went to "Joe's Place" or the "Club Durant" for a good time whether you were a banker, a judge, a salesman entertaining customers, a Senator, or just John Doe taking your wife out to celebrate your tenth wedding anniversary. That the speakeasy was illegal just made it more fun.

Smuggling, illegal manufacture, and transportation of liquor were brand-new businesses; immigrants had as much opportunity as other Americans to get in on the ground floor. Traditionally, immigrants worked long hours at low pay; but those who became bootleggers got rich quickly. The United States was divided into sales districts, controlled by various gangs. Rum-runners smuggled in thousand of cases of British whiskies from the high seas or across the Canadian border. Trucks sped over the nation's highways, feeding whisky from the bootleggers' hidden distilleries to garages and other secret hideouts. From the hideouts, local deliveries were made in florist's wagons, hearses or baby carriages.

The most important results of the Eighteenth Amendment were that it placed hundreds of millions of dollars into the hands of gangs of criminals in the biggest cities of the United States and caused a decline in respect for the law.

THE BIG BINGE

In general, the details of daily living changed more during the ten years following the World War than they had in any fifty years before. The most noticeable change was in the way women looked and acted. Perhaps, having gained the vote and freedom to support herself away from home, the gentle sex had to see how far she could go in changing her position. In any case, her dress was altered radically. Since earliest times the legs had been regarded as among the "hidden charms," and the skirts even of active pioneer women had swept the ground. At the end of the war, skirts had been lifted a few inches, enough to reveal the ankle, or the tops of high-button shoes. Now, they went up as far as the knee. At the same time, girls decided to change their shape. As if tired of the softness and curves that had always distinguished them from men, they adopted fashions that made them look angular. And they cut their hair short, began wearing paint and lipstick, and smoking cigarettes.

The new President, Warren G. Harding, advocated a "return to normalcy." To most Americans, normalcy seemed to mean having a good time. For some reason, they were convinced they deserved it.

STANDARDIZATION OF EXPERIENCE

The motor car came into its own during this decade, and Americans knew a new freedom of movement. "Up the road a piece" was suddenly right next door. The old isolation was gone. A family could go shopping every day, visit friends, and go to the movies.

Motion pictures, one of Edison's many inventions, had been a curiosity at the turn of the century. City people paid a nickel to sit on funeral parlor chairs in a darkened empty store, and to scream and squirm with delight as a steam engine bore down at them from a white sheet on the wall. A man named David Wark Griffith figured out how to tell real stories on film. Now 35 million people visited 20,000 movie palaces two or three times a week to watch William S. Hart put a bullet in a Mexican bad man, to see Douglas Fairbanks kiss Mary Pickford.

Through the movies and radio, more Americans were sharing the same experiences than ever before. Differences between sections of the country became smaller as young girls everywhere tried to cut their hair like the movie star Clara Bow; as young boys in Portland, Maine, and St. Paul, Minnesota, hummed "You're the Cream in My Coffee," which they had both heard on the radio the same day.

Not the least of the influences toward the standardization of American life was the national market. More and more Americans were buying similar products in similar surroundings as stores operated by national retail chains opened in their communities. Between 1914 and 1917, the A&P opened 2,200 new stores. By 1928, there were 17,500 A&P's doing an annual business of $750 million and 1,600 Woolworths selling $272 million worth of items. United Cigar and United Drug bought out a good many local stores and even the restaurant and hotel businesses seemed to lend themselves to chain management.

National advertising, too, was exposing all Americans to like slogans and products. Soaps, cigarettes, canned goods, shirts, and automobiles were sold coast to coast, their virtues proclaimed from the pages of magazines and newspapers, from the billboards that lined the new highways, and over the radio. In some cases, as advertisements for tooth brushes, carpet-sweepers, or shampoos reached isolated farms, they performed a real educational service. But once the advertisers had reached everyone who could afford their products, increasing sales came to depend on taking buyers away from rivals; and there was more emphasis on the arts of influencing people.

It was found that in the basic, primitive human emotions lay the keys to persuasion. People purchased toothpaste or cigarettes not because they were impressed by how they were made or by what they were made of, but in order to satisfy some primitive need.

Where once the public had been informed that a cigarette was made of the "finest Turkish tobaccos," it now was told to "Reach for a *Lucky* instead of a sweet." In other words, smoking would make one thin and beautiful. Terrible fates awaited those who did not follow

Section 1 | "All the News That's Fit to Print." | **The New York Times.** | THE WEATHER Generally fair today and tomorrow; moderate to fresh southerly winds. | Section 1

VOL. LXXVI....No. 25,320. NEW YORK, SUNDAY, MAY 22, 1927. FIVE CENTS

LINDBERGH DOES IT! TO PARIS IN 33½ HOURS; FLIES 1,000 MILES THROUGH SNOW AND SLEET; CHEERING FRENCH CARRY HIM OFF FIELD

COULD HAVE GONE 500 MILES FARTHER

Gasoline for at Least That Much More Flew at Times From 10 Feet to 10,000 Feet Above Water.

ATE ONLY ONE AND A HALF OF HIS FIVE SANDWICHES

Fell Asleep at Times but Quickly Awoke—Glimpses of His Adventure in Brief Interview at the Embassy.

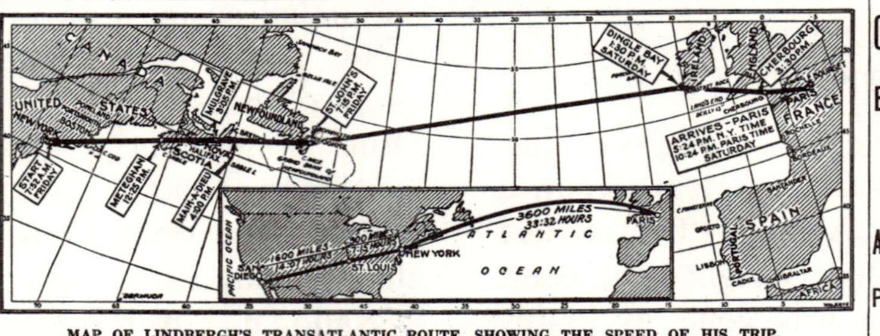

MAP OF LINDBERGH'S TRANSATLANTIC ROUTE, SHOWING THE SPEED OF HIS TRIP.

CROWD ROARS THUNDEROUS WELCOME

Breaks Through Lines of Soldiers and Police and Surging to Plane Lifts Weary Flier from His Cockpit

AVIATORS RESCUE HIM FROM FRENZIED MOB OF 25,000

Paris Boulevards Ring With Celebration After Day and Night Watch—American Flag Is Called For and Wildly Acclaimed

Headlines sold newspapers. The ideal was one big story that dragged on for weeks, supplying headline after headline. Lindbergh's feat made perfect newspaper copy, but it was a need to worship something other than money that enshrined "Lucky Lindy" in the hearts of his countrymen.

the advice of the advertisers — pyorrhea, a dreadful disease of the gums, affected four out of five people who did not use Forhan's toothpaste; halitosis (bad breath) would drive people away from the girl who did not rinse her mouth with Listerine. Worse, she might never get married but, like Edna, be "often a bridesmaid but never a bride." But even if you rinsed your mouth with Listerine you still had to worry about B.O. (body odor), prevented only by using Lifebuoy soap. Having rid yourself of halitosis and B.O., were your worries over? Not by a long shot. What would you say to your friends who no longer objected to your flavor? "When Your Guests Are Gone — Are You Sorry You Ever Invited Them? . . . Be Free From All Embarrassment! Let the Famous *Book of Etiquette* Tell You Exactly What to Do, Say, Write, or Wear on Every Occasion . . ."

"They laughed when I sat down to play the piano," another famous ad proclaimed, promising popularity as a result of taking music lessons. If the appeals of the advertisers were to be believed, Americans cared only about being beautiful, antiseptic, and universally loved. As the poet E. E. Cummings said,

"Take it from me kiddo
believe me
my country, 'tis of
you, land of the Cluett
Shirt Boston Garter and Spearmint
Girl with the Wrigley Eyes (of you
land of the Arrow Ide
and Earl &
Wilson
Collars) of you i
sing: land of Abraham Lincoln and Lydia
E. Pinkham,
land above all of Just Add Hot Water
And Serve —
From every B.V.D.
let freedom ring . . ."

STANDARDIZATION OF THE POPULACE

The great historic movement of immigrants to America's shores was ended by new laws aimed at fixing the character of the population.

The greatly increased immigration from southern and eastern Europe had aroused fears that the "old American stocks" of northwestern Europe would be submerged. Beginning with an act passed in 1917 over President Wilson's veto, several attempts were made to limit this new immigration. The Immigration Act of 1924 set annual quotas based on the proportions of various immigrant groups in the country in 1890, when there were relatively few foreign-born Americans from southern or eastern Europe. Thus, 34,007 British or North Irish, and 28,567 Irish, and 51,227 Germans could enter the United States each year, but only 100 Greeks, 3,845 Italians, 5,982 Poles, and 2,248 Russians. (The law did not even follow its own rule. According to the make-up of the 1890 population, 250 Japanese should have been admitted yearly. The law allowed for none, and gravely offended the Japanese.) From 1925 on, the quota would permit no more than 164,667 persons to enter the U. S. A. from the non-American continents. In 1924, 707,000 people had sought a haven in America. In 1925, the first year of the new law, immigration was reduced to 294,000.

STANDARDIZATION OF THE NEWS

A greater proportion of Americans were attending high school and college than ever before. But if more Americans were being equipped for the difficult responsibilities of democratic citizenship, it was becoming harder to obtain the information needed to make sensible judgments.

For one thing, much more information was needed as affairs in strange and distant places influenced and were influenced by the United States. For another, a mechanical device, the telegraph, had caused a diminishing of local reporting. As members of press associations, newspapers wired their news to other member newspapers in other cities. The cost of news received over the UP or AP wire was far less than the cost of hiring reporters to find and write news stories. The result was that while newspapers were carrying more news, less of the news was of local importance, and the total amount of reporting was less than before.

Equally serious was the decrease in the number of newspapers. Rising costs of paper and of production made it necessary that daily newspapers be fairly large in order to survive. The result was a great many mergers. From 1914 to 1924, the number of newspapers in New York City decreased from seventeen to eleven. In fifteen years, Chicago lost five out of seven morning papers. Formerly even a fairly small city like Rochester had had two daily papers, each representing the viewpoint of one of the major political parties. In 1928 it was estimated that in a thousand American cities there was no more than one newspaper publisher.

This was partly compensated for by the broadcasting of news by radio stations, by the circulation of news magazines, and the growth of public libraries. Yet the over-all effect was of a loss of the vitality of competition.

As The New York World noted, "Today real discussion is being submerged. . . . A great and growing section of our population has no choice but to take a newspaper that is either colorlessly neutral or wholly one-sided." (Three years later The World itself was sold and merged with another newspaper.)

Warren Harding (left) was a kindly man who looked like a President. Two members of his Cabinet betrayed his trust by giving away government oil reserves. Following Harding's death, Calvin Coolidge (right) became President. He believed "The chief business of the American people is business." Here, with his wife's help, he dons overalls to pose as a New England farmer.

PROSPERITY

During the Coolidge Administration, peace and prosperity made the burning beliefs of the Progressives seem out of date. Businessmen sat high in the councils of government. A "new era" had come, they said, in which business had learned its responsibilities. No longer were businesses run simply for profit. The new statesmen of business ran their companies for the benefit of all. There was no need, under such conditions, for government supervision. Federal agencies like the Federal Trade Commission and the Federal Power Commission were taken over by businessmen. Andrew Mellon, the millionaire Secretary of the Treasury, secretly returned billions of dollars of income tax payments to other wealthy men. After all, what was good for business was good for the country. (But, as one of Roosevelt's aides had written, "Life is something more than a matter of business.")

Actually, business in the "new era" differed little from business in the old era. With the sale of toasters, fans, radios, and other appliances, use of electrical power doubled during the 1920's. At the same time, three-quarters of the companies producing electricity fell into the hands of ten great holding companies — corporations formed just for the purpose of holding stock in other corporations. Since holding companies could themselves issue unlimited shares of stock, a group of business operators could buy shares in electrical utilities with money they received by sale of shares in their holding company. As long as the holding company paid out a smaller return on its shares than it received from the utilities, the system was foolproof. And holding companies could be combined into super-holding companies. It was magic.

The success of the device resulted in competition between holding companies for shares in utilities. Utility shares went way up. As the price of utility shares rose, the holding companies had to raise larger sums of money, the end result of which was that the utilities had to charge higher rates for electricity. The expense of the finagling of the business operators was thus passed on to the consumer.

And farm prices, as seemed always the case in time of peace, remained low.

In 1928, the American people made the Republican Herbert Hoover their President. No American was better equipped than he to make the New Era work. As a brilliant organizer and administrator, he had been assigned the difficult task of supplying food and other assistance to Belgium after the German invasion of 1914. In Washington, after America entered the war, he had served as Wilson's Food Administrator. So impressed was the war-time capital with Hoover's intelligence and industry, that many began looking on Hoover as a successor to Wilson. As Secretary of Commerce, Hoover had been the most active member of the Harding and Coolidge Administrations. His Commerce Department had sponsored conferences on unemployment, fostered trade associations, supported far-reaching engineering projects like Hoover Dam, and led the way toward the standardization of industrial products. "The aggregation of great wealth . . ." he had declared in 1920, "presents social and economic ills which we are constantly struggling to remedy."

Now, as President, Hoover would have a chance to show what efficient administration, working closely with business leaders, could do for the American people. "I have no fears for the future of our country," said the new President in his inaugural address in March, 1929. "It is bright with hope."

SACCO AND VANZETTI

The differences between men who thought there was more to life than business, and those who did not, were made clear by a murder trial in Massachusetts. In May, 1920, at the height of the Red scare, two admitted anarchist aliens and draft-dodgers had been convicted of murdering a paymaster in South Braintree. After sentencing the two Italians, Nicola Sacco and Bartolomeo Vanzetti, to death, the trial judge had boasted of what he had done.

Protests were made. Lawyers, suspecting the judge had been unfair, made new appeals for new trials. To one faction of Americans, Sacco and Vanzetti had become a symbol of injustice and oppression. To another faction, they became a symbol of all the alien forces that threatened their comfortable world. Much of the evidence used against Sacco and Vanzetti was later proved to be inexact. But such legal details were obscured by the bitterness between the factions. Finally, in 1927, the Governor of Massachusetts, having consulted a committee of three prominent citizens, denied the prisoners a new trial. "The momentum of the established order," said Robert L. O'Brien, publisher of The Boston Herald, "required the execution of Sacco and Vanzetti . . ." A generation after the events, it appeared that Sacco may have been guilty; that Vanzetti was almost certainly innocent.

"The United States," wrote the historian Samuel Eliot Morison, "has evolved from a country of political experiment, a debtor to Europe, a radical disturber of established government, the hope of the oppressed and an inspiration to all men everywhere who wished to be free; into a wealthy and conservative country, the world's banker and stabilizer, the most powerful enemy to change and revolution. American residence, once the right of the 'poorest child of Adam's kin,' has become a jealously guarded privilege . . ."

THE BIG BULL MARKET

Early in 1929, the Federal Reserve Board had warned member banks that money ought not to be lent for the purpose of buying stocks.

Behind the warning was the fear of several New York banks that too much money had been borrowed for this purpose. Stockbrokers' loans amounted to more than $3.5 billion at the end of 1927. In 1929, they were climbing to more than $6 billion.

All this money was being borrowed to buy stocks because stocks had been rising at unprecedented rates for four years, and especially so since 1928. Everybody, it seemed, was buying stocks. When you heard "Radio" mentioned on the elevator, you knew it meant Radio Corporation of America. With $100 cash a man could borrow $300 from his broker and buy $400 worth of stocks. If the stocks went to $800, the investor had $500 left for himself after he paid back the $300 he had borrowed. He had made $500 on a $100 investment!

Investment was hardly the right word. Speculation, the oldest of American opportunities, suddenly seemed open to any man with a few dollars to spare. And if a man didn't have a few dollars, he could always mortgage his home.

Fortunes were made as the market climbed up and up and up. Between March 3, 1928, and September 3, 1929, American Can went from 77 to 181⅞; American Telephone and Telegraph from 179½ to 335⅝; Anaconda Copper from 54½ to 162; and Radio from 94½ to 505. To thoughtful men, it was clear that Radio at 505 or G. E. at 396¼ were selling at prices much higher than what they were worth. It was the future "bright with hope" that speculators were betting on. Speculators always bet on the future. In simpler times men had sought to buy their speculations cheap. George Washington had bought Ohio land at 1760 prices, betting on what it would be worth in 1780. The speculators of 1929 were paying 1950 prices, and were betting on what values would be in 1970.

The Big Bull Market had its origin in the booming economy of the 1920's. New machinery and new methods had increased production greatly. By 1929, factories were turning out sixty per cent more goods per man-hour than they had in 1920. From 1920 to 1929, industrial profit had risen eighty per cent.

The increased profits were a sensible

Mr. and Mrs. Herbert Hoover.

reason for an advance in the price of stocks. But once the advance started, more and more people had sought to share in it, and they bid stock prices upward and upward. An article in The Ladies Home Journal stated that any man who invested $15 a week in good common stocks would have at least $80,000 and an income of $400 a month, at the end of twenty years. "He will be rich . . . anyone not only can be rich, but ought to be rich." How long would the stock market continue to rise? When shares sold for five or ten times their real worth they sold on hope. Suppose hope were to turn to fear?

STOCK EXCHANGE THE NEW

TRANSACTIONS O

1929. High.	1929. Low.	Stock and Dividend Rate.	First.	High.	Low.	Last.	Net Ch'ge.	Closing Bid.	Closing Ask.	Sales.
57⅞	38	Abitibi Power & Paper.	40	40	38	38	− 6¼	38	40	1,800
112½	106	Abraham & S. pf. (7)*	107¼	107¼	107¼	107¼	− 2¾	106	108¼	20
96	84¾	Adams Express pf. (5)	87⅞	87⅞	87⅞	87⅞	+ ⅞	87⅛	88	200
35⅞	24¾	Adams Millis (2)	26	26	24¾	24¾	− 2¾	20	25	700
104⅞	73	Advance Rumely	8¼	8¼	7	7	− 6¾	7	9	2,600
119	15	Advance Rumely pf....	20	20	15	16	− 7	..	16	1,300
4⅞	¾	Ahumada Lead	1	1	¾	¾	− ⅜	¾	1	6,500
223⅜	95⅛	Air Reduction (†4½)...	125⅛	128	100¼	120	−25	118	120	23,500
48⅞	25	Air Way El. Appl. (2½)	25	25	25	25	− 3½	25	27	3,000
11¼	2½	Ajax Rubber	2½	2½	2½	2½	− ¼	2½	2¾	7,200
10¼	4½	Alaska Juneau	5¼	5⅞	5	5⅞	..	5⅝	5⅞	14,600
25	5	Albany Perf. W. Paper	5	7	5	7	− 1	6	7	2,400
56½	18⅛	Alleghany Corporation.	24¼	24¾	18⅛	20⅝	− 8½	20½	21	224,100
92	80⅛	Alleg. Corp. pf., x w. (5½)	88⅝	88⅝	88½	88½	− 1¼	..	..	600
354¾	204¾	Allied Chem. & Dye (6)	205	218	204¾	210	−35	210	215	32,100
125	120¼	Allied Chem. & D. pf. (7)	122	122	121	121	− ¼	120½	124	400
75½	37¼	Allis-Chalmers Mfg. (2)	46½	47½	37¼	41	− 5	41	44	15,500
30½	29	Alpha Port. Cement (3)	30	30	30	30	− ¼	29¼	30	400
11⅛	3⅞	Amalgamated Leather.	3⅞	3⅞	3⅞	3⅞	− ⅜	3	4	700
42⅝	17½	Amerada Corp. (2)	20¼	21	17½	17½	− 4	17½	19	11,000
23⅝	4	Am. Agricult. Chemical	7¼	7⅞	4	4	− 3⅜	4	5	5,700
73¾	25½	Am. Agricult. Chem. pf.	26	28½	25½	25½	− 5¾	25½	29	2,400
60¼	46	Am. Beet Sugar pf....	49	49	49	49	..	45	50⅞	200
76½	30	Am. Bosch Magneto ..	30	30	30	30	− 5	19	30	2,000
62	44½	Am. Br. S. & F. (2.40)	49	49½	44½	44½	− 5½	44	46	8,200
34¾	4⅛	Am. Brown Bov. Elec.	4¼	5½	4⅛	4⅛	− 6⅞	4⅛	7	11,100
104	49¾	Am. Br. Bov. E. pf. (7)*	64	64	64	64	− 1	52	65	30
184½	107¾	Am. Can (†5)	130¼	134	110	120	−16	116	120	140,100
142	136½	Am. Can pf. (7)	136⅞	136⅞	136⅞	136⅞	− 1⅜	..	137	200
106½	76	Am. Car & Fdy. (6)...	81⅛	87½	76	87	+ 6⅞	87	89	10,100
120	110½	Am. Car & Fdy. pf. (7)	113	113	113	113	..	113	114½	200
81⅝	35	Am. Chicle (2)	38½	38½	35	35	− 9	35	37	2,900
55	20	Am. Com. Alco. (k1.60)	20	30	20	30	− ¾	29	30	17,100
199¼	50	Am. & Foreign Power.	68	73	50	55	−22½	54½	57	89,500
108½	104	Am. & F. Pwr. pf. (7)	106½	106½	106	106	− 1	105½	107	1,400
103	87	Am. & F. Pw. 2d pf. (7)	89½	90	87	90	− 2½	89	90	2,000
42	21½	Am. Hawaiian S. S. (1)	21½	21½	21½	21½	− 1½	..	21½	500
10	5	Am. Hide & Leather...	5	5	5	5	− 1	5	6	500
52¼	30¼	Am. Hide & Leath. pf.	32⅞	32⅞	31	31	− 4¼	31	32	300
85⅝	43½	Am. Home Prod. (3.60)	46¼	49	43½	47	− 3	45	47	9,500
54	30	Am. Ice (3)	33	35	30	35	− 2½	34½	37	8,200
96	89¾	Am. Ice pf. (6)	90	90	90	90	..	90	93	600
96¾	30	Am. International (‡2).	30	41½	30	41½	− 2½	41	42	71,400
8⅞	2½	Am. La F. & Foamite..	3	3	2½	2½	− ⅞	..	2½	900
136	99	Am. Locomotive (8) ...	101	101½	99	100	− ½	100	101	10,500
119⅞	112	Am. Locomotive pf. (7)	115	115¼	115	115	− ¾	114½	115	500
279¾	147¼	Am. Mach. & Fdy. (†5)	185	185	175¼	175¼	−25¾	175	183	1,000
81¾	41⅛	Am. Metal (3)	41⅛	46	41⅛	46	− 7	45	50	16,000
98¼	65	Am. Nat. Gas pf. (7)*	78¼	78¼	78¼	78¼	− 1¾	..	80	50
17⅞	3½	Am. Piano	4	4	3½	3½	− 1½	3	5½	300
55	18	Am. Piano pf. ....*	19	19	18	18	− 1	..	20	100
175¾	73¾	Am. Pwr. & Lgt. (¶1).	75¼	76¼	73¾	73¾	− 5¼	73¾	74	58,400
104	92¼	Am. P. & L. pf. (6)..	98⅛	98⅛	92¼	92¼	− 5¾	92	95	800
84¾	78	Am. P.&L. pf., A, sta. (5)	82⅛	82¼	80	80	− 2	79⅜	80	1,000
55⅜	28	Am. Rad.&Sd. San. (1½)	30	32	29	32	+ 4	31½	32½	141,000
64¾	15	Am. Republics	15	20⅛	15	17⅞	− 4¼	15	18	7,100
144⅝	72	Am. Rolling Mill (c2)..	85⅛	89¾	72	72	−13	70½	71	22,800
74¾	52	Am. Safety Razor (†5).	56⅞	56⅞	52	53¾	− 4¼	53½	54	4,100
41⅞	29½	Am. Seating (2)	30	30	29½	29½	− ½	29	30	3,400
7	⅜	Am. Ship & Commerce.	1	1	⅜	⅜	− 1¾	¼	1	1,800
112⅛	70	Am. Shipbuilding (8)..*	70	78	70	70	−10	..	75	630
130¼	81	Am. Smelt. & Ref. (4).	81	84¾	81	84	− 6	..	85	14,500
49	39	Am. Snuff (3)	40⅛	40½	39	39	− 2	38½	40	2,300
79⅞	35¾	Am. Steel Found. (3)...	42½	43	35¾	40	− 5¼	39½	40	23,200
114	110	Am. Stl. Found. pf. (7)*	111	111	110½	110½	− ½	111	112	160
85	40	Am. Stores (2½)	45	47	40	47	−13	47½	58	6,000
94¾	66	Am. Sugar Refining (5)	70	70	66	66	− 6¾	66	68	7,500
111	102	Am. Sugar Ref. pf. (7).	103⅞	103⅞	102	103⅞	− ⅛	102	104	1,100
60	28	Am. Sumatra Tob. (3)..	32	33	28	29¾	− 3¼	29½	30	4,200
310¼	193¼	Am. Tel. & Tel. (9)....	225	230	204	204	−28	204	205	131,100
232½	160	Am. Tobacco (8)	190	194½	182	191	− 5	189	192	10,100
235	160	Am. Tobacco, B (8)....	190	194¾	182	186	− 9¼	185	188	41,800
121¼	115	Am. Tobacco pf. (6)....	117	117	117	117	− 1	117	118	200
112	107¼	Am. Type Fdrs. pf. (7)*	109	109	108½	108½	− 1½	108½	109	60
199	65	Am. Water Works (c1).	70	71	65	[illegible]	−12	68	70	38,600
[illegible]04	97	[illegible] W. 1st pf. (6)	[illegible]	[illegible]	[illegible]	[illegible]	[illegible]¾	102⅝	103	400

Financial page shows what happened October 29, 1929, as desperate men sought to dump their holdings. Note "Net Ch'ge" column. Stock prices continued to plunge. Three years later, the former president of a big New York bank would remark, "The word 'securities' has almost become obsolete. An investment that drops in price . . . perhaps . . . to a twentieth of its former range is not a security; it is a jeopardy . . ."

THE GREAT DEPRESSION

THE TIDE turned toward the end of October. More than 12 million shares of stock changed hands on Thursday, October 24. On Tuesday, October 29, after some brief rallies, 16 million shares were sold. With everyone frightened and trying to sell at once, prices plunged downward with meteoric speed. General Motors went from 72¾ to 36; Radio Corporation common from 101 to 26; U.S. Steel descended from 261¾ to 150. In a few days $15 billion in market values was lost; by year-end the loss amounted to $40 billion. Stockbrokers jumped out of windows; old ladies who had been tempted by the boom suddenly saw paper profits disappear. They found themselves penniless and giving up their homes.

All the stocks held on credit created a situation in which any drop in prices could cause a lot of selling as alarmed creditors called in the money they had lent against the stocks.

Some investors had become concerned with such things as the falling-off of automobile sales in the spring of 1929. Dealers had to lower prices to sell cars. Inventories of other articles grew "heavy" as sales of radios, textiles, shoes, toothpaste, furniture, and electric irons slowed. The construction industries also declined. New housing dropped to the lowest it had been since 1921.

Periods of growth and prosperity had always been halted by crashes or "panics" followed by spells of readjustment and depression. Astute observers of the American economy watched certain "indicators" like the loadings of freight cars. Noticing that "carloadings" were falling all through early 1929, they began to "get out of the market." A point was reached where more people wanted to sell stocks than wanted to buy them. This started an avalanche.

UNEMPLOYMENT

When the crash came, in October, 1929, 1,500,000 Americans had been looking for jobs and some 31 million had been working. By March, 1930, some 4 million were looking for jobs. Inventories piled up even more, sales campaigns fizzled, production slowed, sometimes stopped. Workmen found pink dismissal slips in their pay envelopes; banks closed, mortgages were called in, and older people who thought themselves taken care of on small incomes swelled the army of unemployed as their incomes shrank to nothing. By March, 1931, unemployment had doubled. Eight million Americans were walking the streets, looking for work.

Winter was the bad time. The homeless shivered in box-cars, stuffed old newspapers under their clothes. They froze on the streets, lined up for free cups of watery soup and slices of stale bread, wandered from factory to factory in shoes flapping open at the seams to read the same big unfriendly signs posted on the gates: "NOT HIRING . . . NO HELP WANTED . . ."

There had been depressions before: in 1837, 1857, 1873, 1893, and 1907, and each time the country had recovered and gone on bigger and better than ever. People waited for "the thing to shake itself out," but things kept getting worse. In October, 1932, three years after the first shock of panic, 12 million men were out of work and the national income had fallen $42 billion, to less than half what it had been in 1929. In Danbury, Connecticut, a thirty-three-year-old woman and her daughter were found starving under a rude canvas shelter in a patch of woods. They had been living on wild berries and apples.

"INEQUALITY IN THE DISTRIBUTION OF INCOME"

Economists picked over the records of the 1920's, seeking clues to the debacle. Had American industry reached a point where it could make more than the American people could use?

What they found was something quite different — industry could make more goods than the people could buy.

As a Brookings Institute study showed, three out of five American families in 1929 had less than $2,000 a year. "At 1929 prices," said the Brookings economists, "a family income of $2,000 may be regarded as sufficient to supply only basic necessities."

All through the 1920's, too many Americans had insufficient incomes. On the one hand, there were cars, rubber tires, shirt, nails, vacuum cleaners, and gasoline with no buyers. On the other hand, there were farmers needing new cars, reapers, and clothes with no money to pay for them. A Detroit machinist, his wife, and five children slept in two rooms in a crowded two-family house. And there were carpenters, masons, plumbers, and electricians looking for work because the people who needed new houses couldn't pay for them.

Between 1920 and 1929, while output per man-hour rose 60%, workers' wages

March, 1931. Local relief agencies were running short. The impoverished sought fuel at abandoned coal mines.

barely increased, and business and banking profits soared. President Hoover would afterwards comment "the debacle . . . was largely contributed by a failure of industry to pass its improvement (through labor-saving devices) to the consumer."

The 60,000 families with the highest incomes had been able to save almost as much money as the remaining millions of families. As the Brookings economists noted, "There has been a tendency, at least during the last decade or so, for the inequality in the distribution of income to be accentuated."

THE ENGINEERING APPROACH

At the time of the depression of 1837, President Van Buren had refrained "from suggesting to Congress any specific plan . . . from a conviction that such measures are not within the constitutional province of the General Government." Grant and Cleveland had followed similar policies in 1873 and 1893, pretending that a government that regulated the economy through tariffs, land grants, and courts of justice could do nothing about unemployment and business failure.

That Herbert Hoover was in the White House in 1929 seemed most fortunate. Who would be better fitted to cope with economic disturbance and the plight of suffering millions than the engineer who had run the Commerce Department with such efficiency and fed the starving Belgians during the World War?

When it no longer seemed that a restoration of confidence in the country's future would end the depression, the Hoover Administration began buying cotton, wheat, and other staples to keep farm prices up, and to lend money to banks and other business concerns. As Hoover would say in 1932. . . . "No government in Washington has hitherto considered that it held so broad a responsibility . . . in such times."

But no matter how much farm produce the Government bought, the farmers grew more. Corn slid down to 15¢ a bushel, cotton to 5¢ a pound, hogs to 3¢, and beef to 2.5¢. To buy one of his children a four-dollar-pair of shoes, a farmer

Angry farmers pour milk out of cans in protest against low milk prices, while children of the unemployed starve. Such waste when there was such want had a kind of Alice-in-Wonderland craziness.

had to sell a whole acre of wheat. In some areas, unused crops beginning to rot on the ground were offered free to anyone who would come and cart them away. The President asked businesses not to cut wages; but pay envelopes of workers still employed in leading industries shrank from $28.50 a week in 1929 to $22.64 in 1931. In July, 1932, the Pennsylvania Department of Labor reported that saw mills were paying 5¢ an hour. Women in Tennessee mills were getting as little as $2.39 for a fifty-hour week.

All this represented increased hunger, worry, sickness and blank despair. Against this human suffering President Hoover confined himself to certain technical, almost surgical measures. Hoover was no doubt correct in feeling that if the economy were straightened out everything would be all right. The human suffering might be merely a symptom rather than the cause of the disease, but such knowledge was neither bread to eat nor shelter against the rain.

Hoover's engineering approach to problems was reenforced by his belief that income was fairly distributed and by his theory that Federal relief would create paupers who would prefer handouts to working for a living. Thus he gave food to starving cattle in Arkansas but not to starving farm families. Congress had authorized the RFC to lend up to three hundred million to the states for relief purposes. Hoover lent only one-tenth of this money for relief, while he unhesitatingly lent $90 million to save a bank in Chicago.

Ground between insufficient local charities, and a Federal Government that would not provide relief, many Americans grew desperate.

Iowa farmers blockaded the roads leading to Sioux City. They and other Western farmers turned back trucks or dumped milk and other produce in an effort to maintain farm prices. "If you continue to confiscate our property and demand that we feed your stomachs and clothe your bodies we will refuse to function," they proclaimed. Armed Nebraska farmers threatened the sheriffs and marshals who tried to take away the farms that had failed to meet mortgage payment or taxes. Twenty thousand World War veterans bummed rides on freight cars and came to Washington to demand early payments of the soldiers' bonus. In Oklahoma City, Minneapolis, and St. Paul, hungry people broke into groceries and meat markets. Respect for law and order was breaking down in great sections of the country. A Mason City, Iowa, lawyer, recounting how neighbors had lost everything after years of hard work wrote:

"I wondered if it was proper to place the responsibility for the breakdown of a faulty human economic system on the shoulders of the Lord."

Summer gave way to fall. To break the tension, people made bitter jokes. The sad little shanty towns that grew up around city dumps, or in a rocky glen in New York's Central Park, became known as "Hoovervilles." "Hoover blankets" were newspapers wrapped inside the clothing for warmth; broken-down automobiles hauled by mules were "Hoover wagons"; empty pockets turned inside out were "Hoover flags"; wild jack-rabbits were "Hoover hogs."

The mood of the nation was perhaps best summarized by an expression coined by a character in a new radio show. Since 1929, "Amos and Andy" had been sounding off weekday nights at seven. Andy would say "I'se regusted," and millions of listeners would chuckle.

THE NEW DEAL

"LET it be from now on the task of our Party to break foolish traditions," Franklin Delano Roosevelt told the Democratic National Convention in Chicago. He had flown there in July, 1932, to accept the nomination for the Presidency. Before that, a candidate had always received notification weeks later, from a visiting delegation.

Reviewing the past dozen years of Republican rule, Roosevelt suggested that the theory that government ought to help just a favored few, whose prosperity would then "leak through, to labor, to the farmer, and to the small business man," had been discredited.

"What do the people of America want more than anything else?" he asked. ". . . Work and security . . . They are . . . the true goal toward which our efforts of reconstruction should lead." An "era of selfishness," for which all must "blame ourselves in equal share," was coming to an end.

"I pledge you, I pledge myself," Roosevelt exclaimed, "to a new deal for the American people."

The Democratic Party had also pledged itself to lowering tariffs and ending Prohibition. Roosevelt's campaign struck many different chords. There were echoes of his cousin Theodore Roosevelt's New Nationalism. In September, in San Francisco, the candidate sounded like the Woodrow Wilson of the New Freedom, but with overtones of despair, of a great adventure finished:

"A glance at the situation today only too clearly indicates that equality of opportunity as we have known it no longer exists," he said. "Our industrial plant is built; the problem just now is whether under existing conditions it is not overbuilt. Our last frontier has long since been reached, and there is practically no more free land. . . . We are not able to invite the immigration from Europe to share our endless plenty. We are now providing a drab living for our own people...The independent businessman is running a losing race . . . If the process of concentration goes on at the same rate, at the end of another century we shall have all American industry controlled by a dozen corporations, and run by perhaps a hundred men. . . . Our task now is not discovery or exploitation of natural resources, or necessarily producing more goods. It is the soberer, less dramatic business of administering resources and plants already in hand . . . of meeting the problem of underconsumption, . . . of distributing wealth and products more equitably, of adapting existing economic organization to the service of the people."

Such an economy would probably only work, he said, with the Government playing an even more important role as adjuster and balancer of different interests.

Toward the end of the campaign, Herbert Hoover, running for re-election, began attacking his opponent's talk of a "new deal." "This election," he said, "is not a mere shift from the ins to the outs. It means deciding the direction our Nation will take over a century to come."

There were candidates advocating a radical change of direction. But the Socialist Norman Thomas received only two per cent of the popular vote, and the revolutionary Communist Party, only one-quarter of one per cent. Roosevelt was decisively elected with almost sixty per cent of the popular vote. The system would get another chance.

Franklin Delano Roosevelt had been born fifty years before in a big house overlooking the Hudson River, about eighty miles north of New York City. The child of his father's old age, he communicated with a distant past. His father, born during the administration of John Quincy Adams, had known men who had known Washington, Jefferson, and Adams.

FDR in 1920, squire of Hyde Park and Democratic candidate for Vice President.

During Franklin's last years at Harvard College, a distant cousin, Theodore Roosevelt, had become President of the United States. Elected to the New York State Senate in 1910, Franklin quickly established a reputation for himself as an independent fighter for good causes. As the 1912 elections approached, he disregarded the state Democratic machine to give early support to Woodrow Wilson.

Wilson rewarded him by naming him Assistant Secretary of the Navy, a post cousin Theodore had held sixteen years before under McKinley. (In war-time Washington, Franklin Roosevelt and Hoover had been quite close friends.) It would not be surprising, therefore, if Franklin was beginning to wonder if he might not eventually follow his cousin all the way to the White House.

In 1920, Franklin Roosevelt was named the Vice-Presidential candidate of his party. Following a strenuous and unsuccessful campaign, he returned to private life. In August, 1921, after a swim in the chill waters of the Bay of Fundy, he was stricken with infantile paralysis. As he slowly recovered, Franklin desperately tried to regain some power of movement. He learned how to crawl along the floor and haul himself upstairs with shoulders and arms, how to push himself up from a wheelchair to crutches.

In July, 1924, he was well enough to attend the Democratic Convention at Madison Square Garden, New York City, where he placed Alfred E. Smith's name in nomination for the Presidency. (After 103 ballots, the convention named John W. Davis.)

In 1928, at Smith's urging, he ran for the Governorship of New York. During his two two-year terms as Governor, Franklin Roosevelt combined Smith's concern with the public welfare with a country gentleman's interest in conservation and agriculture.

When the depression came, Roosevelt set up a state Temporary Emergency Relief Administration to supply money to depleted local charities. Jobs were found for the unemployed on such state conservation projects as planting trees and reclaiming swamps and other wastes. An economist told him that the only hope for the country was to let the depression go along until it struck bottom. Roosevelt replied, "People aren't cattle. . . ."

THE BANKING CRISIS

"No longer is it an apt metaphor to say that anything is 'as safe as a bank,' " the former president of the big National City Bank of New York wrote in The Saturday Evening Post on November 5, 1932. ". . . . Almost $3,000,000,000 of our daily-used cash funds were sequestered in the doubtful assets of the 4,835 insolvent banks. . . . Nowhere else in the world at any time, were it a time of war, or of famine, or of disaster, has any other people recorded so many bank failures in a similar period as did we."

Banks closed because people lost confidence in them. In the business of lending money, banks keep on hand only a small fraction of their total deposits. Usually this is sufficient to pay withdrawals. But when people get worried, and too many try to take out their money at once, the bank must either borrow from another bank, or close its doors and try to call in money it has out on loan.

As more and more banks failed, the entire banking system of the nation was in jeopardy. Through February, 1933, the situation steadily worsened. As of March 2, 23 states had suspended or restricted banking operations. The new

Big parades were one of the ways in which General Hugh Johnson tried to get voluntary support for the NRA. The blue eagle, displayed in store, on cartons, and on labels, showed compliance with NRA codes regulating prices, wages, working conditions, and production. People were asked not to buy anything not marked with the blue eagle. "Ironpants" Johnson sought voluntary support because he feared the NRA was unconstitutional and could not be enforced in the courts. He was right.

President was to be inaugurated on Saturday, March 4. That morning, Governor Lehman closed New York State's banks; then the Illinois banks closed. The only hope was a special holiday that would forcibly close all banks.

Congress was due to reconvene on March 9. On Sunday, March 5, having received assurance that the Secretary of the Treasury would have emergency banking laws ready when Congress met, Roosevelt proclaimed a three-day bank holiday.

THE HUNDRED DAYS

"This is pre-eminently the time to speak the truth," Roosevelt said at his inaugural: ". . . . Nor need we shrink from honestly facing conditions in our country today. This great nation will endure as it has endured, will revive and will prosper.

"So first of all let me assert my firm belief that the only thing we have to fear is fear itself — nameless, unreasoning, unjustified terror which paralyzes needed efforts to convert retreat into advance."

He pledged himself to action, and the people cheered. But their loudest cheers, some uneasily noted, came when he mentioned the possibility that he might have to ask Congress for special powers "to wage a war against the emergency as great as the power that would be given me if we were in fact invaded by a foreign foe."

Across the Atlantic, in Germany, a man named Adolph Hitler had just been granted unusual powers by a feeble democratic regime. The American people seemed as ready as the Germans to hand over their sovereignty. Would Franklin Roosevelt become a dictator?

Working day and night, treasury officials, bankers, "brain-trusters," as Roosevelt's college professor advisers were coming to be known, hammered out an act to save the banks of the country. There were legislators, advisers, and even bankers who hoped the emergency would bring the banks into the Government like the Post Office. But Roosevelt preferred saving the existing order of things.

The banking act was presented to Congress shortly after noon on March 9. With hardly a word of discussion, it was passed by the House at 4 P.M., and by the Senate at 7:30 P.M. One hour later, it was on the President's desk for signature.

Working at the same feverish pace, the President and Congress drafted and passed fourteen more major pieces of legislation during the following hundred days. When it adjourned on June 15, Congress had:

Established the Civilian Conservation Corps, to put unemployed young men to work reclaiming lands and forests;

Set up a Federal relief system to distribute money to overburdened state relief agencies;

Provided a means of raising the purchasing power of farmers by paying them to raise less and by guaranteeing minimum prices for certain quantities of produce (Agricultural Adjustment Act);

Provided for the refinancing of farm and other home mortgages, to prevent foreclosures;

Formed the Tennessee Valley Authority to develop the huge and neglected Tennessee Valley;

Reformed the operations of the stock market by providing for full information on new securities;

Passed the National Industrial Recovery Act, setting up a means of Government coordination of business and providing for a $3,300,000,000 public works program;

Guaranteed bank deposits;

Reformed commercial banking, agricultural credit, and the currency.

Never had so many major pieces of legislation been passed during the term of any one President, let alone during the brief period of a hundred days. And almost all were administration measures, devised by the President and his staffs, and sent over to Congress on the "Hill" for speedy enactment into law. Not that Congress did not play an important role in shaping the legislation, but the inspiration, the drive, came from the White House. Not since the first year of Woodrow Wilson's tenure had a President exerted such forceful leadership.

Overnight, the spirit of the nation was transformed. A government that guaranteed bank deposits, that prevented foreclosures, that provided relief, was a government that cared about the problems of ordinary people.

What was in the air was the fresh wind of experiment. It acquired a language of its own. New agencies, formed to administer the new programs, had names too long for constant repetition. The Civil Conservation Corps became the CCC; the Security and Exchange Commission became the SEC; the National Recovery Administration became the NRA; the Agricultural Adjustment Administration became AAA or "Triple A."

The New Dealers were unafraid to use Federal power. Their philosophy was a mixture of the progressive spirit of the years preceding the World War and of the devices used to manage the economy during World War I.

Although it was generally recognized, by bankers and industrialists as well as college professors, that the roots of the depression lay in the unequal distribution of wealth, the New Deal at first attempted no far-reaching reforms. Faced with a near-dead economy, Roosevelt had sought simply to revive it.

The easiest way to revive the economy had been to give more powers to those who had already been running it. The banks were saved by lending Federal support to the bankers. The NRA sought to save business by lending Federal support to trade associations with power to regulate prices, wages, and production. Agricultural prices were to be kept up by encouraging farm owners to take land out of production. If such programs particularly benefited prosperous farmers, bankers, and bosses, they had the best chance of yielding quick results.

THE EXTREMISTS

There was bitterness among the unemployed. A man could be told to "Move along, Mac," once too often and he would start looking for someone to blame for his troubles. In 1934, Senator Huey Long of Louisiana was proclaiming in the Senate, and wherever men would listen, that the Government should guarantee every family $5,000 a year and provide free college educations to deserving young people. The wealth of the country was concentrated in the hands of a few families, he said. He wanted to tax all income over $1 million and all inheritances over $5 million. He wanted to "share the wealth." He wanted, he said, to make "every man a king."

Long started a Share Our Wealth Society and told Americans to organize local chapters. His chief assistant, an organ-voiced fundamentalist preacher named Gerald L. K. Smith, announced that "Huey Long is a superman."

Many older, retired people remained dissatisfied by the New Deal. They had lost the savings they had counted on and were too feeble for work relief. In California, a kindly, elderly doctor proposed that the Government give a pension every month to all persons over sixty, with the provision that the money be spent before the next pay day. Although no one was ever able to offer a clear explanation of where the Government would get enough money to make all the payments, Dr. Francis Townsend soon had half a million enthusiastic followers.

At least as influential as Huey Long and Dr. Townsend was a Detroit priest, Father Charles E. Coughlin. The Father had begun giving religious talks over Radio Station WJR in 1926. His forthright prose, couched in an attractive Irish brogue, gained him an ever-widening circle of devotees. When the depression came, the Father shifted his attention to politics. He saw the economic problem in the same elemental terms as the Greenbackers and Populists of an earlier West. To Father Coughlin, inflation was the sure cure for the evils of unequal distribution. If generations of poor Southern whites spoke through Huey Long, the voices of Mary Lease, James Weaver, Henry George, and William Jennings Bryan echoed the Father's orations. He warned of "the Red Fog of Communism" and called for nationalization

Huey Pierce Long, Jr., struts between two Louisiana State University bandleaders. The "Kingfish," built schools, roads, and hospitals, and used the resulting graft to make Louisiana a police state subject to his will alone.

of banking and national resources. He blamed the country's misery on "Wall Street" and the money-changers of the East and predicted revolution.

By 1934, he was broadcasting to 10 million Americans each week. He received more letters a week than anybody else in America, and probably half a million dollars a year in voluntary contributions.

The appeal of the Communists, in the early 1930's, was the appeal of simple, direct action. Like Father Coughlin and Senator Long, known as "the Kingfish," they had a simple explanation of the ills of society: "Put one more S in the U.S.A.," sang the talented Negro poet Langston Hughes,

"To make it Soviet
One more S in the U.S.A.
Oh, we'll live to see it yet.
When the land belongs to the farmers
And the factories to
the working men —
The U.S.A. when we take control
Will be U.S.S.A. then."

When nine Negroes were accused of attacking two white girls on an Alabama freight train, the Communist Party induced a celebrated attorney to defend the Scottsboro boys for nothing, and kept the million dollars they raised in contributions. The boys' eventual acquittal dismayed Southern bigots and Communists (who plotted to assure their convictions) alike.

The New Deal offered no simple remedies, nor did it tell people what to do. It made it profitable for them to do what was required. The theme was individual dignity, personal responsibility.

The New Deal was illogical. It helped unions organize and lent money to bankers. It provided work relief to millions of unemployed so they could buy food, and encouraged farmers to kill millions of baby pigs and to plow under corn and wheat to keep food prices high. It was as illogical as life itself, trying to keep paths and choices open against almost unbearable pressures.

To those baffled by the illogic of freedom, the logic of Huey Long, the Communists, and other radicals made everything seem simple.

The United States Constitution accepted the evil passions of men as a fact of existence. It sought to curb evil, and maintain freedom, through such devices as separation of powers. The Communists believed that evil resulted from private ownership of land and factories and preached that their system would make men so perfect that, ultimately, they would require no government at all. With the fervor of a young religion, they plotted the subversion of the United States.

But the Third International, a convention of Communist parties, had made the preservation of the Soviet Union the first concern of world Communism. American Communists were, in effect, foreign agents. This was not always clear to those who served the Communist cause in the 1930's. Americans who joined the Communists in protesting against war and fascism, for instance, could feel that war and fascism menaced the United States as much as they menaced Russia. If they didn't know that the German Communist Party had, in conspiring against the Weimar Republic, helped bring Hitler to power, it was on such ignorance that the Communist Party fed.

Americans drifted in and out of the Communist Party. It is doubtful if there were ever 50,000 members at any one time or that many were aware that concealed spy rings were stealing secrets from Government agencies.

At a convention in Michigan in 1922, the delegates had resolved, "The Communist Party will never cease to maintain its underground machinery until after" it had taken over the country.

REFORM AND REACTION

If the vigorous actions of the spring of 1933 had indeed saved the Republic, this was another way of saying that a free battleground for contending forces had been preserved.

Dr. Townsend, Huey Long, Father Coughlin, and the Communists attacked the New Deal from the left, and some conservative Democrats and Republicans formed the American Liberty League to attack the New Deal from the right.

The New Deal answered these attacks and signs of discontent by turning from temporary restoratives to permanent reforms. Where it had formerly offered relief and sought to restore industries and banks, it now sought to raise up the underprivileged.

"We find our population suffering from old inequalities, little changed by past sporadic remedies," President Roosevelt told the Congress in 1935. "In spite of our efforts and in spite of our talk, we have not weeded out the overprivileged, and we have not effectively lifted up the underprivileged . . ." Never had any President asserted such control over the economic life of the people.

In its second phase, the New Deal created a Social Security Act which provided Federal unemployment insurance, and old age pensions to citizens sixty-five and older. Congress raised income tax rates on higher incomes (from 31.4 per cent to 33.4 per cent on incomes above $100,000 a year; from 57.2 per cent to 68 per cent on incomes above $1 million), and passed an act to regulate the huge public utility holding companies that forced consumers to pay unnecessarily high electric rates. The Administration also began borrowing money to finance relief measures. This defied an economic principle held dear by most of the college-educated elite of the country, that only the emergency of war justified the Federal Government's spending more money in any one year than it earned.

Huey Long, who found echoes of his "share-the-wealth" propaganda in these new moves, planned to run for President in 1936, and it was expected he would draw 6 million votes. His assassination prevented this, and an alliance of Long, Coughlin, and Townsend followers behind William Lemke polled less than a million votes. Roosevelt defeated the Republican Landon with a landslide victory, carrying every state but two.

Woodrow Wilson had once told Roosevelt that American history showed that a reform administration came to office only once in twenty years, and that its forward impulse did not outlast one term. "What we do not accomplish in the first term," Wilson had said, "is not likely to be accomplished at all." As he began his second term, the President was increasingly preoccupied in fighting off attacks on the changes he had made.

The most effective attacks on the New Deal came from the Supreme Court. In 1934, 1935, and 1936, the Court struck down the NRA and the AAA and ruled against minimum wage laws.

"I suppose no intelligent person likes very well the way the New Deal does things," said Justice Harlan Stone as the Court recessed in May of 1936, "but that ought not to make us forget that ours is a nation which should have the powers ordinarily possessed by governments, and that the framers of the Constitution intended that it should have. . . . We finished the term of Court yesterday, I think in many ways one of the most disastrous in its history."

Roosevelt met his first serious defeat when Congress refused to give him power to reform the Court by appointing additional justices; but the Supreme Court was thereafter to prove more in tune with the needs of the 1930's.

"IN UNION WE MUST BE"

One of the acts of the "Hundred Days" started a process of far-reaching change. Into the NRA, Senator Robert Wagner of New York had succeeded in inserting the following section:

The Wagner Act set off a "no holds barred" struggle between companies and unions.

". . . employees shall have the right to organize and bargain collectively through representatives of their own choosing, and shall be free from the interference, restraint, or coercion of employers of labor, or their agents, in the designation of such representatives . . . no employee and no one seeking employment shall be required as a condition of employment to join any company union or to refrain from joining, organizing, or assisting a labor organization of his own choosing."

Many labor leaders viewed Section 7a with mistrust, unready to believe that the United States Government would really assist them. But to John L. Lewis of the United Mine Workers, it seemed the opportunity of a lifetime.

"From the standpoint of human welfare and economic freedom," Lewis announced in stentorian tones, "we are convinced that there has been no legal instrument comparable with it since

President Lincoln's Emancipation Proclamation."

Working through the coal fields of Kentucky, West Virginia, Pennsylvania, Illinois, and Alabama, the union quickly brought its strength up to 400,000 members. The miners sang:

"In nineteen hundred an' thirty-three,
When Mr. Roosevelt took his seat,
He said to President John L. Lewis,
'In Union we must be.' "

A few other unions took the cue. The Amalgamated Clothing Workers added twenty per cent to its membership. The International Ladies Garment Workers Union tripled its numbers.

Following the Supreme Court decision against the NRA, Senator Wagner drew up another, stronger law. The Wagner Act provided a means of enforcing its provisions. It set up a powerful National Labor Relations Board (NLRB).

"It is hereby declared to be the policy of the United States," the Wagner Act declared in no uncertain terms, "to encourage . . . the practice and procedure of collective bargaining" and to protect "the exercise by workers of full freedom of association, self-organization, and designation of representatives of their own choosing, for the purpose of negotiating the terms and conditions of their employment or other mutual aid or protection."

John L. Lewis formed a new organization, the CIO, to unionize the two biggest industries in the country: automobile and steel. Union membership rose from 4 million in 1936 to 7 million in 1937, to 10 million in 1941. The unions provided many men with better working conditions, higher pay, health insurance, and a sense of increased control over their destinies. Important to the country as a whole was the establishment of labor as a powerful, permanent force in the nation. Henceforth, utilities propaganda would be balanced by CIO propaganda, and the lobbyists of banks, insurance companies, and steel mills would find themselves rubbing elbows with, and often opposed by, lobbyists from the Steel Workers, the Electrical Workers or the Auto Workers.

Since Roosevelt's inaugural, national income had increased 50%, farm income had doubled, and corporations had begun making money again. (In 1932, U. S. corporations had lost $4 billion; in 1936, they showed a profit of $6.5 billion.) Booming prosperity had not been restored, but the downward cycle that had commenced in the fall of 1929 had been halted. Hope had replaced despair. In 1936, one could have more confidence, than in 1932, that democratic government had a future. And this, after all, had been the President's main concern. As Roosevelt said in accepting renomination in the fall of 1936 (rephrasing Lincoln at Gettysburg), "We are fighting to save a great and precious form of government for ourselves and for the world."

"Governments can err, Presidents do make mistakes," he had previously conceded in that same speech, "but the immortal Dante tells us that divine justice weighs the sins of the cold-blooded and the sins of the warm-hearted in different scales.

"Better the occasional faults of a government that lives in a spirit of charity than the consistent omissions of a government frozen in the ice of its own indifference.

"There is a mysterious cycle in human events. To some generations much is given. Of other generations much is expected. This generation of Americans has a rendezvous with destiny."

Peace parades were fed by disillusionment and the old isolationist belief that America was self-sufficient. A series of Neutrality Acts (1935-37), forbade the U.S.A. from supplying arms to belligerents. Pacifist in aim, they deprived America of world influence.

RENDEZVOUS WITH DESTINY

IF THE fear of revolution was lifted from the United States, it hung heavy over the rest of the world. France was deeply divided, and in most of the countries of Europe rebellions were prevented only by stern repression. In Italy a crisis of the early 1920's had elevated a dictator named Benito Mussolini. The depression had brought Adolf Hitler and his brown shirts to power in Germany. These two regimes sought, like the Communists, to turn all interests to the purposes of the State.

Crises and war ruled in a world of injustice and want:

1932 — Japan resigned from the League of Nations because her conquest of Manchuria was not recognized.

1935 — Italy invaded the African kingdom of Ethiopia.

1936 — the five-year-old Republic of Spain was torn by civil war. Hitler fortified the Rhineland, in violation of the Treaty of Versailles. In August began the first of a lengthy series of "show" trials in the Soviet Union. In three years, an insecure and oppressive regime would kill all but 41 of the 139 highest ranking Communists, and would enslave at least seven million of its subjects.

1937 — Japan renewed its armed conquest of China.

In the case of the Italian aggression, the League of Nations failed to act, as it had four years earlier when Japan first invaded China. Thereafter, the League could claim no respect as a guardian against war.

The American people had displayed no desire to follow the recommendation of Hoover's Secretary of State, Stimson, that Japan be boycotted. Nor did England and France act against Italy and Germany. Everywhere, the forces of aggression seemed free to trample people into submission.

DR. NEW DEAL BECOMES DR. WIN-THE-WAR

Painfully, the British and French learned that letting Hitler have his way made him more, rather than less, aggressive. After German occupations of Austria and Czechoslovakia, in 1938 and the spring of 1939, they became determined to aid Poland against German attack.

Public opinion in the United States was also shifting, as it was perceived that the revolutionary Socialist regime treated the German people like cattle and displayed toward other nations a ruthless disregard for truth and honor.

"There comes a time in the affairs of men," President Roosevelt told Congress early in 1939, "when they must prepare to defend not their homes alone, but the tenets of faith and humanity on which their churches, their government and their very civilization are founded . . ."

Many Americans had justified isolationism out of a belief that two broad oceans protected them from harm. Roosevelt warned them that the airplane was making such thinking obsolete.

". . . The world has grown so small," Roosevelt said, "and weapons of attack so swift that no nation can be safe. . . . Survival cannot be guaranteed after the attack begins . . ."

The success of the aggressors had been at least partly due to division among their opponents. The Russians hoped that the democracies and fascist nations would weaken each other in a war; and England and France hoped that Germany, Italy, and Japan would attack Russia, rather than themselves. The aggressors cleverly played on these hopes and fears by forming what became known as the "Rome-Berlin-Tokyo Axis," dedicated to the overthrow of Communism. But on August 23, 1939, Germany and the Soviet Union signed a pact in which they agreed not to attack each other. The German Army invaded Poland on September 1, and England and France, having pledged to protect Poland, declared war on Germany.

Unlike Wilson, Roosevelt never attempted to keep his countrymen neutral in thought or deed. Poland had fallen in six weeks. Norway, Denmark, Belgium, and Holland were quickly overrun, and France was humbled in a savage twelve-day campaign. On June 10, 1940, the day after Italy invaded an already defeated France, Roosevelt announced that:

"Overwhelmingly we, as a nation, . . . are convinced that military and naval victory for the gods of force and hate would endanger the institutions of democracy in the Western World . . . the whole of our sympathies lie with those nations that are giving their life blood in combat against those forces."

Saying, of Mussolini's attack, that "the hand that held the dagger has struck it into the back of its neighbor," Roosevelt pledged that America would ". . . . extend to the opponents of force the material resources of this nation and prepare itself for any emergency."

On September 3, the United States gave Britain fifty destroyers in exchange for leases for air and naval bases on British possessions in the Western Hemisphere. Two weeks later, Congress courageously passed a military conscription bill, the first ever enacted in time of peace, and about a million young men were drafted for military service.

Some Americans opposed these moves. Well over a million participated in a movement that reaffirmed the old isolationist beliefs. Among the leaders of America First was Charles Lindbergh, who had become convinced that Germany could not be beaten. Among its members were many heirs of the Populist tradition that Eastern bankers and money-traders led the nation into foreign wars for personal profit. Among its enthusiastic supporters were American Communists who, since the Nazi-Soviet Pact, had been dedicated to keeping America from helping Germany's enemies.

But the American people's approval of their President's belligerent course was demonstrated by his election in 1940, to an unprecedented third term.

In the two years since 1939, a startling change had come over the American scene. It was possible for a boy to grow up in the America of the 1920's and 1930's without ever seeing an American soldier, except in an Armistice Day parade. Now buses and trains were checkered with young men in army browns and navy blues.

Businessmen, in the "doghouse" since 1936, were welcomed in Washington for their ability to help the nation produce huge amounts of military equipment. Shipyards and aircraft plants went on three shifts; welding torches shattered the night sky with flashes of blue; quiet country roads were heavy with traffic as the gates opened after the midnight shift. Almost without anybody's noticing it, prosperity had returned.

Steadily the country drifted into war. A lend-lease enactment effectively canceled all the reservations of the neutrality acts, actually putting the United States in the position of supplying a great part of the British war machine. In June, 1941, Hitler invaded Soviet Russia, violating the most recent and successful of his treaties. As lend-lease aid was extended to the Soviet Union, Roosevelt and British Prime Minister Winston Churchill met at sea, off Newfoundland, to issue a joint statement of war aims. American merchant ships were armed, and American naval vessels escorted convoys halfway across the Atlantic Ocean.

Although the "Open Door" policy had appeared to oppose Japanese designs on China, the United States had on many occasions shown at least a reluctance to back up her words. In 1900, for instance, a few months after his "Open Door" note, Secretary of State Hay had himself told the Japanese that the United States was "not at present prepared . . . to enforce these views in the East by any demonstration which could present a character of hostility to any other Power."

In July, 1941, America imposed an embargo against the Japanese, who had threateningly sent their armies southward, through Indochina. The flow of oil and scrap steel, on which Japan's war machine fed, was halted. Japan was faced with the choice of ceasing her conquests or of seizing the oil fields of the nearby Dutch East Indies. But the United States and Great Britain had warned that they would brook no invasion of Dutch possessions. The Japanese were faced with exactly the same sort of dilemma Lincoln had created for the South in 1861.

At 7:55 in the morning of December 7, 353 Japanese fleet-based bombers and 28 submarines surprised Pearl Harbor. In a quick, well-executed assault, the quiet harbor became a fiery, smoke-filled cauldron. The American Pacific Fleet was devastated — 8 battleships had been disabled, of which two were total losses; 3 cruisers had been seriously damaged; 3 destroyers had been wrecked; and most of the aircraft lined up wing-to-wing on Kaneoke and Ewa Airfields were destroyed. Some 2,400 Americans were killed and 1,100 were wounded.

Even more than the assault on Fort Sumter, this attack created a united opposition. On December 11, Germany and Italy declared war on the U.S.A. The President would soon quip, "Dr. New Deal has been replaced by Dr. Win-the-War."

"ARSENAL OF DEMOCRACY"

Engaged simultaneously in two great wars, one in the Pacific, and one in Europe, and supplying her allies as well as herself, the United States became an immense armed workshop.

The harsh years of the depression had placed continued emphasis on factory efficiency. Since 1929, output per man had increased twenty-eight per cent. In 1944, these efficient factories, running on three shifts a day, were producing twice as much as they had in 1940. The shipbuilding industry turned out 746 large vessels and 24,000 landing craft in four years. Aircraft production increased to 100,000 a year in 1944. By June, 1943, 5 million tons of food, 13,000 airplanes and 300,000 trucks, jeeps, and scout cars had been sent to Britain and Russia.

The Federal budget jumped from $9 billion in 1940 to $79 billion in 1943 and reached a high of $98 billion in 1945. Much of the money was borrowed. The national debt rose $229 billion during the war.

A lot of the money flowed into the economy through the hands of working people. By 1944, the depression seemed to have been turned inside out. Where people had looked for jobs, jobs now looked for people, and housewives were earning forty dollars a week fastening wires or inspecting copper pipe. Where there had been too many goods and not enough buyers, now shelves were empty and customers were being turned away. Hotel rooms were scarce, people stood in line for a seat in a restaurant, and fur coats, jewelry, and grand pianos sold like hot cakes. After Pearl Harbor, rationing had been instituted to control demand. Private cars were limited to five gallons of fuel a month. Housewives could obtain meat, sugar, butter, and other essential foods only in exchange for OPA stamps. Along with rationing the Federal Government instituted price and wage controls, allocated raw materials, built plants, moved and housed workers.

As the common purpose of the wars of 1898 and 1917 had helped draw North and South together, the Second World War brought the sons and daughters of the 1900-1914 immigrant flood into the mainstream of American life. And the labor shortage and needs of the armed services gave Negroes new opportunities.

MACHINES AND WAR

Advances in technology had changed the nature of war since 1918. During the First World War, the internal combustion engine had been harnessed to crude little airplanes and to a British invention called the tank, which had

Light army trucks roll through a General Motors assembly line that once made automobiles.

shown an ability to advance past the machine gun. Using massed tanks and dive bombers, the Germans demonstrated that fast movement had been restored to war.

Aircraft, with their ability to attack supply centers, bridges, roads, and railroads behind enemy lines, were assuming particular importance. If control of the air could not by itself win a battle, it was becoming clear that without it, few campaigns would be victorious. As control of the air was becoming decisive to land warfare, so carrier-based aircraft replaced the battleship as the key to sea power. In the decisive naval battle of the Pacific War, off Midway Island, planes attacked ships, with neither of the fleets coming within sight of the other.

It was even thought that aircraft might destroy a nation's ability to wage war. As preached by General William C. "Billy" Mitchell and other early theorists of strategic bombing, the destruction of factories, military stores, and transportation from the air, could weaken an enemy in much the same fashion as a blockade. The United States entered the war with a small fleet of four-engined strategic bombers. The B-17 Flying Fortress, equipped with a precision bombsight and oxygen-breathing apparatus, and bristling with defensive machine guns approached its targets from 40,000 feet. Eventually thousands of Flying Fortresses and other four-engined machines would lumber over Germany. American and British fleets would drop thousands of tons of bombs on German cities; but their blows would not be decisive.

Tanks, aircraft, and submarines had

American soldiers land in northern France, June 6, 1944. Eleven months later they will meet Russians crossing Germany from the east, and the war in Europe will end. Meanwhile, in the Pacific, the American Army and Navy were engaged in the other part of the great global struggle. Commanding allied forces in Europe was Dwight D. Eisenhower; in the Pacific, Douglas MacArthur.

clearly shown the dependence of military power on technology. Radar, a means of detecting aircraft by radio waves, had helped save the British Isles from German invasion and conquest. One reason for the American and British decision to conquer Germany before Japan was Germany's outstanding record of technical and scientific achievement.

A new German weapon, Vengeance Weapon One, or V-1, first appeared in the English sky on June 13, 1944. Soon 100 such robot bombs were exploding in the area around London every day. In September, an even deadlier weapon began wreaking havoc on the city. A huge rocket, V-2, ascended sixty miles into the stratosphere and came down without warning, at a speed of one mile a second. But this revolutionary weapon came too late to turn the tide of the conflict.

BIRTH OF THE UNITED NATIONS

Never had an American President exerted such influence as did Roosevelt during the Second World War. His picture,

February 1945. With their armies probing into Germany from the West and East, Roosevelt, Churchill, and Stalin met at the Crimean resort town of Yalta. They agreed to invite their allies to San Francisco to form a United Nations organization. The principal strategic concern of the U.S.A. was to obtain a Russian commitment to attack the Japanese in Manchuria. U.S. Chiefs of Staff feared the American invasion of Japan would cost a million casualties. Russia sought sway over Eastern Europe.

torn from newspapers or magazines, was tacked behind closet doors throughout blighted Europe. It hung in Tunisian bazaars, in the huts of Russian peasants, in shacks in the western hills of China. Of the three war leaders — Churchill, Stalin, and Roosevelt — Roosevelt was the first. It was he who devised the strategy of unconditional surrender. It was he who tried to commit Britain and Russia to a world in which conflicts would be settled by peaceful means. Except for a hard core of fanatical Nazis and Japanese imperialists, all the world looked hopefully to America and her President.

Ever mindful of the failure of Wilson's long-range plans for world peace, Roosevelt sought to commit his allies to a new world organization before the war was over. He had opened the discussion with Churchill even before America entered the war. Nor was the subject neglected after Pearl Harbor as grand strategy was discussed with the British, French, Chinese, and Russian leaders in Canada, Africa, and Persia. Roosevelt was taking advantage of the warmth of war-time alliance before it had a chance to cool. He would not, like Wilson, wait for a Versailles Conference at which former allies would be quarreling over the spoils.

Three months after beginning a fourth

term as President, two months after meeting with Churchill and Stalin in Russia, Roosevelt was dead and the Vice President, Harry S. Truman, was suddenly confronted with a series of crucial decisions. During the three months he had been Vice President, Truman had spent but a few hours with Roosevelt. He had not been invited to Yalta, nor had he been kept informed of all the great concerns and commitments of the Administration. ("The President, by necessity, builds his own staff, and the Vice President remains an outsider," Mr. Truman explained some years afterwards. ". . . There are many reasons for this, but an important one is the fact that both the President and his Vice President are . . . astute politicians, and neither can take the other completely into his confidence.")

While Cabinet members and agency heads urgently sought to tell their new President what they had been doing, Truman decided to go forward with the United Nations Conference. The organization that took shape in San Francisco was a confederacy of nations, with little power of compulsion over members. Most of its powers were vested in a Security Council consisting of five permanent members (China, France, the United Kingdom, the U.S.A., and the U.S.S.R.) and six non-permanent members. All member nations were to be represented in a General Assembly and special agencies were created to deal with health, trust territories, and for the collecting and dissemination of information. That America joined the UN was to some extent due to the efforts of a former isolationist Senator from Michigan. ". . . Pearl Harbor," Senator Vandenberg once said, ". . . ended isolationism for any realist." Remembering 1919, when American participation in the League of Nations became a political issue, President Roosevelt had invited Senator Vandenberg and other prominent Republicans to help plan the new world organization.

On May 9, two weeks after President Truman had addressed the delegates at San Francisco, Germany surrendered. At Potsdam, Germany, on July 17, Truman, Churchill, and Stalin worked out the details of occupying Europe and issued an

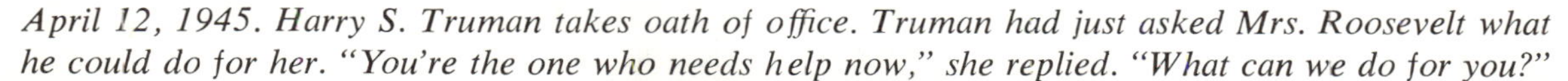

April 12, 1945. Harry S. Truman takes oath of office. Truman had just asked Mrs. Roosevelt what he could do for her. "You're the one who needs help now," she replied. "What can we do for you?"

ultimatum threatening Japan with total destruction.

While in Potsdam, Truman learned that a huge secret project, of which he had been ignorant when he took office, had borne deadly fruit. An atom bomb had just been successfully tested in New Mexico. Another grave decision was made, and shortly before 8 A. M. on August 6, there was a blinding flash over the Japanese city of Hiroshima.

Of the 343,000 people in Hiroshima, 150,000 were killed and wounded. The city was destroyed by one bomb. Three days later, another atom bomb destroyed the city of Nagasaki. The next day, Japan sued for peace.

In the fall of 1945 the United States stood supreme in the world as no nation had ever stood supreme. America had turned out more tanks, aircraft, and ships than all the other warring nations combined. She had fed and armed her allies and built the greatest Navy and Air Force in the world. Where Germany, England, and Russia had struggled to maintain their industrial production against the devastation of war, American capacity had almost doubled.

Pre-eminent in industrial production, sea power and air power, controlling chains of islands scattered throughout the Pacific Ocean, and with sole possession of the atom bomb, the United States seemed destined for a long period of unchallenged world leadership. As delegates from 51 nations assembled in London in January, 1946, to hold the first meetings of the United Nations, the future seemed bright.

THE ATOM

The almost unlimited destructive power of modern weapons made the quest for peace more urgent than ever before. Scientists predicted that it would be possible to make bombs hundreds of times more powerful than those used in Hiroshima and Nagasaki. Such weapons, capable of devastating twenty or thirty square miles, would be delivered by rockets similar to the German V-2's, but with ranges measured in thousands of miles. They would arch hundreds of miles above the surface of the earth, traveling at speeds measured in miles-per-second.

A world in which two nations possessed such weapons, the scientists said, would be a world of mutual terror. With cities subject to instant destruction, only instant readiness to retaliate could ward off danger. As tension mounted, some accident could eventually cause one of the nations to launch its missiles, and a good part of the world would go blazing into oblivion.

The only hope, they said, was that all nations agree to some kind of international control to prevent the making of such weapons.

In 1946, it seemed the time was ripe for such a move. Only the United States possessed atomic bombs, and the United States was willing to turn over its weapons and atomic plants to an international authority with the power to make certain that no other nation made nuclear weapons. The talks began in the United Nations on June 14.

As they had with regard to a host of other issues, the Soviets demurred. The inspection necessary to insure that they manufactured no bombs would, they said, open their country, to subversion. The discussion ended, to be resumed at some future time, but the American people didn't worry. After all, no one else had the "bomb." And didn't the scientists say it would be 1952, maybe even 1955, before the Russians had it?

WORLD RESPONSIBILITY

Within a month after Yalta, President Roosevelt had been troubled by Russian delays in providing for free elections in Poland. Nevertheless, America and Britain continued to honor commitments. "If they [the Russians] were firm in their way [by insisting on cheating]," Truman wrote, "we could be firm in ours. And our way was to stick to our agreements and keep insisting that they do the same." But moral pressure would not move the Soviets and the countries of eastern Europe remained armed camps dominated by puppet Communist regimes. In March, 1946, to everyone's amazement, Soviet delegate Gromyko left a Security Council meeting on the

An atom bomb explodes under water in test at Bikini Atoll in the Pacific, summer of 1946. Tiny dark objects on the water are battleships and other naval vessels. The huge column of water soared more than a mile into the sky.

continued presence of Soviet troops in Iran. This was the first of many Soviet departures and vetoes. (Unready for world government, the great powers had all insisted on the right to veto UN measures contrary to their interests.)

In the spring of 1946, Winston Churchill, now an ordinary British Member of Parliament, accepted an invitation to speak at Westminster College in Fulton, Missouri. With President Harry S. Truman sitting on the platform, Churchill reminded his audience that he had warned of the coming of World War II and that no one had listened. Now, he said, the world was faced with a similar threat.

"From Stettin in the Baltic to Trieste in the Adriatic, an iron curtain has descended across the Continent. . . . I do not believe," Churchill said, "that Soviet Russia desires war. What they desire is the fruits of war and the indefinite expansion of their power and doctrines."

The warning went unheeded. Most Americans still thought of Russia as a friendly nation. They sympathized with the hard tasks of reconstruction before her. In any case, the Soviet Union could hardly be considered a serious threat. She might continue to keep more men under arms than any other nation, but in case of a showdown the United States always had the atom bomb.

America continued to disarm, scrapping planes and tanks, putting ships in moth balls, in a rapidly changing world. Japan, under the guidance of General Douglas MacArthur, was transforming herself into a Western-style democracy. Elsewhere in the Far East, Chinese Communists were defeating the armies of Chiang Kai-shek. In western Europe, the inabilities of even such advanced nations as France and Italy to provide jobs and a secure living for many of their people, swelled the ranks of Communist parties.

On July 4, 1946, in accordance with a fourteen-year-old promise, the United States gave the Philippines their independence. In 1947, the 400 million people of India received their promised independence from the British. People everywhere now felt the dignity of independence to be suddenly attainable. Indonesians and Indochinese sought to keep their old Dutch and French masters from returning after the defeat of the Japanese. There were stirrings among the people of Africa.

This turmoil created a dilemma for the United States. On the one hand, the American people sympathized with the efforts of others to free themselves from colonial subservience. On the other hand, the loss of colonies weakened the already exhausted European democracies. Further, the anti-colonial revolutionaries were sometimes Marxist in philosophy and friendly to, if not agents of, the Soviet Union.

In general, the United States encouraged her friends to withdraw from colonies: the Dutch from Indonesia, the French from Indochina. But where the British had evolved a means of transferring power in an orderly manner to democratic native regimes, most of the former colonies, unprepared for free institutions, were governed by small groups of soldiers.

The United States could not remain a mere bystander. In February, 1947, the British suddenly informed Washington that they could no longer meet the expense of defending Greece from armed Communist revolutionaries. To prevent sudden change everywhere, there remained only the United States.

The exhaustion of England and France had thrust upon America the main responsibility for Western civilization. The first response of the Truman Administration was to obtain $400 million to arm Greece and Turkey. The policy, as announced by President Truman, would be to arm all free peoples to resist armed subversion.

The Truman Doctrine, as the policy was called, was only a temporary measure. As a first move against Soviet imperialism, it marked a turning point in American policy. On April 17, 1947, a new phrase was added to the language. "Let us not be deceived," said elder statesman Bernard Baruch, "today we are in the midst of a cold war." But it was seen that the world-wide unrest had many causes and that America would be menaced by Communism or other alien philosophies for many generations to come. Against such a broad and long-lasting challenge, resources must be husbanded. If the United States tried to assist too many nations at once, it might defend none effectively. Nor was the only danger that of armed insurrection.

The two biggest threats in 1947 were to western Europe and China. To help China, where a civil war raged, the United States would have to supply great quantities of arms and men.

In Western Europe, on the other hand, it seemed that if the economy was restored by large grants of money, the threat of Communism would subside. Besides, a Communist take-over of industrialized Europe would be a more immediate threat to America than the conquest of backward China.

Early in June, Secretary of State George Marshall told the American people of a program to save western Europe.

"Our policy," he declared, is "directed

not against any country or doctrine, but against hunger, poverty, desperation, and chaos. Its purpose should be the revival of a working economy . . . so as to permit the emergence of political and social conditions in which free institutions can exist . . ."

The world conflict had brought imaginative response from the United States.

When the Republican Eightieth Congress reassembled early in 1948, it was asked to consider $17 billion in requested aid. A Communist coup in Czechoslovakia, and forthcoming Italian elections, which the Communists were given an even chance to win, helped Congress make up its mind. The huge sum was approved, to be spent over a four-year period. On a vast scale, American money, raw materials, productive and technical skills were committed to restoring Europe. Two years later another program, called "Point Four," sent 2,000 American technicians to undeveloped areas of the world. Knowledge, as well as money, was being used to fight poverty, disease and ignorance. Never had any nation mobilized so large a portion of its resources to preserve peace.

Events in Europe and Asia moved to a climax. The Marshall Plan restored hope to western Europe. And from June, 1948 to May, 1949, American and British aircraft defeated a Russian blockade of Berlin by flying in 5,000 tons of supplies a day.

Soldiers wave discharge papers as they leave separation center in Pennsylvania. They want to get home to the steaks, the cars, and girls they had been missing. A grateful nation gave millions of veterans college educations and on-the-job training. While American forces in Europe shrank, large Russian armies stayed in Germany, Poland, Bulgaria, Hungary, and Rumania.

Meanwhile, all through 1948, the armies of Chinese Communist leader Mao Tse-tung pushed southward. In January, 1949, Chiang Kai-shek's government fled to the island of Formosa. It seemed that a new regime, unfriendly to America, was well on its way to establishing firm control of the most populous nation on earth.

The shock of China was swiftly followed by other shocks:

In September, 1949, President Truman announced that the Soviet Union had tested an atom bomb, at least three years sooner than expected.

"There is only one thing worse than one nation having the atomic bomb," commented scientist Harold Urey — "that's two nations having it."

In January, 1950, the President ordered the Atomic Energy Commission to proceed with developing the so-called "hydrogen or super-bomb," a weapon with hundreds, or even thousands of times the power of the biggest "atom" bombs.

On February 3, 1950, the British Government announced that an atomic scientist had admitted turning over valuable secrets to the Soviet Union. The information Klaus Fuchs gave Russia had speeded the Russian development of the atom bomb by "at least a year."

June 24, 1950: In the U.S.A., it was a drowsy, summer Saturday afternoon. While Americans played on their beaches and mowed their lawns, tanks and trucks raced through the cool morning dark 11,000 miles to the west.

The news was on the radio Sunday morning. The Republic of South Korea had been invaded by troops from North Korea. Most Americans wondered where Korea was.

The 38th parallel of latitude, dividing the two Koreas, had been intended as a temporary line between the American and Soviet zones of occupation at the end of World War II.

By June, 1949, American and Soviet troops had left Korea. What had been planned as a temporary line became a border between two unfriendly regimes. It was to be one of the duties of the UN to supervise free elections in Korea. But the Russians had established a puppet Communist government in North Korea, and the Republic, formed in South Korea under UN auspices, had pledged itself to unifying the country.

In January, Secretary of State Dean Acheson had told the National Press Club that the United States would defend Japan, Okinawa or the Philippines, but that Formosa and the Republic of Korea ought to place their reliance on the United Nations.

It is possible that this speech encouraged the Communists to invade the Republic of Korea. What, after all, could the United Nations do against an army? Ethiopia had gone before the League of Nations for protection against Italian aggression, and what good had it done her?

But President Truman ordered American air and naval forces to help the South Koreans, and on Tuesday, June 26, after its request for a cease fire was ignored, the United Nations summoned members to "furnish such assistance to the Republic of Korea as may be necessary to repel the armed attack and to restore international peace and security in the area." The UN was not, after all, to be another League of Nations.

A Soviet veto of the strong Security Council stand was prevented by the fact that they had walked out because of another dispute.

American soldiers were rushed to Korea and, a few weeks later, President Truman asked Congress for $10 billion. The long decline in American military spending was reversed. In September, General Douglas MacArthur launched an offensive from the southern tip of Korea. Two months later, the United Nations forces were approaching the border between China and Korea. The North Koreans were overwhelmed.

"The war," General MacArthur told reporters, "very definitely is coming to an end shortly."

Two days later, thirty-three Chinese Communist divisions struck the UN army. There was another long retreat, then another advance as the United Nations forces pushed their way back to the 38th parallel. In a dispute over whether or not to extend the war to the Chinese mainland, General MacArthur was dismissed. There could be no real debate over the Administration's decision to confine the war to Korea; the President has absolute authority in defense and foreign affairs. But the controversy it caused was another example of the way the nation's world-wide commitments would strain the Constitution.

In June, 1951, peace talks began between the UN commanders and North Koreans and Chinese in a tent at the 38th parallel. All through 1952, the truce talks sputtered along and it became harder and harder for Americans to understand what the fighting in Korea had been all about.

Yet, in terms of the drives of Soviet imperialism and Communist world conquest, the United States was doing the best it had done since 1945. The Marshall Plan had saved western Europe from Communism; a new military agreement had forged fourteen nations of the West into the firm NATO alliance; and a Communist conquest had been, for the first time, halted in its tracks.

In Korea, for the first time in history, nations fought for international justice. UN troops of the British Commonwealth, Holland, Turkey, the Philippines, Thailand, France, Greece, Belgium, Luxembourg, Ethiopia and Colombia; and medical detachments from Denmark, Norway, Italy, Sweden, and India gathered there. But the main burden was proudly borne by the United States.

THE FAIR DEAL

The new role of the Government as protector of prosperity was clearly stated in the Employment Act of 1946:

"Sec. 2. . . . use all practicable means . . . of creating and maintaining, in a manner calculated to foster and promote free competitive enterprise and the general welfare, conditions under which there will be afforded useful employment opportunities, including self-employment, for those able, willing, and seeking to work, and to promote maximum employment, production, and purchasing power."

As a result of the New Deal and the war, the country enjoyed a better distribution of income than ever before. In the 1920's, sixty per cent of American families had had less than $2,000 a year. In 1949, only one-third of American families had such small incomes, and a great many had doubled their earnings. Five million families had incomes of more than $7,500 a year.

As one small indication of what gains in buying power by some 20 million families meant: In 1900, the 75 million people of America bought some 155,000 pairs of silk stockings. In 1949, a population about twice as big bought 3,500 times as many pairs of nylon stockings. Before the war, the average American family had eaten macaroni and cheese, noodles, or spaghetti three or four nights a week. In 1947, very few American families did not eat meat five nights a week. That year, manufacturing workers were earning an average of $1.23 an hour.

The gains in buying power took place in spite of a decline in the value of the dollar to sixty-seven cents (in terms of 1942 purchasing power) in 1948. As workmen won wage increases and

In the spring of 1951, President Truman dismissed General MacArthur from his Far Eastern command for seeking to influence public opinion in favor of all-out war against Chinese Communists. MacArthur returned to a hero's welcome; but there could be no appeal from the President's decision.

management increased prices, everyone seemed to benefit except those living on incomes of fixed numbers of dollars. (Each war had brought inflation.)

President Truman's Administration brought little that was new to the domestic scene. It merely continued to be friendly to the changes brought by the New Deal, and sought to defend them against attack when the Republicans won control of Congress in 1946.

President Truman called his policy the Fair Deal. With it, he won re-election in 1948, despite the defection of some Southern Democrats and the formation of a third party.

SIGNS OF STRAIN

The swift, massive shift in American foreign policy had left many Americans confused and dismayed.

The first evidence of strain came in the fall of 1946, when President Truman fired Secretary of Commerce Henry Wallace because of differences over foreign policy. In 1948, Wallace polled 1.1 million votes as the Presidential candidate of a third party whose platform criticized the Administration's increasing toughness toward the Soviet Union.

Other Americans found it equally difficult to understand why their country could not prevent China from falling to the Communists. Wallace's followers had mumbled about conspiracies of American military men to destroy Russia. Those bewildered by events in China murmured that Communist conspirators within the U. S. Government had betrayed China.

As the Truman Doctrine and the Marshall Plan had fed the suspicions of one group, the Hiss case fed the suspicions of the other. Alger Hiss, a former high State Department official, was convicted of lying when he denied having passed secret documents to a Communist agent in the years before World War II.

Until Americans learned a lot more about the kind of world they lived in, they would keep looking for conspirators and betrayers. It was hard to learn that in a world of violent change, not all change benefited the United States, nor created free republics in the image of America.

Six days after the news of atom spy Fuchs, a Republican Senator from Wisconsin began making charges of Communism in high places. None were substantiated, but they were widely believed. Senator Joseph McCarthy became very influential. Here, the Senator holds up a 1935 newspaper as evidence that CBS newsman Edward R. Murrow was an "adviser" to a Moscow University summer session. The facts were different. In 1954, the Senate censured McCarthy.

Not the least of the dangers of a long "cold war" was that it would impair the rights of Americans. Government employees were fired for disloyalty after summary military-like proceedings. In 1954, Dr. J. R. Oppenheimer was denied security clearance. In 1963, the Government would award him the Fermi medal.

AMERICA AT MID-CENTURY

With everyone owning cars, the trend toward city-living, observed since the first census in 1790, was reversed. New suburban communities mushroomed. In many Northern cities, the pattern seemed to be that the old neighborhoods, the blocks full of Irish or Italians, or Polish, were dying. Middle income white people were moving out to the suburbs and new groups, Negroes from the South and Puerto Ricans, were taking their place. Increasingly, big cities were becoming havens of the poor.

Airline pilots flying north from Florida noticed that after they reached Virginia, the seaboard was one continuous village of winking lights. The dark patches had disappeared. Pastures, potato farms, and woodlands had been turned into one-family homes and garden apartments. This huge new community spread across old regional lines and there was a question as to whether town, county, and state governments could cope with the new pattern of living. Certainly, the shift in population would shake many traditions.

The link between the automobile and the growth of the suburbs demonstrated how one change could create other changes. American industry was now operating in a revolutionary way, producing, by organized research, new substances and techniques, deriving wealth from nature instead of from the exploitation of men. (The most novel element in American life after 1945 was television. By 1951, 10 million homes had television sets. Families stayed home more, huddled around the bright little screens. Movie theaters reported tremendous drops in attendance.)

During the hard times of the depression the number of births per thousand people had zigzagged down from 21.3 to 18.4. This decline in births continued a long-term trend. (The birth rate had been 55.2 in 1820, 30.1 in 1910.)

In 1946, the birth rate began to climb. Medical Science was also permitting more Americans to live to a ripe old age. There was a higher proportion of non-producing young and old people than ever before.

America's big corporations had emerged from World War II bigger than ever; 135 corporations owned forty-five per cent of the industry of the United States. This represented about a quarter of all the manufacturing volume in the world. If the New Nationalism, the New Freedom and the New Deal had kept these huge institutions from destroying the Constitution, if they had prevented monopolies, each industry now seemed dominated by a few giants whose prices and products were more similar than not. There were General Motors, Ford, and Chrysler in the automobile field; G.E.

In a time of confusion, Dwight D. Eisenhower reminded Americans of the certainties of a war that had been won and his popularity was a unifying influence. But when he left office in 1961, he warned that the combination "of an immense military establishment and a large arms industry is new in the American experience. . . . In the councils of government we must guard against the acquisition of unwarranted influence, whether sought or not, by the military industrial complex. The potential for the disastrous rise of misplaced power exists and will persist. . . ."

and Westinghouse in electricity; U. S. Steel and Bethlehem Steel; General Foods and General Mills.

And, strangely, the owners of American industry, the stockholders, no longer ran it. Control of the biggest corporations in the country had shifted to expert managers who owned little, if any, stock. These enterprises had also become independent of bankers and investors. They made so much money that they could finance new plants and facilities without outside help. On the other hand, Federal law safeguarded union elections, and regulated minimum wages and other working conditions, and Federal taxes often determined the ways in which profits were used.

Beholden to the public interest, increasingly sensitive to public opinion, America's big corporations had evolved into half-socialistic enterprises. And if corporations were half-socialistic, labor unions often seemed at least half-monopolistic. The battle for collective bargaining had been won. Every big industry was unionized. The "open shop," (in which union members and non-members could be alike employed) had in many cases been replaced by the "closed shop" in which all workers were compelled to join the recognized union. The closed shop insured the power of the union, but where the union was not democratic, it forced the worker to pay the costs of membership without giving him commensurate privileges. At its best, the undemocratic union deprived the worker of a voice in union affairs; at its worst, it doomed him to the results of corrupt bargains — to substandard pay and working conditions.

In the decades after World War II, undemocratic unions were not rare. The men who controlled them, like James Hoffa of the Teamsters' Union, often resembled the business monopolists of the nineteenth century. There were bloody struggles in the histories of most unions, and memories of an era in which unions had to fight for the right to exist. Whether union intolerance to internal opposition was a hangover from a desperate time, or whether freedom of action and independence of thought were against the nature of most unions, the future would tell.

A NEW CONSENSUS

Events must unfold before they can be understood and judged. Recent years can be compared to a printed page close under one's nose. There are large and grainy details, but their meaning is still obscure.

With the perspective of just a few years, one can surmise that Dwight D. Eisenhower's two terms as President (1953-1961) will be remembered as a period of consolidation and rest between the turbulence of two wars, World War II and Korea, and acceptance of the new challenges of the Space Age.

Eisenhower was elected at a time when Americans were deeply divided. McCarthyism and the reaction over General MacArthur's dismissal were symptoms of differences in Americans' definitions of loyalty — indeed of their traditions — differences which threatened the foundations of the venerable Republic. The 6,000,000 majority that had elected Eisenhower to his first term represented a broad consensus of opinion. People trusted the General. He didn't embark on any adventures nor exert the power of his office in any new directions, but he did end the Korean War by moving atomic weapons to Oki-

"All the News That's Fit to Print"

The New York Times.

LATE CITY EDITION
U. S. Weather Bureau Report (Page 33) forecasts:
Cloudy and cool today and tonight. Mostly fair tomorrow.
Temp. range: 65—53. Yesterday: 62.4—49.2.

VOL. CVII..No. 36,414. © 1957, by The New York Times Company. Times Square, New York 36, N. Y. NEW YORK, SATURDAY, OCTOBER 5, 1957. 10c beyond 100-mile zone from New York City FIVE CENTS

SOVIET FIRES EARTH SATELLITE INTO SPACE; IT IS CIRCLING THE GLOBE AT 18,000 M. P. H.; SPHERE TRACKED IN 4 CROSSINGS OVER U. S.

HOFFA IS ELECTED TEAMSTERS' HEAD; WARNS OF BATTLE

Defeats Two Foes 3 to 1 —Says Union Will Fight 'With Every Ounce'

Text of the Hoffa address is printed on Page 6.

By A. H. RASKIN
Special to The New York Times.

MIAMI BEACH, Oct. 4—The scandal-scarred International Brotherhood of Teamsters elected James R. Hoffa as its president today.

He won by a margin of nearly 3 to 1 over the combined vote of two rivals who campaigned on pledges to clean up the nation's biggest union.

Senate rackets investigators and Hoffa critics in the union rank-and-file immediately opened actions to strip the 44-year-old former warehouseman from Detroit of his election victory.

A jubilant Hoffa exhibited, however, greater concern over the possibility that his union might be ousted from the American Federation of Labor and Congress of Industrial Organizations. He appealed for time to prove that he could make the teamsters "a model of trade unionism."

The parent organization has ordered the 1,400,000-member Teamsters Union to get rid of corrupt leadership by Oct. 24 or face suspension. Hoffa said he felt actions by the union at its week-long convention here should satisfy the federation.

Warns Union Will Fight

He made it plain to the 1,700 cheering delegates that he did not intend to go before the convention in the role of suppliant. He said expulsion would not destroy the teamsters. He warned that the union would fight "with every ounce of strength we possess" if it found itself outside.

In such a civil war the teamsters would start with a war-chest of $38,000,000 in the hands of the international union and much more at the disposal of its locals. The teamsters also could count on their strategic power over other unions through their control of trucks and warehouses.

The Hoffa victory brought warnings of repressive legislation from James P. Mitchell, Secretary of Labor, and Senator John L. McClellan, Democrat of Arkansas. The Senator heads the Select Committee on

Associated Press Wirephoto
IN TOKEN OF VICTORY: Dave Beck, retiring head of the Teamsters Union, raises hand of James R. Hoffa upon his election as union's president. At right is Mrs. Hoffa.

FAUBUS COMPARES HIS STAND TO LEE'S

Says He Will Remain Loyal to People of Arkansas— All Is Quiet at School

By HOMER BIGART
Special to The New York Times.

LITTLE ROCK, Ark., Oct. 4—Gov. Orval E. Faubus said today that he had made a decision as painfully difficult as the one that had confronted Robert E. Lee at the outset of the Civil War.

"Lee was offered command of the Federal Army in 1861," Governor Faubus recalled. "Lee decided to remain loyal to the people of his state.

"The Democratic party of the North wants me to go along with them on the integration issue. I will remain with the people of Arkansas."

Governor Faubus said he had come under no local pressure to change his stand on integration at Little Rock Central High School. It was a stand that forced President Eisenhower to send Federal troops into this city to uphold Federal Court decisions and to safeguard the nine Negro students registered at Central High.

Winthrop Rockefeller, chairman of the

Flu Widens in City; 10% Rate Predicted; 200,000 Pupils Out

By ROBERT ALDEN

Asian influenza continued to spread through the city yesterday.

Commissioner of Hospitals Morris A. Jacobs reported that there were ten times more respiratory infections than during the comparable period a year ago.

Attendance in the city's schools fell again. The Board of Education said that close to 200,000 of the city's 941,000 pupils were not in their classrooms yesterday. On Thursday 160,000 pupils were absent.

The attendance estimates were based on a sampling of the schools by the board. The sampling showed that in some schools in the Harlem area—the section hardest hit by the epidemic—more than 50 per cent of the pupils were absent. The board estimated that the over-all city absence rate was 20 per cent.

3,000 Teachers Absent

About 3,000 teachers out of about 39,000 were not in their classrooms yesterday, compared with 2,700 absent on Thursday.

The city's acting Health Commissioner, Dr. Roscoe P. Kandle, said he expected that the

ARGENTINA TAKES EMERGENCY STEPS

State of Siege Proclaimed in Buenos Aires Region —Arrests Reported

By Reuters.

BUENOS AIRES, Oct. 4—A state of siege, suspending constitutional guarantees, was proclaimed tonight in Buenos Aires city and Province.

The Under Secretary of the Ministry of Interior, Garcia Puente, announced the state of siege at a news conference.

He said the emergency move suspended for thirty days the constitutional guarantees in the capital and the Province of Buenos Aires, but not in the remainder of the nation.

He said the measure was aimed exclusively "at defending the normal development of the Government's political plan, jeopardized through sabotage and social unrest."

The proclamation of the state of siege followed the arrest of scores of labor leaders during the day. The number arrested was estimated by observers as 100 to 300.

Bankers, telephone workers, oilworkers, seamstresses and other unions reported tonight that their leaders had been detained or taken aboard

COURSE RECORDED

Navy Picks Up Radio Signals—4 Report Sighting Device

By WALTER SULLIVAN
Special to The New York Times.

WASHINGTON, Saturday, Oct. 5—The Naval Research Laboratory announced early today that it had recorded four crossings of the Soviet earth satellite over the United States.

It said that one had passed near Washington. Two crossings were farther to the west. The location of the fourth was not made available immediately.

It added that tracking would be continued in an attempt to pin down the orbit sufficiently to obtain scientific information of the type sought in the International Geophysical Year.

[Four visual sightings, one of which was in conjunction with a radio contact, were reported by early Saturday morning. Two sightings were made at Columbus, Ohio, and one each from Terre Haute, Ind., and Whittier, Calif.]

Press Reports Noted

Soviet newspapers reported several weeks ago that the Soviet satellites would broadcast on frequencies in the neighborhood of twenty and forty megacycles. More exact frequencies were given by Soviet scientists at a conference on rockets and satellites that took place here this week.

Presumably the Naval Research Laboratory, which is responsible for the United States satellite program under the National Academy of Sciences, immediately set up receivers on those frequencies.

The tracking system established in this country to monitor its own satellites uses 108 megacycles, since much more accurate positions can be obtained with the higher frequencies. The Russians at first agreed to use equipment "compatible" with that of the United States, but then announced the lower frequencies.

Deception Ruled Out

American scientists believe this was because of a shortage of Soviet receivers capable of handling the higher frequency. It was not thought to be designed to hide the satellite since the Soviet signals are within easy reach of American listeners.

This was demonstrated last night as amateur and commercial radio stations, as well as the Naval Research Laboratory, reported hearing them.

Teams of visual observers at 150 stations in the United States and other Western nations were alerted

The New York Times — Oct. 5, 1957
The approximate orbit of the Russian earth satellite is shown by black line. The rotation of the earth will bring the United States under the orbit of Soviet-made moon.

Device Is 8 Times Heavier Than One Planned by U.S.

Special to The New York Times.

WASHINGTON, Oct. 4—Leaders of the United States earth satellite program were astonished tonight to learn that the Soviet Union had launched a satellite eight times heavier than that contemplated by this country.

Dr. Joseph Kaplan, chairman of the United States program for the International Geophysical Year, described the 184-pound weight as "fantastic." The heaviest American satellites are to weigh twenty-one and a half pounds.

The actual launching, nevertheless, did not take the American scientists by surprise. At the end of working sessions on the International Conference on Rockets and Satellites, which has been taking place here, some said they thought the pitching of a Soviet satellite into the sky was imminent.

The satellite must fly at a speed of about 18,000 miles an hour to counteract the force of gravity at an altitude of 560 miles. The initial announcement in Moscow did not make it clear whether or not the rocket that placed it in orbit was aimed north or south.

Its Direction in Doubt

This would determine whether or not the satellite's initial crossing of the United States was northbound or southbound. Since the earth rotates within the orbit the satellite should in one day traverse almost all nations of the world.

With an orbit inclined 65 degrees to the equator, its sweep would cover virtually the entire region between

SATELLITE SIGNAL BROADCAST HERE

Impulse Carried on Radio and TV—First Reported by Long Island Station

By ROY SILVER

Radio signals from the first satellite launched yesterday by the Russians were broadcast to radio and television audiences here last night.

The first word that the signals had been received in this country was reported by RCA Communication, Inc. It said that its receiving station at Riverhead, L. I., had picked up what it believed to be impulse signals from the Soviet satellite.

The National Broadcasting Company and the Columbia Broadcasting System broke into their radio and television programs to enable their audiences to hear the pinging sound of the "moon's" signal. The British Broadcasting Corporation in London said it had tuned powerful receivers to the Soviet earth satellite frequencies. Reuter's radio station north of London ... hearing the signals

560 MILES HIGH

Visible With Simple Binoculars, Moscow Statement Says

Text of Tass announcement appears on Page 3.

By WILLIAM J. JORDEN
Special to The New York Times.

MOSCOW, Saturday, Oct. 5—The Soviet Union announced this morning that it successfully launched a man-made earth satellite into space yesterday.

The Russians calculated the satellite's orbit at a maximum of 560 miles above the earth and its speed at 18,000 miles an hour.

The official Soviet news agency Tass said the artificial moon, with a diameter of twenty-two inches and a weight of 184 pounds, was circling the earth once every hour and thirty-five minutes. This means more than fifteen times a day.

Two radio transmitters, Tass said, are sending signals continuously on frequencies of 20.005 and 40.002 megacycles. These signals were said to be strong enough to be picked up by amateur radio operators. The trajectory of the satellite is being tracked by numerous scientific stations.

Due Over Moscow Today

Tass said the satellite was moving at an angle of 65 degrees to the equatorial plane and would pass over the Moscow area twice today.

"Its flight," the announcement added, "will be observed in the rays of the rising and setting sun with the aid of the simplest optical instruments, such as binoculars and spyglasses."

The Soviet Union said the world's first satellite was "successfully launched" yesterday. Thus it asserted that it had put a scientific instrument into space before the United States. Washington has disclosed plans to launch a satellite next spring, Oct. 4."

The Moscow announcement said the Soviet Union planned to send up more and bigger and heavier artificial satellites during the current International Geophysical Year, an eighteen-month period of study of the earth, its crust and the space surrounding it.

Five Miles a Second

The rocket that carried the satellite into space left the earth at a rate of five miles a second, the Tass announcement said. Nothing was revealed, however, concerning the material of which the man-made moon was constructed or the

Until October 5, 1955, no American doubted his country would be first at anything, from milk production to orbiting an artificial satellite. But Sputnik weighed nine times as much as the proposed American Vanguard satellite. This meant that the Russians had bigger rocket engines, and ended a comforting illusion that free societies were bound to be first in technology. It began to seem possible that the U.S.S.R. might, one day, make good its boast of catching up with the U.S.A.

nawa and threatening to bomb Chinese bases; and he did continue the policies of Roosevelt and Truman. Eisenhower was a Republican and considerable isolationist sentiment remained in his party; as a supporter of the NATO Alliance and advocate of the UN he did much toward reconciling differences among his countrymen.

From 1954 until the end of his second term, Eisenhower, working with Democratic Congresses, became a kind of coalition President; and national power, for the first time in 20 years, helped Republicans to understand the problems of Western leadership and of running a government with a $64 billion budget. (In 1925, in the Coolidge years, the budget had been $3 billion.)

Seemingly without special effort on the President's part, McCarthyism lost its influence, and the anxieties and divisions that marked the early 1950's became remote and unimportant. As the Presidential campaign of 1960 approached, it was possible that Americans could be summoned to new efforts.

THE NEW FRONTIER

"Let the word go forth from this time and place, to friend and foe alike, that the torch has been passed to a new generation of Americans — born in this century, tempered by war, disciplined by a hard and bitter peace, proud of our ancient heritage. . . . Let every nation know . . . that we shall pay any price, bear any burden, meet any hardship, support any friend, oppose any foe to assure the survival and the success of liberty. This much we pledge — and more." Thus did John Fitzgerald Kennedy, on a cold bright January day in 1961, call his countrymen to action. Present at the inaugural, to request that the new President be more Irish than Harvard, was poet Robert Frost. The New Frontier, to which Kennedy urged Americans, was to be marked by a new respect for artistic and intellectual achievement, and by confidence in the power of reason. College professors, lawyers, young business executives, and journalists — men who had been on the outside looking in and to whom the calm and self-satisfaction of the Eisenhower years had appeared as drift and indecision — were summoned to Washington to try new ideas, establish new agencies, and reform old departments.

No President, not even Lincoln, came to office at a more crucial time than did John Fitzgerald Kennedy. The spectre of world destruction was just one of a host of novelties. Western colonialism was almost dead. Africa suddenly held more independent nations than any other continent. America's population was approaching 200,000,000, and there was concern that even her continental spaces might become crowded. Six European nations had formed a Common Market, comparable in size to America's continental trade area. Their economies were overtaking that of the United States, and it seemed likely that even France and Germany's rivalry would dissolve in so fruitful an association. A Cuban revolution had put a Communist regime 90 miles from Florida.

The New Frontier of which the President spoke was really many frontiers. New kinds of diplomacy to be explored; and new industries and techniques, to be exploited. An explosion in scientific knowledge and its application was making the whole universe a new frontier. President Kennedy committed the United States to a race with the Soviet Union

John Fitzgerald Kennedy was the first President to move into a capital that could be destroyed any second by enemy missiles. With the nervous coolness of his generation — at once witty, sardonic, and tough — this youngest of all elected Presidents, and the first born in the 20th century, bravely sought to convert the challenges of the new era into new achievements. Here he talks to astronaut Walter Schirra at Cape Canaveral (renamed Cape Kennedy a few months later).

to land men on the moon. Beyond the moon lay Mars, other planets, and their moons; beyond them, the stars and other worlds. In this frightening time, Americans had turned their backs on the past to choose as their President the youngest man ever elected to that office, and the first who was not of the Protestant faith.

When Kennedy came to office, the cold war, "the hard and bitter peace," had been nagging at men's hopes for fifteen years. One of the new President's aims was to somehow end the conflict. "How is it possible," Senator Brien McMahon had asked in 1950, "for free institutions to flourish or even to maintain themselves in a situation where defenses, civil and military, must be ceaselessly poised to meet an attack that might incinerate fifty million Americans . . . in . . . moments?" The cold war was inconsistent with American ideals and if the rivalry between Russia and America would not cease, ways in which it would bring out the best in each nation, rather than the worst, had to be found.

Kennedy's opportunity came during a terrible week in October, 1962, when the USSR and the United States found themselves on the brink of nuclear war. The place of confrontation was Cuba, where American reconnaissance aircraft had discovered missile sites from which most American cities could be destroyed. The Soviets had moved the missiles into Cuba in a desperate effort to equalize American nuclear superiority. President Kennedy blockaded Cuba to prevent the importation of arms, and threatened further action unless the missiles were promptly withdrawn.

The United States, as the President had stated in his inaugural, was prepared "to pay any price . . . to assure the survival of liberty" and the Soviets, convinced at last that this included the supreme price of nuclear destruction, withdrew the missiles. During the year after the Cuban crisis, the USSR and the United States signed a treaty banning nuclear tests everywhere except underground and a subsequent agreement not to put weapons into space. It seemed possible that both nations were trying hard to insure that if their rivalry did not abate, it would at least be channeled into less dangerous paths. The peace remained "hard and bitter," but if both powers now trusted each other's restraint in the launching of nuclear weapons, a small thaw in the cold war had been achieved.

The election of Kennedy, a Roman Catholic, represented a lessening of old prejudices. But, ironically, his most urgent domestic problem was the growing impatience of Negroes in their quest for equal rights. In May, 1954, the Supreme Court had unanimously ruled that school segregation was illegal. Two years later, only five of twelve Southern states had begun to comply with this decision. Ten years later, the great majority of Negro children still attended inferior schools in most of the states of the union. President Kennedy recognized that refusal to grant Negroes equal rights tested the morals of *all* Americans. The ghettoes which confined Negroes in northern cities were symptoms of the same lack of compassion that existed in the Southern back country.

As the third year of Kennedy's term of office drew to a close, it was clear that the test would be long and painful, and that patience and courage would be tested, as well as beliefs. In Mississippi, a young Negro leader was shot in the back, and there was rioting in Birmingham, where a church bombing had re-

President Lyndon B. Johnson meets the press on the White House lawn. His style folksy and intimate, President Johnson proved himself a shrewd and forceful politician with an ability to get men to work together for practical ends.

sulted in the deaths of several children.

Then, on November 22, 1963, the Friday before Thanksgiving, President Kennedy was assassinated. There was a shocked and silent weekend when everything except feverish news from Dallas, Texas, and the slow funeral procession seemed to stop. Television showed it all: the scene of the crime, the murder of the assassin, the lowering of the coffin into the ground, and the new President standing on a rain-drenched airfield invoking help, human and divine.

Vice President Lyndon Baines Johnson came to the White House prepared by a long and distinguished Congressional career. With Johnson as President, Congress finished legislating two major parts of the Kennedy program, a tax cut and a civil rights act. President Johnson, directing his attention mainly toward domestic matters, proposed to attack poverty (it was estimated that 20% of American families had incomes under $3000 a year) and forcefully supported the Negro struggle for equality.

The tendency of the two-party system is to play down differences in principle in order to gain broad national support. (Meanings are softened so that the desires of one class or section will not prove indigestible to other classes or sections.) In the unusual 1964 election, differences of principle were emphasized. Senator Barry M. Goldwater and his adherents, in control of the Republican Party, believed that the menace to individual liberty posed by the growth of federal power outweighed any possible benefits therefrom; and that all efforts to reach an understanding with the Communist world were doomed to failure. Preaching states rights and a militant foreign policy, the Goldwater Republicans confronted the American people with a choice between the status quo and radical change. Faced with such a choice, Americans gave President Johnson and his running-mate, Senator Hubert Humphrey of Minnesota, almost sixteen million more votes than their opponents, a record plurality. (Senator Goldwater, losing the support of many moderate Republicans, carried only six states: his native Arizona and the five southern states most opposed to racial equality.)

It is true, of course, that the growth of power of any kind is cause for concern; but a large majority of the American people had demonstrated their support of the new uses of federalism formulated by the New Deal, the New Frontier (and even by Woodrow Wilson, for Goldwater attacked all the changes brought by the 20th century). And if the words of the Declaration of Independence are used as a measure of the Republic's health, one could not say that the 1960s found freedom and individual dignity rare among Americans, nor that the fight for more liberty and equality was not proceeding more vigorously than ever. Horizons of opportunity were broadening, not narrowing.

So far, through two turbulent centuries, Americans have shown that free men, making their own decisions, can cope with a wondrous and baffling array of problems. They have kept their system working as it expanded over a continent, and as the center of life shifted from the country to the city. They have absorbed millions of immigrants with diverse languages and traditions. They have wiped out slavery. They have survived the growth of huge concentrations of capital and have harnessed an immense productive power.

In accepting renomination in 1936, President Franklin Roosevelt announced, "This generation of Americans has a rendezvous with destiny."

Destiny had been met, but the outcome remains in doubt. It always will. Freedom — the right to personal beliefs, the maintenance of individual dignity against the power of governments, corporations, and other combinations of men — has never been safe — and if it has never been fully achieved, still the struggle is worthwhile — indeed, it is everything. As Longfellow put it more than a century before:

". . . sail on, O Ship of State!
Sail on, O Union, strong and great!
Humanity with all its fears,
With all its hopes of future years,
Is hanging breathless on thy fate!"

BIBLIOGRAPHY

General:

A History of American Life, 13 volumes, edited by A. M. Schlesinger and D. R. Fox, MacMillan
Documents of American History, edited by H. S. Commager, Crofts
Constitution of the United States of America, legislative reference section, Library of Congress, E. S. Corwin, editor
The Columbia Encyclopedia, 2nd Edition
Historical Statistics of the United States, Colonial Times to 1957, U.S. Department of Commerce
West Point Atlas of American Wars, chief editor Col. V. J. Esposito, Praeger
American History Atlas, Hart, Bolton, Matteson, Denoyer Geppert
The American Past, R. Butterfield, Simon and Schuster
The Stages of Economic Growth, W. W. Rostow, Cambridge
The Negro in the United States, R. W. Logan, Anvil
Basic History of American Business, T. C. Cochran, Anvil
Rendezvous With Destiny, E. Goldman, Vintage
The American Political Tradition, R. Hofstadter, Vintage
Frontier and Section, F. J. Turner, Spectrum
Immigration as a Factor in American History, O. Handlin, Prentice-Hall
The American Language, H. L. Mencken, 4th edition, Knopf
Critics and Crusaders, C. A. Madison, Holt
Indians of the Americas, J. Collier, Mentor
The American Indian, C. Wissler, McMurtie
Harvard Guide to American History, O. Handlin et al, Harvard U. Press
Atlas of the Historical Geography of the United States, C. O. Paullin, Carnegie
Dictionary of American Biography, 22 vol., Scribner
Dictionary of American History, 5 vol., edited by J. T. Adams, Scribner
Encyclopedia of American History, R. B. Morris, ed., Harper

General, periodicals:

Niles' Weekly Register 1811-1849
Frank Leslie's Illustrated Newspaper 1855-1900
Gleason's Pictorial Drawing Room Companion 1851-59 (known as Ballou's after 1855)
Harper's Weekly 1857-1900
Charleston City Gazette 1822
New York Journal 1774
Illustrated London News 1842-1900
Cincinnati Advertiser 1829
Daily Richmond Whig 1840
Charleston Evening News 1859
U.S. Magazine and Democratic Review 1837-59
American Whig Review 1845-52
New York World 1898
New York Journal 1898
New York Herald 1915
New York Times 1920-date

Sources for particular chapters:

Revolution through An Emerging Nation

American Archives, 9 vol. P. Force, ed., Washington 1837-53
Journals of the Continental Congress, 34 vol., W. C. Ford, et al, eds. Washington, 1904-37
The Colonial Craftsman, C. Bridenbaugh, N.Y.U.
England in America, L. G. Tyler, Harper
Colonial Self-Government, C. M. Andrews, Harper
Provincial America, E. B. Greene, Harper
Home Life in Colonial Days, A. M. Earle, Macmillan
Child Life in Colonial Days, A. M. Earle, Macmillan
George Washington, D. S. Freeman, Vol. I-VI, Scribner
Autobiography, B. Franklin, Bantam
The First American Revolution, C. Rossiter, Harvest
Writings of Thomas Jefferson, edited by P. L. Ford, Putnam
Thomas Jefferson, S. Padover, Mentor
John Adams and the American Revolution, C. D. Bowen, Universal Library
Alexander Hamilton and the Founding of the Nation, R. Morris, Dial
Common Sense and The Crisis, T. Paine, Dolphin
Andrew Jackson, the Border Captain, M. James, Universal Library
The Federalist, A. Hamilton, J. Jay, J. Madison, Modern Library
The Living U. S. Constitution, S. Padover, Mentor
The Complete Madison, S. Padover, Harper
Letters From an American Farmer, St. J. Crevocouer, Dutton
Papers of John Adams, edited by C. F. Adams, Vol. I, II, Little Brown
The Presidency of John Adams, S. G. Kurtz, A. S. Barnes
Origins of the American Revolution, J. C. Miller, Stanford
The New Nation, M. Jensen, Knopf

The North

March of the Iron Men, R. Burlingame, Universal Library
Grandfather Stories, S. H. Adams, Random House
The Age of Jackson, A. M. Schlesinger, Jr., Little Brown
The Law of Civilization and Decay, B. Adams, Vintage
Walden and Other Writings, H. D. Thoreau, New American Library
The Golden Day, L. Mumford, Norton
The Flowering of New England, V. W. Brooks, Dutton
Dairy of J. Q. Adams, A. Nevins, Longmans
Two Years Before the Mast, R. H. Dana, Jr., Bantam
The Education of Henry Adams, H. Adams, H. Mifflin
Gangs of New York, H. Asbury, Avon
Tammany Hall, M. Werner, Doubleday Doran
Bulletin U.S. Department of Labor Statistics No. 499
A Chronology of American Railroads, Association of American Railroads

The West

History of the American Fur Trade in the Far West, H. M. Chittenden, Academic Reprints
Rise of the New West, F. J. Turner, Harper
Andrew Jackson, the Border Captain
Life on the Mississippi, M. Twain, Bantam
Abraham Lincoln, the Prairie Years, Vol. I & II, C. Sandburg, Harcourt Brace
Jefferson Davis, H. Strode, Harcourt Brace
The Journals of Lewis & Clark, B. DeVoto, Houghton Mifflin
Harrison and Tecumseh, H. Adams, in A Henry Adams Reader, E. Stevenson, Anchor

Notes: 1. Author and publisher given only with first listing of book
2. Many of these books are available in paperback

Tippecanoe, H. Adams, in A Henry Adams Reader
U. S. Grant and the American Military Tradition, B. Catton, Universal Library

The South

The Rise of the New West
The Education of Henry Adams
Slave Trading in the Old South, F. Bancroft, Ungar
Cannibals All, G. Fitzhugh, Harvard
The Mind of the South, W. J. Cash, Vintage
The American Slave Trade, J. R. Spears, Ballantine
The Slave States before the Civil War, F. L. Olmstead, Capricorn
The Flush Times of Alabama and Mississippi, J. G. Baldwin, Sagamore
Jefferson Davis

Crisis

Cannibals All
The Impending Crisis, H. R. Helper, Capricorn
Abraham Lincoln, the Prairie Years, Vol. I & II
The Antislavery Origins of the Civil War, D. L. Dumond, Ann Arbor
Diary of J. Q. Adams
The Education of Henry Adams
Uncle Tom's Cabin, H. B. Stowe, Dolphin
Degradation of the Democratic Dogma, H. Adams, Capricorn
The Flowering of New England
The Age of Jackson

End of Innocence

A Short History of the Civil War, F. Pratt, Pocket Books
Eyewitness, The Civil War as We Lived It, O. Eisenschiml & R. Newman, Universal Library
U. S. Grant and the American Military Tradition
Lincoln Reconsidered, D. Donald, Vintage
The Confederacy, A. Kirwan, Meridian

Restoration of the Peace and The New Nation

Reunion and Reaction, C. V. Woodward, Little Brown
The Road to Reunion, P. H. Buck, Vintage
Chapters of Erie, C. F. Adams, Jr. & H. Adams, Cornell
The Education of Henry Adams
The Law of Civilization and Decay
Grandfather Stories
March of the Iron Men
The Day of the Cattleman, E. S. Osgood, Phoenix
The Great Plains, W. S. Webb, Universal Library
The Oregon Trail, F. Parkman, Bantam
How the Other Half Lives, J. Riis, Sagamore
The Autobiography of Lincoln Steffens, L. Steffens, Harcourt Brace
The Shame of the Cities, L. Steffens, Doubleday Page
The Upbuilders, L. Steffens, Doubleday Page
The Great Pierpont Morgan, F. L. Allen, Bantam
Theodore Roosevelt, H. F. Pringle, Harvest
The Story of My Life, C. Darrow, Universal Library
The Mind of the South
The American Commonwealth, J. Bryce, Macmillan

World Power through Peace Without Victory

The Influence of Seapower upon History, A. T. Mahan, Sagamore
Theodore Roosevelt
The Philosophy and Policies of Woodrow Wilson, edited by E. Latham, U. of Chicago Press
The Story of My Life, C. Darrow
Autobiography of Lincoln Steffens
The Crisis of the Old Order, A. M. Schlesinger, Jr., Houghton Mifflin
Roosevelt in Retrospect, J. Gunther, Harper
Our Times, M. Sullivan, Scribners
American Diplomacy, G. Kennan, Mentor
The American Commonwealth
Henry Cabot Lodge, a biography, J. A. Garraty, Knopf

The Automobile Revolution

Henry Ford, R. Burlingame, Signet
Ford: The Times, The Man, The Company, A. Nevins & F. E. Hill, Scribners

The New Era and The Great Depression

The Crisis of the Old Order
Only Yesterday, F. L. Allen, Bantam
Roosevelt in Retrospect
The Great Depression, D. A. Shannon, Spectrum
The Big Change, F. L. Allen, Bantam
The American Communist Party a Critical History, I. Howe & L. Coser, Praeger

The New Deal

The Coming of the New Deal, A. M. Schlesinger, Jr., Houghton Mifflin
The Great Depression
The New Age of Franklin Roosevelt, D. Perkins, U. of Chicago
Roosevelt and Hopkins, R. Sherwood, Harper
This I Remember, E. Roosevelt, Harper
Roosevelt in Retrospect
I Remember Distinctly, F. Perkins, Viking
The American Communist Party a Critical History,
The Big Change
The Folklore of Capitalism, T. Arnold, Yale
The Politics of Upheaval, A. M. Schlesinger, Jr., Houghton Mifflin

Rendezvous With Destiny

Roosevelt and Hopkins
Roosevelt in Retrospect
The Big Change
The New Age of Franklin Roosevelt
Year of Decision, H. S. Truman, Doubleday
The Pocket History of the Second World War, edited by H. S. Commager, Pocket Books
The Price of Power, H. Agar, U. of Chicago
The Crucial Decade and After, E. Goldman, Vintage
Day of Infamy, W. Lord, Bantam
Crusade in Europe, D. D. Eisenhower, Doubleday
The American Communist Party a Critical History
Two Minutes Till Midnight, E. Davis, Bobbs Merrill
Comparisons of the United States and Soviet Economies, Joint Committee Congress of the U. S., U. S. Govt. Ptg. Office
The 20th Century Capitalist Revolution, A. A. Berle, Harvest
General Account of the Military Use of Atomic Energy, H. D. Smyth, U. S. Govt. Ptg. Office
Witness, W. Chambers, Random House
But We Were Born Free, E. Davis, Bobbs Merrill
The McCarthy Record, Wisconsin Citizens Committee
American Capitalism, J. K. Galbraith, Sentry
Power and Policy, T. Finletter, Harcourt Brace
U. S. Relations with China with Special Reference to Period 1944-49, U. S. Dept. of State

INDEX

Note: Italicized numerals refer to pictures and captions.

N

O

P

Q

R

S

PICTURE CREDITS

Ansco Brady Collection: 158. Atomic Energy Commission: 264-5. Bella C. Landauer Collection, New-York Historical Society: 42, 60, 64, 180, 185. Brown Brothers: 210, 211, 215, 229, 232, 247. C. F. Adams, Jr., Dover, Maine: 48. Consolidated Edison Company of New York: 195. Eastman House, Rochester, New York: 188, 241. European Picture Service: 236, 245. Ford Motor Company: 216, 218, 219. General Motors Corporation: 259. Harris and Ewing: 212. Historical Society of Pennsylvania: 94. Metropolitan Museum of Art: bequest of C. A. Munn – 9, 36; gift of E. S., A. M. and M. A. Hawes, 1938 – 84; gift of I. N. Phelps Stokes, E. S., A. M. and M. A. Hawes, 1937 – 100, 126 (daguerrotype), 128, 130; gift of Wilfred Wood, 1956 – 22; Rogers Fund, 1942 – 62, 63; the collection of J. H. Grenville Gilbert of Ware, Mass., gift of Mrs. Gilbert – 23. New-York Historical Society: 4, 6-7, 14, 18, 20-21, 24, 51, 52, 59, 65, 66, 68-9, 70, 73, 74-5, 76, 78, 79, 80, 81, 82, 83, 87, 88, 103, 105, 108, 109, 112, 114, 115, 116, 117, 120, 121, 124, 126, 130 (right), 131, 133, 135, 138, 142, 143, 146, 147, 150-1, 153, 154-5, 156, 164-5, 174, 176, 177, 178, 179, 183, 184 (left and right), 187, 189, 192, 193, 194, 199, 203, 222. New York Public Library: 26-7, 57, 97. New York Times: 234, 240, 275. Smithsonian Institution: 95. The Library of Congress: 19, 33, 38-9, 90, 127, 136, 157, 163, 167, 170, 172, 184 (center photo), 191, 202, 204, 208, 221. The Whaling Museum, New Bedford, Mass.: 1. Thomas Alva Edison Foundation: 169. Underwood and Underwood: 197, 206, 209, 227, 239, 251. Union Pacific Railroad: 2-3. U.S. Army: 260, 269. Wadsworth Atheneum, Hartford, Conn.: 47. Wide World Photos: 226, 231, 242, 244, 250, 253, 255, 261, 262, 267, 270, 271, 272, 273, 277, 279. Yale University: 12, 93. End papers, courtesy New York Historical Society.

WASHINGTON
OREGON
CALIFORNIA
UTAH TERRITORY
FREMONT BASIN
NEBRASKA
KANSAS
TERRITORY OF NEW MEXICO
TEXAS
NEBRASKA
BRITISH
Nº 6
MAP OF THE
GOLD REGION
OF
CALIFORNIA.
Scale of Miles
GOLD REGION
UTAH
PACIFIC OCEAN
Uninhabited Region
Open Prairies